Van Tyne, Claude
    Halstead

    The causes of t'
    war of independ
    ence

THE FOUNDING OF
THE AMERICAN REPUBLIC

VOLUME I

THE CAUSES OF
THE WAR OF INDEPENDENCE

THE
CAUSES OF THE WAR
OF INDEPENDENCE

BEING THE FIRST VOLUME OF
A HISTORY OF THE FOUNDING
OF THE AMERICAN REPUBLIC

BY

CLAUDE H. VAN TYNE

PROFESSOR OF HISTORY IN
THE UNIVERSITY OF MICHIGAN

NEW YORK
PETER SMITH
1951

PREFACE

IT is my purpose here to relate those outstanding facts and movements in American history which best describe the founding of the American Republic. In the first volume, the effort has been to explain the growth of the spirit of independence which made Americans discontented with their subordinate position in the British Empire. The second volume I plan shall tell the story of the war for independence, and the effort of Americans to set up new political institutions in their several provinces and to solve the problem of imperial organization which England had failed to solve in time to preserve the loyalty of her colonies. The third volume will be concerned with the failure of the first American experiment in organizing an effective union and the story of the successful attempt which wrought the Constitution of the United States.

The unity of the three volumes lies in the undertaking, failure, and final solution of a problem of imperial organization for a large body of people settled in an area of continental extent. Besides this common theme and the particular subjects of the individual volumes, one should note three salient features of the years 1763–89. One of these was the successful struggle of thirteen English colonies in America for independence. The second was the revolution of political institutions which was brought about in the process of creating the new American Republic. The third, necessary for the success of the first, and more spectacular, was the effort of an envious world to destroy the prestige of England, to take from her the rule of the sea, while she strove to prevent the dismemberment of her empire.

During the last twenty years the industry of a number of historians in the field covered by this work has greatly changed the old way of viewing its problems. Dr. George L. Beer's studies of the British colonial and commercial policy have softened the earlier judgments as to its character. Professor C. M. Andrews, with his guides to the British Archives and his illuminating books on various phases of colonial history and British methods of government, has brought new light to the whole subject. Professor C. W. Alvord's scholarly study of British politics as they touched the problems of the American West in the pre-Revolutionary days has rendered a great service to the general historian. Professor A. M. Schlesinger has thrown a flood of light upon the economic causes of the Revolution by his study of the merchants' attitude toward it. Professor A. C. McLaughlin has rendered a splendid service to those who would understand the growth of political ideals and constitutional principles. Though dealing with the whole field of American history on a scale hitherto unattempted, Professor Channing found time in his volume covering the period to make contributions for which all who come after must be indebted. Sir George O. Trevelyan has given us in charming literary form a more intimate acquaintance with the social and personal history of the time. Local studies by Becker, Lingley, Eckenrode, Lincoln, Wallace, and others have greatly smoothed the road for the historian who would traverse the whole territory. There is danger, I know, in selecting for mention these few workers in the field, for many others have put us under obligations with magazine articles, biographical studies and monographs, which can only be recognized in the footnotes throughout this work.

Great as would be my pleasure in acknowledging my many obligations to librarians and archivists in London, Paris, Washington, Philadelphia, New York, and Boston, I must forego it, and speak only of my great obligation to Waldo G. Leland for the assistance rendered in Paris by placing all of his rich knowledge of the archives at my disposal. To the Honorable William L. Clements I wish to express my gratitude for the pains he has taken during recent years to add to his splendid collection of *Americana*, already rich in the discovery and colonial period, an almost unrivaled collection in my special field. Finally, my chiefest obligation is to my friends and colleagues, Professor Arthur L. Cross, Professor Edward R. Turner, and Dean Henry M. Bates, who have carefully read my manuscript, saving me many errors, and some misunderstandings which their larger knowledge in their special fields corrected. Dr. O. W. Stephenson also rendered the great service of checking up all quotations and references. My wife, like all patient wives of needy authors, has borne the wearisomeness of the comparison of written and type-written manuscripts and the fiery ordeal of proof-reading.

C. H. V.

August, 1921

CONTENTS

x CONTENTS

THE CAUSES OF
THE WAR OF INDEPENDENCE

THE CAUSES OF
THE WAR OF INDEPENDENCE

. .

CHAPTER I

CONDITIONS WHICH FORMED THE
AMERICAN SPIRIT

JOHN ADAMS lived to that ripe old age which delights
in philosophic reflection upon the activities that
absorb the prime of life. He never tired of corre-
sponding with Thomas Jefferson or William Wirt or
some prospective historian of the revolutionary era
wherein he had been one of the heroic figures. In a
reminiscent letter, written in his declining years, he
declares that the history of the American Revolution
ought to be divided into four periods ranging from
1620 to 1781.[1] "The Revolution," he asserted, "was
effected before the war commenced. The Revolution was in the minds and hearts of the people."
The principles and feelings which led the Americans
to rebel ought, he added, "to be traced back for two
hundred years, and sought in the history of the
country from the first plantation in America."[2]
John Adams had many quaint conceits which do not
carry conviction, but any student of the colonial
era would agree with this opinion. Back two hundred years, therefore, from the date (1818) of

---

[1] John Adams, *Works*, v, 492.   [2] *Ibid.*, x, 282–84, 313.

Adams' letter, we must go in order to trace the evolution of "the spirit of 1776," the will to be independent, and the desire to set up new political institutions which would secure the "rights of man."

In the very genesis of English settlement, the leaders of the English colonists were liberal and even radical when they first set foot on the shores of the New World. Their early migrations had in the main been caused by the political and religious conflicts of the age.[1] This is true in spite of the contemporary impression that England was over-populated, and that migration was necessary to relieve her of her surplus. The delusion arose from the fact that for the first time, due to uneven distribution of the rising prosperity, Dives and Lazarus were seen daily side by side. While wealth increased, pauperism became an established and little understood evil. Though the delusion of over-population led the State to approve of the movement to America, it was true, in New England at least, that the bulk of the people had left the homeland for religious and political reasons, and not, as Winthrop declared, because the homeland "grew weary of her inhabitants," or, in another's quaint phrase, because swarms of idle persons having no labor to relieve their misery do swarm "in lewd and naughtie practices." [2] The company, which secured the charter and financed the venture, might be greedy and think only of its twenty per cent, but the people of

---

[1] *Political Science Quarterly*, XXIII, 94. (Article by G. L. Beer.) The Pilgrims did, it is true, leave Holland to better their condition.
[2] *Ibid.*, 85.

the colony were more heavenly minded. Tell the
financiers of planning a church, of converting ten
thousand souls to God, and, we are told, they were
senseless as stones, and "stirred no more than as
if men spake of toys and trifles," but those themes
spoke trumpet-tongued to numbers of the future
colonists.[1] The majority of those destined to people
New England insisted upon going to Heaven in their
own way, and from this chronic and incurable non-
conformity in religion, developed political opposition
to rulers who would drive them along the Episcopalian road to salvation. The idea of sovereignty of
the people, the modern world's dominant ideal of
democratic rule, may be said to have originated, in
the days of Elizabeth and James, with those small
congregations of separatists who asserted their right
to meet and worship in their own way. They denied
the right of Government to "compell religion, to
plant churches by power, and to force a submission
to Ecclesiastical government by lawes and penalties."

It must be remembered also that the American
colonies were founded when Sir Edwin Sandys and
Richard Hooker were attacking the old political
faith from every quarter. Rebellious John Hampden
was intimately interested in the Puritan migration
to Massachusetts.[2] Later, Algernon Sidney, doomed
to be an English martyr to the cause of freedom,
seems to have been consulted by William Penn in

---

[1] Crashaw, who seems to have been a disciple of Izaak Walton,
declared that you had only to tell them of twenty per cent gain and
"Oh, how they bite at it, oh, how it stirres them!" Brown, *Genesis
of the United States*, I, 360.

[2] A. P. Newton, *Colonizing Activities of the English Puritans*, 84.

preparing his first constitution. Harrington, another prophet of political freedom, surely influenced Penn.[1] Both Pym and Hampden planned at one time to go to America.[2] Few liberal leaders in England during the early colonial period failed to lend mind and energy to the furtherance of the growth of free institutions in America. These men were preaching the new political faith which found, in the seventeenth century, a refuge on the farther shore of the Atlantic, there to grow in the seclusion and aloofness of the wilderness, until, in the latter half of the eighteenth century, it was to confound the less advanced government of the mother country.[3] The tenets of the new political philosophy were boldly set before the House of Commons in 1614 by Sir Edwin Sandys.[4] The fragments which the unaccustomed ears of the clerk could gather are "no successive king, but first elected. Election double of person and care; but both come in by consent of people, and with reciprocal conditions between king and people." With these words the "judicious" Hooker, anticipating with "dove-like simplicity" the social compact theory, later developed by Locke, would have agreed. Years later, Milton was to make this idea of "government by compact" even more clear, asserting that "the power of kings and magistrates is nothing else but what is . . . committed

---

[1] R. Smith, *Harrington*, etc., 167–70.

[2] Newton, *Colonizing Activities of the English Puritans*, 71, 172. Perhaps even Cromwell had like intent. Gardiner. x, 78.

[3] C. P. Gooch, *English Democratic Ideas in the Seventeenth Century passim.*

[4] *Journal of the Commons*, I, 493.

to them in trust from the people to the common good of them all." Four years before Sandys had given public expression to his principle which cut at the very roots of the idea of the divine right of kings, King James had declared to Parliament, whom he had warned against "meddling with the mysteries of state," that "kings are not only God's lieutenants upon earth and sit upon God's throne, but even by God himself they are called gods"; and, he concluded, "it is seditious in subjects to dispute what a king may do in the height of his power." Again in a moment of kingly rapture, he asserted, "I am the husband, the whole isle [England] is my lawful wife: I am the head and it is my body; I am the shepherd and it is my flock." [1] To this sharp conflict of opinion had come the old faith and the new, and in the early days of migration to America there came to the shores of New England at least few Englishmen capable of thinking who had not made the choice of the new.

When the British Government rendered life so wretched for Dissenters that they felt moved to leave England and flee to America, it simply put off for one hundred and fifty years, and removed to another land, the final struggle between those who represented the Established Church, feudal practice, and tradition, the king's prerogative, landed property, and privilege, on the one side, and their opponents on the other side, the radicals and liberals in Church and State, with antagonistic ideas as to Church and secular government. The Pilgrims and

[1] Prothero, *Statutes and Constitutional Documents*, 283, 293, 400.

Puritans of Plymouth and Massachusetts Bay, pioneers in the philosophy of Locke and the thinking of Milton, did not bring to America the conservative views of the divine right of kings, of monarchy, or of ecclesiastical tradition. Had these radicals been retained in England, and there lived in constant touch with the old traditions, their views might have been moderated in time. Across the seas, released from all restraint, they pressed on to the logical conclusion of their new faith.[1] It was a fateful day for the British Empire when its government through intolerance sent the Puritan away, a scapegoat into the wilderness. Not only the pressure of the new conditions, but the democratic bias of the Puritan leaders gave them a push toward a simpler form of social organization than the Old World had known.

The simple essentials of democracy could hardly be stated with more wisdom than by John Robinson in his parting letter to the Pilgrims. "Whereas," said he, "you are become a body politik, using amongst yourselves civill governments, and are not furnished with any persons of spetiall eminencie above the rest, to be chosen by you into office of government, let your wisdome and godlines appeare, not only in chusing such persons as doe entirely love and will promote the commone good, but also in yeelding unto them all due honour and obedience in their lawfull administrations; not behoulding in them the ordinarinesse of their persons, but Gods ordi-

[1] Chief Justice William Smith, of New York, declared after he, as a Loyalist, had fled to Canada, "All America was at the very outset of the plantations, abandoned to democracy." C. P. Lucas, *History of Canada*, 256

nance for your good, not being like the foolish mul-
titud who more honour the gay coate, than either
the vertuous minde of the man, or glorious ordinance
of the Lord. But you know better things, and that
the image of the Lords power and authoritie which
the magistrate beareth is honourable, in how meane
persons soever. And this dutie you both may the
more willingly and ought the more conscionably to
performe, because you are at least for the present
to have only them for your ordinarie governours,
which your selves shall make choyse of for that
worke." [1]

Thus spoke the "common father unto them," as
Bradford calls him, who not only excelled in divine
things, but "was also very able to give directions in
civil affairs." They were leaving a world ruled by
noblemen and gentlemen, where the common man
merely obeyed his betters, and, lacking the "bright
presence" of rulers provided by the gracious hand
of their king, they would choose "meane persons,"
perhaps, to "promote the commone good." To these
they must not be less obedient because of the "ordinarinesse of their persons." Not only were many
of the first American colonists dissenters from the
established religion, leaving the English shores just
as the old political faith was being insistently questioned, but they were in a large majority poor men,
dissatisfied with the existing order and easily lured
by radical ideas. Although to some extent the planters of the new colonies had heeded Sir Francis

[1] Jameson, *The Arrival of the Pilgrims* (Brown University Imprint),
22-24.

Bacon's advice that "the people wherewith you plant ought to be gardeners, ploughmen, laborers, smiths, carpenters, joiners, fishermen, fowlers, and some few apothecaries, surgeons, cooks, and bakers," yet they had to some extent drawn his splenetic denunciation that "it is a shameful and unblessed thing to take the scum of the people and wicked condemned men to be the people with whom you plant." Whichever the colonists might be, men with honest trades or "sturdy beggars," they were almost to a man comparatively poor. The anticipated hardships of the life in the American wilds barred the way thither to the well-to-do, as to the neurotic and the weak. The rude frontier conditions made all hesitate who, like Homer's Phæacians, loved the banquet and the harp and the dance and the warm bath and love and sleep. The fear of hardships was like the flaming sword that kept the way of the tree of life. It deterred the rich and the well-born, but the indigent and the land-hungry and those eager to rise heeded it not and passed by unscathed. There the poor, and even the improvident and criminal, became — either they or their descendants — sober and prosperous citizens, thus demonstrating St. Augustine's thesis that "out of the children of the night and of the darkness, children of the light and of the day are made." [1] But their prosperity was of the modest sort, and, up to the time of the American Revolution, there were no Americans of great wealth as it was estimated in England and only a moderate proportion with more than a mere com-

[1] *Confessions of St. Augustine*, book XIII, chap. XIV.

petence. Great numbers of the colonists either of
Virginia, Maryland, or Massachusetts were people
of good morals, law-abiding, and God-fearing, but
they were liberal in their political ideas partly because they had no reason, based upon their prosperity, to desire to conserve the old order of things.

In old civilizations like that of Europe, men of
radical or even liberal tendencies are held in check
by the enveloping conservative forces, by traditions,
by the fear of displeasing those in high social position, by the nearness of government itself; but on
the frontier, three thousand miles away, in the case
of these American colonies, these restraining forces
did not exist, and men moved forward rapidly, even
recklessly, on the path of political and social experiment. This liberation from the compulsion of established social relations was felt by all classes of
American colonists. This was true, either of the
Separatists, when their church was forced "to fly
to the wilderness," or of the forerunners of Malthus
— who seemed to show belief in the doctrine that
bears his name by leaving their country for their
country's good; it was true of those who went with
a desire to spread the gospel, or of the criminals who
were reprieved on the condition that they would go
to America. The colonist might be one who wished
to take up "the white man's burden," or one who
merely disliked the English humdrum life of quiet
and ease; he might be an idealist who left the British
Isles when Sandys, Hooker, Locke, and Milton were
giving expression to the new political philosophy, or
he might be merely a poor debtor like Micawber

leaving the land that gave him birth, but which did not give him employment. Whatever the cause of quitting the homeland, he could not long remain on the farther shore of the Atlantic before he felt the trammels of the old social order fall away and became a freer man. It took, perhaps, a century to drive the colonists utterly away from the sentiments and ideals and traditions which still bound men who continued to live in England, but the divergence began very early.

The thought of three thousand miles of tossing seas had a most tranquillizing effect upon any fears that the American colonist might entertain of vengeance by the British Government for disobedience to its will. It confirmed their belief that the Lord had provided a shelter and a hiding-place for them. Peter Oliver, a Chief Justice of Massachusetts just before the Revolution, found there a prevailing maxim that when Jove was distant the lightning was not to be feared. Men who were three thousand miles distant across an unfrequented ocean could not get it into their heads, he wrote, "that an English church or state scourge could be made of such length as to reach them." [1] The effect of this distance was inevitably to weaken government, and as Burke warned Parliament, it was of no use to "fret and rage and bite the chains of Nature." They might have "winged ministers of vengeance" to carry

[1] British Museum, *Egerton MSS.* 2671 F 13.

A famous example of the way the storms of the seas preserved the colonists, at least temporarily, from the power of the English Government was in 1686 when Randolph with his *quo warranto* arrived too late. See Channing, *History of the United States*, II, 164.

their power "to the remotest verge of the seas," but there distance steps in to limit arrogance. "Seas roll, months pass, between the order and the execution." Until 1755 there was no regular mail service and the Government's instructions to colonial governors, as well as the latter's reports, were often six months in transit on the merchant vessels, and there were many cases where the delivery followed several years after the sending.[1]

A colonist who had crossed the sea under conditions that prevailed in the seventeenth and eighteenth centuries had every reason to regard it as a mighty barrier against the agents of despotism. A passage in seven weeks was fairly common; but a ship that left Rotterdam with one hundred and fifty Germans from the Palatinate landed one third of them twenty-four weeks later. In the great migration of the Palatines in 1710, over six hundred, or twenty per cent, died on the voyage, which lasted from January to June.[2] Those who landed were a crushed, sick, and dispirited band of exiles. As high as one hundred and thirty, out of one hundred and fifty passengers, are recorded as dying on one trans-Atlantic voyage. The ship which brought the Governor's wife to Virginia in 1639 was "so pestered with people and goods . . . and so full of infection that after a while they saw little but throwing people over-board." Yet it may be presumed that a governor's lady would enjoy the best transportation available. Even Lord Carlisle, on a mission of vital

[1] Dickerson, *American Colonial Government*, 133–36.
[2] Jacobs, *The German Migration to America*, pt. III, 76–77.

interest to a whole empire, was six weeks in passage
from England to America.

The ships were small, the cabins close and crowded.
Not even the use of rue and wormwood, which William Penn advised, nor the sprinkling of vinegar
about the cabin could preserve sanitary conditions.[1]
A medical commission, appointed by the legislature
of Pennsylvania, in 1754, to investigate the diseases
incident to ocean travel, reported that "the steam
of bilge water and the breath of great numbers of
people betwixt the decks of a ship make the air moist
and in some degree, putrid, and, like that of moist
and boggy places, will produce fevers on persons
that are a long time in them."[2] On immigrant ships
the ravages of smallpox are often recorded, and the
stifling to death of children crammed in the hold.[3]
Mittelberger (1756) wrote that during a voyage
"there is on board these ships terrible misery,
stench, fumes, horror, vomiting, many kinds of
seasickness, fever, dysentery, . . . scurvy, cancer,
mouth-rot, and the like, all of which come from old
and sharply salted food and meat, also from very
bad and foul water, so that many die miserably."[4]

[1] Under such conditions in a small vessel the terrors of a storm can
be imagined. John Wesley was ashamed of his fear, but to him the
waves of the sea "rose up to the heavens above, and clave down to
hell beneath." Added to this fear was the danger from pirates who
were so common in that day that if a ship were sighted it was the
custom to make ready to fight it. *Va. Mag. of Hist.*, xxiv, 12–15.

[2] Jacobs, *The German Migration to America*, pt. iii, 65. The whole
report is a curious revelation of the crude colonial medical ideas. See
also Georgia Historical Society, *Collections*, iv ("Itinerant Observations in America," 62).

[3] *American Historical Review*, vi, 66. (Diary of James Mill.)

[4] G. Mittelberger, *Journey to Pennsylvania* (1754) (translated by
C. T. Eben), 20.

Little wonder that John Harrower heard between
decks such things as he had never heard before,
"some damning, some blasting their legs and thighs,
some their liver, lungs, lights, and eyes," and some,
to make the scene odder, "cursed Father, Mother,
Sister and Brother." [1] After a voyage on which the
water had "tasted like ink," and the biscuit had to
be broken with an axe, and after men had been
fifteen weeks on the high seas, without sight of land,[2]
a lively sense of the breadth of the Atlantic was not
unnatural. The Government could not change this
fact. "The ocean remains," said Burke, "you cannot pump this dry; and so long as it continues in its
present bed, so long all the causes which weaken
authority by distance will continue." The fear of the
scourge of either King or Parliament was sure to be
greatly diminished at so great a distance.

Added to the fact of remoteness was the novelty
of life in the American wilderness. If the chains of
tradition were ever to be struck off, it must be in
this environment so utterly unlike that of England.
From a land of populous towns with highly complex
life, a land of open fields where the forest was the
exception, they had come to a continent bordered
with forests, and with more forests stretching across
its vast extent farther than the wildest imagination
of the most poetic colonist dared to dream. Virginia
was, as John Smith pictured, "all overgrowne with

---

[1] *American Historical Review*, VI, 74. (J. Harrower's Diary.)

[2] *Narrative of J. C. Buethner*, 22–24. It was only rhetorical exaggeration when an officer of the Guards summed up the voyage as "the
pox above board, the plague between decks, hell in the fore-castle,
and the devil at the helm."

trees and weedes, being a plaine wildernes as God first made it." And that "Honorable gentleman," Master George Percy, saw "goodly tall Trees, with such Fresh-waters running through the woods," that he was "almost ravished at the first sight thereof." [1] Indeed some of the early comers to the American shores wrote of them as did Dr. Johnson of the "Happy Valley," where dwelt Rasselas, the Prince of Abyssinia. America seemed in their pages a place where "the blessings of nature were collected and its evils extracted and excluded." This idealized wilderness was of vast extent. John Muir, the most affectionate of the students of the American forests, pictures them at the time of the coming of the white man as composed of about five hundred species of trees, covering the continent.[2] "Wide-branching oak, and elms in endless variety, walnut and maple, chestnut and beech, ilex and locust, touching limb to limb, spread a leafy translucent canopy along the coast of the Atlantic, over the wrinkled folds and ridges of the Alleghanies. . . . To the southward stretched dark, level-topped cypresses in knobby, tangled swamps, grassy savannas in the midst of them like lakes of light, groves of gay, sparkling spice-trees, magnolias and palms, glossy-leaved and blooming and shining continually. To the northward, over Maine and Ottawa, rose hosts of spicy, rosiny evergreens, white pine and spruce, hemlock and cedar." Into this forest environment, on the

---

[1] *Narratives of Early Virginia* (Tyler, *ed.*), 10, 83; *William and Mary College Quarterly*, xix, 90–91, 103.
[2] J. Muir, *Our National Parks*, 332–33.

shores of the great drowned-river valleys of Virginia
and Maryland, and of the bays of New England, came
city and town bred men and women, fated to be
forced by nature to change their mode of life, to
give up a life which emphasized the importance of
the community for one that put the stress, as population moved westward, on the importance of the
individual.[1]

On the Atlantic seaboard, at Jamestown, Plymouth, and Massachusetts Bay, the English race
was to have a rebirth, the first of these destined to
occur perennially as the race marched westward
toward the setting sun. The next was to be beyond
the fall-line, a second beyond the Appalachians, and
more to follow as the frontiersmen pressed on to the
Pacific. In the first settlements on the Atlantic seaboard, the frontier of Europe, the early colonists
experienced many of the influences of life on the
outer edge of civilization which the foremost student
of the westward movement attributes to the purely
American frontiers beyond the falls, beyond the
mountains, or beyond the "Father of Waters."[2]
The colonist came to the Atlantic coast clothed
in European habit, and moved in all matters by
European traditions. The Virginia planters paid to
exacting Nature one thousand men to learn the

[1] This tendency was modified at first somewhat in New England
by the custom of moving to new settlements in groups, the whole
congregation of a church.

[2] See articles by F. J. Turner in Wisconsin Historical Society, *Proceedings*, 1893, pp. 79–112; *Atlantic Monthly*, LXXVIII, 289; Bullock,
Select Readings in Economics; American Historical Association,
Report, 1893, p. 199; F. J. Turner, *The Frontier in American History*,
passim.

lesson of the wilderness and to unlearn the customs of their native land.[1] So unprepared were they that one of the first settlers wrote, "Our drinke was water, our lodgings, castles in the aire." The adjustment to the forest life with which they were forced to "bukle and incounter" cost the Puritan fathers of New England many deaths and much suffering from cold and hunger and disease. The Puritan antipathy to sport nearly led to their extinction during the first few years in America.[2] Knowing nothing of hunting and fishing, they nearly starved when their crops failed them, though there was plentiful game in the woods and fish in the sea. Before Nature would let them prosper, they gave up the food of their fathers and learned to enjoy the food of the Indians. The newcomers to America could not reproduce the cottage of the English countryside, but they built the log cabin of the Indian.[3] Emulating the aborigines, they sought the openings of the forest in which to raise their grain. The wilderness itself appealed to their imaginations. "Oh, how sweet," wrote William Penn from his principality in the American wilds, "is the quiet of these parts, freed from the troubles and perplexities of woeful Europe." And John Pory found that "among these Christall rivers and odereferous woods, I doe escape muche expense, envye, contempte, vanity and vexation of mind." [4] The world of the forest was new, untouched by tradi-

[1] Channing, *Hist. of the U.S.*, I, 189.
[2] *Magazine of American History*, XIII, 477.
[3] Parkman, *Frontenac* (Boston, 1848), 390.
[4] *Narratives of Early Virginia*, 286.

tion; it had no society held rigid in the cake of custom. Not since the dawn of civilization had such possibilities for the trial of new ideas, and for the advancement of democratic principles opened to the sons of man. This potential American democracy was not, in Harrington's phrase, an oak planted in a flower pot, but had "the Earth for her Root, and Heaven for her Branches." Resources lay all about the new settlers, and more lands full of them stretched away to the westward horizon. It was but natural that "God's people" should turn with eyes of longing to these "free and open spaces of the New World, whither they might flee to be at peace." Here was a chance to start over again, to fashion in a better pattern that social fabric, so sadly warped by man's failures in the past. Penn's "Holy Experiment in Government" simply expressed substantially what in other minds was only of such stuff as Utopias are made. Many colonial leaders had their visions of a new order, and if their plans for a changed society were not clear, at least they gloried in their escape from the bonds of the old. "There never was," declared Increase Mather (1677), "a generation that did so perfectly shake off the dust of Babylon both as to ecclesiastical and civil constitution, as the first generation of Christians that came into this land for the gospel's sake." [1]

Everything in their new environment tended to make the settlers forget the power or even the need of the British Government. The fundamentals of political organization remained the same, but a

---

[1] Thornton, *The Pulpit of the Revolution*, xviii.

thousand laws, needed to keep order in the highly complex English society, became irrelevant and useless in the sparsely settled forest. New laws of the colonists' own making took the place of those discarded. America did not exactly realize the poet's dream of "happy shores without a law," but men felt government less frequently. The very service which the British Government had been wont to render to the citizen seemed in large part to vanish. In England when an enemy threatened, the subject had looked to the King or Parliament to organize the national force to meet the attack, but in Virginia or Massachusetts, a John Smith or a Miles Standish took the enterprise into his own hands and led his fellows forth to repel the invader.[1] Having little cause to fear and often able to dispense with government, the colonist became individualistic; he expected to look out for himself; he developed hatred of restraint. Frontiersmen were "inclined to doe when and how they please or not at all." [2]

As time went on and he conquered the wilderness, he might be pardoned a spirit of independence and of confidence. Certain that there could be no harder worlds to conquer, he had a fine enthusiasm about the future. If the undrained swamp and the ugly tree stumps, and the general air of the rude frontier seem to belie his praise of his new home, the pioneer replied to criticism, with the sublime optimism of Mark Tapley, that his Eden was not all built yet.

[1] I do not here refer to cases like that of Nathanial Bacon who went forth to repel the Indians in spite of the colony's governor.

[2] Mass. Hist. Soc., *Proceedings*, XLIII, 506.

He idealized the barren wilderness; he found its soil
fertile, its air healing. The Puritan fathers, though
they "felt the pinch harshly" at first, refused to
long for the city they had left, but "lifted up their
eyes to the heavens, their dearest country, and
quieted their spirits." And this they did in spite of
the grinding toil, the long, cold siege of winter, and
the ever-present fear of the lurking Indians. If New
England got into a "peevish and touchy humor,"
as John Evelyn wrote in 1671, it was not from want
of strength to meet its hardships, but because its
somber temper would not brook interference.

There were a number of conditions and facts of
colonial life which began early to make differences
between English and colonial political experiences,
differences fated in the course of time to make them
view great questions of imperial organization at
such conflicting angles as to imperil the unity of the
British Empire. The peopling of America began at
a time when in England local administrative bodies
of a popular character, like the county, town, and
parish, still kept some of their original vigor.[1] It was
from parts of England where control in local matters
was still with the people that most of the colonists
of New England came. The landed gentry, in England, who were engaged in a struggle with James and
Charles, for the mastery of the central government,
were still strong in the counties, towns, and parishes,
and those like Winthrop who removed to New
England reproduced oversea the local government
forms which were flickering out at home, while those

---

[1] Channing, *Hist. of the U.S.*, I, 421–26.

who remained and who were interested in Virginia, secured for it the county organization and the settlers' representation in the colonial legislature. The troubles of the Stuarts and Cromwell left them so preoccupied that the American colonists enjoyed fifty years of freedom in which to develop on lines divergent from English tendencies. When these popular political institutions had once been set going in America, they went on evolving along the lines originally laid down, but in England, after the Restoration (1660), political methods and forms were set back as far as possible on the wonted ways of the times before Cromwell.[1] For a hundred years, thereafter, England seemed, as far as the freedom of local government from control by the central was concerned, positively to walk backward with averted face, while the American colonies passed on to even more independent local government and liberal political forms suited to a people pushing ever onward into the wilderness. This historical course of development in local government constantly widened the breach between England and her colonies in the matter of political ideals.

We have here reviewed certain basic conditions and facts which affected American life and institutions from the outset. All of them tended to bring about such differences between home-staying and emigrating Englishmen, and such variations in their political institutions, that if the time ever came when their interests pulled in opposite directions, a rupture of their political relations would be likely.

[1] Channing, *Hist. of the U.S.*, II, 2-3.

Political and religious conflicts of the age were dominant causes of the early migrations. The first colonies were founded when Hooker, Sandys, Locke, Milton, and Harrington were assailing the old political faith. A major part of the settlers were men very reasonably discontented with the existing order of society. In America, these discontented men found themselves in a novel environment which lacked the restraining forces found in the old complex European society. Class chains fell away at least in part. The very distance from England, the three thousand miles of storm-vexed sea, lessened the fear of the home government and left the colonist more free to develop his own local government. Town-bred men became, on the new continent, denizens of the wilds. Life there had an absorbing novelty which broke the shackles of tradition, and they shook off "the dust of Babylon, both as to ecclesiastical and civil" customs. As the years went on, they came to depend less and less on the home government. Their pride in the conquest of the wilderness and their triumph in overcoming their difficulties gave them confidence and nourished a spirit of independence. Successful experience in local government — a system carried over from England just as the relation between the center and the local units was changing there — gave them confidence in their ability to care intelligently for their own affairs. Between the decks of the Susan Constant and the Mayflower voyaged men whose present convictions and whose destined experiences boded ill for any statesmen who should ever try to gainsay their will.

CHAPTER II

CONDITIONS OF COLONIAL GOVERNMENT
WHICH BRED INDEPENDENCE

THE political unrest in England, contemporary with the early migrations, the character of the colonists, and the conditions which influenced their lives in the American environment, all gave to colonial political life a trend in a direction leading whither Providence only knew. If the genius imagined by Burke had drawn aside for John Winthrop the curtain which concealed the future, he might truthfully have declared that "Whatever England has been growing to by a progressive increase of improvement, brought in by varieties of people, by succession of civilizing conquests and civilizing settlements of seventeen hundred years," your children's children in their old age shall have seen added to America in the brief span of three generations.[1] And it was the ingenious political methods by which the colonists attained this end, in spite of British imperial designs, which drew from Burke the admiring declaration that when he reflected on these effects, he "felt all pride of power sink, and all presumption in the wisdom of human contrivances melt and die away" within him.

From the first the American colonists profited by the fact that they not only inherited the traditions of England's long struggle for political liberty, but

[1] Burke, *Works* (ed. 1871), II, 114–15.

that, in a formal fashion in Virginia's first charter, it was fixed that English colonists were to enjoy there all liberties, franchises, and immunities "as if they had been abiding and born within this our Realm of England," [1] — to them were to belong the Magna Charta and the common law. That provision set up a new colonial policy, not like that of Spain or France or the nations of antiquity. When Englishmen migrated they went out "with all the first great privileges of Englishmen on their backs." [2] Aside from this concession in the charter the colonists were always to insist, and the Crown's legal advisers to grant, that Magna Charta, the great constitutional statutes, and the common law were the birthright of all Englishmen on English soil in whatever clime or place. Let an Englishman go where he would in lands claimed by England, he carried as much of law and liberty with him as the nature of things would bear,[3] but Frenchmen, Spaniards, Greeks, or Romans who became settlers in new lands had never had the same rights as home-dwellers. As a foundation principle of a new colonial policy this provision of the charter was most significant, but the colonists were to learn that only eternal vigilance would secure to them the rights of Englishmen. They insisted upon that principle under any and all circumstances as the whole colo-

---

[1] Macdonald, *Documentary Source Book of American History*, 7 (clause xv).

[2] *Hansard Debates*, xvi, 196.

[3] The words of Richard West, legal adviser to the Board of Trade, 1720. George Chalmers, *Opinions*, i, 194. It would seem that the colonists had this right whether the King willed it or not.

nial history bears witness,[1] and by this insistence they entered fully upon their inheritance of all the preceding ages of English constitutional history.

In the early days, when their powers of resistance were weak, they were aided in holding fast to their heritage by an arbitrary assumption of the English King. James II took the stand that Virginia and New England were got by conquest and were not subject to control by Parliament. By the King's prerogative, therefore, they were to be governed, by the powers which the King could exercise of his own initiative without the sanction of Parliament. The colonies were to profit greatly by this temporary elimination of parliamentary interference, for the kings of England for years to come were too weak and preoccupied to enforce their will, and meanwhile the colonies waxed strong and grew in their own way, before Parliament could bring its greater strength to the task of moulding them to its imperial policy. The result was that after a half of a century, one group of them at least could say with a full heart, "We have long drunk of the cup of as great liberties as any people that we can hear of under the whole heaven." [2]

Almost from the moment of setting foot upon the new continent, the colonists began to rear the fabric of the English laws and constitution — a law-making

[1] An interesting case was that of the settlers on Long Island, who, after the overthrow of the Dutch power, at once claimed the rights of Englishmen when Nicholls undertook to set up a government there which assumed that they were conquered people. See also Wells, *Life of Samuel Adams*, I, 96.

[2] Letter to Sir Harry Vane, 1654. *Rhode Island Colonial Records*, I, 288.

assembly, a representative system of government, and recognition of the common-law guarantees of personal liberty.[1] The liberal faction of the Virginia Company in London, having got the upper hand, proceeded in November of 1618 to ratify the "great charter of privileges, orders, and lawes." Bearing the Company's commission, which provided for setting up in Virginia a governor, council, and general assembly,[2] Sir George Yeardley arrived at Jamestown in April of the next year. The several settlements, on Sir George's invitation, sent two delegates each to meet with their new governor and six councillors in the choir of the church at Jamestown.[3] Here was planted in the New World the first seed of the English Parliament. Although this elected House of Burgesses with power to govern the colony did not arise out of demands by the colonists, yet they took to it as birds to the free air. On the first day, apparently within an hour, the new assembly began to exercise a privilege which the House of Commons had wrung from the King. The Speaker, though sickly and not able "to pass through long harangues," took exception to the qualifications of Captain Warde and Captain Martin. The assembly, in imitation of the English Commons, proceeded to

[1] Royal Historical Society, *Magna Charta Commemoration Essays*, 185.

[2] Pownall ascribed the preservation to American colonists of the essential rights of Englishmen to the fact that the Island of Jersey had, by its constitution, "a shadow and semblance of an English parliament," a meeting of the three orders or estates of the island whenever money was to be raised to supply public occasions. This precedent, he claimed, made it easy to put the idea in early American charters. Snow, *Administration of Dependencies*, III.

[3] See proceedings in *Narratives of Early Virginia*, 249 *et seq.*

exercise the right to judge of the qualifications of its own members. In due time, they began to make such laws "as may issue out of every man's private conceipte,"[1] or, in different phrase, such laws as were so peculiar to their new home that no English law of the kind had ever been enacted. They passed a law, for example, that no man could sell or give to the Indians any hoe or any dog "of the Englishe race,"[2] neither could he sell arms or powder and shot "upon paine of being held a Traytour to the colony" and of being hanged without redemption. Already the legal enactments of this little England across the sea were beginning to diverge, though slightly and harmlessly enough at first, from those of the British Parliament. It was but the thin point of the wedge which in time was to help split the British Empire.

Like institutions with like tendencies were set up in New England. Though the terms of their charter seemed to permit the Massachusetts Bay Company to give John Winthrop and twelve assistants — the only members of the Company residing in Massachusetts — the power to govern some two thousand subjects,[3] the iron logic of the new conditions ruled otherwise. When in October, 1630, some persons, to the number of one hundred and nine, applied to Winthrop and the others to be made members or "freemen" of the corporation,

---

[1] They had already passed "the lawes drawen out of the Instructions given by his Maties Counsell of Virginia in England," selecting those suited to their environment.

[2] *Narratives of Early Virginia* (Jameson, *general editor*), 270.

[3] Macdonald, *Documentary Source Book*, 24–25.

the little aristocracy was confronted by a dilemma. If they refused the demand, the petitioners, whose numbers and labor were much needed, would go to the free lands beckoning them either to the north or south, to Maine or to New Plymouth. If the demand were granted, the tenfold increase in the resident members of the company would swamp the oligarchy and hasten the rule of the people. Winthrop, a modern Pharaoh, unwilling to let his people go, tried the halfway course of admitting them, but concealing some of the privileges which their membership conferred. For a time they were allowed only the privilege of electing the assistants who ruled and taxed them. This device, though it caused some grumbling,[1] succeeded for a little over three years, when in April, 1634, the "freemen" desired a sight of the patent and there saw plain as the way to the parish church that all of their laws should be made at the general court wherein the freemen had acted hitherto only as electors.[2] This right they now demanded of the Governor, and he with some shiftings granted what they claimed. This was a perfectly logical outcome of the political convictions of the New England settlers who had left their old home in part because of their belief in the right of the people to govern themselves.

The next step was the evolving of a representative system. Those colonists, living in towns some distance from Boston and exposed to Indian attack

---

[1] For the Watertown protest see Original Narratives, *Winthrop Journal*, I, 74.

[2] Original Narratives, *Winthrop Journal*, 122.

if the settlers should leave in any considerable number, could not all come to the meetings of the General Court. It was arranged that they might send deputies. As new settlements grew up, it became the custom here as elsewhere in America to demand as a right the admission of a representative in the provincial assembly. Thus it came about that representation in America developed under the care of the communities represented, and not, as in England during the formative period, a matter guided by the King's necessities and fixed in the cake of custom so that it did not change with changing conditions. Thus in the growth of yet another institution, England and her colonies were drifting apart.

Even with the changes which gave political influence to more people, Massachusetts had become not a democracy but an aristocratic republic, governed only by the representatives of those who were members of the colony's churches. As the law-making body built up the code of laws for governing the colony, the Word of God was as much in evidence as Magna Charta and the English common law. Here again, as in Virginia, the driving force of the wilderness needs brought new laws into being, laws unknown in the statutes of Parliament. Sometimes these enactments were quite contrary to the English laws, even violating the terms of the charter under which the legislators held their lands. The methods of administration also wandered from the ways that custom had established in the home-land. It was not unusual for Winthrop and his fellow magistrates in this "Bible Commonwealth"

to detain or even set behind the bars men who
disputed their methods of rule, and who wished to
appeal to the tribunals of England.[1] Here, too, in
this "Nation of God," divergence was beginning
and would go on until, all unaware of the widening
breach, Englishmen and Americans would discover,
in the latter half of the eighteenth century, that
they differed irreconcilably in certain basic political
principles.

As new colonies one after another were founded
in America, there evolved in various ways similar
institutions, given to like divergences from the English legal and constitutional development. There
were interesting variations in the historical experiences of the several colonies, but all were subject to
the same forest influence, all had the same sense
of safety from effective interference by the home
government. In Providence, an extreme example
of this variety of political experience, there was set
up the nearest approach to a real democracy that
the English-speaking world had seen. At first the
wanderers from the older settlements in Massachusetts had only squatted on land to which they
had no right except a title from the natives. The
English King had not given Roger Williams license
to govern, but he and his fellows shifted for themselves until the royal will could be known.[2] Williams
sought equality and freedom in religious matters,

---

[1] Channing, *Hist. of the U.S.*, I, 350; *Political Science Quarterly*,
XIII, no. 1, p. 53 (Osgood article).

[2] It was not until 1663 that a charter secured their lands and right
to govern English subjects. Macdonald, *Documentary Source Book*
67–72.

but his fellow settlers somewhat alarmed him by the extent to which they demanded like principles in civil affairs. Yet they did not propose that their democracy should "prove an anarchie, and so a common tirannie," for, as their records declare, they were "exceeding desirous to preserve every man safe in his person, name and estate."[1] To Sir Harry Vane they expressed their delight in the freedom of their forest life. "We have . . . been long free . . . from the iron yokes of wolfish bishops; . . . we have sitten quiet and dry from the streams of blood spilt by the war in our native country. We have not felt the new chains of the Presbyterian tyrants, nor (in this colony) have we been consumed with the over zealous fire of the (so-called) Godly and Christian magistrates. . . . We have not known what an excise means. We have almost forgotten what titles are."[2] Holding fast to the memory of such blessings, men could forget the fear of the Indian and the rigor of a New England winter. Moreover, the very absence from their lives of bishops, civil war, excises, and titles wrought changes in their attitude toward government, and altered their concept of it from that which still held with Englishmen who did not migrate.

Among the many instruments of government in which the colonists embodied their new-fashioned methods of political activity, with their frontier variations from the English type, none is more

[1] 1647.
[2] *Rhode Island Colonial Records*, I, 288 (spelling slightly modernized).

marked than that known as the Fundamental Orders
of Connecticut. The makers did little more than
to write on paper (January, 1638–39) the political
forms which had grown out of the governmental
experience in Massachusetts Bay, yet these "Orders" deserve to be characterized as "the first written constitution known to history, that created a
government." A church community of Massachusetts Bay, seeking the cheap and fertile lands of the
Connecticut valley, had gone thither with their
children, cattle, and household goods. "Knowing
that where a people are gathered together the Word
of God requires that to mayntayne the peace and
union of such people there should be an orderly and
decent Government," they associated themselves
"to be as one Public State or Commonwealth." [1]
They drew up no mere social compact or Church
covenant, but a true frame of government, describing its form, its officers, and its powers. It is interesting to speculate whether this "land of steady
habits" was more so politically because it had civil
forms fixed in writing to which succeeding generations might refer. At least the "Orders" gave to the
men living under them a sense of political self-
control which could not make them easier to bend
to any future imperial plan.

Written fundamental law like the Connecticut
"Orders" [2] and Pennsylvania's "Charter of Privi-

[1] Macdonald, *Documentary Source Book*, 36.
[2] The New York "Charter of Liberties" was merely an act of the
assembly, but while it lasted had much the same authority as the
"Orders." The Pennsylvania "Charter of Privileges" (1701) had
many features common to all written constitutions. It remained in
force until 1776.

ieges," or else documents in the form of the charters which each colony received from the English Government, had a profound influence upon American political ideals. This fundamental law, as written in charters, took several forms, fancied in varying degrees by the colonists. There were charters given by the British Crown to companies like the Massachusetts Bay Company, to individual proprietors like Penn, to joint proprietors as in the Carolinas, or to trustees as in the case of Georgia. Although Governor Bernard thought such charters all too liberal, amounting as he declared "to an alienation of the dominions of Great Britain" and "in effect, acts dismembering the British Empire," [1] yet the colonists often found the charters weak bulwarks for their rights, and learned that theoretical defense based upon them made little impression upon King or Parliament if actual conditions argued otherwise.

The seventeenth-century colonial era was marked by the rise and decline of this system of chartered colonies, either like the corporate colonies of New England, or the proprietary colonies such as Maryland and Pennsylvania. By the close of the century all of these colonial systems had suffered temporary eclipse and some had wholly disappeared.[2] Royal provinces had been substituted. Inhabitants of corporate colonies, like Massachusetts, had always resisted this change, because under their charters, by hook or crook, they had enjoyed for nearly a half-

---

[1] Sir Francis Bernard, *Select Letters on Government.*
[2] *Political Science Quarterly*, xvii, no. 2, p. 206 (Osgood article). The Penns and the Calverts lost their colonies for a time, but both regained and held them up to the American Revolution.

century *de facto* self-government, but the proprietary governments, as South Carolina was at first, were not so satisfactory to the colonists, and they rather welcomed government by the Crown.[1] In either case government was foisted upon them from the outside, and the colonial spirit rose against it intuitively.

One of the first cases of colonial defiance of the English Government was (1664) when Charles II sent commissioners to "regulate" New England. At the mere hint that Massachusetts was to be asked to permit the substitution of a new charter establishing a royal colony in place of their corporate charter with its self-rule, the Puritan rulers put their charter in safe hands, manned the harbor fort, set new guns on its ramparts, and petitioned the King to let their "laws and liberties live." Fearing lest they were to lose their charter, they spoke humbly of being in that case ready to perish or at least to seek new habitations. When the royal commissioners tried to assert their authority by summoning the Governor and company to appear before them at the house of Captain Breedon, a trumpeter was ordered to warn all persons loyal to the King and dutiful to God not to heed their summons.[2] The last sounding of the trumpet was under the very window of Captain Breedon's house, upon which the commissioners gave up. How the magistrates reconciled loyalty to the King with disobedience to

[1] *Life and Writings of Benjamin Franklin* (Smyth, *ed.*), IV, 314. (Petition asking the King to resume control of Pennsylvania.)

[2] New York Historical Society, *Collections*, 1869, pp. 62–68.

his commissioners, Puritan logic does not explain. Their diplomacy is more easily understood than their logic, for they sent the King a shipload of masts, and provisions to His Majesty's ships in the West Indies.

The next serious attempt to take the Massachusetts charter was in 1681 when Randolph appeared with a legal demand that the corporation appear in London before the Court of the King's Bench to defend their right to their charter. Undecided what to do, the magistrates and deputies "sought the face of the Lord," which meant consulting the ministers of the colony. Their unanimous advice was that it was the undoubted duty of the authorities of Massachusetts Bay "to abide by what rights and privileges the Lord our God in his merciful providence hath bestowed upon us." They argued that it was better to obey the God of their fathers than to put their trust in princes.[1] To sin by giving away the inheritance of their fathers "would be to incurr the high displeasure of the King of Kings." It being persistently argued that they had legally forfeited their charter, they made reply that "though, according to some corrupt and unrighteous laws, they might have done so, yet according to the laws of righteousness and equity they had not done so."[2] This appeal to natural law was prophetic of the days of England's trial when James Otis and Samuel Adams would forge this theory

[1] Mass. Hist. Soc., *Collections* (3d ser.), I, 78.

[2] *Ibid.*, 80. This was not an isolated case of their disobedience to the King's will. See *Calendar of State Papers* (*America and West Indies*, 1681–85), 236–39.

into a flaming sword for the colonial defense.
Neither the appeals to the King, nor to Providence,
nor to natural laws saved the charter on this occasion, and in 1684 it was withdrawn. A few years
later, 1691, a new and modified charter was granted,
wherein Massachusetts was obliged to accept a
governor appointed by the King. In all cases, and
there were others like this, when a colony had enjoyed a liberal charter and then was robbed of it —
to become a royal province in which the governor's
commission took the place of the charter — the
colony felt aggrieved and never ceased to pine for
its liberties. They felt the loss as Englishmen might
have mourned the loss of Magna Charta.

Such conflicts with the King as that of Massachusetts Bay over the possession of her charter were
rare, at least only occasional, but the whole colonial
history abounds in struggles between the assemblies
elected by the people and the governors, the appointed agents of King or Parliament.[1] Though the
governors were in the main men without any natural
bent toward tyranny, and were merely commonplace
Englishmen anxious to carry out instructions and
draw their salaries, yet they represented to the
colonist the dangerous spirit of prerogative, an ever-
present menace to their liberties. The King's use
of prerogative, of those powers which he could exercise of his own will and initiative, continued, in
theory at least, without diminution, in the American
provinces, and governors there were expected to do

[1] Except in Connecticut and Rhode Island where the people chose
their own governors.

the royal will. As a result ink was not black enough to paint them in their proper colors. Even the benign Franklin overdrew his picture of them. "Their office," he wrote, "makes them insolent; their insolence makes them odious; and, being conscious that they are hated, they become malicious. Their malice urges them to continual abuse of the inhabitants in their letters to Administration, representing them as disaffected and rebellious, and (to encourage the use of severity), as weak, divided, timid, and cowardly. Government believes all; thinks it necessary to support and countenance its officers. Their quarreling with the people is deemed a mark and consequence of their fidelity. They are therefore more highly rewarded, and this makes their conduct still more insolent and provoking." [1] This was written on the eve of the Revolution, and is indicative of critical spirit at its height, but descriptions nearly as bitter are to be found in all colonial records.

Needy politicians and adventurers there were, no doubt, and at times, as Junius expressed it, "It was not Virginia that wanted a governor but a court favorite that wanted a salary." Lord Cornbury, Governor of New York, was a spendthrift, immoral and dishonest, but he was cousin-german to Queen Mary and Queen Anne, he was burdened with debt, and the court had to find him a place. The poor relatives of high officials must be cared for,[2] and the

---

[1] Trevelyan, *The American Revolution*, I, 16. See also Hotblack, *Chatham's Colonial Policy*, 173.

[2] *N. C. Colonial Records*, II, 154–58; III, 80.

Ministry could not have it said that "the hungry sheep look up and are not fed." A writer who observed this process in another part of the empire made the acrid comment that the Ministry acted "as if justice and public virtue were best administered and promoted by men most distinguished for ignorance and profligacy, and that they would prove the best protectors of other people's fortunes who by vice and profusion had dissipated their own!" [1] Rawdon Crawley, in "Vanity Fair," Governor of "Coventry Island," was a character in fiction, but his counterpart might have been found in the actual history of any eighteenth-century colonial empire. A few men of ability were made governors, but they seem to have been little more successful from the British Government point of view than those who were inefficient or lacking in experience. The colonists opposed them whether good or bad. If governors were not Stuart kings, yet one could make the most of their tyrannous attributes. If they had no crowns that made their heads uneasy, their official robes reminded the colonist of the source of their power and made them seem natural political enemies. It was the duty of the colonial governor to assume royal prerogatives, and that too with attributes of the royal power which Parliament in the days of Charles I and James II had wrested from the King. Things the monarch could no longer do in England his representative in the colony could do. A governor could summon, prorogue, and dissolve a colonial assembly,

[1] B. Edwards, *West Indies*, II, 390 (bk. VI, chap. 1).

but the King, at least in practice, dared not so treat Parliament.[1] The colonists naturally strove to reduce the governor's power with reference to their assemblies within the same limits as the King's power with reference to Parliament. Mere provincial tendency to imitate the homeland would lead them to do that.[2] They never forgot or forgave that "haughty bashaw," as Samuel Adams dubbed Governor Dudley, when he bitterly asserted (1702) that "the King's subjects in New England did not differ much from slaves, and that the only difference was, that they were not bought and sold."[3] He had taunted them too with the sneer that they "must not expect their liberties would follow them to the ends of the earth." But they did expect that very thing, and they would follow to the ends of the earth any provincial leader who would boldly demand those English-born liberties.

In spite of the colonial fear of the royal governor, there were conditions controlling his relations with the colonists which as a rule rendered him powerless enough to cope with them. Though the governors were at first instructed to give profitable offices and to make grants of land to influential provincials and in this way secure their aid in controlling the colony,[4] time was to prove that, when the climbers had

[1] Channing, *Hist. of the U.S.*, ii, 246; E. B. Greene, *The Provincial Governor*, 229 (Bernard's Commission), 92–93.

[2] *Minutes of the Council of Pennsylvania*, i, 494; W. R. Anson, *Law and Custom of the Constitution.*

[3] *Andros Tracts*, i, 82; Palfrey, *New England*, iii, 526. Wells, *Samuel Adams*, i, 96.

[4] Becker, *The History of Political Parties in the Province of New York*, 8 12.

secured their titles to land grants or been enriched
with their sinecures, they were apt to scorn the
ladder by which they had ascended and to seek
provincial popularity by embracing the cause of the
assembly rather than that of the governor.[1] In later
days, as Sir Guy Carleton discovered in his Canadian
province, "the governor having little or nothing to
give away can have but little influence." Moreover,
as he pointed out, it was "impossible for the dignity
of the throne or peerage to be represented in the
American forest," and for that reason the British
form of government transplanted to America could
never produce "the same fruits as at home." [2] The
governor was unfortunate, Carleton said, in having
the duty of keeping all the colonial officers in proper
subordination and of restraining those officers who
live by fees "from running them up to extortion."
All such officers, "finding themselves checked in
their views of profit," are "disposed to look on the
person who disappoints them as their enemy."

Another source of gubernatorial weakness in most
of the provinces was dwelt upon by Cadwallader
Colden of New York. "The proper Ballance of
power essential to the English Constitution is
destroy'd in the Colonies . . . owing to the Governours having no subsistence but from the Assembly."
They may resist for a time, he admitted, but after
all are obliged to comply "or starve or be sunk in
debt." One governor complained bitterly that while

[1] Robert Livingston was a good example. See Becker, *Political
Parties in the Province of New York*, 12.
[2] Andrews, *The Colonial Period*, 151.

trying to carry out the instructions of the British Government, "I was left to begg my daily bread from a hard-hearted Assembly here."[1] Franklin thought the proprietary governor was "the most wretched thing alive." Having two masters, he was "certain to live in perpetual broils" and "uncertain whether he shall be able to live at all."[2] Sir William Keith, we are told, was of a philosophical mind and in his first address to the assembly made hints, that could not be misunderstood, "that in case they would pay him well he would serve them well." The assembly, Franklin dryly remarks, were sensible enough to see "that this was all that could be required of a Man who had a Family to maintain with some degree of Splendor, and who was no richer than Plantation Governors usually are. In short they believed in him, and the Returns he annually made them were suitable to the Confidence they plac'd in him."

Most of the colonies refused to grant a permanent civil list out of which the British Government might pay the governors' salaries, and Parliament paid no attention to the recommendation of the Board of Trade that the salaries be paid out of the royal treasury.[3] Franklin struck a chord to which the colonial heart responded when he declared, in his "Gazette," that there ought to be mutual depend-

[1] Keys, *Cadwallader Colden*, 235; *New York Colonial Documents*, v, 451; D. D. Wallace, *Life of Henry Laurens*, 112; Dickerson, *American Colonial Government*, 155.

[2] Franklin, *Works* (Sparks, *ed.*), III, 187.

[3] There were repeated threats to do this. Beer, *British Colonial Policy, 1754–1765*, 37–38; Spencer, *Constitutional Conflict in Massachusetts*, 70–88; E. B. Greene, *The Provincial Governor*, chap. IX.

ence between governor and governed.[1] If there were
a governor, wrote Samuel Adams, "independent of
the people for his *support*, as well as of his *political
Being*," he would be in fact a master and soon a
tyrant.[2] Nevertheless, there were nearly independent governors, who in spite of the fact made little
progress on the royal road to tyranny. In Virginia
the governor was able to pay himself out of quit-
rents and fees received for various functions, and
these, with the permanent grant by the House of
Burgesses of two shillings on each hogshead of tobacco sent out of the province, left him almost independent of the legislature. Only in times of war
or poor harvests could he be coerced by his need of
money.[3] The colonist knew how to make the most
of all English precedents as to modes of coercing an
executive. Most of the colonists, like the Massachusetts settlers, retained the tradition of their
struggle as Englishmen with King Charles I and
Archbishop Laud, and they never forgot how to
starve an executive into obedience. Neither Massachusetts Bay nor the other plantations of New
England ever made the mistake of leaving the
governor independent in money matters. They dis-
tinctly favored the arrangement, quite contrary to
scriptural wisdom, by which the governor had two
masters, one who gave him his commission, and one

[1] Franklin, *Works* (Temple Franklin, *ed.*), I, 66. For another defense of the colonial view see Franklin, *Writings* (Smyth, *ed.*), v, 83.

[2] Samuel Adams, *Writings*, II, 248.

[3] Channing, *Hist. of the U.S.*, I, 520–21; II, 80; Andrews, *The Colonial
Period*, 170. In the Carolinas also the governors were paid out of
export dues, quit-rents, and small duties. E. B. Greene, *The Provincial Governor*, 60–63.

who gave him his pay. When, on the eve of the Revolution, an act of Parliament provided funds for a governor's salary which he would not have to beg from the hard-hearted assembly, Samuel Adams' wrath knew no bounds.[1] He wanted to know if it was not an indignity "to have a Governor, an avowed advocate for ministerial measures, and a most assiduous instrument in carrying them on, modelled, shaped, controlled, and directed totally independent of the people over whom he is commissioned to govern, and yet absolutely dependent upon the Crown; pensioned by those on whom his existence depends, and paid out of a revenue established by those who have no authority to establish it, and extorted from the people in a manner most odious, insulting and oppressive." Though Adams "required the gall of the dragon" to express his bitterness, he only voiced the colonial view, but the governors looked at the problem from a different angle. One declared that the colonies would be governed as they ought to be when governors were made independent of their assemblies, and then hanged up when they failed to do their duty. They had not advanced beyond the seventeenth-century wisdom of Francis Bacon, who, taking all knowledge to be his province, had declared, with an air of finality, "For government [of colonies] let it be in the hands of one, assisted with some council."[2] The American colonial governors were witnessing the dawn of true democracy, but autocratic tradition

---

[1] Wells, *Samuel Adams*, i, 486.
[2] Bacon, *Essays* (1893 ed.). 174.

had dulled the coördinating nerves so that what the eye saw the mind did not comprehend.

An important cause of friction between governor and provincial legislator was an unconscious tendency of the colonials to ape the great parliamentary figures of "Old England." They could not resist trying to fancy themselves at Westminster, or writing under the name of Pym or Hampden when they were not imitating those heroes in the modest legislative halls of the colony. The colonial Solons, therefore, drew no small satisfaction from virtuous conflict with the governor. Even if these vice-regal officers did not try "to bashaw it over Englishmen," but were only able and efficient, as in the case of Nicholls, Lovelace, and Dongan in New York, the colonists were, nevertheless, discontented, and clamored for self-control. Not even the appointment of their fellow colonists to the governor's seat gave them satisfaction.[1] The colonial politicians rather enjoyed clothing themselves in the Roman toga of Brutus, and thinking of their governor as another Cæsar. It made the small affairs of colonial politics swell with importance. John Adams classed himself with that "mighty line of heroes and confessors and martyrs who since the beginning of history have done battle for the dignity and happiness of human nature against the leagued assailants of both." To strut for an hour on the colonial stage in the part of an heroic defender of the people's liberties was not without pleasing sensations. For such heroics the governor was the inevitable victim.

[1] E. B. Greene, *The Provincial Governor*, 48–49.

One of them swore that he proceeded with as much caution in everything as if he were walking between red-hot irons, and acted with the same sincerity as if he were to die to-morrow, but all to no purpose.

Peter Oliver, a Loyalist, tells how the New Englanders played the devil with all the governors sent there — "Governor Burnet they worried into his grave. . . . They were continually adding fuel to the flame of contention which like the Vestal Fire — they made it a part of their religion to keep alive." The "demagoges," he said, "boasted that they could, when they pleased, remove any governor from his post." [1] If a governor made trouble by trying to carry out his instructions, he might be replaced by another who created the illusion of success through clever concessions to the assembly.[2] On the whole, however, it must be said that the British Government supported the governors against colonial complaints, especially if the officers incurred criticism only because they tried to carry out instructions.[3] There were exceptions, however, even to this, and Codrington, Governor of Barbados, a wrathful victim of colonial contumacy, declared that "if an English gentleman was to be perjured, clamoured, and voted out of his reputation without being allowed a hearing, then a Frenchman or even a Turk had no reason to envy an Englishman." His experience made him long for a furlough rather than a new commission. But it was not merely the

---

[1] British Museum, *Egerton MSS.*, 2671 F 16.

[2] Becker, *The Beginnings of the American People*, 164; Andrews, *The Colonial Period*, 169, 181.

[3] But see Dickerson. *American Colonial Government*, 156–57.

governor's activities in obeying his royal master that estranged him from the people of his colony. Even his sectarian preferences usually made him odious.

All governors, lieutenant-governors, secretaries, councillors, attorneys-general, chief justices, customs officers — all colonial officers, in fact, who were appointed by the British Government — were "ruffle-shirted Episcopalians," and attended the Anglican Church.[1] This fact, especially in the northern colonies where an opposing sect was established, served to keep the British officials aloof religiously and to make the Dissenters less willing to yield obedience to them. Moreover, these officers, thus isolated at this important point of social contact, lost that opportunity of understanding and sympathizing with the people. If they took religion at all seriously, they were sure to give offense by merely encouraging Anglican Church practices.

It was the Episcopalian zeal of Andros, in the last years of the seventeenth century, that so much aroused the wrath of the Puritans. In spite of their laws penalizing every observance of Christmas, Andros attended Anglican service on that day, "a red-coat . . . on his right hand and Captain George on his left," and sixty red-coated soldiers in the rear. In the spring, as if again to flout the "immodest

[1] For nearly one hundred years before the Revolution, royal governors were instructed to see that the Book of Common Prayer was read "each Sunday and Holy Day" and "the Blessed Sacrament administered according to the rules of the Church of England." *Documents Relating to the Colonial History of New York*, VII, 362. Note a curious result recorded in *Literary Diary of Ezra Stiles*, I, 294–95.

godliness" of the Puritans, he even caused a Maypole to be set up, and thereupon Increase Mather solemnly wrote that "the Devil had begun his march of triumph." When the governor, in his Anglican zeal, established an Episcopal minister in Boston, Puritan intolerance could see in him only "Baal's priest," and his prayers were "leeks, garlic, and trash," while his church was "Egypt's Babylon." [1] When he, finally, compelled the Puritans to share the south meeting-house, and ordered them to close their shops on the anniversary of the "martyrdom of Charles I," their indignation knew no bounds.

The ever-recurring clash between the provincial governor, symbol of the monarchical principle in government, and the assembly, symbol of the democratic principle, worked increasingly to awake the colonial sense of a divergence between American interests and those of England. No cause of the final rebellion is more profound, perhaps, than this nagging conflict. As time went on, the assemblies by fair means or foul, took over the functions of the governor, and even of his council which he had carefully selected from among such colonists as promised to be docile supporters of the royal power. Even the chief law officers of the colonies grew subservient as they became dependent upon the assembly for their salaries. The whole center of gravity of the colonial administration shifted grad-

[1] Mass. Hist. Soc., *Collections* (7th ser.), VII, 133; Oliver, *The Puritan Commonwealth*, 446–50; Mass. Hist. Soc., *Proceedings* (2d ser.), XIII, 410–11; Hutchinson, *Collection of Papers relative to Massachusetts Bay*, 525–76; Osgood, *The American Colonies in the Seventeenth Century*, III, 390.

ually from London to the capitals of the American
provinces. "Thus, little by little," wrote Governor
Glen of South Carolina (1743), "the people have got
the whole administration in their hands and the
crown is by various laws despoiled of its principal
flowers and brightest jewels." [1] "The whole frame of
government was unhinged," he wrote, "and the
governor divested of his power."

What flowers and jewels Governor Glen had in
mind we can in part determine from his own complaints. In defiance of the King's instructions, the
assembly, and not the governor, elected the holders
of all Church preferments. This might seem a small
matter, but at least it was a feather plucked from
Cæsar's wing. So independent were the clergy, as a
result, that the governor was not even prayed for,
he lamented, though the assembly did enjoy their
benediction. Almost all officers owed their places
to the truculent assembly. The treasurer, the Indian
commissioner, the comptroller of duties, the powder
receiver, were responsible to and removable only by
the assembly. It was the old English struggle over
again to win for the representatives of the people a
voice in the appointment of ministers of government.
All executive power was parceled out among commissioners — appointees of the Commons House of
Assembly — so that they had the sole direction
of everything. If the governor merely asserted that
all forts and castles belonged to the King, he would
not be listened to by the assembly, Glen declared.
In a word, by controlling the raising and spending of

[1] Wallace, *Henry Laurens*, 35, 37, 40.

taxes, and by choosing their own auditors, the Commons House of Assembly, as the lower house was called, were the real arbiters of the use of all public monies.[1] The very smallness of the affairs with which this "Parliament in miniature" dealt made it meticulous. No use of power was too small to be magnified into tyranny, if the governor tried to exercise it. Finding their power to be in "holding the purse-strings of the people," the members of the assembly never ceased their vigilance in that respect. They kept the same tight hold upon the public wallet that marked the early days of the British Parliament, even to learning to ape that ancient body in the trick of putting off the voting of supplies until the last day of the session.

Other colonies gained the same power over the governor. In Virginia, the burgesses supervised most expenditures, aside from the salary of the governor, by insisting on their right to appoint their own treasurers. To demand this right and gain it was but to repeat in an American province the exercise of a right which Parliament first successfully asserted over Henry IV, two centuries before. Some colonial assemblies in the British Empire had the brazen effrontery to appoint their own officer to receive and issue the public money even though a Crown officer was actually commissioned for that duty.[2] In New York the assembly persisted in elect-

[1] Wallace, *Henry Laurens*, 165. In England, Parliament had compelled Edward III to permit auditing of his accounts by their commissioners (1341), though the custom had not become definitely established until after the Restoration.

[2] Royal Hist. Soc., *Transactions* (4th ser.), I, 204.

ing its own treasurer, limiting all appropriations to
one year, making money bills specific, both as to
the purpose and as to the agent who should spend
the money.[1] By this constant, even excessive, use
of specific grants of money, governors were made
mere figureheads. Not only in New York and the
Carolinas, but in Massachusetts, New Jersey, and
Pennsylvania, the assemblies, repeating the ancient
methods and victories of Parliament, gained in time
full power over the finances. The victory was so
complete in New York (1754) that the Privy Council informed King George II, "The Assembly have
taken to themselves not only the management
and disposal of such publick money, but have also
wrested from your Majesty's Governor the nomina-
tion of all offices of Government, the custody and
direction of the publick military stores, the muster-
ing and direction of troops . . . and in short, almost
every other executive part of government." [2] By
the middle of the eighteenth century the lower house
in nearly all colonies had affected, in practice at
least, the powers and privileges of the British House
of Commons, and, protest as they would, the English authorities seemed unable to curb them.

The opposition of the assembly was by no means
always personal and directed against an unpopular
governor. It was more fundamental than that, for
it extended to any representative of the Imperial
Government. All appointees of the Crown, chief

[1] Becker, *Political Parties in the Province of New York*, 7; E. P.
Tanner, *The Province of New Jersey* (Columbia University Studies),
chap. XXII.

[2] *Documents Relating to the Colonial History of New York*, VI, 831-32.

justices, attorneys-general, customs officials, secretaries, deputy auditors, and receivers-general, had to expect trouble with the assembly, if by hook or crook that body could reach them.[1] The judiciary was a special object of the assembly's solicitude, and with reason in some cases, for, as Colonel Barré charged, men had been "promoted to the highest seats of justice" in the colonies, who to his knowledge "were glad by going to a foreign country to escape being brought to a bar of a court of justice in their own." The chief justice and the attorney-general sent to North Carolina by His Grace, the Duke of Newcastle, were declared not to know enough law to be "clerkes to a justice of the peace." [2] In New York where the governors won the technical points as to tenure and salary of judges, the assembly through an organized colonial bar was able, nevertheless, to control the judiciary.[3] Especially, the members of the governor's council appointed by him, and meant to act as an upper house in the colonial legislature, met with continual hostility. When the two houses in South Carolina clashed over the question of control of money bills, the Commons accused the Council of "seditious doctrine" for claiming such a control.[4] The Commons regarded the Council as representing an outside power, and believed that the principle of constitutional self-

---

[1] The South Carolina Assembly's effort to punish Chief Justice Wright illustrates the spirit of rancor. Wallace, *Henry Laurens*, 39.

[2] Dickerson, *American Colonial Government*, 144.

[3] Becker, *Political Parties in the Province of New York*, 7.

[4] Wallace, *Henry Laurens*, 38, 39, 40, 112, 115, 169; Channing, *Hist. of the U.S.*, I, 513.

government was at stake. The New York Assembly also asserted its supremacy as a legislature, and refused to allow the Council to amend money bills.[1] Again an American assembly was merely insisting upon the fruits of the victory of the British House of Commons (1678) won in conflict with the House of Lords over this same question in the reign of Charles II. The assemblies were not at all abashed by the rebuke of the Board of Trade declaring that "No assembly in the plantations ought to pretend to all the privileges of the House of Commons in England, which will no more be allowed them than it would to the council, if they should pretend to all the privileges of the House of Lords here." [2] In South Carolina, the Council and Commons quarreled over the matter of correspondence with the colonial agent in London and the Commons vindicated its power to control his election.[3] It was a matter of some moment whether this agent represented the popular element in the colony or those who supported royal prerogative. Neither Virginia nor Maryland was ever able to get its agents wholly under the control of the lower house.[4] As a result of the large measure of success which the lower houses of the colonial legislatures won, they came, like the Commons in South Carolina, to measure their privileges by those of the British House of Commons. Unmoved by the

[1] Becker, *Political Parties in the Province of New York*, 6; Channing, *Hist. of the U.S.*, II, 310.

[2] *New York Colonial Documents*, IV, 1171–72.

[3] Wallace, *Henry Laurens*, 96. See A. G. Waldo, in *Americana*, February, 1912.

[4] *Political Science Quarterly*, XXXV, 373–392 (B. Bond, art. on "The Colonial Agent").

adverse decisions of ministers and imperial law officers, they never ceased to claim the distinctive
powers of their more ancient model. Throughout
America the colonial lower houses of assembly,
through various stages of evolution strangely like
those experienced by the House of Commons in
England, attained a position of supremacy.[1] There
were, it is true, some of the battles which Parliament
had fought and won, which the provincial legislatures
did not have to fight over again — freedom of debate
for example; but on the other hand there was at
least one parliamentary victory which the American
assemblies desired, but never won — the exemption
from the royal veto upon their laws.

The assemblies, though often justified in their
attitude of opposition, were on many occasions
merely factious and unreasonable. They prevented,
or hindered till useless, measures both wise and for
their good. Never did they appear at worse advantage than in their opposition, during the French and
Indian War, to the imperial efforts to get them to
prepare for their own defense.[2] Their views were
often narrow, prejudiced, and unstatesmanlike.
Slowly and surely they inevitably encroached upon
the executive. Sometimes their motives for this
encroachment were even sinister, as when the members of the South Carolina Commons strove for a
large share of political power to save themselves
from loss after taking part in an illegal land-grabbing

---

[1] Dickerson, *American Colonial Government*, chap. v.

[2] *University of California Publications*, I, no. 1, pp. 1–98 (McCormac
article), "Colonial Opposition to Imperial Authority." *Political Science Quarterly*, XIII, no. 1, 55. (H. L. Osgood article.)

scheme.[1] But this was unusual, and, in general, they were merely narrow-minded, provincial politicians, watching with Argus eyes the petty interests which, after all, were their own. It is easy to give wise counsel after the event, but the opinion of Chief Justice William Smith is not unworthy of consideration. That distinguished Loyalist found Canada a more congenial land than New York when he had fled from the wrath of the patriots of that province, and after the Revolutionary War, he wrote reflectively:[2] "I trace the late revolt . . . to a remoter cause than those to which it is ordinarily ascribed. The truth is the country had outgrown its government and wanted the true remedy for more than half a century before the rupture commenced. . . . To expect wisdom and moderation from near a score of petty parliaments consisting in effect of only one of the three necessary branches of a parliament, must . . . appear to have been a very extravagant expectation. An American Assembly, quiet in the weakness of their infancy, could not but discover in their elevation to prosperity, that themselves were the substance, and the governor and Board of Counsel were shadows in their political frame. . . . It belonged to the administrations of the days of our fathers to have found the cure in the erection of a power upon the continent itself to control all its own little republics and create a partner in the legislation of the empire capable of consulting their own safety and the common welfare." Exile seemed to have

[1] Wallace, *Henry Laurens*, 42.
[2] C. P. Lucas, *History of Canada*, 256 (see 259).

given the banished Loyalist a prophetic vision of that Commonwealth of Nations which bitter experience was in the course of time to form out of Imperial Britain.

CHAPTER III

BRITISH EXPANSION CREATES IMPERIAL PROBLEMS

In 1763 British imperial attainment had reached the crest of the wave upon which it had been rising since the days of Raleigh. Not even the most dismal Cassandra would then have prophesied an approaching loss of half the empire which had been growing so rapidly for one hundred and fifty years. It had been two centuries and a half since Columbus's discovery had profoundly changed England's strategic position among the commercial nations. The Mediterranean was no longer the heart of the trading world. The change did not come at once, but with the growing use of the Atlantic and the firing of men's imagination with dreams of a Northwest Passage to India, England was awakened to her advantage. The Cabots, voyaging to Newfoundland and Labrador, seemed to have accomplished little toward stirring the English mind to grasp the opportunities, but at least their discoveries laid foundations for later claims to the North American coast.[1] Children who might have heard of Cabot were in the vale of years before England made further notable efforts to enter upon her heritage of the sea. Then came Drake and Hawkins and the piratical raids on Spanish settlements, during which the English "sea-dogs" acquired

---

[1] *American Historical Review*, IV, 60–61 (H. Harrisse, "The Outcome of the Cabot Quarter-Centenary").

the seamanship which in 1588 with the aid of fortune overthrew "the Invincible Armada." After that victory began the decline of Spanish sea-power and the rise of England's. With the growing sense of power, Englishmen began to have visions of a dominion beyond the sea which would rival if not destroy that of Spain. Essex, Gilbert, and Raleigh dreamed these dreams, and early in the seventeenth century, Sir Edwin Sandys, John Smith, George Calvert, John Winthrop, and many others gave them a reality on the Chesapeake and on Massachusetts Bay. From this time on, Venice was not more wedded to the Adriatic than England to the Atlantic. Thinking Englishmen came more and more to endorse the words of Sir John Boroughs in his "Sovereignty of the British Seas," "And therefore, the Sovereignty of our seas being the most precious Jewell of his Majesty's Crowne and (next under God) the principall meanes of our Wealth and Safetie, all true English hearts and hands are bounded by all possible meanes and diligence to preserve and maintaine the same, even with the uttermost hazzard of their lives, their goods and fortunes."

The extension of the British Empire beyond the seas was further secured by the strong Puritan navy fostered by Cromwell to fight at sea those who would overthrow the Protestant power.[1] This was the beginning of England's sea dominion. The English were forced as never before to comprehend their manifest destiny to rule the sea, to understand the

---

[1] See F. Strong, "Causes of Cromwell's West India Expedition,' in *American Historical Review*, IV, 228, 245.

advantage that geography had placed in their grasp. The destiny was not to be wholly won without the duel with Holland which we follow in such absorbing detail in Pepys' immortal diary. Holland at least saved herself from destruction in 1674, when the combined attack of England and France seemed to fail. But the Dutch strength had been overstrained, and thereafter her sea-power waned as England's forged ahead. Holland's merchant marine suffered from the British Navigation Laws, and her tenuous hold on the American coast at the mouth of the Hudson was lost during the reign of Charles II, when England's colonies became an unbroken series of settlements along the Atlantic coast. Aside from her waning sea-power, Holland had not the surplus population to people the Atlantic seaboard. The population of the English colonies doubled every twenty-five years, for, in addition to constant immigration from Europe, the exuberant economic promise of America did not tend to cause the most prudent colonist to reflect upon the deterrent theories of Malthus. English fecundity, as well as English sea-power, assured British hold upon the western shore of the Northern Atlantic.

The next phase of England's imperial expansion was initiated when she, with Holland, began to resist the efforts of Frenchmen, under Colbert's inspiration, to build a greater France in North America. Though France had begun early the competition for a place under the sun in America, she had been retarded by strife at home. The French Cartier had preceded the English Drake or Frobisher; Coligny ventured earlier than Raleigh or Gilbert; and the Pilgrims were but the contemporaries of the French founders of Acadia and Quebec; yet France, supreme in Europe, at the close of the Thirty Years' War had, because of the European struggle, fallen behind in the colonial race. Her prolonged struggle with England and Holland, which seemed at first a religious conflict, Catholic against Protestant, became in the days of Queen Anne the most commercial of wars. The American and Indian trade of the English and Dutch traders was imperiled. A union of the French and Spanish powers would probably close the American world to the English and the Dutch, so that in its wider aspects the War of the Spanish Succession was a competition for the New World. At the Treaty of Utrecht (1713), England for the moment won the race for America, and became, if not the dominant authority in the world, at least superlative in maritime power. France was still to be a dangerous rival in America and India, but for the time England gained Acadia, Nova Scotia, and Newfoundland, and the control of the lucrative slave-trade with the Spanish West Indies. British possessions in America were still small as compared with the empire of Spain, or the vast claims of France in Canada and the Mississippi Valley, but they were compact and peopled with Europeans. The conflict with France was not yet at an end, but dragged on until the great victory in the Seven Years' War, when Boscawen "made the Indies echo with his thunder" and the full might of English sea-power was revealed. The strategic genius of Hawke and

"Old Dreadnaught" had given England the command of the sea. That and the European war restrained the armies of France within her low-water mark, left her brave soldiers at Quebec and Montreal dependent on inadequate resources, and gave the English colonies the full support of the mother country. At the Treaty of Paris (1763), France, as the price of "a Christian, universal, and perpetual peace," gave up the remainder of her American empire — Canada and her claims east of the Mississippi to England, and Louisiana to Spain as compensation for the loss of Florida.[1] With that consummation, England became an object of jealousy for all Europe, and was everywhere denounced as the "tyrant of the seas." It was not strange that Horace Walpole talked of burning all day his Greek and Latin books, those "histories of little people." It had taken the Romans three hundred years to conquer the world, while his England, he boasted, had subdued the globe in three campaigns, a globe "as big again" as it was in the Roman's day. Yet the truth was that little by little the British, conquering and peopling half the world without any ambitious plan, had taken up the burdens of empire, forced by a fate whose decrees they could not honorably refuse to obey.

Though Great Britain roused the jealousy of the world by the rapidity with which she had added cubits to her imperial stature, yet had her enemies realized the magnitude of the problems of organization which accompanied that growth, all emotions

[1] *Revue des questions historiques*, XLIII, 420, lxxi, 1.

of envy would have died within them. At the dawn of the era of expansion the problems of empire had seemed easy of solution. All were answered by the simple formula of the mercantile theory as to colonies. Every governmental act which concerned the American colonies was determined by the political and economic theory that colonies were not worth while unless they could be so managed as to bring gold into the home country. No other motive was thinkable in that age. The aim was not to transplant English men and women to new homes across the sea where they might create a greater Britain, but to transport some laborers to a plantation in a distant land whose natural products were such as England could not raise herself. Swift's satire causes Gulliver to explain to the Houyhnhnms the kind of lands which his countrymen think worthy of colonization. As to those which "do not abound either in gold, silver, sugar or tobacco, I did humbly conceive that they were by no means proper objects of our zeal, our valor or our interests."

In their eagerness to force the American colonies to produce what England could not, the directors of colonial affairs flew in the face of nature. A new China and a new India were to be created by governmental magic on the American shores. Drugs and spices and silks were ordered grown where Nature had decreed that only tobacco or rice and indigo would grow. Since there were not mines of the precious metal in England, colonists were ordered to search for gold in Virginia. In order to escape dependence on the Dutch and Portuguese spice islands, the West Indies and Florida were to raise nutmegs, cloves, and ginger. Virginians must plant vines and raise silkworms, in order that wines and silks might no longer be the monopoly of France.[1]

The natural sequence of such ideas was that in the seventeenth century British statesmen had an attitude of positive dislike toward New England. These northern colonies were not serviceable as were the West Indies to the commercial system. Sandwich told Charles II to "hinder their growth" as much as possible. The goods they produced too nearly resembled those of England. As late as 1763 that idea still had advocates, and Parliament was urged to encourage growth in the South and check it in the North.[2] Only one use was conceived for them. In the New England pine forests the British Government caused to be marked with the King's broad arrow all trees of a size and kind to make good masts for the royal navy; the colonists north of Pennsylvania were ordered to produce tar and pitch and turpentine. But the New Englanders preferred the West Indian lumber trade in planks, beams, and clapboards for building of houses there, and for a half century they defied the Government agents, sued or drove them off when on their lawful business. New England maintained its economic independence for a generation before it ventured to assert political independence. Some part of the foundation for that assertion may be found in the irritation of these New

---

[1] Andrews, *The Colonial Period*, 110–11.
[2] Alvord, *The Mississippi Valley in British Politics*, I, 53; Beer, *The Old Colonial System*, II, 233–34.

England woodmen, determined to earn their living in their own way.[1]

By 1760, however, manufactures were increasing by leaps and bounds, and progressive statesmen, of whom William Pitt was the leader, began to grasp a new theory of the place of colonies in an empire. New Englands might profitably be set up beyond the seas, whose citizens would wear English clothes, adorn their houses with English furniture, and eat their food on English plates and with English cutlery. In a word, dependencies might be useful merely as market-places, even though they produced no raw materials not grown in England. Men began to argue that a proper aim in planting or acquiring a colony might be "to increase the strength of the mother country by providing room for an increase of people."[2] Settlers on American soil, it was augered, would multiply the English seed as the stars of heaven. It was these new conceptions of the purpose of colonies that made Pitt decide, during the negotiations leading to the Treaty of Paris, to take Canada from France rather than Guadeloupe as one of the spoils of war. Even after that date, however, the city merchants of England seem still to have clung to the old preferences for tropical colonies, while the manufacturers and farmers leaned toward the new theory. Dominated during the formative period by ideas springing from the mercantile theory, England had a commercial and not a colonial policy. England became the "Mother

---

[1] E. L. Lord, *Industrial Experiments*, 56, 87, 123.
[2] Alvord, *The Mississippi Valley in British Politics*, I, 52, 54.

of Nations" in spite of the purpose of her Government, whose remotest wish, perhaps, was to beget "children of Kingdoms," to use Bacon's homely phrase. "Colonies are only settlements made in different parts of the world for the improvement of trade," wrote (1765) one who fully understood the Government's aim. It was not, from the modern viewpoint, an enlightened statesmanlike policy, aiming at the welfare of the colonies, but a policy grown in the market-place, rooted in the idea of gain for the mother country. Nevertheless, it worked very well in an age utterly impervious to any other idea, and perhaps was the only practical way in that stage of human experience.

It was tobacco, the natural product of Virginia's soil, that first determined the British policy.[1] In 1621 orders came to Virginia to ship all tobacco to England and to trade with no foreign merchants. That policy continued unchanged to the opening of the Revolution. Washington and Richard Henry Lee, as their fathers before them, were compelled by law to send all of their tobacco, that "scurvy" but most profitable weed, to England. Though King James had written his "Counterblaste to Tobacco," and reputable writers had declared that men "grew mad and crazed in the brain" if they "sucked the smoke of this weed," yet so great was the number who ventured their wits that tobacco came to be the only colonial product that brought profit to both planter and merchant and which brought satisfaction

---

[1] Andrews, *The Colonial Period*, 114; Beer, *Origins of the British Colonial System, 1578–1660*, chap. IV.

to the British exchequer. In Cromwell's time (1651) an ordinance reaffirmed the earlier trade restrictions and required all trade to be in English or colonial built ships,[1] but it was not until the return of Charles II, ruined in purse and bent on exploiting the colonies to recoup his fortunes, that the full logical development of England's restrictive policy began.

The restrictive system fully entered upon at that time found expression ultimately in three types of laws. The first sort were acts of navigation which protected British shipowners against Dutch and French and Spanish owners and indeed all foreign competition.[2] A second group were acts of trade which aimed to secure a monopoly for English merchants of colonial commerce. A third class sought to secure English manufacturers against the development of rival industry in the colonies, and to put in their hands a monopoly of the colonial markets.[3] Some laws combined two or more of these aims. All three look, to our modern eyes, like class legislation, devised to put gold, not only into the

[1] Beer, *Origins of the British Colonial System, 1578–1660*, 374, 385.

[2] While working together in the Public Records Office in London, R. G. Usher called my attention to a document in P. C. *Register*, 28, Fol. 95, which shows that as early as 1615 the principle of the Navigation Acts was announced by the Privy Council in the matter of shipping fish in foreign bottoms. And, of course, there had been Navigation Acts even earlier, in the time of Richard II, for example. Cross, *England and Greater Britain*, 213.

[3] The important Trade and Navigation Acts in the series can most conveniently be studied in Macdonald, *Documentary Source Book*, 55, 72, 78, 90, 105. By the end of the seventeenth century England had, by the improvement of her customs administration, shown her fixed purpose to limit the trade of her colonies to the bounds of the "mpire within which it could be controlled.

King's depleted treasury, but into the purses of English shipowners, merchants, and manufacturers. The Navigation Acts, it is true, covered under their beneficent ægis the shipowners of the colonies as well as of England, and the building of ships so prospered that it was said of New England that the world "never saw a more amphibious population." What the Government did was not for any despotic purpose, but because in that age nobody saw a reason for colonies except for business ends. It was the only natural thing to do at that time, and contemporary statesmen of any other nation in the world would have thought the British ministers shallow-pated, indeed, had they done otherwise. The American colonies were regarded as great enterprises to be directed by those who would profit by the business. The colonists must not manufacture lest they rival that industry in England. Even William Pitt, "friend of America," declared with a grand gesture that "if the Americans should manufacture a lock of wool or a horse shoe," he would "fill their ports with ships and their towns with troops." [1] These prohibitions, which only affected manufactures on a large scale, did little harm to colonial prosperity, for the want of capital, the high price of labor, the counter-temptation of abundant fertile land made manufacturing the least alluring industry. Men turned rather to commerce and agriculture, and only in the homes were articles made

[1] Knox, *Extra Official State Papers*, II, Appendix XV. Laws against colonial manufacturing were (1699) aimed against woolen industry; (1732), beaver hats; (1750) rolled iron. See 10 and 11 Wm. III, chap. X, 19; 5 Geo. II, chap. XXIII, 23 Geo. II, chap. XXIX.

for domestic consumption. What commercial undertakings the colonists had must be for the profit of Englishmen, not of colonists. The colonial planter or New England trader must sell only to England, and buy only over British counters. Henry Laurens, of South Carolina, must sell his rice and indigo and deer skins to English merchants, and buy his India goods, his furniture, and his hats and gloves from a London or Bristol merchant. Free of British control, he might have sold his goods at greater profit in France or Spain, and bought his clothing and finery cheaper there, but that must not be, since he was a colonist. All of this system was the result of no peculiar selfishness or tyrannous attributes of English business men and their Government, but was in full accord with the dominant theory of the age which ruled at Madrid and Paris as completely as in London. Perhaps Englishmen were more pushing than Frenchmen and Spaniards. Some may have deserved Franklin's slur that "Britain would if she could manufacture & trade for all the World; England for all Britain; — London for all England; — and every Londoner for all London." "Nature," he sneered, "has put Bounds to your Abilities, tho' none to your Desires."[1] But Addison painted the British merchant more charitably. "Our English merchant converts the tin of his own country into gold, and exchanges his wool for rubies. The Mahometans are clothed in our British manufacture, and the inhabitants of the frozen zone are warmed with the fleeces of our sheep." The British merchant,

[1] Franklin, *Writings* (Smyth, *ed.*), IV, 245.

Addison contended, knits "mankind together in a mutual intercourse of good offices, distributes the gifts of Nature, finds work for the poor, adds wealth to the rich, and magnificence to the great." Surely such services must be rewarded, the admiring statesman would urge, and moreover, he might have added Britain was only carrying out logically an idea that swayed every statesman of that age. Moreover, the British Government defended the justice of regulating trade in the interests of the Crown by pointing out that the royal navy, in both peace and war, protected the colonies and all their trade, in an age of real peril from powerful enemies. "These restrictive laws," declared a believer in them, "founded upon principles of the most solid policy, flung a great weight of naval force into the hands of the mother country, which was to protect the colonies, and without an union with which the colonies must have been entirely weak and defenceless." [1] It was hard, nevertheless, for a colonist to realize that British guardianship which the royal navy exercised. That power which kept the enemy from the American shores, and prevented it bringing stores and ammunition to its nationals in Canada, was a power little appreciated by the colonist. When he spoke of fighting his own battles, he thought of repelling Indian attacks and French invasions from the north, but little of that British fleet which by long and weary vigils out at sea kept the French Government from sending aid to its subjects in Canada. Its work was not spectacular, not done in the view of the

[1] Hansard, *Parliamentary History*, xvi, 201.

colonists, rarely obviously performed for their good, and they easily forgot it as one of the obligations to England. Even the colonists, however, would not have disputed the soundness of the mercantile theory, though the logic of their interests forced them to oppose its practical results.

In consequence of this guiding idea, England's administrative system for her colonies had no other object than the regulation of commerce. With such an aim there seemed no reason for developing a department concerned with the colonies alone. One great reason for the failure of the British Government to solve successfully the problem of keeping its colonies loyal to itself, was the fact that in its governmental system there was no organ with independent power to act and evolve colonial policies The Board of Trade and Plantations could advise, but not do things. All other officers or governmental bodies had in the main to look after the business of the kingdom, and attended to colonial matters only as a subordinate duty to which they turned aside at convenience.[1] The King and his Privy Council might give a little time to the affairs of Virginia or of New York, but affairs of the kingdom would loom larger and seem vastly more important. Parliament, as it grew in power, and took into its hands all momentous business of the empire, would lightly touch colonial problems, but it could spare little time to consider relevant facts which assiduous Boards might have gathered. As Richard Bland pointed out, in his

[1] Andrews, *The Colonial Period*, 138, 140; Dickerson, *American Colonial Government*, chaps. II, III.

famous pamphlet (1763), "The ministers in *England* see nothing with their own eyes that is passing amongst us, and know nothing upon their own Knowledge; and therefore are very improper Legislators to give Laws to the Colony."[1] The Secretary of State was a busy man who might initiate policies, but he would be likely to know all other things before the peculiar needs of American provinces. The Treasury and the Admiralty had certain functions to perform in the colonies — functions connected with the customs duties and the trade laws, but a policy in those matters was not their affair. The same was true of the War Office which had charge of the army in America. Finally, the Board of Trade and Plantations, founded in 1696, which, alone of all the governmental organs, was especially concerned with colonial affairs, could, out of its mass of records and reports, merely advise the Privy Council, or Secretary of State or Parliament, but had no power of its own to carry out a policy.[2] Moreover, great as was the attention they gave the colonies, and full as was their information, trade was its single aim, and all that they did was to the end of making the colonies profitable to the Crown. Among all of these offices there was little coöperation or responsibility, and their methods were clumsy and dilatory. Their agents in the colonies were in some cases allowed to serve by deputy. Captain Phipps claimed to have known a person in Virginia who held eleven offices, the emoluments

[1] *William and Mary College Quarterly*, xix, 39.
[2] Channing, *Hist. of the U.S.*, ii, 231-37 (especially page 235).

of which were appropriated to the support of men of bad description in England.[1] Patents of office were farmed out, and plural holdings allowed. Sinecures were common, and with them and the other loaves and fishes of public life Ministers bought political subservience. Methods of appointment were bad, and the appointees were often not above bribery and corruption. A colonial administration with no higher aim than regulation of commerce, having no special organ of government responsible for it, and a lack of coöperation among the many organs that dabbled in it, did not need to be hampered by low political morals to end in failure. Nevertheless, England was not behind but rather ahead, perhaps, of her contemporaries in her colonial efficiency. The art of governing colonies so that they would remain loyal to the mother country was as yet unknown.

In the interest of plans for enriching and strengthening the kingdom, the early free-and-easy ways of leaving proprietors and chartered companies to rule the American plantations gave way to a plan to develop a more uniform and centralized system of control. During the early eighteenth century repeated efforts were made to bring under the Crown all colonial governments not hitherto dependent on it. The heads of the Anglican Church and the Board of Trade gave hearty support, but the Whig party opposed it. Though the Board long clung to the idea, it could never get Parliamentary sanction. The only measure of success they had was that within

[1] Almon, *Debates of Parliament*, IX, 144.

sixty years they increased the number of royal provinces from three to seven. Moreover, as a result of their efforts to unify the empire, colonial laws were, after 1700, more regularly sent back to England for approval by the Crown, and royal governors got fuller and more precise instructions. It should not be forgotten, either, that in spite of the running fight between royal governor and provincial assembly, the extent to which the rod of empire was wielded in American affairs, and on the whole obeyed, was vast, and caused a drift toward unity. Finally, the very system of trade control, wrong as it was, probably tended to give greater cohesion to the empire, though British statesmen had aimed toward a self-sufficient economic empire, rather than one closely knit politically.[1]

Influences and tendencies were not wanting, therefore, to bring about imperial unity, but it was a unity which bound each integral part to the center. As far as there was conscious effort by British statesmen, it was directed to creating ties that bound Massachusetts to England, New Jersey to England, and Virginia and North Carolina to the same imperial center. The maxims of the commercial system argued the wisdom of keeping the colonies weakened by their divisions, and dependent on the strength of the British Government. Even Burke (1769) wrote of the great empire which "we have to rule, composed of a vast mass of heterogeneous governments . . . all to be kept in peace, and kept out of conspiracy, with one another, all to be held in subordination

---

[1] Beer, *British Colonial Policy, 1754–65*, 210.

to this country." [1] The inexorable mercantile theory would permit the growth of governments able to manage American local affairs, but not an American general government competent to deal with the affairs of America as a whole. Samuel Adams, Patrick Henry, and Christopher Gadsden were so bound up in the petty concerns of their respective provinces that the imperial interests touched them not at all.[2] Could they have sat in an American parliament, such as, indeed, was proposed in 1754 by the Albany Congress, which was responsible for all inter-colonial affairs, they must have developed loyalty to the American portion of the British imperial domain, and the assumption of that responsibility would have saved the necessity of the ill-fated interference by the English Parliament. As can be seen to-day, Great Britian was so nearly in sight of the promised land that one wonders why she did not enter in and possess it. Franklin wrote long after [3] "that if the Albany plan of union had been adapted and made effective, the subsequent separation of the colonies from the Mother Country might not so soon have happened. . . . For the Colonies, if so united, would have really been . . . sufficient to their own Defence, and being trusted with it . . . an Army from Britain, for that purpose would have been unnecessary; the Pretences for framing the Stamp Act would then not have existed, nor the other Projects . . . which were the causes of the Breach and attended with such

---

[1] Burke, *Works* (ed. 1869), I, 396.

[2] Note attitude in New York. Becker, *Political Parties in the Province of New York*, 6.

[3] Franklin, *Writings* (Smyth, *ed.*), III, 226–27.

terrible Expense of Blood and Treasure." Franklin
was probably quite right in this, for it was because
of the manifest incapacity of the separate colonial
assemblies to handle the domestic affairs of America,
such as military defense and Indian affairs, that
the British Government undertook those measures
which led to the final break and American independence. The colonies feared the plan because of the
taxing power to be given the Grand Council,[1] yet
that was exactly the power which, after years of bitter experience under the Articles of Confederation,
it was found necessary in 1787 to grant to the new
Federal Government. The Albany plan was feared
by the British Ministry lest it should weaken central
control and make America too strong, and yet it
seems the only device which would have made the
colonies able to cope with the larger problems of
America, and thus have saved Parliament the necessity of stepping in to assume the care themselves.
It is, perhaps, a statesman's greatest task to breed
a devotion in those they govern which will make
them forget their interests and themselves. It was
in that direction that the rulers of the British Empire
had failed in America. They did not seem to know
how that emotion was engendered; their only study
of the question had been in the market. Loyalty to
the empire was sadly lacking in the average American colonist. He clamored for the *rights* of Englishmen, but was unconcerned about the *duties*. The
average colonists felt no sense of duty to maintain

[1] For example, see Mass. Hist. Soc., *Collections* (1st Ser.), VII.
208–09.

the empire as a whole. That sense seemed atrophied through lack of exercise. They had only a petty provincial interest, material interest for which their legislatures fought.[1]

Besides the inability of statesmen to anticipate the solutions of the problems of preserving a united empire — a solution which only time could unfold — there are certain physical facts in the American situation which help to explain the dominant particularism of the colonies. The very forces of physical geography would seem to have conspired far back in geologic ages to make the colonies self-centered, individualistic, and disunited. The rivers of the American coast which faced Europe did not form a system like those of the basin of the Mississippi, but flowed each one more or less directly to the sea. South of New England each flowed in what the geologist calls a drowned river valley. The old bed of the river had been submerged as the sea flowed in upon the edge of the continent, when, as the result of some vast geological change or convulsion, the Atlantic coast had subsided. The lower courses of all the seaboard rivers were much deeper in consequence. The Hudson was navigable to the seafaring vessels of the day as far as Albany; the Delaware as far as Trenton. Chesapeake Bay, with its far-stretching arms, formed by the inrushing sea, gave watery highways to numerous settlements. All the lower courses of the rivers of Maryland and Virginia were overflooded, and deepened. The

[1] Yet not all were wanting in that larger loyalty, as the many thousand Loyalists of the Revolution proved.

Potomac was open to ocean-going ships as far as the present site of Washington, the James as far as Richmond, and each accommodated, along its easily accessible banks, a narrow, isolated border of settlements, hugging closely to the rivers which kept them in touch with the sea and thus with Europe. Joshua Gee argued in 1738 against the theory that in time the colonies would grow rich and set up for themselves and cast off the British government. The fear was groundless, he said, because the colonists nearly all lived on the navigable rivers and bays of America where the British navy could easily reach and subdue them.[1] Behind the settlements in the early days stretched a tangled, often pathless forest through which even bridle-paths but slowly penetrated. Each settlement was a little world by itself, physically isolated, and communicating with its neighbors by river and sea routes. Months went by with no news of the outside world, and the colonists, having no thoughts but of themselves, were absorbed in their own petty problems. Few ventured to pass by land from one colony to another. Trade, that powerful agent for binding people together, was so hampered by the British Navigation Laws that it did but little to knit the colonies together. It was easier for law-abiding merchants to do their trading with England across the sea than with most American colonies. The news, too, that came to most colonies was from the West Indies or England rather than from an American neighbor. Maryland and Virginia were,

[1] Joshua Gee, *Trade and Navigation of Great Britain* (6th ed.), **71.**

of course, bound together by the watery highways of the Chesapeake, and the Delaware preserved an intercourse by means of sloops and shallops and schooners which plied between Pennsylvania, Delaware, and New Jersey. The latter could trade also with Long Island and New York by water routes. New England settlements formed a group by themselves which early coalesced along their borders. South Carolina and Georgia lay isolated from them all. Each of these groups was largely cut off from the rest. In the absence of roads, which the early colonists were too poor to build, the path of intercolonial commerce must be down one river to the sea, along the dangerous coast, unlighted and without mariners' signals, and then up a second river to the other colony. Taking into account the distance, the dangers, and the fact that it was the day of sailing vessels, it is easy to see that there were needed few legal barriers to turn most of the trade to England. The commercial intercourse, therefore, which must have helped unite the colonies was long prevented by Nature, and by statesmen who saw fit to reënact the law of God. It was little wonder that colonies long remained "as much divided in their interest and affection as Christian and Turk." [1]

The results of the selfish provincialism engendered by decrees of Nature, by laws rooted in the commercial policy, and by the failure of statesmen to conjure the spirit of loyalty in American hearts, were fully realized during the seven years' struggle

---

[1] *Documents Relating to the Colonial History of New York*, IV. 73.

with France for imperial expansion and commercial existence. Though America may have been won in Germany, or at least kept there, as Pitt's declaration may be interpreted, the phases of that conflict which affected the colonial relations with the British Government were battles with Indians on all colonial frontiers, and with French in the Ohio Valley and about Quebec. When war began, the Crown urged upon all its agents in America to get every grant and service possible from the colonists to drive out the French and repel the Indians leagued with them. All schemes failed, however, to bring them "to a sense of their duty to the king, to awaken them to take care of their lives and fortunes." The attempt to get united action failed at the Albany Congress, and all that was left to hope was action by individual colonies. That was doomed from the first because the larger motive was wanting. The colonists could see the war only as a struggle for empire on the part of England and France, in which the winning government would reap the spoils and ought to pay. They felt no shame, therefore, that the British Government was obliged to send to America large numbers of regulars to wage the colonial battles and that it was the "red-coats," and not provincial troops, that won the war.[1] When (1765) Colonel Barré resented Townshend's assertion that the colonists had been protected by British arms, and declared that on the contrary "they have nobly taken up arms in your defence," he showed

[1] Beer, *British Colonial Policy*, 270. (The size of colonial levies of troops is discussed in a note.)

that he knew more of feats of broil and battle than of history. His oratory was capital, but the valor which colonists exerted was for their own protection, and in the French and Indian War, at least, was lukewarm even when their frontiers were being drenched in blood. The response to the Ministry's request for provincial troops from the southern colonies was feeble and of little avail. Georgia was poor and weak, needing governmental support even to protect her own frontiers.[1] South Carolina began well and had three hundred men at Great Meadows, but thereafter she was content with warding attacks on her own border.[2] North Carolina, rent with party factions, and wrestling with a bad money system, made plans which she only half executed, and was satisfied with laying the odium on the governor for their failure. The presence of the French in western territory claimed by Virginia might have aroused her interest, but her early efforts were not heartening. No proper military law could be enacted, and all of Governor Dinwiddie's efforts could enlist only such men as were described by Washington as "loose idle persons, that are quite destitute of house and home . . . many of them without shoes, others want stockings, some are without shirts, and not a few have scarce a coat or waistcoat for their backs." [3] The future "father" of his

---

[1] *Colonial Records of Georgia*, XIII, 47, 61.

[2] *Dinwiddie Papers*, I, 249.   South Carolina voted £6000 for the Braddock expedition.

[3] Hening, *Statutes*, VI, 112, *et seq.*;   Washington, *Writings* (Ford, ed.), I, 42.   Many of these wretches seem to have been indentured servants. See Lady Edgar, *A Colonial Governor*, etc., 46.

country found the officer's pay so small that he "would rather dig for a maintenance . . . than serve on such ignoble terms." The Virginia burgesses worried the governor so much about the rights of Englishmen, and did so little for the common cause, that Dinwiddie denounced their pretensions. "I hear you," he sneered, "declaring your knowledge of your country's danger" and "professing the most ardent Zeal for her Service; yet find these declarations only an unavailing Flourish of Words." [1] Later, Virginians responded more freely, and made amends for their early delays. The total contribution, however, of the southern colonies was very inconsiderable, and Braddock fell in 1755 largely because that section and Pennsylvania had failed in their duty not only to the empire but to themselves.

In both Pennsylvania and Maryland disputes with the Penns and Calverts rendered the colonist even more callous to the needs of the empire. In the "City of Brotherly Love" seven years of conflict between the proprietary governor and assembly marked the war period, during which they went, again and more exhaustively, over every subject of controversy that had marked the whole colonial period. [2] The assembly, deaf to argument or reason, would haggle over a theory of their rights under the British Constitution while their border citizens were

[1] *Colonial Records of North Carolina*, v, 138; *Journals of the House of Burgesses, 1752–58*, 205; *Virginia Historical Collections*, III (*Dinwiddie Papers*), I, 302, 328.

[2] Root, *Relations of Pennsylvania with the British Government*, chap. x.

being butchered. Besides the question of rights, the Quaker statesmen would rather die than resist the Indians or French with "carnal weapons." When asked to give to the common cause they refused to dip their money in blood. At one time, they voted five hundred dollars to buy the Indians off, but not to fight them. During the long quarrel with the governor, the assembly accused the Penns of reaping where they had not sown, of trying to make free tenants abject vassals. They agreed to raise money by taxation, if the vast estates of the Penns might be taxed too. While they dallied and made the excuse that they were not obliged to defend the Penns' estate at their own expense, they seemed to forget that it was not a question of estates, but of human beings left to the horrors of tomahawk and firebrand. Both the Penns and the assembly were stubborn, and their "obstinacy invincible" left the colony defenseless. Such troops as were voted were raised under a wretched law, which made them an extremely bad collection "of broken Innkeepers, Horse Jockeys, and Indian traders . . . a gathering from the scum of the worst of people in every Country," who were in a panic at the very name of Indians.[1] In Maryland, Baltimore was more generous than the Penns and gave to the cause some fines and licenses which were wont to yield him revenue. Aside from this action, the controversies with the assembly ran the same course as in Pennsylvania. The chief desire of the colonial representatives seemed to be to discredit the proprietor with

[1] Kimball, *Pitt's Correspondence*, I, 342.

the British Government. "Throwing out a sop . . . to these noisy animals," as Calvert suggested, was not tried. Maryland's assembly, too, would grant no compulsory military law, and, like most of the other colonies, was "parsimonious even to prodigality."

In New York the law-givers granted money, but insisted upon choosing their own committee to spend it, so that the governor, burdened with the colony's defense, must run to the committee with every little item of expense. Moreover, the assembly did not make good even what it voted. New Jersey, on good terms with its governor, and more charitable toward its neighbors than was common in colonial days, was peculiarly alive to the interests of the "King and Country." New England responded more freely than the other sections. Connecticut and Rhode Island are especially noteworthy. They had no existing quarrel with the British Government, and, having governors of their own choosing and charters so liberal as to leave them secure in practical independence, they were conspicuously loyal. It seems strange that no statesman of the time noted the significance of that loyalty, and the conditions that begot it. In Massachusetts Governor Shirley had the wit to know how to go with his people as far as he could without worrying and putting them out of temper.[1] He opened the hearts, and even the pocketbooks of his "wise, free, jealous and moral people," by telling them of Pitt's promise that the money they voted would be repaid. New Hampshire was

[1] Hutchinson, *History of Massachusetts Bay*, III, 17.

the most reluctant colony of her section, and what she did she delayed too long to be of service.

A conspectus of the conduct of all the thirteen colonies during the French and Indian War reveals individual colonies waiting, watching, furtively advancing, or halting until another colony should act. Burnaby, who traveled there during the war, declared: "Fire and water are not more heterogeneous than the different colonies in North America. Nothing can exceed the jealousy and emulation which they possess in regard to each other." [1] "The Want of Union among the Colonies must ever occasion Delay in their military Operations," wrote William Franklin.[2] "The first that happens to be called upon postpones coming to any Determination till 't is known what other colonies will do; and each of those others think they have an equal Right to act in the same Manner. This procrastinating Conduct, owing to the Jealousies and Apprehensions each Colony has lest it should happen to contribute Somewhat more than its Share, is the Reason why the American Levies are sometimes delayed till the Season for Action is nearly elapsed." Such a system which allowed New York or South Carolina or any colony to evade its duty as part of the empire was plainly bad. It made the action of the least zealous become the standard for all; it penalized the active and public-spirited. It was not strange that the royal governors thought them "sunk in profound

---

[1] Burnaby's *Travels* (Wilson, *ed.*, 1904), 152–53.
[2] Wm. Franklin to Board of Trade, March 6, 1764, in New Jersey *Archives* (1st Series), IX, 429.

lethergy, and resigned to stupidity and slumbering."
The French counted upon this lack of team-work,
and even the Indians looked askance at the want
of union. Indeed, the colonial lack of uniform and
just dealings with the Indians, especially in trade
matters, made them lukewarm to the English cause,
and caused them to lean to the French in their
sympathies during the war.[1]

It was plain, long before the end, that the Seven
Years' War had forced to the fore imperial problems,
which, though strictly American, were yet too large
for any of the autonomous colonies to handle alone.
It was, moreover, the strain which the Seven Years'
War put upon the relations between Great Britain
and her American colonies which forced into prominence every subject of controversy which for a
hundred years had been setting by the ears the
royal governor and the provincial assembly. Americans had never so clarified their ideas on constitutional questions, and, aided by the stress of war,
had demanded everything nominated in the bond.
What assistance had been secured by Pitt from the
American colonies had been bought at an alarming
price — concessions which deprived the governors
of all but their pomp, and left the assemblies with
every real power. Moreover, the utter want of any
sense of loyalty to the empire on the part of individual colonists was shown in the extent to which
illicit trade was carried on with the enemy. Not all
the British naval activity could prevent colonial

[1] Wraxall's *Abridgment of Indian Affairs* (H. C. McIlvaine's ed.)
is an excellent survey of Indian affairs up to 1756.

merchants from supplying French colonies with the provisions for want of which they must have capitulated. Fortunes were made in the trade, and so demoralized was public opinion that convictions on clear proof were not to be gotten from colonial juries. William Pitt gave strictest orders to enforce the laws of trade, but all to no purpose.[1] The conviction was forced upon the British Government that the American portion of its empire must be made to assume its duties. No better device occurred to them than compulsion by action of the British Parliament. Even good friends of the colonies believed that such a procedure would be for their good. Governor Hutchinson wrote: "I never think of the measures necessary for the peace and good order of the Colonies without pain. There must be an abridgment of what are called English liberties. I relieve myself by considering that in a remove from a state of nature to the most perfect state of government there must be a great restraint of natural liberty. I doubt whether it is possible to project a system of government in which a Colony, 3000 miles distant from the parent state shall enjoy all the liberty of the parent state. I am certain that I have never yet seen the projection. I wish the good of the Colony when I wish to see some further restraint of liberty, rather than the connection with the parent State should be broken." [2]

[1] Beer, *British Colonial Policy, 1754–1765*, chap. VI.   Rhode Island and Pennsylvania were especially guilty. Governor Denny of Pennsylvania openly sold passes which aided the traders to escape detection.
[2] Belcher, *First American Civil War*, I, 105.

There was a good vein of common sense in
Hutchinson's philosophy, if strong rule from the center were the only alternative to feeble and inefficient
rule by thirteen separate assemblies. The obvious
weakness of the plan of the British Ministry was the
purpose to use compulsion with this grown child of
the empire rather than persuasion. The Ministers
did rot understand, as Pitt begged them to do, that
the colonies had become "too great an object to be
grasped but in the arms of affection." [1] The gods,
bent on the destruction of the empire, seemed to
have made its rulers mad. The pride and haughtiness engendered in the English rulers by their
successes in the Seven Years' War, ending in the
triumphant peace of 1763, made them impatient of
colonial resistance to their will. Horace Walpole
described his contemporaries of the English ruling
class as "born with Roman insolence" and behav-
ing with "more haughtiness than an Asiatic monarch." [2]

It was in this spirit that the English rulers undertook to set bounds to the independence already won,
to establish a system of real British control in America. This aim might have succeeded a century before
when America was "of mean Beginnings" as "was
Rome," but now Pitt warned them that the "scanty
fountain" had become "a large Stream, covered with
Sails and floated with a commerce." [3] It was too
late; "England, victorious in four parts of the

---

[1] *American Historical Review*, xvii, 573.
[2] Walpole, *Letters* (Toynbee, *ed.*), vii, 365.
[3] *American Historical Review*, xvii, 573.

world," could not conjure back into its prison the free spirit of American independence. Stubborn efforts to that end led through ten fateful years to the severing of the empire.

CHAPTER IV

THE WORLD'S COLONIAL EXPERIENCES WHICH MIGHT GUIDE BRITISH STATESMEN

HAVING traced the rapid growth of the British Empire to the year 1763, we have seen what appears from our point of view the attempt to govern the new Englands overseas as if they were mere estates to be exploited for gain, or market-places wherein to enrich English merchants. We have seen statesmen guided, by what we in our greater wisdom might call an economic friar's-lantern, the mercantile theory, to the building up of a restrictive system that seems to unsympathetic modern eyes coolly planned with no other aim than to enrich England at the expense of the colonies. It is easy now to criticize it all, to ridicule such a policy and hold it up to scorn, but that was the way the age did things and from their point of view there was no better way. We have observed, too, the development of an administrative system which, in addition to its crudity and lack of efficient organization, had only a commercial and not a colonial end in view. It rather vaguely and slowly endeavored to attain a more unified system of control. Its failure was demonstrated during the Seven Years' War, and as a result we shall see a firm though ill-judged effort to centralize imperial control, an effort which the colonies met with resistance and rebellion. These facts, and the natural interpretation of them taken by themselves, have tended to give the students of history a rather low opinion of the British statesmen of the period preceding and during the American Revolution. No proper estimate of the praise or blame which readers of history must accord them can be reached without an examination of the accumulated political wisdom of the age in colonial matters and an effort to ascertain the bounds which the experience of mankind placed upon all statesmen confronted with such problems. Pitt, Grenville, and Townshend were met with a new imperial problem to solve; we who are wiser than they have our minds illumined by seven or eight additional generations of human experience

First of all it must be comprehended that superior as were England's political attainments to those of any country in continental Europe, greater still were the political advances of her American colonists, beyond the colonial subjects of any other contemporary government. The very fullness of their political freedom made them sensitive to the least interference, and fierce to resent it. While in Harrington's quaint phrase, they were "yet babes," and could "not live without sucking the breasts of their mother cities," they endured occasional restraint, but when they came of age they fulfilled his prophecy that they would seek to "wean themselves." One of the deepest reasons for their turning away from the mother state was the training in political liberty which England had permitted them from their earliest days. Either by example from the political struggles at home, or in the harsh school of frontier experience, they had learned the sweetness of liberty. The degree of their freedom can be understood only by comparing the English colonial system with that of her great European rivals. With these contrasts clearly in mind, the truth will appear that the freest of colonists were the first to rebel.

Whatever might have been the original condition of English colonies in America, or whatever from time to time the imperial purpose of the British Government, the political fact had come to be, by 1760, that the colonies were self-governing. They possessed assemblies which enjoyed political supremacy within their own boundaries. Through their own laws and committees the colonial legislatures controlled to a large extent the policy of the colonies. Within its own little realm, a colonial legislature was hardly less mighty than the British Parliament. It was but impatient exaggeration when a colonial official declared that "Rhode Island was no more a part of the British Empire than the Bahamas when they were inhabited by Buccaneers." [1] Parliament might pass laws to regulate her commerce, but there were smugglers to set the laws at naught, and as for the great majority of her domestic concerns, Parliament never heard of them.

English emigrants to America seemed to see no other way to manage their political affairs than by an imitation of the methods of England. The English colonies started with the great advantage that the home country understood parliamentary government. The time of conflict between the royal

[1] Josiah Quincy, *Reports of Massachusetts Courts*, 4, 36–37.

claims of the Stuarts and the demands of the more progressive members of Parliament was identical with the era of England's first colonial efforts. Those who strove for the supremacy of Parliament were not always successful in England, but the idea of government by representatives of the people was familiar enough to be very early taken account of in the colonial charters. The earliest of them were meant to be liberal,[1] but at best the first Virginian charters left the colonizing company at the mercy of the King and the colonists at the mercy of the Company. But a dozen years had not gone by before the charter was so changed that the people living in the colony chose representatives to make the laws of the colony.[2] A little later the colonists of Massachusetts, taking heart at the victories of Parliament and thinking complacently of the three thousand miles between their charter and the English authorities, boldly ignored royal orders, and acted pretty much as if they recognized no sovereign but their own legislature.

Though, in royal colonies at least, governors were sent to America to uphold royal authority, and councillors were selected who might be expected to aid their pretension, yet the whole colonial history is a story of the success of popular assemblies in shearing both governor and council of their authority. Brief as is this review of the nature of British rule in colonial America, it will suffice for the purpose of contrast with that of Spain and France and the

---

[1] Macdonald, *Documentary Source Book*, nos. 1 and 2.
[2] *Ibid.*, no. 5 (Ordinance for Virginia).

nations of antiquity. In setting them one against another, we must remember that the comparison of unlike or contrasting social and political institutions is often misleading and even unfair unless the whole background and aim of each are fully known. It must be clearly appreciated, too, that the purpose here is to show that English statesmen were not behind their rivals in that age and that English colonists controlled their own destinies more than any other colonists of the eighteenth century.[1]

Spanish colonies in America had been established a century before John Smith lent color and heroics to England's first successful venture. From first to last, in Peru or Mexico or in the islands of the sea, all Spanish colonists were in theory dependencies of the Crown. Leaders of Spanish expeditions, Cortes or Pizarro, viceroys and governors, justice or ministers of religion, all were appointed by the King and removed at his will. The government was monarchical first of all.[2] In New Spain or Peru the viceroy was the representative of the person of the King. His duty, said one of them,[3] was to be father of the people, patron of the monasteries, and protector of the poor and of the widows and the orphans. Conquerors in new regions might set up governments, but the long arm of the Spanish Government soon reached them. The Spaniards ruled their American colonies from Madrid and from Seville with minute care, with much and often wise legislation.

---

[1] Indeed, one must go back to the Greeks to find freer colonists.
[2] E. G. Bourne, *Spain in America*, 228.
[3] H. H. Bancroft, *Mexico*, ii, 661.

From the Council of the Indies, with its group of "Godfearing men, noble of birth and of pure lineage," radiated supreme legislative and judicial control, under the King, of all Spanish America.[1] Another of the King's instruments was the India House, or *Casa de Contratacion*, which had larger executive functions, more immediate activity in administration. It was the agent of the Spanish King in carrying out the laws relating to the Indies.[2] In theory the English Board of Trade might be said to have had the same dominion over the English colonies, but it was in practice that the two systems differed utterly. During two long centuries of Spanish rule in America, there occurs no instance of a colony's success in gaining control of its affairs, while English colonial history bristles with such examples. Spanish colonies were equipped from the outset with ample legal machinery, and the lever that put it all in motion was manipulated at Seville. Governors, *audiencias*, presidents, viceroys, captains-general, and municipal officers, all drew every political power and direction from the Council of the Indies.[3] All this was not in vain, Spanish administration was a long way from being a failure, but, from the iron rule of this hierarchy, the vast majority of inhabitants of the Spanish colonies gleaned no political lesson but that of obedience. They learned only to follow, not to initiate progress

---

[1] The Council sat in Seville in Spain. Cunningham, *The Audiencia in the Spanish Colonies*, 14–17; Moses, *Spanish Rule in America*, 19.

[2] Moses, *Spanish Rule in America*, 21; Cunningham, *The Audiencia in the Spanish Colonies*, 13.

[3] Leroy-Beaulieu, *De la colonisation chez les peuples modernes*, 20.

in one direction or another. All experience in matters of public concern was denied them. The small power exercised by elected magistrates in the Peruvian or Mexican towns was limited to sanitary and humane legislation and to some regulation of their own interior commerce.[1] The English settlement, independent and feeble in the early days, but gathering strength through struggle, had a chance for more healthy social growth than Spanish colonies, bitted and curbed by the rigid rule of the royal officials. Peru and Mexico, being colonized when the ancient popular liberty of the homeland had been beaten down and subdued to a régime of absolutism, were not likely to fight for political liberty as were Virginia and Massachusetts which imbibed from the England of the seventeenth century a spirit of liberty and local independence.[2] As a general rule, it may be assumed that a colonist's ideas as to the way he ought to be governed will depend in the main upon the nature of the government under which he had lived at home. For that reason, Spanish-American colonists were fairly content under governmental absolutism which would have roused English-American colonists to fierce rebellion.

Quite as interesting in its contrast with the Eng-

[1] Nevertheless, what experience they got in regulating their own affairs was derived from this source. *American Political Science Review*, VIII, 205–06 (Moses, "Government in Spanish America").

[2] Spain, with her Council and Cortes kept on political exhibition, was nevertheless an absolute monarchy, and her colonists carried across the seas the habit of accepting that form of government. The stress was laid on the royal source of political power. England, holding to the King and Lords, was coming, nevertheless, to emphasize the people's representatives in her Commons, and the supremacy of that element her colonists reproduced in America.

lish régime was the French colony in America along the St. Lawrence and other waterways of Canada. It enjoyed less care, but endured quite as much absolutism as Peru or Mexico. French colonial administration centered in the Bourbon monarch "In the fulness of our power and our certain knowledge," the King directed all. He chose governors, intendants, and judges, and set the limits of their power.[1] Louis XIV actually read many of the endless letters from Canadian governors and signed the replies with the royal hand.[2] He attempted to direct everything from the statesman's comprehensive plan to the petty edict forbidding the least of the "habitants" to liberate his feelings in the form of profanity.[3]

In order to symbolize the royal character of the colonial rule, the far-away American wilds were invaded by a royal representative surrounded by young nobles "gorgeous in lace and ribands and majestic in leonine wigs." Twenty-four guards in royal livery, four pages and six valets swelled the pageant.[4] The Canadian governor-general and intendant were the instruments of a powerful centralization. Only the fact that the King and Minister, their sole masters, were three thousand miles away left them any initiative whatever. Even the little left to each was jealously guarded, for intend-

[1] A. H. Snow, *Administration of Dependencies*, 17.

[2] Parkman, *The Old Régime in Canada*, 349.   I am indebted to this work for a large part of the following description of the French colonial government.

[3] Nevertheless, the King's supremacy in colonial affairs was only theoretical, and many agencies besides his will decided such matters.

[4] Parkman, *The Old Régime in Canada*, 238.

ant and governor-general watched each other like
cat and mouse — natural enemies as they were
meant to be.

There was no suggestion of a colonial legislature
like those in the English colonies.[1] The Canadians
were trained to subjection and dependence. The
ordinance of the intendant entered every cranny
of colonial life. That officer settled a question of
boundaries or fixed the pay of a chimney sweep.
His decree fixed the number of horses that a colonist
might keep. He forbade farmers to live in the cities
or the denizens of cities to rent houses to farmers.[2]
The very color of bread was prescribed — all with
a degree of absolutism that would have become
the intendant's royal master, a French Bourbon.
Colonists were children in perpetuity. One intendant
solemnly declared, "It is of great consequence that
the people should not be left at liberty to speak
their minds." [3] There could be no public meeting
for any purpose except with special license from the
intendant. Such meetings were jealously watched,
lest a shred of self-government appear. There seems
to have been little resentment of this, for the French
colonist, accustomed to a paternal rule at home,
was peculiarly devoid of initiative. No man's fate
was left to himself, and politically none seemed to

---

[1] The governor, intendant, and bishop, with resident councillors
(five at first, later twelve), formed a superior council, which exercised
legislative, judicial, and executive functions, but all were appointed
by the Crown.

[2] Parkman, *The Old Régime in Canada*, 342.

[3] No colonist could return to France without permission. There
were cruel punishments for speaking ill of the King, or using profanity.
Servants who left their masters were set in the pillory.

wish it so. Unlike the English colonist, he had no traditions of self-government. An executive without a legislature would have seemed to an English colonist as fanciful as one of Murillo's winged heads, but the French colonist made no complaint on that score. Like the Spanish colonist, the French "habitant" did not mind autocracy while it was kind and meant well.

Under oppression the French colonists clamored for a change of masters, not for a change of the form of government. The people seemed to feel themselves incapable of accomplishing any amelioration on their own account. When the colony weakened because of official folly or corruption, political stimulants were sent, but freedom was denied. Too often, the remedy was merely new officials, henchmen and relatives of the ministers of state, who came like those before them only to return to Paris to spend ill-gotten gains, while the colony was dying of anæmia. As Parkman says, lesser offices were multiplied to care for impecunious retainers so that "lean and starving Canada was covered with official leeches, sucking in famished desperation at her bloodless veins." [1] In the English colonies, if a governor were inefficient, incompetent, or worse, he was faced by a determined body of representatives which was skilled in every parliamentary device to tear away his powers, but the Canadian "habitant" had no escape except to that domain of savage freedom, the vast interior wilderness, whither the lure of the fur-trade drew so many venturous

[1] Parkman, *The Old Régime in Canada*, 348–49.

youths. There they could defy the threats of the
far-off Bourbon. There alone could they escape the
"official jackals" who preyed without fear upon
the sedate farmer and colonist on the banks of the
St. Lawrence. Nearly one third of the "habitants"
took this method of escape, but the remainder only
cried out for new masters instead of seeking some
form of local control that would better their condition. If the French Government failed in its
paternalism as compared with the Spanish Government, it was because it did not devise a system for
keeping in close contact with its distant colonies.
France never developed the naval power, nor any
counterpart of the Spanish convoyed "Indian fleet,"
to control the ocean connection. In a centralized
system colonies needed constant support of a power
that kept always in touch with them. In the administration of justice in Canada we have an example of the tardiness of intercommunication. If
justice went awry in the "Superior Council," [1] it
was a year and a half or two years before an answer
came from France to a complaint. It was little
consolation, even if La Hontan's satirical compliment to Canadian judicial methods were true, that
Justice was more chaste and disinterested there than
in France. "At least," he said, "if she is sold, she
is sold cheaper. We do not pass through the clutches
of advocates, the talons of attorneys and the claws
of clerks. . . . Our Themis is prompt and she does
not bristle with fees, costs, and charges." But

[1] The Superior Council, besides issuing edicts and registering laws,
judged in all civil and criminal cases.

Themis was prompt only if she did not have to cross the seas. Delay in that case was merely of the same nature as all the other governmental dallying sure to result from attempted control of local matters at a distance of a thousand leagues.

Though black by contrast with England's almost self-governing colonies, the Spanish and French colonial governments were given every attention that a benevolent despot could lavish. The vast body of Spanish laws applying to the Indies shows a broad humanity and deep regard for the welfare of the Spanish subjects in America.[1] If viceroys and governors had absolute power, there was endeavor to keep them from tyranny. The *Audiencia*[2] or Supreme Court was a real check upon the personal tyranny of the viceroy or governor. Moreover, at the end of every viceroy's term there was an inquest. Every man with a grievance could there complain to the Spanish commissioners who then made a report to the Council for the Indies. It was in their power to correct abuses. Yet, as we are told, "Those who know the seductive influence of Plutus over the feeble and pliant Themis" may judge how successful was this device. It could not, of course, have the effectiveness of the ever alert colonial legislature in the English colony. The Spanish inquest was all too likely to resemble a whirlwind in the street, "which served only to raise the dust, chaff and other refuse and set it on the colonist's head." [1]

---

[1] E. G. Bourne, *Spain in America*, 226.
[2] Cunningham, *The Audiencia in the Spanish Colonies*, chap. VI.
[3] Helps, *Spanish Conquest in America* (new ed.), III, 102-09.

In the French colony in Canada the Bourbon Government tried to guard the subject against tyranny by the mutual check which governor-general and intendant gave each other and also through the deliberations of the Superior Council. Against the complete success of either of these absolutist devices worked the eternal truth that no man will so well stand guard at the gates of the temple of liberty as he who there protects his own welfare.

This brief comparison of English colonial government with that of other countries of that day might be continued with examples from lesser aspirants for colonial achievement, but there is little to learn from such examination. The Dutch colonies were never founded for motives other than commerce. The whole control of a Dutch colony was placed in the hands of a mercantile corporation. This gradually became more and more centralized in power and authority. Although the Commonwealth of the United Provinces was a republic, the Dutch East India Company grew into an aristocracy — haughty, absolute, and unmerciful as any autocrat in Christendom. It forged the chains of political slavery upon millions of its subjects.[1] Tea and silk, pepper and cinnamon, camphor, copper, ebony-wood, and opium were the objects of the Company's deepest concern. The souls of human beings, the rights of man, the guardianship of liberty of fellow-citizens, did not interest them. The Dutch, therefore, though they enjoyed freedom at home, contributed nothing toward solving the problem of imperial organization

[1] Morris, *History of Colonization*, I, 315-16.

in the interests of the liberty of the colonist. Nor did Portugal lend aid in solving that problem. Though its colonial system strongly resembled that of Spain, it was much less fortunate in the character of its viceroys who seem to have been utterly faithless to the interests of the fatherland.

It will be seen, from this brief sketch of colonial governments of the seventeenth and eighteenth centuries, that the English colonist of that age could not reasonably compare his colonial government unfavorably with the colonial régime of any other contemporary nation. Chatham's figure was not without truth when he declared (May 26, 1774), "Had the British Colonies been planted by any other Kingdom than our own, the inhabitants would have carried with them the chains of slavery, the spirit of despotism." Moreover, the statesmen at the head of British imperial affairs could not learn wisdom in liberal colonial management from any government then in existence. Even if they turned to historical sources of light, there was little to guide their search for a colonial régime that would enable them to breed democracies loyal to England.

Greek colonies, for example, had been free enough. Whether it was Agrigentum, Pindar's "most beautiful abode of mortals," or Sybaris, with its illrepute for luxury and ease, the Greek colony had been wont to set up for itself in the new land and there enjoy absolute political freedom. Though the Mediterranean, as Cicero put it, wore a Greek fringe, each individual settlement had its own constitution. These were so varied that monarchies and republics, aristocracies and democracies, freedom and tyranny all might be found among the many colonies. Whether the emigrant was going to Cyprus or the far-away land of "Thule," the home state usually approved and encouraged the remove. It relieved the homeland of discontented spirits and of a surplus of laborers. If Greek genius spread to distant lands; if Thales, Euclid, Lysias, Xenophon, and Herodotus were colonists of Greece; if Æolians, Ionians, and Dorians carried her culture to colonies in Asia Minor; if Pythagoras and Homer were reputed citizens of the colony of Samos, the mother country merely took pride in the fact that they were her children, but it made no claim to political control. Leaving home to shift for themselves on an alien shore, they carried the blessing of the fatherland, but no advantage was expected by the State; no support by the colony. The only bond was commerce, and a moral sentiment, the result of common origin.[1] Had the English statesmen of the seventeenth and eighteenth centuries chosen this method of treating England's colonial children, the most eloquent defenders of the rights of the colonies would have declared them cruel and heartless to leave Englishmen at the mercy of French and Spanish enemies. Though Tucker, Dean of Gloucester, had actually proposed (1766) "a separation, parting with the colonies entirely, and then making leagues of friendship with them, as with so many independent states," the suggestion got no favorable response even from the most ardent advocates of

[1] Morris, *History of Colonization*, chap. IV.

colonial liberty. ʻIndeed, under American conditions, and in the period of settlement, protection by England and a degree of dependence by the colonist were the inevitable conditions of success in making a permanent plantation.

If the perplexed statesman, studying the past for help on the problems of the present, had turned from Greek to Roman history,[1] he would have found only precedents to avoid. Rome, indeed, had developed to the utmost perfection that very centralization of control which English statesmen were trying to establish when the American colonists rebelled. The end and aim of Rome's colonial undertaking was to bring more of the earth under Roman dominion. As a rule her colonies were towns conquered from other people. The former inhabitants, in whole or in part, were driven out, robbed of their lands, which were then given to Romans, usually the poor.[2] Plutarch pictures these prospective Roman colonists drawn up in military fashion and the entire troop herded by their commissioner, marching to the sound of martial music, setting out for the distant lands assigned them. Often, indeed, they were little more than garrisons in conquered fortified places.[3] Rome was master of her citizens; she selected for this purpose whom she pleased, chose their abode, gave them leaders and a code of laws. In leaving Rome colonists lost their Roman citizenship, and, therefore, the rich and talented seldom chose to go out

---

[1] That British statesmen did do this is shown in F. W. Hirst, *Adam Smith*, 147–49.

[2] Sir G. C. Lewis, *Government of Dependencies*, 115–16.

[3] Niebuhr, *History of Rome*, II, 51.

from the shadow of her walls. Greek architects and artists, historians and poets, philosophers and orators were to be found in all her far-flung colonies, but Rome's genius and talent remained for the most part within the circle that bound her seven hills. Every stratum of society thought it a hardship and a sacrifice to be forced to leave the imperial city. In the Roman scheme there was little opportunity for spontaneous emigration; nothing was left to mere chance or individual caprice.[1] Rome exercised supreme control. Hers was not a colonial system that could be applied to a liberty-loving British colonist.

Though there is little doubt that Roman provinces, as her dependencies outside of Italy were called, were governed less tyrannously than others in the ancient world,[2] yet the worst of tyrannies could exist there. The conscience of a provincial ruler like Cicero or Agricola might save their subjects from plunder, but without that moral restraint the rapacity of a Verres was possible. "All Roman provinces are mourning," cried his eloquent accuser. "All free peoples are complaining; every kingdom is protesting against our covetousness and our injustice; there is no place on this side of the seas, none so distant, so out of the way, that in these days, the lust and iniquity of our citizens has not reached it."[3] And it is recorded by Dion Cassius that when

[1] Morris, *History of Colonization*, i, 129.

[2] Polybius tells us that the Carthaginians admired and honored the governors who levied the largest tribute and employed the harshest measures for levying it. Sir G. C. Lewis, *Government of Dependencies*, iii.

[3] Cicero, *Verres*, ii, Lib. iii, c. 89.

Tiberius asked Cato why the Dalmatians revolted from Rome, he replied that it was "because the Romans sent not dogs or shepherds, but wolves to guard their flocks." [1] Until late in the empire the governor of a province was supreme in all respects. He combined both judicial and military functions Under such conditions, wolves like Verres were possible, and after all allowance is made for Cicero's rhetoric, it may safely be asserted that the worst of English colonial governors had neither the power nor the ambition to rival Verres.

If, therefore, we are to understand England's position and that of her colonies ready to "wean themselves," we must place ourselves in the eighteenth century, in a world not wholly unhappy under absolutism, and for which the curtain had not yet been wholly lifted upon a stage where Democracy was to take the leading part in the political drama. We must see England, not yet fully prepared, compelled to solve at once the problem of imperial organization, and with such dim light as the experience of mankind then offered. It was not as if Wisdom cried out in the street and no man regarded, for it was only with generations more of experience that England could find the solution. Though she was then, and continued to be, the greatest of colonizing nations, she had much to learn, which only bitter experience could impart. Even imaginative minds like those of William Pitt and Adam Smith could soar only a little way above the solid ground of human experience. The lessons of history, the lamp

[1] Dion Cassius, I, VI, c. 16.

of reason, the observation of contemporary colonizing nations were not sufficient guide to the upper
regions of imperial statesmanship. Unable to pene-
trate the veil that hid Great Britain's own successful
future in Canada and Australia, and her other self-
governing dependencies, the choice seemed to her
statesmen to lie between letting the colonies set
up for themselves like Greek cities — a heartless
method from the colonists' point of view — or in
mild imitation of Rome and Spain to keep them in
a state of at least partial subordination. To make
them integral parts of the nation seemed impracticable because of the distance. The plan actually
attempted, that of centralizing the control of the
colonies, was chosen with perfectly good intent on
the part of the British Government, but because of
the whole colonial experience in the freedom-giving
life of the American forest, it looked to the colonist
like a plot to establish tyranny. The leveling effects
of the primitive life on the frontier of the British
Empire had developed a spirit of individualism and
separatism. Isolation had made the colonists provincial; they had shaped their institutions to their
own needs and not those of the empire. Every year
of colonial life advanced them toward independence.

CHAPTER V

GROPING FOR SOLUTIONS OF THE IMPERIAL PROBLEMS

In a passage of the "Confessions" of St. Augustine, that worthy post-Nicene father discourses on the rashness of those who inquire what God did before He created heaven and earth. It may appear a like temerity to have gone back to the days of Edwin Sandys, William Bradford, and John Winthrop to seek the causes of American independence. One would not need to be unduly disputatious to argue that all of the "fundamental causes" considered in the preceding pages might have led merely to the creation of a different variety of English-speaking people than that produced by the environment and experiences in Cornwall or Northumberland or London. One might point to Canadians, Australians, and the English colonists of Cape Town, as examples of people radically changed by a new environment into a race quite different from the English who stayed at home, but a race which, nevertheless, had retained loyalty to the British Empire. The rebuttal, however, would emphasize the fact that before any of the other oversea colonies of England had attained the strength that America had gained in 1775, the British Government had learned not to allow its relations with them to become strained, but to yield, if not gracefully, at least in time to keep their allegiance.[1] Even that process has led to their becoming self-ruling members of a commonwealth of nations, loyal to the motherland, but hardly less independent than the United States. In considering the immediate causes of the American War for Independence, in the period of 1763–1775, it will be seen that trouble was brewed not at all because of any cruel tyranny on the part of George III and his ministers, but because their honest though mistaken efforts to rule for the best interests of the empire were misinterpreted by a people with a different theory of what constituted political liberty. All argument as to the true nature of the British Constitution, all appeals to the "natural rights of man," all clever deductions from the past history of the English struggle for liberty, only rendered the debaters more distrustful of each other, less ready to be reconciled. Their differences lay in those ultimate springs of conduct, their ideals of human justice and the best interests of mankind.

After the Treaty of Paris (1763) British imperial affairs seem, to one looking backwards, to have been at the cross-roads where one turning would lead to the political Delectable Mountains, and the other to the Slough of Despond. The British Ministry then met a great problem, and a new one, because the vast domain in Canada and the Mississippi Valley had been taken from France during the momentary triumph of a new theory as to the value of colonies. William Pitt, after wondering which he

[1] Cross, *History of England*, 930–32; Curry, *British Colonial Policy*, *passim*.

should be "hanged for not keeping," decided to keep Canada, rather than Guadeloupe, and his judgment was accepted by the makers of the Peace of Paris. That decision became the star which pointed out the course of British colonial policy for a decade thereafter.[1] Canada and Pitt's gorgeous dream of a continental empire having been chosen, the Ministry was pledged to a policy of western expansion, to some plan which would make of the Ohio and the Mississippi Valleys an imperial possession of more value than a West Indian island. They must exploit the peltries and the fertile plains, and found colonies so that England might in time clothe "unnumbered nations" with her manufactures. Up to this time, as Adam Smith phrased it, English rulers had only amused their people with pictures of their great empire to the west of the Atlantic. It was, in fact, "not an empire, but the project of an empire; not a gold mine, but the project of a gold mine." The time had come to develop both the old and the new territory and make them true parts of the empire.

Any plans for Canada and the great region of the "Western Waters" would be sure to meet with opposition. The old theory of the reason for colonies still had many adherents who refused to follow Pitt in his flights of imagination about the real grandeur of nations. His vision of new realms filled with Englishmen, increasing British power and wealth with

---

[1] The excellent and exhaustive study of this whole subject is C. W. Alvord's *The Mississippi Valley in British Politics*, 2 vols The following treatment of the matter is largely based on this work.

new populations and new markets, could not drive
out the old prepossession about the value of sugar
from Guadeloupe. To the sugar merchants Goldsmith's dream of "peopling the deserts of America
. . . with the waste of an exuberant nation " was a
poet's rhapsody, but not such stuff as trade is fed on.

Few Englishmen had imagination, and knowledge
about the transmontane spaces of America was even
rarer. The British mind had little acquaintance
with the classic books about Canada by Charlevoix,
Hennepin, or La Hontan. The Great Lakes, the
Falls of Niagara, the courses of the Ohio and the
Mississippi, the trading posts at the portages or narrow waters, the open prairies of this vast inland
empire were as unknown to the intelligent Londoner
in 1763 as the physical features of the Philippine
Islands are a mystery to the New Yorker to-day.
An under-secretary for the colonies, thinking this
region as barren as the omniscient Dr. Johnson had
pictured it, declared that he expected the West to be
given up to barbarism for ages, "like the plains of
Asia, and that the population would be as unsettled
as the Scythians or Tartars." [1] In Canada, Boswell's
hero saw only a "cold, uncomfortable, uninviting
region, . . . nothing but furs and fish," inhabited by
people "living in perpetual regret of . . . their native
land." [2]

The opponents of Pitt's choice of the spoils of
war argued that the conquest of Canada was glorious, dazzling, perhaps, but dangerous. "A neighbor

[1] Knox, *Extra Official State Papers*, II, 49.
[2] Alvord, *The Mississippi Valley in British Politics*, I, 79.

that kept the colonies in awe, was not a bad neighbor." That awe preserved the colonial feeling of dependence on England. "Give the American provinces continental extent," it was objected, and they would have ten times the area of England. These provinces had "richer soil in most places, all the different climates you can fancy, all the lakes and rivers for navigation one could wish, plenty of wood for shipping, and as much iron, hemp, and naval stores as any part of the world; such a country at such a distance, could never remain long subject to Britain." [1] In fact, some eight years before the Treaty of Paris, John Adams had written, "If we can remove the troublesome Gallicks, our people . . . will in another century become more numerous than England itself," and since we "have all the naval stores in our hands, it will be easy to obtain the mastery of the seas, then the united forces of all Europe will not be able to subdue us. The only way to keep us from setting up for ourselves will be to disunite us." [2] There were prophetic souls in those days who saw clearly America's manifest destiny, but who differed widely as to whether its fate would be left to Providence, or an effort made to deflect it by act of Parliament.

The British Ministry, seeking to determine a policy for Canada and the Mississippi Valley, was heading into a stormy sea. A score of clashing interests would buffet any government that tried to

[1] "Reasons for Keeping Guadeloupe . . ." London, 1761. Quoted by W. L. Grant, "Canada or Guadeloupe," in *American Historical Review*, xvii, 740.

[2] John Adams, *Works*, i, 23.

compose them. Land speculators and fur-traders, philanthropic friends of the "noble red man" and cynical imperialists eager to take up the "white man's burden," would shout their conflicting arguments. Colonies with western claims and those without, statesmen of the old school, and their opponents of the new school in colonial affairs, military men with opposing theories as to methods of control, all would demand a hearing and be content with no solution but their own. Greatest danger of all would be in the oppugnancy of imperial rights to colonial rights of domain. Almost until the outbreak of the French and Indian War, the British Government had permitted the colonies, each in its own selfish way, to settle all questions arising in their hinterland. Fur-trade problems, Indian policies, and land company conflicts were all subjects of fierce intercolonial rivalry, which left the "forest children" at the mercy of the greedy traders and land speculators. The hit-or-miss control of these matters led to deadly feuds between the colonies, and to an abuse of the Indians through land frauds and trade that was mere robbery. The success of the French in getting the support of the Indians in the struggle for the possession of the Ohio Valley was due to their better control of the fur-trade and resultant fairer treatment of the aborigines. Nevertheless, the failure of the colonies in these relations made them no less opposed to any plan of imperial control. Even their own vain efforts at Albany (1754) to devise some plan for unity in these matters did **not** alter their opposition.

There could never be peace in the western wilds until a single strong power put the fear of the law into the hearts of the rival factions. The differing interests of the fur-trade and land companies created deadly feuds. The trader wished to preserve the wilds where the Indian might freely hunt the fur-bearing animals, but "gentlemen adventurers" with a project for a colony wished to hasten civilized conditions as fast as possible. The trader did not hesitate even to urge the Indians to attack new western settlements in the hope of discouraging and retarding the clearing of the forest. The very methods of the unregulated traders created Indian unrest and imperiled the lives of settlers. The fur-buyers cynically boasted that better bargains were made with the Indians if rum was used, and "certain strength'ning drugs." The trader's scales were honest, of course, they said with a leer, but a slip would "turn three pounds to one." Indians who were mad with drink did not notice slight errors.[1] No wonder that Franklin called the traders "the most vicious and abandoned wretches of our nation,"[2] and General Amherst wrote that they used every low trick and artifice to defraud the untutored savage. In all this, each trader suffered no interference by his own colony, and in the Hudson's Bay Company he had a powerful friend at court if the British Government threatened action.

But the trader's rival, the land companies, had friends, too, for to their support came those states·

---

[1] Alvord, *The Mississippi Valley in British Politics*, I, 184.
[2] Franklin, *Works*, [Smythe, *ed.*] IV, 469–70.

men who advocated the new colonial principle that growing populations meant growing markets for the homeland. Nor were these statesmen always without financial interests in the cause, for often their names stood high on the lists of members of land companies whose stock would rise if the British Government embraced their principles.[1]

The eighteenth century, also, had its "immoral alliance" between "big business and those in political power." But even the tribe of land speculators and of politicians who embraced the new theory, that dependencies should be fostered for the sake of their markets, were divided on the western policy. Englishmen and colonials who had bought large tracts in the region east of the Appalachians looked with disfavor on plans of extensive land grants in the West beyond the mountains, because such grants would by competition lower the values of their land.[2] With them were joined men of conscience, who opposed, on principle, such plans as made certain that hordes of settlers would rush over the mountains and possess the ancient homes of the Indians. They argued that these wards of the empire must be protected by imperial officers stationed in the West. The trade with the Indians and the purchase of their lands would then be under proper control. The fate of the empire of the "western waters" was to be wrangled out among these conflicting factions and interests in London.

[1] Alvord, *The Mississippi Valley in British Politics*, I, 112, 213.

[2] Lord Dartmouth, Charles Townshend, and Richard Oswald had twenty to forty thousand acres each. (Alvord, *The Mississippi Valley in British Politics*, I, 112, 213.) Lord Holland and Grenville also had investments in American land.

There were colonial interests also which would have to be handled with the greatest delicacy. Virginia had long been making land grants to companies of capitalists, not only in her territory east of the Alleghenies, but beyond them in the region where she recognized no bounds short of the "South Sea." By 1757, she had ceded in that way two million acres. Her soldiers of the French and Indian War were rewarded with bounty lands which increased these grants.[1] Virginia felt greatly aggrieved when in October, 1761, Colonel Bouquet, leader of the British troops in Pennsylvania, issued a proclamation, later approved by General Amherst, British Commander-in-Chief in America, and by the Board of Trade, prohibiting all settlements west of the mountains.[2] Officers and soldiers of the Virginia militia were injured and angered by this action of the Government, but members of the Ohio Land Company were especially afflicted. Out in this forested West was America's land of promise from which many colonials expected riches, but uncontrolled exploitation of the wealth of the "Great Valley" was contrary to the interests of the empire as a whole. If the British Government could control the sale of land, and gather the returns therefrom, the imperial treasury might be filled with the income. To realize this the Government must take

[1] Alvord, *The Mississippi Valley in British Politics*, I, 88–89.

[2] The aim of this was to put an end to the irritation to the Indians, due to new settlements which cleared the forest and frightened away the game. Hitherto the Indian preference for the French had been a mystery to the British Government officials. Bouquet's action enlightened them,

from the colonies, and make a function of its own, the purchase of Indian lands, and it must delimit the western bounds of colonies whose charters gave them grounds for vague claims far into the western wilderness. Here, then, Virginia's interests, and, indeed, those of other colonies, clashed with imperial interests. Colonies like Pennsylvania with definite western bounds could look with favor on imperialistic plans which proposed to ignore ancient charter grants of land in the West, but colonies like Virginia, with vast charter claims in the West, resented this threat to "vested rights." Indeed, some British "imperialists" would not go that far. In spite of the indication which Bouquet's proclamation gave as to the new policy of the British Government, there was, after the Treaty of Peace (1763), a veritable land craze among the colonial speculators. In the "Old Dominion," Colonel George Washington pressed the claims of his companions in arms, the Virginia militia. On June 3, 1763, gentlemen from Maryland and Virginia founded the Mississippi Company. New York land speculators planned the colony of New Wales on the Upper Ohio. It was plain that the hour had struck when the British Government must decide and apply its policy to its western dominion, or else resign that region forever to the capricious wills of the several colonies.

Both the hour and the man were at hand.[1] When Lord Bute resigned in 1763 as the head of the

[1] Professor Alvord declares that Lord Shelburne was the man who exercised greater influence on the development of Western America than any other British statesman. *The Mississippi Valley in British Politics*, I, 140.

Ministry, and selected his own successors,[1] Lord Shelburne was made President of the Board of Trade and sat in the Cabinet, where he was entitled to equal weight with the Secretary in colonial matters. Indeed, he came to manage American affairs as an independent department. Although he had a tendency to radicalism, and in later years saw "with sincere delight" the beginnings of the French Revolution, yet he was on intimate and confidential terms with Lord Bute, the King's favorite. His theory that men of independent fortunes should be "trustees between the king and the people . . . without being slaves to either," made such a relation possible even for a radical. Though he was a believer in the free-trade ideas of his friends, Adam Smith and David Hume, yet his conception was a free trade between colony and mother country so managed as to be of value to both. Thus modified, his economic theory would not make him intolerable to George Grenville and Lord Halifax, his colleagues in the Ministry, both of whom he disliked and to whose plans he was lukewarm. He was rather imperious in temper and suspicious of men with whom he dealt, both of which faults came, perhaps, from his never having enjoyed strict mental discipline. His friend, Jeremy Bentham, thought his "head was not clear"; his mind was full to overflowing, but not logical or just.[2] He was original, all agreed, but lacking in judgment; on the scrap of an idea

[1] The so-called triumvirate, consisting of George Grenville, Lord Halifax, and Lord Egremont.

[2] The third Lord Holland agreed with Bentham. See Fitzmaurice, *Life of Shelburne*, I, 487.

he would build a whole philosophical system. His catholic taste and wide intellectual interest brought him into friendly relation with the greatest minds of his time, Dr. Johnson, Oliver Goldsmith, Price, and Priestley, and from all he took his toll of ideas. Lord Camden and Dunning were his political friends, and William Pitt was his idol. He often consulted with Benjamin Franklin. He had at Oxford listened to the lectures of the famous Blackstone, and he had been a deep student of modern history. Besides his touch with men and books, he had enjoyed at least one experience of life at high tension, when in a campaign under Wolfe in Germany. From this range of experience and intellectual contact he developed a character for learning and boldness in speech, which was neither polished nor coherent. He was not a great orator, but a man to beware of in debate. If he deserved Disraeli's epithet of "the ablest and most accomplished minister of the eighteenth century," it was because of his imagination and industry. His favorite mode of solving a government problem was to make the most exhaustive research in documentary and other sources. He even overdid his research and made his colleagues impatient with his assiduous study of " those silly manuscripts." He was exasperatingly slow in making up his mind. That was one of his weaknesses, and another that limited his influence was a prevailing belief that he was insincere. Walpole declared that "falsehood was rather his profession than his instrument," though Priestley thought him "frank, plain and open." Friends explained his unfortunate reputation by saying that he was not accustomed to explain the full meaning of measures which he advocated, so that when all was revealed he was reproached for deceit. His own theory, that "men required to be bribed into doing good " reveals a cynical spirit that may easily have reflected back upon himself those attributes which he so freely suspected in others. He was one of those positive personalities which either won wholly or repelled men. They were either his warm friends or implacable enemies, and they saw in him either a noble, generous idealist, or a cunning betrayer of the cause of the people. This man in his strength and his weakness was destined to affect deeply the fate of America.[1]

On taking office, Shelburne began with characteristic thoroughness to make a complete study of the whole matter of the western policy. He sought advice from every source and gathered quantities of documents which would inform him upon what seemed the three main questions: (1) the regulation of Indian trade and relations; (2) whether an army should be maintained in America; and (3) whether there should be a contribution by the colonies for the support of the imperial establishment. As a result of his investigations and reports, the Ministry planned to secure happy relations with the Indians by making them sure that their hunting grounds, those "immense wastes of savage country," would not be encroached upon until an honest purchase

---

[1] This attempt to portray the character of Shelburne is based upon Fitzmaurice's *Life of Shelburne*, and upon the excellent account of him in Alvord's *Mississippi Valley in British Politics*, I. 140–52.

should open them to settlement. A boundary line between the Atlantic seaboard colonies and the Indian country of the trans-Allegheny region was considered, but Shelburne made clear that his idea was a boundary which was to be slowly abolished or moved westward as the lands were purchased.[1] It was planned to send twenty battalions, or ten thousand soldiers, to America, the expense to be borne at first by England, but in time to be cared for by the colonies. Such a contribution by the colonies was to be as little "burthensome and as palatable to the colonies" as possible. Of this plan even Edmund Burke, "friend of the colonies," and later repealer of the Stamp Act, approved "when a more calm and settled season comes." William Pitt, too, seems to have approved.[2] In fact, only the question of the distribution of the troops — whether in the eastern settlements or scattered among the western posts — seems to have caused dispute between political factions. This carefully conceived plan of Shelburne's was prevented by factional politics from ever coming to full fruition, but it had great influence upon all later actions of the Government. By July, 1763, the Ministry was ready to issue proclamations unfolding its plan to the governors of the colonies. Then new and interesting tidings from America, and later some important ministerial

[1] Alvord, *The Mississippi Valley in British Politics*, I, 172. It was not part of Shelburne's plan, but proposed by Lord Egremont and approved by others of the Ministry, that the western lands reserved behind such a boundary line be controlled by the Government of Quebec. There was no ulterior motive in this; certainly no wish to offend the thirteen American colonies.

[2] Alvord, *The Mississippi Valley in British Politics*, I, 130–60.

changes, delayed this promulgation until October, which led to significant changes in the form of their policy.

The untoward news from oversea was that of the outbreak of the Indian war called in Parkman's fascinating volumes "The Conspiracy of Pontiac." [1] Packet after packet from America brought news of savage warfare on the unprotected settlements throughout the West. The fraud and violence of the fur-trader and the land speculator had roused the vengeance of the Indians, and, led by an able and ambitious warrior, Pontiac, they ravaged the western posts and frontiers. The whole West was lost in a few weeks; only Fort Pitt and Detroit survived the onslaught. There were two immediate occasions of the outbreak: one was the anger of the Indians because, on Amherst's advice, the British Government, in a fit of economy after the making of peace, had ceased making gifts to the Indians; another was because the Indians, "with an uneasy and jealous eye," saw the English settlers pouring out of the Appalachian passes into the Great Valley, and no doubt were warned by the French fur-traders in words not very different from those of DuQuesne to the Iroquois. "Are you ignorant," DuQuesne asked, "of the difference between the King of England and the King of France? Go see the forts that our king has established, and you will see that you can still hunt under their very walls. They have been placed for your advantage in places which you

---

[1] There is an excellent short account in L. S. Mayo, *Jeffrey Amherst*, chap. XI.

frequent. The English, on the contrary, are no sooner in possession of a place than the game is driven away. The forest falls before them as they advance, and the soil is laid bare so that you can scarce find the wherewithal to erect a shelter for the night." [1] It is certain that the Indians were assured by the insidious French traders that the King of France was sending an army to drive out the English. Pontiac believed that he was only preparing the way for the French hosts who would push the English into the sea.

When the news of the Pontiac uprising reached England, the members of the Board of Trade were not wholly surprised, but they did realize that their plan for the protection of the Indian, and thus the settlers from his vengeance, had been delayed too long. They at once proposed to the Ministry a proclamation of the boundary suggested by Shelburne, which would allay the fears of the Indians and restore peace in the West. Action was delayed, however, by a whole summer's political uncertainty in London. George III had determined to have a change in the make-up of the Ministry, and had put the negotiations in the hands of his favorite, Lord Bute. An effort to secure the aid of William Pitt and some of the Old Whigs failed, as did an endeavor to bring Pitt and the Duke of Bedford's followers together, both undertakings being based on the King's wish for a "broad-bottomed" ministry which would assure a strong and permanent government. It seems a pity that Pitt's genius could not have

[1] F. J. Turner, *The Frontier in American History*, 14.

been summoned to his country's service at that critical moment. That spirit, supported by fleets and armies, which, in Barré's phrase, had "set Great Britain at the head of the world," might have knit its scattered provinces together. But few men of spirit could work with Pitt. He was never a congenial colleague. Men who worked with him must obey without question, sign state papers without reading them. He scorned Lilliputian statesmen and their plans. He alone could save England, he cried, and he did it. In his dramatic way, he loved to be shrouded in mystery. Men felt that his mind had a touch of the infinite, that his imagination roamed the whole world. His career was fascinating to watch, but no careful statesman wished to be tied to the tail of a comet. Noble as were Pitt's ideas, they often seemed beyond human attainment. Men did not mind venturing step by step into the unknown, but to dive into the infinite at the command of a ministerial colleague was both risky and undignified. All efforts to surround Pitt with obedient colleagues failed. The King in desperation was finally obliged to dismiss Lord Bute in order to gain the Duke of Bedford's aid in forming a new ministry. Thereupon George Grenville was enlisted, and the Grenville-Bedford régime, with its fatal consequences for the British Empire, began its course, vain of its power, but soon distrusted by the King.[1] Before its attention could be called to the American situation, Shelburne resigned, and the Earl of Hillsbor-

---

[1] An excellent account of these negotiations is in Alvord, *The Mississippi Valley in British Politics*, I, 189–97.

ough took his place. Into Hillsborough's hands came Shelburne's plan, ready, but delayed by the tottering ministry. Something must be done at once, but Hillsborough had never held a position which dealt with colonial affairs, and it was fortunate that most of the work on the western policy had already been done by Shelburne. Hillsborough had little to do but to incorporate the decision of the recent ministry in a proclamation, already urged by Shelburne, to quiet the fears of the Indians. Precious months had gone by, and it was already October. Within six days, Hillsborough, with the aid of Lord Halifax, prepared this important state paper, so fateful in American affairs. The chief change, important to note at this time, was in the location of the Indian boundary line.[1] Something rough and ready was needed to meet the emergency of the Pontiac war, a natural boundary like the Appalachian divide, rather than a carefully surveyed line to run in and out and embrace villages already in the upper Ohio Valley. This neglect to exempt settlements already made west of the mountains, and the prohibition of sale of Indian lands except to the Crown, gave great offense to the powerful land interests, already described, in the colonies, as well as to political factions in England.[2] Moreover, much of the reserved

[1] For other changes and some unintended provisions in the proclamation see Alvord, *The Mississippi Valley in British Politics*, 1, 202–10. The serious blunder in respect to the property laws of Quebec will be taken up later.

[2] The proclamation may be found in Fitzmaurice's *Life of Shelburne*, II, 439, and in Macdonald's *Documentary Source Book*, 113. The territory ceded by France was divided into four governments, Quebec, East Florida, West Florida, and Grenada. All the remaining

territory lay within regions long ago granted in charters to the older colonies, regions in which those colonies had plans of their own. Thither thousands of their people were even then preparing to "swarm." Neither the fur-traders nor the land companies liked the imperial regulations, though Sir William Johnson and John Stuart, the two men who knew most about it, believed that the western chaotic conditions could be cured only by putting all Indian affairs under imperial control. The proclamation of 1763 left the King's hand on October 7, and the British Government was committed to a policy of imperial control of its new western domain.

In addition to the nature of this imperial plan, it is important to note that the British Government, having acquired the West in the Treaty of Paris, felt pledged to prove to the nation the value of this acquisition. To do this, now that Shelburne's plan was fairly entered upon, required money to support the military establishment proposed for the western posts, as well as to keep up government in the new regions, and that, too, at a time when England was laboring under a war debt of nearly £130,000,000.[1] The new accretions to Great Britain's empire had swelled the annual budget for naval and military expenses alone from £70,000 to £350,000. Having taken one step, the Grenville-Bedford Ministry was pledged to the next, and that implied the acceptance of Shelburne's plan to raise the money needed for

acquired territory was set aside as an Indian reservation by the boundary line described in the text.

[1] *Commons Journal*, XXIX, 760; *Bowdoin and Temple Papers,* pt. I, 77.

imperial expenses in America from the American colonies themselves. Unfortunately this plan was not to be carried out by Lord Shelburne, whose liberal mind conceived of a system which would give all of the colonies as much self-rule as was enjoyed by Connecticut, but was to be jammed through by the Bedford faction, which believed in the complete subordination of the colonies. Their thought was that the old charters had recklessly granted away imperial rights, which ought now to be regained by the mother country, even if vested rights had to be attacked. Like their pensioned pamphleteer, Dr. Johnson, they asked superciliously whether nothing could be done toward "demolishing these pernicious charter governments, and reducing them all to one form in immediate dependence on the king." [1] American colonial governors had advised them repeatedly that the colonies must be organized upon a new plan, that the old had failed. Governor Bernard hoped (1763) that there would soon "be only one common rule in all American parts." [2] All circumstances, all advice urged them on to try, now that "the East and West Indies were in their hands," as Barré told them, whether their infant fingers were "able to grasp the world." They had conquered; could they organize their conquests?

The Molasses Act of 1733, which was about to expire, had been devised to force New England distillers and sellers of rum to buy their molasses and sugar and rum from British sugar planters, and to

[1] *Life of Samuel Johnson,* 279.
[2] British Museum, *King's MSS.,* 205 F 200.

keep colonial traders out of the French and Spanish
West Indies, confining their traffic to the British
Islands.[1] It seemed to the colonists a bad piece of
class legislation, seeking to enable "a few pamper'd
Creolians" to "roll in their gilded equipages thro'
the streets" of London, at the expense of two million
American subjects.[2] Smuggling, on such a scale
that it was the rule rather than the exception in
colonial trade, had made the statute a dead-letter.
In addition to administrative reforms, Grenville
now turned (1764) to Parliament for legislation,
which properly enforced would bring a revenue into
the imperial treasury. He could no longer tolerate
a customs service which cost the Crown seven
thousand pounds to support, and which collected
only two thousand pounds revenue. Urged on by
the sugar planters of the British West Indies, whose
political influence was fairly proportioned to their
wealth, an act was passed which aimed to make
perpetual "the old Molasses Act" (1733) and to
prevent "the clandestine conveyance of goods to
and from the said colonies," so "happily enlarged
by the recent peace."[3] The duty on French and
Spanish molasses was reduced from six pence to
three pence that the profits of evasion might not
offer so great temptation to the smuggler. New
duties, also, to be collected with the utmost rigor,
were imposed upon wine from the Azores and
Madeiras, and upon white sugar, coffee, pimento,
and indigo from the foreign islands of the West

---

[1] For the act see Macdonald, *Documentary Source Book*, 103.
[2] Schlesinger, *The Colonial Merchants, in the American Revolution*,
42–43.   [3] *Ibid.* 117.

Indies.[1] The trial of indicted smugglers in colonial
courts having proved futile, the British admiralty
courts were given jurisdiction in such cases and
British naval officers given power to collect the customs duties. The greatest burden of all, as colonial
agitators interpreted it, was a provision that all
duties and forfeitures were to be paid into the "Re-
ceipt of His Majesty's Exchequer." [2] This was asserted to mean silver and gold, which would thus
be drained from the colonies. In fact it was to be
used in America to buy supplies for the British troops
stationed there.[3] Finally, as if to exhibit at once his
knowledge of sound finance, and his ignorance of
colonial conditions, Grenville induced Parliament
later in the year to enact a law "to prevent paper
bills of credit hereafter issued in any of His Majesty's colonies from being made legal tender." The
time set for sinking old issues of such money was not
to be extended.

Like many other clever epigrams, the assertion
that "Grenville lost America because he read the
American despatches" is untrue. However assiduous and precise his study of finance, his arid mind
had absorbed little knowledge of colonial life and
spirit. In no previous service of his in the Govern-

---

[1] There were certain provisions meant to help the colonial trade.
Some duties were repealed and bounties granted to that end.

[2] Clause XI of the Sugar Act. See also *Annual Register*, 1765, p. 22.

[3] Channing, *Hist. of the U.S.*, III, 43–44. Franklin claimed, however, during his examination at the bar of the House of Commons that
"it will be spent in the conquered colonies (Canada, Florida, etc.)
where the soldiers are, not in the colonies that pay it." Resolution no. 17 of the measures proposed by Grenville on March 10,
1764, definitely stated that the duties were to be paid in "sterling
money." Hansard, *Parliamentary Debates*, xv, 1428.

ment had he dealt with colonial affairs. Only a year earlier than the Sugar Act, Governor Bernard of Massachusetts had reported to his Government: "The inhabitants of the trading towns of New England, Men, Women, and Children, have their whole supply of Clothing from Great Britain. Most of the Women in all other towns have the principal part of their clothing of British Manufactures, the Men have more or less. The poor laboring people of the country towns wear their common Cloaths principally of coarse home spun Linnens and woollens. Shoes are to be excepted . . . Furniture . . . is British . . . and Nails, Glass, lead, locks, and hinges."[1] To pay for all these manufactures of Great Britain, the New England provinces had long depended in part for the requisite gold and silver upon an illicit trade with the French and Spanish Islands.[2] The Puritan provinces had no staple like tobacco or rice or indigo with which to pay for their English-made glass and locks and hinges, or the manufactured finery with which they were clothed. To take away their molasses trade or to burden their slave trade, in which rum was an essential item, was to take away the balance in gold and silver or bank exchange, with which they gave satisfaction to their English creditors.[3] John Adams, years after, did not blush to confess that molasses was an essential

[1] British Museum, *King's MSS.*, 205 F 198.
[2] H. C. Bell, "West Indian Trade before the Revolution," in *American Historical Review*, XXII, 274, an excellent detailed description of trade with the West Indies.
[3] See Wells, *Samuel Adams*, I, 81, for instructions to the colonial agent in London. John Adams, *Works*, X, 345.

ingredient in American independence. Governor Bernard had assured his royal master that "even illegal trade, where the balance is in favor of these British subjects, makes its final returns to Great Britain." [1] When so fundamental a source of the medium of exchange was thus snatched away, there would be little gratitude in New England because to their fishermen, whom Burke pictured as "pursuing the whales among the tumbling mountains of arctic ice, or following them beneath the frozen serpent of the South," were remitted the duty on whale fins.[2] It was too small a sop to mollify the Puritan Cerberus.

Although the southern colonies, with bountiful staple products to exchange for British goods, were little injured by the Sugar Act, the middle colonies felt its effect only less than those of New England. They had enjoyed devious ways of getting hard money with which to pay for English manufactures. Their merchants carried their lumber, wheat, and meat to the West Indies,[3] and exchanged them there for cotton, indigo, and sugar, which were good as gold for remittance to their English creditors. Rum and molasses got in the Indies were by the alchemy of trade turned into gold and silver to the same end. The fur-trade, too, furnished exchange welcome to the English merchant. To limit their trade, as the Sugar Act intended, to the British sugar islands, would woefully cut down their market for lumber

[1] British Museum, *King's MSS.*, 205 F 198.   [2] 4 Geo. III, c. 15.

[3] This was their chief market, for the importation of grain and meat into England had been prohibited in a statute of the reign of Charles II.

and foodstuffs. This would reduce greatly the supply of silver needed to square accounts in London. Finally, it was maddening to colonial vanity to have the interests of a small coterie of West Indian sugar planters made an object of greater concern to Parliament than the interests of the thirteen colonies of the Atlantic seaboard. All of the colonies north of Virginia were suffering a real blow to their economic well-being. Though many laws in earlier days might have been burdensome if enforced, their ill-effects had been nullified by individual enterprise joined with a moral obtuseness to the crime of smuggling. Though illicit trade had always been common, and though it was smuggling that lost Massachusetts her charter as early as 1684, yet in the general colonial import trade there had not been a serious amount of contraband trade.[1] This was due to no moral scruples of the colonists, for they evaded any restrictions when it was profitable to do so, but smuggling was not good business when better bargains were to be obtained from England than from France or the Netherlands. It was in this sense that the Trade Acts were approved by James Otis. "Very good," he said, "we have submitted to this. The act of navigation is a good act, so are all that exclude foreign manufactures from the plantations, and every honest man will readily subscribe to them."[2] It was the Molasses Act which had created

---

[1] That in colonial exports was very small also.

[2] The Virginia Committee of Correspondence (1762) admitted this, "provided the mother country supplies all the Colonies want." *Virginia Magazine of History*, XI, 137. J. Otis, *Rights of the British Colonists*, etc. (Boston, 1764), 54, 55.

the greatest incentive to illicit trade. The great
mass of contraband trade was in molasses, rum,
and sugar.[1] From the French and Spanish West
Indies, and therefore paying no duty, came 11,500
hogsheads of molasses out of the 14,000 hogsheads
imported into Rhode Island every year.[2] Indeed,
the entire output of the British islands would not
furnish two thirds of the quantity imported into
Rhode Island, and, moreover, the British planters
asked a price more than twenty-five per cent higher
than the foreign islands.[3] It was estimated that the
loss each year to the English treasury, due to the
success of the New England smugglers, was not less
than £100,000.[4]

There is no doubt that this illicit trade maintained
the prosperity of the individual colonies, but its
effect on British national welfare was demoralizing.
This evil was at its worst during the Seven Years'
War, when the colonial smugglers, especially those
of Pennsylvania and New York, neutralized the
advantage of British naval supremacy by supplying
the French colonies with flour, beef, and pork, the
very articles of trade which the navy's activity
aimed to cut off. Flour concealed in claret kegs,
or carried under flags of truce — flags sold even by
colonial governors for twenty pounds sterling —
"nourished and supported" the French enemies.[5]
Yet when the colonists were reproached for this
treasonable trade, they asked how they were to pay

[1] Schlesinger, *The Colonial Merchants*, 42.
[2] *Ibid.*, quoting *Rhode Island Colonial Records*, VI, 378–83.
[3] *Ibid.*, 43.   [4] Beer, *The Old Colonial System*, pt. I, vol. II, 269.
[5] Beer, *British Colonial Policy. 1754–65*, 87–88.

their share toward the support of the war without
money gained from commercial dealings with their
best customers, their good friends, the enemy.[1] The
Livingston family of New York were said to have
made a fortune out of this trade, and many fortunes
in New England and New York and Pennsylvania
were reputed greatly swollen by this illicit trade. In
the first Continental Congress, Lynch, of South
Carolina, blurted out, "Many gentlemen in this
room know how to bring in goods, sugars and others,
without paying duties."[2] The colonial conscience
omitted smuggling from the catalogue of crimes.
John Hancock was no less respectable because he
was suspected of smuggling. Indeed, this suspicion
was only an ornament of his respectability. So common was the crime that all distinction between a
merchant and a smuggler was lost. Smuggling and
respectability went hand in hand in the market-
place. Franklin, with homely philosophy, explained
that "there are those in the world who would not
wrong a neighbour, but make no scruple of cheating
the King. The reverse, however, does not hold; for
whoever scruples cheating the King will certainly
not wrong his neighbour." In the colonial mind, in
fact, "smuggling" was not a well-chosen word to
describe evasion of the trade laws, which was, after
all, only a defiance of the British sovereignty by the
individual colonist. The acts of smugglers refusing
obedience to the trade and navigation laws, and

[1] Hall, "Chatham's Colonial Policy," in *American Historical Review*, v, 666.
[2] Hansard, *Parliamentary History*, xvi, 125; John Adams. *Works*
II, 394.

rhetorical defiance by Patrick Henry and James Otis, were only preludes to ultimate defiance by all the American colonists. Like any laws which do not appeal to the understanding and sympathy of the honest citizens of a state, the trade laws which ran counter to the interests of the colonial merchants were not enforceable. James Otis only overstated when in a moment of excitement he declared that "if the King of Great Britain in person were encamped on Boston Common, at the head of twenty thousand men, with all his navy on our coast, he would not be able to execute these laws."[1] There were many wily devices by which the law was evaded, and the New England coast, with its creeks and coves and rocky inlets, offered easy sanctuary in fog or darkness to the Puritan smuggler. Yet such daring methods were unnecessary, for we may read to-day the solemn oaths of informers that collectors of His Majesty's customs were known regularly to receive from captains of vessels casks of wine or boxes of fruit, portions of which went even to the governor — on the condition that the collector's eye pass charitably over prohibited cargoes of wine and fruit.[2] In the customs records the vessel was set down as entering only with salt or ballast. The fees of customs officers were so small that, it was said, without bribery and corruption they must starve. They could make the job lucrative only by shutting their eyes or opening them no further than

[1] W. S. McClellan, *Smuggling in American Colonies*, 78.
[2] *Boston Gazette*, June 12, 1769; Palfrey, *History of New England*, v, 40.

to see a bribe. Governor Bernard, who ought to know, since there is sworn testimony that he shared in the proceeds, declared (1764), "if conniving at foreign sugars and molasses and Portugal wines and fruits is to be reckoned Corruption, there never was, I believe, an uncorrupt Customs House Officer in America until within twelve months." [1] If, perchance, cargoes were seized for evasion of duties, there was always the probability of rescue by rioters. The fate of one who tried to aid the British Government in rooting out the trade evil is suggested by the spirit of a colonial journal, which urged the seizure of a customs spy. "All lovers of Liberty will make a diligent search, and having found this bird of darkness, will produce him tarred and feathered at the Coffee-House" to expiate his sins. Benedict Arnold caused an informer to be tied to the public whipping post and given forty lashes, for which p'easure Arnold and his fellows paid a fine of fifty shillings. [2] Even if a smuggler were caught redhanded, it was difficult to convict him, because, we are told by one who knew, the jury was made up of men "equally concerned in carrying on an illicit trade, and its hardly to be expected that they will find each other guilty." [3] That they might free a smuggler of Irish soap, a jury in Jamaica solemnly decided that soap was a foodstuff upon which a man could live for a month. It was therefore "provisions," which under the trade laws might be freely imported from Ireland. Candles were put into a

---

[1] Josiah Quincy, *Reports*, etc., 423, 424.
[2] Barber, *Historical Collections of Connecticut*, 166.
[3] Hart, *American History Told by Contemporaries*, II, 87.

similar category for a like purpose by another jury.[1] These facts exhibit the true nature of colonial acquiescence in the trade and navigation laws before 1764. Burke could have had little understanding of these conditions when he declared, "The Acts of Navigation attended the Colonies from their infancy, grew with their growth, and strengthened with their strength. They were confirmed in obedience to it, even more by usage than by law." [2] The only element of truth in his assertion was that the colonists did not object to them, if they were not enforced in such parts as opposed colonial interests. In 1764 the new measures offered by "that two penny monarch, George Grenville," were so planned as greatly to increase the hazards of illicit trading, and in addition to the reforms in the administration of the trade laws, which Pitt had introduced during the Seven Years' War, Grenville had instructed all colonial governors to give insistent enforcement to the trade laws, and, besides increasing the force of revenue officers, had ordered all holders of sinecures in customs offices to hie them from London to their American posts. He had increased the number of war vessels on the American coast, and authorized the use of general writs to aid the searchers for smuggled goods. Indeed, it is a fair question as to whether American traders were more alarmed over the new Sugar Act or over the new efficiency of the customs administration. The strait-jacket of trade seemed securely fastened upon the colonial victim,

[1] Beer, *The Old Colonial System*, pt. i, vol. i, 306–08.
[2] Burke, *Speeches* (ed. 1816), i, 202.

and his reactions were the more frantic because of his feeling of impotence.

Nevertheless the effect in America of the Sugar Act and of the new administrative measures was not alarming to those accustomed to colonial protest and bluster. Many individuals complained bitterly of the burden to commerce, but there was no mass reaction or rebellion.[1] Adam Smith expressed only a truism when he declared that "to prohibit a great people making the best of their resources was a violation of the most sacred rights of mankind"; but to go further and declare with Arthur Young that the cause of the American War was "that baleful spirit of commerce, that wished to govern great nations on the maxims of the counter," is to express a small part of the truth, and to ignore that long training in self-government which had made the English colonist utterly different from the French or the Spanish inhabitants of the colonies of those empires. Frenchman and Spaniard in America endured the trade restraints fastened on them by the "baleful spirit of commerce." These restraints were not merely on the statute books, but were much more rigorously enforced than in English provinces. Moreover, even the colonists of England were not to be aflame along a thousand miles of the Atlantic seaboard, until another parliamentary enactment, attacking more plainly a fundamental principle of political liberty, should awake in the colonial mind every memory of the long struggle by which they had reached their actual political independence.

[1] W. F. Ashley, *Surveys, Historic and Economic*, 309.

CHAPTER VI

THE STAMP ACT REVEALS WEAKNESS IN THE IMPERIAL FABRIC

WE have seen how the Seven Years' War had forced into prominence problems which, though strictly American, were yet too large for any one of the self-ruling colonies of America to handle. We have noted how the British Ministry realized its lack of powers and revenue to solve these problems, and how, instead of creating a suitable legislature in America, they tried to get from America what they needed by use of the agency of the existing legislature in England. It was not a new device, this use of the British Parliament to give force to the royal prerogative in America. Obstinate Massachusetts had been threatened (1729) with intervention by Parliament. Indeed, Americans had not denied before 1763 the right of Parliament to succor the waning power of the King's prerogative in matters of trade and revenue acts and of other regulative measures.[1] That to put such purely colonial matters in the control of Parliament would, if successful, destroy the American sense of responsibility, that it would leave that sense "unexercized and unbreathed" save in purely local affairs, seems to have been an idea foreign to the minds of that age. Even Pitt, whose penetrating mind opened up political vistas unsuspected by duller men, did not suggest, until

[1] Andrews, *The Colonial Period*, 241.

the Continental Congress actually sat in Philadel·
phia, that the way to tax America was to let those
delegates from the thirteen colonies make "a free
grant to the King . . . of a certain perpetual revenue," fixing *themselves* the quotas and proportions to be borne by each province. He alone saw
that this "mighty continental nation" had found
in its Congress an articulate voice.

Even if the implied imperial reorganization was
unthinkable in that age, one might conceive of devices to lessen expenses or increase revenue, to
which it might seem to our generation Grenville
could have turned. If the new ministerial plan for
America demanded money, why not cut off £400,000
of pensions by which the Government cared for
impecunious relatives and friends, or why not take
action against Rigby, paymaster of the forces, who
"put into his private wallet the interest on a million
pounds of public money in the Bank of England"? [1]
Such thoughts were beyond the reaches of eighteenth-century souls. Grenville and his contemporaries could no more imagine such reforms than
they could have imagined wireless communication
with America. The suggestion of them would have
been taken no more seriously than some of the
bizarre suggestions by angry colonists. A minister
of finance, as James Otis insinuated, might "go
nabob hunting on this occasion" or "the great
Mogul be obliged to contribute" to pay the national
debt. "He is a pagan, an East Indian, and of a

---

[1] Grenville himself had profited by drawing the interest on the
nation's money while he was treasurer of the navy.

dark complexion," all quite as good as those offered
for taxing the American colonists. Or, as another
American radical might suggest, why not raise the
taxes on the land of country squires in order to
increase the revenue? The answer of Grenville to
such a query would have been that no ministry could
survive such temerity, and it was far easier to tax the
distant Americans. Moreover, there was some truth
in the blunt declaration of an eccentric Englishman
to Josiah Quincy. "Very true," he said, "Great
Britain has no right to tax you. The ministry know
it as well as you, but money must be had somewhere.
Everything is strained to the utmost at home."
"Why," he exclaimed in closing, "all the world are
slaves, and North America can't hope to be free." [1]
After all, except for the method of taxing, the logic
was not ill, which held that Americans ought to pay
for their own defense and government. That logic,
whether good or bad, was all that might have been
expected of Grenville, whose pedantic mind was
absorbed in the details of his office, while he blindly
passed by the really great issues. He was one of
those dread individuals with "a fund of useful
knowledge." [2] The stiffness that was in his manner
was also in his mind, which always placed above
common sense the letter of the law in which he was
so deeply versed. To come, as Pitt scorned to do,
armed at all points, with law cases and acts of Parliament, with the statute book "doubled down in

[1] Mass. Hist. Soc., *Proceedings*, XLIX, 433.
[2] Historical MSS. Commission, *Reports* (*Various Collections*), VI,
94–101.

dog's ears," exactly suited his genius and his character. It was not in him to arrive at the wisdom of Sir
Philip Francis, who declared that "the fate of nations must not be tried by forms." Sir Philip admitted that he used to be able to reason most
logically against the Americans, but since he had
studied the book of wisdom he had dismissed logic
out of his library.

Grenville's efforts toward administrative efficiency
and his new measures, the Sugar Act and the Currency Act, were but the few cautious steps in the
direction of his final purpose. As if he sensed danger,
he moved slowly. On March 10, 1764, in a series of
resolutions which outlined the terms of the Sugar
Act, a resolve was included that asserted the purpose
of charging "certain stamp duties" in the colonies.[1]
The warning was a whole year in advance of the
actual execution of the plan, allowing time, as
Burke later sarcastically pointed out, "for all the
discontents of that country to fester and come to a
head, and for all the arrangements which factious
men could make toward an opposition to the law."
The stamp tax idea was not original with Grenville:
Pitt later asserted that even when he was minister,
men had proposed to him to "burn his fingers with
an American Stamp Act." Such an act had been
recommended by several provincial officials of long
experience; it was now proposed, Grenville declared,
"from a real regard and tenderness" for the colonists, and it was to be imposed only if the colonial

[1] Hansard, *Parliamentary Debates*, xv, 1427 no. 14; *Grenville Papers*, II, 373–74.

agents could not tell him of a better. "If the colonies prefer some other tax, let them signify," said Grenville. The only reply to his request for suggestions was a proposal to try the old plan of requisitions on the several colonies, but remembering its miserable failure in the Seven Years' War, he asked, "Can you agree on the proportions each colony should raise?" Getting no answer except remonstrances "carefully concealed from the eye of Parliament," he pressed on his financial plans regardless of their political consequences. He was wont to say that "the most important word to him, next to that of liberty, was revenue," but for the moment, at least, liberty fell to the rear.

Before a Parliament more ill-informed than himself Grenville brought his stamp measure. Such knowledge as the members had of colonial conditions came, second hand, strained through the reports of the Board of Trade or the Secretary of State, colored by the aims and purposes of these officials. Grenville's arguments only vexed the dull ear of either friend or foe, for he was a poor debater, unaware of the charms of brevity. It was enough that he assured them that the method was "easy," would fall only on property, and be collected by few officers, who would not give offense by entering and searching houses. He could easily show them, with "delusive geometrical accuracy," that the stamp duties were lighter than those levied at that moment in England, and that a few English taxes like those on marriage certificates and pardons had been omitted.[1]

[1] Mass. Hist. Soc., *Collections* (6th Ser.), IX, 49.

It was to fall chiefly on bonds, newspapers, legal and commercial documents, and insurance policies.[1] Offenses against the law were to be tried in admiralty courts in America or England. The proceeds were to go wholly to defray the expense of governing and defending the American colonies. It was all reasonable enough as a revenue measure, and had it been passed by an American Congress would have provoked only the usual grumbling which has greeted taxation in all ages. Grenville even tried to commend the poisoned chalice by selecting American colonists as the stamp agents rather than sending English officers. Franklin nominated his friend Hughes for the office in Pennsylvania; Richard Henry Lee sought the office in Virginia; and Jared Ingersoll, who, from the visitor's gallery had watched Parliament enact the measure, accepted, on Franklin's advice, the office of distributor in his own colony of Connecticut.[2] When such men failed to forecast the results of the measure it is little wonder that when only two or three members spoke against it, without force or apparent interest, Horace Walpole could write to his friend, the Earl of Hertford, "There has been nothing of note in Parliament, but one slight day on the American taxes, which Charles Townshend supporting, received a pretty heavy thump from Barré, who is the present Pitt." [3]

Barré had, indeed, disturbed the slumbers of many members who were taking lightly this momentous

[1] Macdonald, *Documentary Source Book*, no. 33.
[2] British Museum, *Egerton MSS.*, 2671 F 30. See C. M. Andrews, *Guide*, etc., II, 102, for complete list of all colonial receivers.
[3] Hansard, *Parliamentary History*, XVI, 37.

bill. This fiery young man of twenty-nine, the Irish-
born son of a French refugee, was unrivaled in political opposition. His massive, swarthy figure was, as
Walpole said, the "dread of all vociferous Norths
and Rigbys, on whose lungs depended so much of
Mr. Grenville's power." [1] Barré had received a face
wound while he was fighting by Wolfe's side when
that hero fell on the Plains of Abraham, and it gave
an additional terror to the glare which went with the
invective so feared by his opponents.[2] In his opposition to the Stamp Act he was representing the views
of Pitt, as Walpole suggested, and of his patron,
Lord Shelburne, who was absent being married that
day, and who complimented him handsomely when
told of his defense of those "sons of Liberty," the
Americans.[3] Perhaps Barré was the more bitter
against Grenville, because that minister had dismissed him but a year before from a post worth
£4000 a year. No doubt, too, his brilliant speech
influenced Pitt to restore him later to the lost post
when the "Great Commoner" was again in power.
Certainly, it made him loved and famous in America, where his assertion that the men sent to rule
Americans, "sent to spy out their liberties, to mis-
represent their actions, and to prey upon them," had
"caused the blood of these *sons of liberty* to recoil
within them," was received with vast applause, and

[1] H. Walpole, *Letters* (Toynbee, *ed.*), vi, 187–88.
[2] While in America he had passed through New York, New Jersey,
Pennsylvania and Massachusetts. Gordon, i, 438; Mass. Hist. Soc.
Proceedings, l, 452.
[3] Hansard, *Parliamentary History*, xvi, 39. Fitzmaurice, *Life of
Shelburne*, i, 225.

the epithet he had given them was adopted as the name of numbers of patriotic clubs.

Barré warned Parliament that the spirit of freedom actuated Americans, that though loyal subjects, they were jealous of their liberties and would "vindicate them if ever they should be violated." His friend Jackson, dubbed by Dr. Johnson "the all-knowing," also warned them that though Parliament was undoubtedly "the universal, unlimited legislature of the British dominions," yet it should voluntarily set bounds to the exercise of that power.[1] Otherwise, he added, "the liberties of America, I do not say will be lost, but will be in danger, and they cannot be injured without danger to the liberties of Great Britain."

But all these warnings could not take America's fate from the knees of the gods. Members of Parliament could not see what is so clear to-day, that each new adventure of Grenville in the field of colonial regulation only added to the offense given by the last legislative foray. Sugar Act, Currency Act, and now the Stamp Act; each new act seemed cunningly devised to swell the burden laid upon colonial shoulders by the last. The Sugar Act, by its dislocation of colonial trade habits, was most troublesome of all. Having by this measure blocked the West Indian source which flowed with gold and silver for trade with England, the blundering minister fostered the Currency Bill, which acted to cut down still further the available specie for British trade. By the Stamp Act, then, he increased

---

[1] Quoted by Bancroft, *History of the United States*, v, 238.

the yearly need for gold and silver by £60,000. All this followed the Proclamation of 1763, seeming to close the West to settlement, in the interest of the very Indian tribes who had but yesterday wrought such havoc in the border settlements, and this exclusion was proclaimed just as the desire to migrate thither was likely to be increased, because the demand for laborers was reduced by the restrictions on commerce. Finally, the time selected to add all this burden was at the close of the Seven Years' War, when local colonial taxes were high owing to their own war debts, and the reason advanced was that they were to be protected from foes whom they now considered vanquished. Moreover, the "protection" was to be given by a standing army of ten thousand men to be maintained out of the proposed revenues, and to be billeted upon American communities.[1] Little wonder that the whole plan, benevolent as it doubtless was in purpose, looked to the colonists like a dark design of a would-be tyrant. Moreover, the Stamp Act itself, with its symbols of tyranny, the stamped paper, brought to the fore the whole question of colonial rights.

The warning which Grenville had given America of his proposed Stamp Act had aroused the whole hive of colonial legislators. They had denounced the Sugar Act in memorials and addresses to which no heed had been given, and to the mere threat of a stamp duty the retort was made that it was contrary to their rights as British citizens to be taxed by Parliament. Though the Stamp Act was passed in the

[1] Macdonald, *Documentary Source Book*, 131

spring, its actual going into force had been, at the request of colonial agents, delayed until fall. In the meanwhile restless discontent was fanned into something dangerously like the flame of rebellion, and, most alarming of all, it was no longer local, but spread from north to south. One of the most important effects of the Stamp Act was to enlist the planting provinces of the South in swelling the protest already rising in volume from the northern commercial provinces because of their losses under the Sugar Act.[1] The plane of the controversy was now raised, and appeals to natural rights furnished common ground for North and South. Indeed, it was in Virginia that the first "trumpet of sedition" was blown.

It would be easy for Diderot's Rameau, believing that the end of all man's effort is to "place something between his teeth" and thus obey the laws of mastication, or easy, indeed, for any disciple of the "dismal science" to prove that the whole basis for rebellion in Virginia was economic and due to the desire of debtor tobacco planters to be rid of British creditors, but deeper students of that history assign other causes. Andrew Barnaby, traveling in Virginia in 1759, found the public or political character of the Virginians to correspond with their private one; "they are haughty and jealous of their liberties," he said, "impatient of restraint and can scarcely bear the thought of being controlled by any superior power. Many of them consider the colonies as independent states not connected with Great

[1] Schlesinger, *The Colonial Merchants*, 34–39, 65.

Britain otherwise than by having a common king and being bound to her with natural affection." [1]

A successful Virginia tobacco planter enjoyed an income great enough to give him — like the English country gentleman whom he aped — leisure not only for dicing and horse-racing, but for reading and attention to public affairs. From a perusal of history and English law the planters had imbibed ideas which opened their minds to the liberal theories which, in the middle of the eighteenth century, seemed to radiate like electric waves throughout the civilized world. Moreover, in the county courts, or as members of the parish vestries and of the colonial legislature, they had become masters of the art of self-government. [2] Though there was a comparatively liberal franchise [3] the actual political control in the dominant seaboard section was confined to a small group of planters who had great interests at stake which hostile lawmaking might imperil, and it behooved them to agree upon men of ability to represent them. Members of certain families, attaining their positions through wealth and social standing, were returned to the House of Burgesses, decade after decade, a Cabell from Amherst, a Fleming from Cumberland, and a Randolph from Williamsburg. [4] Nevertheless, factional rivalries made ability necessary as well as family ties. Besides this intensive training in the best school of statecraft, it has been shown that twenty-seven out

[1] Andrew Barnaby in *William and Mary College Quarterly*, no. 18, p. 15.
[2] Lingley, *The Transition in Virginia*, 112, 113.
[3] *Ibid.*, 117.   [4] *Ibid.*, 111.

of the forty-one most influential burgesses in the pre-Revolutionary period had been educated in British educational institutions, or at William and Mary in Virginia.[1] Moreover, these men and their American ancestors had from the earliest time enjoyed the privilege of self-taxation. This ruling clique, silk-stockinged, socially exclusive, aristocratic in bearing and spirit, took an absorbing interest in self-rule for Virginia, but cared not a straw for the rights of the common man.

Ablest and foremost in defending this passion for local self-government was Richard Bland, of Prince George County. Most of the remonstrances which the House of Burgesses made against the new British policy were the work of this genial, good-mannered, classical scholar who was also both farmer and lawyer.[2] The study of history and law at William and Mary and at the University of Edinburgh had forged for him the weapons with which in 1760 he defended the assembly's constitutional right to enact needed laws without interference from England.

Besides these planter lawgivers there was a group of burgesses representing the upland counties, the Piedmont and mountain sections of Virginia, men not so endowed with the goods of this world nor so cultivated in intellectual and spiritual matters, but hostile to any government except their own. In the Piedmont region were many dissenters and in the Great Valley, beyond the first mountain range,

---

[1] Lingley, *The Transition in Virginia*, 114.
[2] H. J. Eckenrode, *The Revolution in Virginia*, 11, 12.

many Scotch-Irish and Germans, non-English people, little moved by English traditions, and if not dissenters, at least belonging to some sect not Episcopalian, which was the church almost universally attended by the tide-water planters. This sectarian difference, and the greater social democracy of the western region caused a lack of harmony between the upland and the lowland representatives. Yet the latter, weak in numbers and lacking in political experience, had little influence until in the heat of the quarrel with the British Government a leader was vouchsafed them in the obscure young lawyer, Patrick Henry.

This "forest born Demosthenes," in Byron's phrase, was a natural tragedian to whom the rude frontier had denied any stage but the county court or the floor of the House of Burgesses. Two years before the Stamp Act he had won local renown by taking the popular side in the "Parsons' Cause." [1] This case grew out of a long-standing dispute over the method of paying the salaries of the clergy of the Established Church — salaries once fixed at so many pounds of tobacco, the Virginian accepted medium of exchange. The "sublime" weed was a bad form of money, fluctuating with every harvest, yet Virginians had agreed to use it as a circulating medium and had made legal enactments, equivalent to contracts, providing for paying the Anglican clergy in that lucre. When poor harvests caused the

---

[1] Excellent accounts of this case may be found in Eckenrode, *The Revolution in Virginia*, 9–12; Lingley, *The Transition in Virginia*, 27–34; Tyler, *Patrick Henry*, i, 45; Wirt, *Patrick Henry*, 23.

price to rise, the burgesses proceeded in effect to violate their contract by a new law the "Two Penny Act," a legal nullification of the old law. The clergy had suffered when the price was low, but were not to gain when the price was high. When, therefore, as a probable result of their appeal to the Bishop of London, the "Two Penny Act" received the royal veto, the clergy were encouraged to sue for their salaries on the basis of the old act, which had been approved by the King.

The question of the royal veto was a burning one, and more than a dozen years later much was made in the Declaration of Independence of the King's tyranny in vetoing or disallowing laws held to be for the good of the colonies. The colonial legislatures had always watched and imitated Parliament in its struggle for power, and they regarded the royal veto as obsolete. The royal veto had, indeed, fallen into disuse since 1707 so far as it affected the laws of Parliament, and the advanced spirits in the colonial legislatures demanded a like freedom for themselves. Royal colonies were expected to send their laws at once to England for approval or disallowance, while charter and proprietary colonies had certain privileges which did not, however, wholly exempt them. Since years might pass between the making of a law and its disallowance, all acts under the law were valid until the day of their disapproval.[1] The King was usually blamed for this disallowance because

[1] Dickerson, in *American Colonial Government*, 227, says that there were over four hundred cases of disallowance of colonial laws between 1696 and 1765. This paragraph is based upon Dickerson's chapter v, the best treatment to date. See also E. B. Russell.

the notification of such action stated that it was done by "the King in Council"; but in fact the King's part was a mere governmental fiction and the Board of Trade was wholly responsible. The reasons for their action were many. Colonial acts that hampered the home government or trenched on the royal prerogative were pretty sure to be negatived. The Bishop of London watched with a jealous eye all ecclesiastical legislation and pressed the Board for nullification of all laws offensive to the established Church's interests. Laws inconsistent with the laws of England were annulled, and the action in some cases was not unlike our national custom which permits a court to declare null and void laws contrary to the national constitution and laws. English merchants could usually get the Board of Trade to disallow colonial laws which laid a burden on their commerce or placed trammels on intercolonial trade or the Indian trade. Colonial attempts to curb the slave-trade unduly were vetoed by this power of the Board of Trade. It was obliged at times to secure the repeal of unjust laws and those laying legal obstacles in the way of collecting debts. In the method of doing this work every due form of legal procedure was observed by the Board. Less ceremony is observed by our Supreme Court in declaring state laws unconstitutional than this Board employed in the disallowance of colonial acts.[1] Moreover, they meant to cause as little trouble as possible, and often refrained from the veto because of the inconvenience it might occasion. It was irri-

[1] Dickerson, *American Colonial Government*, 271.

tating, of course, just as the invalidation of laws by
the courts to-day is so, but the purpose was good,
and the machinery on the whole worked better than
that of other parts of the British administration.
Though there was, doubtless, too much red tape, the
plan did effectively mould and shape certain colonial
institutions. Nevertheless, the interference was at
times maddening from the colonial point of view,
and in the case of the "Two Penny Act" the majority of Virginians felt greatly aggrieved, especially
as the action touched their pockets.[1]

In a famous case in the Hanover County Court,
before a jury manned in part by Presbyterians,
Patrick Henry pleaded the popular cause. He made
an adroit appeal to the frontier disregard of law,
declaring that the King, in vetoing the assembly's
reasonable and beneficial enactments, had ceased
to be the father of his people and degenerated into
a tyrant, thus forfeiting all right to his subjects'
obedience. He pleaded with the jury not to rivet
the chains of bondage on their own necks, and with
innuendoes against the Church and clergy appealed
to some of the least admirable prejudices of ignorant
frontiersmen. The soundest part of his argument,
in which he held that the Virginian burgesses had
the constitutional right to pass, without interference
from the King, all legislation necessary to the colony,
was based upon Richard Bland's scholarly pamphlet
written three years earlier. In a passage, in which
Henry alluded to what he called "the original com-

[1] For American opinion on imperial review, see E. B. Greene's
article in *American Historical Review*, XXIII, 104.

pact between king and people," we have good reason
to think that he was following Samuel Davies, the
eloquent Virginia preacher to whom Henry had
listened for more than a decade, and who doubtless influenced both his oratorical style and his
political philosophy. The jury, "bewildered" by his
eloquence and "thoughtless even of the admitted
rights" of the clergy, gave Maury, the plaintiff, a
verdict of one penny damages. In a highly cultured
community, an honorable lawyer, influenced by the
highest standards of the bar, and wishing an honest
legal basis for his argument, could hardly have taken
the case at all. It was easy for the unsympathetic
to hold that Henry abused the courts of justice for
political ends. The verdict secured was plainly an
injustice to the clergy, though the motives of the
assembly, which had to consider the whole community, were probably just, and doubtless Henry,
"prophet of young freedom," was right in protesting
against a dangerous system of government. Unfortunately for Henry's reputation, it was not the only
time in his life that he was on the side of injustice
and made it prevail.[1]

Though Henry's name rang through the Virginia
forests, and he became at once a hero of the lower
classes, he was not so highly rated by the contemporary rulers of the colony, the clergy or the upper
classes in general. His work seemed to be to set the
masses against the high-born. The most flaming
figure, perhaps, in Virginian history, he stood as a

[1] See Hook case, Randolph murder case, and Jones *vs.* Walker in
Morgan's *Henry.*

rallying-point for revolutionists and dissenters, not as a great leader toward solid reform. All agreed as to his mastery of the art of oratory, but many disagreed as to his wisdom, depth of thought, or even honesty of reasoning. One of his admiring contemporaries declared that in religious matters he was a "saint, but a very devil in politics — a son of thunder"; [1] but opponents classed him with political demagogues who seek to strengthen their own power by haranguing the masses, urging them to force legislatures, courts, or executive officers to respond at once to the impulse of the hour. They classed him with those who reck not "what crimes it costs to be a moment free and famous through all the ages." Edmund Randolph, who knew him well, fairly estimated his mentality when he wrote of Henry that: "In pure reasoning he encountered many successful competitors; in the wisdom of books many superiors; but though he might be inconclusive he was never frivolous, and arguments which at first seemed strange, were afterwards discovered to be select of their kind, because adapted to some peculiarity in his audience." It is certain that he had real genius in selecting the arguments and phrases which would appeal to the popular mind, voicing its deepest convictions.

Before the Stamp Act was considered by the Virginia Assembly, Henry had entered as a member from Louisa County, and when the colony's attitude toward that measure was being discussed in the committee of the whole, May 29, 1765, he sprang to the

[1] W. W. Henry, *Patrick Henry, Life and Correspondence*, I, 197.

fore with a set of resolutions written hurriedly on the leaf of his copy of "Coke upon Littleton." [1] The resolutions were afire with passion, but contained in substance an assertion of colonial rights not new to the House of Burgesses. Against their heat and virulence, however, there was bitter opposition by men like Peyton Randolph, Edmund Pendleton, Richard Bland, and George Wythe, all of whom were soon to lead open rebellion against the British Government. These gentlemen of the tide-water aristocracy were especially offended when Henry, in the "torrent of his sublime eloquence," somewhat overstepped the Virginian conventions of propriety. A French agent, seeking to sound the colonial loyalty and find how deep it was, happened to reach Williamsburg just in time to get invited to visit the House of Burgesses in the very hour of Henry's speech. "Shortly after I came in," the agent reported to the French Government, "one of the members stood up and said he had read that in former times tarquin and Julus had their Brutus, Charles had his Cromwell, and he Did not Doubt that some good American would stand up in favor of his Country, but (says he) in a more moderate manner. And was going to continue, when the Speaker of the house rose and said, he, the last that stood up, had spoke traison and was sorey to see that not one of the members of the house was loyal Enough to Stop him, before he had gone so far. Upon which, the Same member stood up again, (his name is henery) and said that if he had affronted

---

[1] Henry, *Patrick Henry*, I, 93.

the Speaker, or the house, he was ready to ask pardon, and he would show his loyalty to his majesty, King G the third, at the Expense of the last Drop of his blood, but what he had Said must be atributed to the Interest of his Country's Dying liberty which he had at heart, and the heat of passion might have lead him to have said something more than he intended, but again, if he had Said anything wrong, he beged the Speaker and the houses pardon; some other members Stood up and backed him on which that afaire was droped." [1]

This irreverent allusion to "the best of kings" shocked men, who would have hesitated at nothing to flaunt the will of their sovereign, but who had real respect for his person. It was not the first time Henry had been charged with treason, less dangerous to one accused in the Virginia forest than in Westminster, a thousand leagues away. Moreover, Henry was lawyer enough to come within a hair's breadth of treason without being guilty of an overt act, to use the words of the British Attorney-General, three years later, speaking of American lawyers in general. [2] If the passage of the resolutions was to seem to give approval to such sentiments as Henry's, it was not strange that the excited Randolph rushed by Jeffer-

[1] This document was discovered by Monsieur Abel Doysié in the *Archives* of the Hydrographic Service of the Ministry of the Marine in Paris, in the course of an investigation which he was conducting for the Carnegie Institution of Washington, under the direction of W. G. Leland. The report is in marked contrast to the conventional story, which has Henry cry, "If that be treason make the most of it." The spy's account was an entry in a diary written up from day to day The old story is based on memory.

[2] Bancroft, *Hist. of U.S.*, epoch III, chap. 37.

son, hanging about the door, swearing that he would give five hundred guineas for a single vote to help defeat Henry. Contemporary accounts are confusing as to how many of Henry's resolutions were finally passed — supported, as Governor Fauquier informed his King, by the "young, hot and giddy members" [1] from the upland regions — but six, known as the "Virginia Resolves," were published in newspapers from Savannah to Boston, becoming, as Governor Bernard of Massachusetts wrote, an "alarm bell to the disaffected" everywhere. This much Henry surely did, and his act spread the spirit of revolt from the assembly to the people, but the claim, made long after by Jefferson, that the eastern members, forming a sort of British faction, opposed resistance to Great Britain, and that Henry, backed by the western members, took the lead in opposition, is not borne out by the facts.[2] There was no English party in the House of Burgesses, and the up-country men and the seaboard planters seem to have agreed that the House of Burgesses alone could make laws to regulate the internal affairs of Virginia, but the seaboard planters wished to be moderate and tactful in asserting this claim, while the more robust frontiersmen preferred a fighting attitude. Speed and dash was their method. It was that which made a sympathetic New Englander cry, "Those Virginians are men, they are noble spirits." [3] Henry did not originate the spirit of resistance; he merely

[1] *Journal of House of Burgesses, 1761–1765.* preface, lxviii.
[2] Lingley, *The Transition in Virginia,* 123; Eckenrode, *The Revolution in Virginia,* 18.
[3] Bancroft, *Hist. of U.S.* (ed. 1884), iii, 115.

made it reckless, demanding instant action, and that suited the temper of a great number of Americans in that trying hour. His work done, with better judgment than any other act of his brilliant career, Henry was seen in the afternoon "clad in a pair of leather breeches, his saddle bags on his arm, leading a lame horse," passing down the street on his way home.[1]

There was plenty of dry tinder in the colonies to be fired by the spark of Henry's eloquence. "Behold, a whole continent awakened, alarmed, restless and disaffected," cheerfully exclaimed an opponent of the act. The merchants, lawyers, and newspaper men were the most injured and the most aroused by the menace of the Stamp Act. John Hancock, the rich Boston merchant, declared that the act would "stagnate trade." He feared he must shut up his warehouse doors, since there was not cash enough in New England to support such a tax. In his mind and that of all merchants the Sugar Act, cutting down the West Indian supply of ready money, and the Currency Act, forbidding reckless issues of paper money in the colonies, had reduced the ready cash with which the stamps, now needed on all ship papers, could be bought. "Unless we are allowed a paper currency they need not send tax gatherers," wrote Daniel Coxe, "for they can gather nothing — never was money so scarce as now." Indeed, that was a general opinion voiced in nearly every colony, some holding that in a few years the act would take off all the cash.[2] Moreover, under existing trade

[1] Grigsby, *Virginia Convention of 1776*, 150.
[2] Wells, *Samuel Adams*, I, 83. The Stamp Act Congress later endorsed

conditions John Dickinson doubted whether commerce could bear the stamp taxes on policies, fees
with clerks, protests, notarial acts, letters, and even
advertisements.[1] The lawyers, too, foresaw great
inroads on their business, because the act assessed
duties on all legal documents, on letters of administration, deeds, bonds, licenses and leases. To John
Adams it seemed that, after thirty years of his life
passed in preparation for business, "this execrable
project was set on foot for my ruin as well as that
of America in general." [2] It was one of the most serious errors of the British Government to arouse the
American lawyers. Burke a few years later did not
fail to point out this folly. The study of law, he
said, "renders men acute, inquisitive, dexterous,
prompt in attack, ready in defence, full of resources.
In other countries, the people, more simple, and of
a less mercurial cast, judge of an ill principle in
government only by an actual grievance; here
[America] they anticipate the evil, and judge of the
pressure of the grievance by the badness of the principle. They augur misgovernment at a distance, and
snuff the approach of tyranny in every tainted
breeze." [3] Lieutenant-Governor Colden thought the
lawyers of New York more powerful than elsewhere,
and that nothing was "too wicked for them to at-

this idea; asserting that the act would render the colonists "unable
to purchase the manufactures of Great Britain." Macdonald, *Select
Charters* (1606–1775), 315.

[1] John Dickinson, *Writings* (Ford, *ed.*), 227–30. Merchants seem
not to have understood the modern device of putting the whole burden
on the consumer.

[2] John Adams, *Works*, II, 156.

[3] Burke, *Works* (1869 ed.), II, 125.

tempt," and he added the press was to them "what the pulpit was in times of Popery." [1] The press, indeed, stirred by the tax levied on all newspapers and pamphlets, was never so unanimous at any later time in opposition to the Government. The thirty-odd newspapers of America, "crammed with treason" and published defiantly for the most part without stamps, carried on a most effective propaganda against the Stamp Act.[2] Pamphleteers, too, were never so united. Dulany, of Maryland, whose famous pamphlet against this act the immortal Pitt had held in his hand and eulogized before the admiring House of Commons, was opposed to no other later tax and in time became a Loyalist. The clergy, too, was almost of one voice, and John Adams was not unduly rhetorical, when he wrote in his diary, "Our presses have groaned, our pulpits have thundered, our legislatures have resolved, our towns have voted; the crown officers have everywhere trembled, and all their little tools and creatures been afraid to speak and ashamed to be seen." [3]

The opposition to the Stamp Act was almost universal aside from actual Crown officials and their lawyers. Joseph Galloway, who soon was to become the leader of the King's American supporters, Thomas Jones, Chief Justice in New York and fated to be sympathetic historian of the Loyalist cause, Colden and Hutchinson, the King's own agents in America, and thousands of others who

---

[1] *Letter Books of Governor Colden,* II, 71.
[2] Schlesinger, *The Colonial Merchants,* 70–71.
[3] John Adams, *Works,* II, 154.

would within a decade be flying from the wrath of
their rebellious neighbors because of their loyalism,
were now at one with the Adamses, the Lees, Gadsden, James Otis, and Patrick Henry in their assertions of the injustice of the Stamp Act. The main
difference of opinion was as to the device for de-
feating the purpose of this hateful act of Parliament.
Laurens, planter and merchant in South Carolina,
destined within fifteen years to be the president of a
Continental Congress, directing a war for independence from Great Britain, defied "all the grumble-
tonians from Quebeck to West Florida" to point
out any other way but "graceful obedience" until
the act could be annihilated in a "constitutional
way" — unless they would "beat to arms." A mere
suspension of it would involve all in "ruin and
destruction." All would be on their knees within a
fortnight praying the governor to give life to the
law.[1] Planters as a rule approved of dignified protests by legislative bodies, but, aside from them,
Laurens's plan of action was unusual, for most men
favored either nullification or the giving up of all
business that required stamps. Was the act to be
nullified or merely passively defeated? Should the
courts close that no stamps might be needed, or
should they do business as if no Stamp Act existed?
Was commerce to cease and the customs houses
close, or were ships to go and come without stamps?
The temperament and interests of men determined
which horn of the dilemma they would seize. To the
disgust of John Adams, Massachusetts at first chose

[1] Wallace, *Henry Laurens*, 117.

the legal method of avoiding the tax. In his diary, neglected for some busy months, he wrote disconsolately, December 18, 1765, "the probate office is shut, the custom house is shut, the courts of justice are shut, and all business seems at a stand . . . I have not drawn a writ since the first of November. Debtors grow insolent, creditors grow angry." "How long," he asked, "are we to have this passive obedience to the Stamp Act?" It acknowledged the authority of Parliament to tax. He thought it cowardly. The bar behaves "like a lot of shot pigeons," he wrote scornfully.[1] "Indolence and idleness make a large chasm in my affairs," he confessed, thus revealing the personal interest that moved his wrath. The radicals generally preferred actual nullification, doing all business without stamps, and they declared that the stoppage of business was a sly device of the friends of Government, intended in the end to lead to the necessity of complying with the law.[2] Even Edmund Pendleton, who as a rule was conservative, preferred open nullification, but his friend George Washington favored the legal method of abstaining from all business that required stamps.[3] With exceptions the northern colonies closed the courts, while the southern provinces kept them open, ignoring the stamps. Both methods defeated the Stamp Act.[4] In general merchants kept the ports open, while lawyers, at

[1] John Adams, Diary, in Works, ii, 155; Wells, Samuel Adams, i, 110.
[2] Becker, Political Parties in the Province of New York, 37.
[3] Rives, James Madison, i, 70; Bancroft, Hist. of U.S., iii, 146.
[4] R. H. Lee, Letters, i, 15; Bancroft, Hist. of U.S , iii, 147.

first, with perhaps more reverence for the law, suspended all legal business. Shipowners induced governors to issue "let-passes" for their departing ships or forced customs officers to write them statements that stamped clearances could not be had.[1] By hook or crook all classes contrived to convey to Grenville the impression that they were a stiff-necked people bent on ruling and taxing themselves.

The spirit of the colonists was too high to stop with mere lying down in the political traces or even with nullification, and an active campaign to force Parliament to repeal the act was soon on. The pressure upon British merchants to that end was, perhaps, unconscious at first. Economic distress, resulting from some one or all of the oppressive acts, had forced economies which soon diminished the volume of British commerce. Fashionable mourning was simplified, domestic sage and sassafras took the place of imported tea, spinning schools aimed to supplant English textiles, societies arose, pledged to the culture of flax and the making of linen, hitherto purchased in the British Isles, and patriotic maidens gathered in social groups to spin and weave. "A garment of linsey-woolsey, when made the distinction of real patriotism, is more honorable," declared Daniel Dulany, "than all the pageantry, and the robes and the plumes and the diadem of an emperor without it." [2] Soon it became the fashion to

---

[1] In South Carolina commerce seems to have suffered an embargo. See Wallace, *Henry Laurens*, 121. If a British cruiser seized vessels with such papers, the colonists intimidated the captain so that he released them. See R. D. W. Conner, *Cornelius Harnett*, 33.

[2] D. Dulany, *Considerations on the Propriety of Taxing the Colonies*, 64, 65.

wear homespun. It now dawned on the excited colonial mind that these measures could be used as political arguments, more convincing, perhaps, to the members of Parliament than legislative addresses and remonstrances filled with appeals to the rights of Englishmen or to charter guarantees. The colony of New York was first to take formal action to boycott British manufactures. A few days before the Stamp Act was to come into force, the merchants met and two hundred of them agreed to make all their orders for goods from England contingent on the repeal of the obnoxious act. A week later, four hundred Philadelphia merchants organized for a like purpose, and circulated printed forms for countermanding orders already given. They united in memorials to London merchants urging them to bring pressure upon Parliament to repeal all offending acts. Within a month Boston merchants agreed upon non-importation on like conditions. The loyal Colden, Lieutenant-Governor of New York, sneered that this meant no sacrifice to the thrifty merchant who had laid in a big stock, and that people only "paid high prices for old, moth-eaten goods which couldn't have been sold but for the patriotic fervor." The London merchants felt the pinch, nevertheless, and, indeed, three months before these agreements they had noted a decline in American orders. Ships sailed to the colonies not half laden, and summer orders fell off £600,000, never so small "in the memory of man." After the non-importation agreements, if goods did arrive at American ports, contrary to the compact, a committee of merchants ordered them locked up or put in the care of the "Sons of Liberty" until the act should be repealed.[1] In Virginia, Richard Henry Lee, quick to see which way the wind blew, dropped his stamp collectorship and swept into popular favor with a draft of "articles of Association" binding the citizens of Westmoreland to import no goods from England and "at every hazard, paying no regard to danger . . . or death," to prevent the execution of the Stamp Act.[2] If the British merchant had an economic nerve, the colonists were bent on torturing it until he should turn to Parliament for relief.

Not all of the colonial conduct was as decorous as that hitherto recounted. Merchants, lawyers, and planters might restrain themselves from physical violence, but not so laborers, artisans, or the rougher element in the port towns. All these classes were possessed of the high-strung, nervous temper common to frontier peoples, and when they were distressed by the unemployment due to the suspension of business, did not reason as to whether the fault was that of the merchants who for the purpose of coercion ceased trading or that of the Government which laid the tax. Nor did they distinguish finely between the responsible Ministry three thousand miles away and its agents, governors, or customs officers or stamp distributors in America, sworn to do their duties. They wreaked their vengeance on those whom their leaders designated as responsible.

[1] This paragraph is largely based on Schlesinger, *The Colonial Merchants*, 76–79.
[2] R. H. Lee, *Letters*, I, 15; *Virginia Historical Register*, II, 16.

Hutchinson in Massachusetts, who suffered severely
at their hands, explained to a friend how the business was managed. "The rabble of the town of
Boston" were employed, he wrote, "headed by one
Mackintosh . . . a bold fellow, and as likely for a
Masaniello as you can well conceive." "When there
is occasion to burn or hang effigies or pull down
houses," these are the agents, but "they are somewhat controlled by a superior set consisting of the
master-masons and carpenters, etc." When a customs house is to be opened "these are under the
direction of a committee of merchants, Mr. Rowe at
their head, then, Molyneux Soloman Davis, etc." [1]
Toward the middle of August, nearly three months
before the Stamp Act would go into force, riots
began in Boston. An effigy of Andrew Oliver, the
nominated stamp distributor, later forced to resign
that office, was swung all day on the "Great Tree,"
and after dark an "amazing" multitude, shouting
"liberty, property and no stamps," bore the image
on a bier, through the State House and under the
very chamber where sat the Governor and Council.
With the débris of the demolished stamp office they
made a funeral pyre for the execrated effigy. Twelve
days later the mob sacked the home of the customs
officer, burned the vice-admiralty records, gutted the
mansion of Lieutenant-Governor Hutchinson, beating down the very partition walls, wrecking the
furniture, and defacing family plate and portraits.[2]
The greatest loss to posterity was the destruction of

[1] Hosmer, *Life of Hutchinson*, 103–04.
[2] Hansard, *Parliamentary History*, xvi, 126–28, 130.

books and records of the colony gathered by Hutchinson during thirty years. Only the manuscript of his history, based on these records, was saved, and that still bears on its edges the mud of Boston streets. The Governor, Bernard, thought the province was "on the brink of a precipice;" and John Adams, though he confided twenty reasons to his diary why the people committed such excesses, did not approve these "atrocious violations of the peace."[1] Conservative patriots did not mind "a little rioting," but it must be kept within bounds. Jonathan Mayhew, the radical Boston divine, who on August 25th before the last riot had excited the people with his sermon from the text, "I would they were even cut off which trouble you," wrote a letter of regret to Hutchinson. Indeed, reaction was rapid, and the Boston town meeting expressed "utter detestation" of this "violent proceedings."[2] Nevertheless, the Governor could write to the Board of Trade his solemn conviction that the "real authority of the government is at an end; some of the principal ringleaders in the late riots walk the streets with impunity; no officers dare attack them; no Attorney General prosecute them; and no Judges sit upon them."[3] It was plain to all thinking men that the mob's violence was but another crime committed

---

[1] John Adams, *Works*, II, 150–51.

[2] *Boston Town Records* (1758–69), 152. The rioters were never punished, and compensation for the sufferers was obtained from the Massachusetts legislature only after a bitter debate between the Governor and the assembly as to whether the "respectable inhabitants had suffered in the opinion of the world for having been tame spectators of the violence committed." *Massachusetts State Papers*, 95–101.

[3] Force, *American Archives*, I, 14.

in the name of Liberty. Boston was not singular in
its riotous conduct. In the North there were notable
riots at Newport and in New York.[1] Southward, in
North Carolina, the people burned the effigy of
an offending "Honorable Gentleman," and forced
others, who would have preferred remaining quietly
at home, to drink toasts to Liberty and confusion
to the stamps. With drums and flying colors they
marched the stamp distributor to the court-house,
got his resignation, and bore him home in an arm-
chair. A printer's life was spared only on condition
that he issue a stampless paper. In Charleston,
South Carolina, Henry Laurens was awakened at
midnight by "a most violent thumping and confused noise at my western door and chamber window, and soon distinguished the sounds of ' *Liberty*,
Liberty and stamp'd paper, *Open your doors* and let
us search your house and *cellars.*' I opened the
window, saw a crowd of men chiefly in disguise, and
heard the voices and thumping of many more on the
other side, assured them that I had no stamped
paper or any connection with stamps." In vain he
parleyed with them a few minutes, and finally the
desire to save his sick wife prompted him "to open
the door which in two minutes more they would
have beat through: — a brace of cutlasses across
my breasts was the Salutation, and, 'Lights, Lights
and Search' — was the cry. I presently knew
several of them under their thickest disguises of
soot, sailors habits, slouch hats, etc.; and to their
great surprise called no less than nine of them by

[1] Becker, *Political Parties in the Province of New York*, 32, 35, 48.

name." [1] After searching his house, they desired him to take a "Bible Oath" that he did not know where the stamps were. "When they found this attempt fruitless, a softer oath, as they thought, was propounded — I must say, 'May God disinherit me from the Kingdom of Heaven' if I knew where the stamped papers were." This, too, he refused, even though they should "barbicu" him, and at last they retired with "God bless your Honor." "Is it not amazing," he asked, "that such a number of men many of them heated with liquor and all armed with cutlasses and clubs did not do one penny damage to my garden not even to walk over a bed and not 15/ damage to my fence, gate or house." [2]

These "apings" of the "infamous, inglorious feats of riot and disipation" to the northward, Laurens believed, were engineered by the leader of the South Carolina "Sons of Liberty," Christopher Gadsden, who retorted by calling his conservative fellow citizen a "mercantile patriot" more concerned for his property than for the rights of America. Though in time both came to work for the same end, they rarely agreed in method, but each worked according to his own character and bent. The "Sons of Liberty" whom Gadsden led in South Carolina seem to have been the same indefinite organization as elsewhere in America. The term appears to have been applied everywhere to groups of radicals who gathered at times openly, but again secretly. They held parades, burned effigies, attended dinners, en-

---

[1] Wallace, *Henry Laurens*, 118.　　　[2] *Ibid.*, 119.

joyed punch, wine, pipes and tobacco, and sang together the liberty songs. In Massachusetts and New York they were, perhaps, more active than in all the other places in the colonies.[1] There seems to have been no stable membership, but in any particular place numbers waxed or waned as occasion required. Messages were sent from a group in one colony to the "Sons" in another, but the only authentication was the signature, "Sons of Liberty." From their meetings, which "sprang into being like magic" and "usurped authority from the skies," they issued resolutions signed only "President" or "Secretary." They sent out post bills, so intangible as to time and place that the source of authority was a complete mystery, yet their orders were in the main obeyed. Their committees could maintain "a sort of Holy Inquisition into the sales and purchases of every man of business . . . and into the reported opinions of individuals," and they would be obeyed. Recruited from the poorer classes, they alienated the better class, and seemed to prefer, said a critic, "that the gentlemen of fortune did not join them." [2] John Adams attended one meeting, where he mentioned a brazier, a painter, a printer, a distiller, a jeweler, and a master of a vessel. He heard there "no plots, no machinations." When there was work of violence to do, buildings burned or stamps "purified," workingmen were used, though the leaders in the "dirty matters" might be higher up.

[1] Becker (*Political Parties in the Province of New York*, 43–50) gives an excellent account of them there, when they first are heard of in New York at the time of the November riots.

[2] *Montressor Journals*, 348; *American Historical Review*, I, 247

It was the opinion of governors that this "licentious rabble" ought to be suppressed.[1] The heyday of their existence was at the time of the Stamp Act, but they were heard of in crises for years after.

Throughout the colonies the stamp collectors were intimidated into resigning the office, and as a result of this and various other modes of opposition to the Stamp Act, no stamps were issued except in rare instances, and Georgia won a dark notoriety as the one continental colony where any number were used.[2]

The reaction of the British Government to all this rebellious conduct is worthy of consideration. If the Ministry aimed at tyranny, it was of a very weak and nerveless kind. It was only a braggart major of artillery who boasted that he would "cram the stamps down the throats of the people" with the end of his sword.[3] When the London authorities learned that the only safe place for stamps in America was on the King's ships or in the forts under His Majesty's guns, where they were surely not revenue-producing, they issued a few brave orders. "Let a sloop of war be off Annapolis until the stamps are secure," wrote a secretary; "send the 'Viper' to Boston until the tumults subside," commanded another,[4] and General Gage was told in an order in

[1] Colonial History of New York, *Documents*, VII, 868; VIII, 143.

[2] Governor Lyttelton, of Jamaica, wrote that the Stamp Act "has been fully carried into execution here." Historical MSS. Commission, *Reports (Various Collections)*, VI, 92. It seems not to have been disputed in Quebec or Nova Scotia, and at least only passively resisted. Coffin, *The Province of Quebec*, xx, 316–17.

[3] Bancroft, *Hist. of U.S.*, III, 148.

[4] *Calendar of Home Office Papers, 1766–69*, nos. 4, 27, 41, 83, 84.

council that it was the King's pleasure that he issue orders to all commanders in America to aid the civil with military power, but only on requisition by the civil magistrates, and even then not to "repel force by force unless in case of necessity." [1] Governor Bernard was criticized because he had not "nipped the spirit of sedition in the bud," but he was given no orders to do anything but "hit soft." The true tyrants of the world's history have not been wont to deal so gently with their rebellious subjects.

[1] War Office, Oct. 24, 1765; Public Record Office, *W. O.* 4, 988, F 46.

CHAPTER VII

THE REPEAL OF THE STAMP ACT

BESIDES the universal activities of merchants, law-yers, and printers in opposition to the Stamp Act and the ubiquitous riots of the rabble in the colonies, nothing more clearly proved the unanimity of distaste for the Stamp Act than the response to a circular letter sent out (June 8, 1765) by the Massachusetts House of Representatives urging the other colonies to send committees to New York in October to consult together on the evils of the late acts and to implore relief from the King and Parliament. A leader in bringing about this significant meeting with its augury of future union was James Otis, who, clogged with two conservative, unsympathetic colleagues, was chosen a delegate to the proposed Stamp Act Congress, a bearer of the sentiment of the Massachusetts radicals. An enemy saw in Otis "the first who broke down the barriers of government to let in the hydra of Rebellion," [1] but it was John Adams' solemn judgment that he had never known a man whose love of his country was more ardent or sincere, whose services were so important and essential to the cause of his country. In one of Otis' early pamphlets (1762) was concentrated, Adams declared in after years, the Declaration of Independence, the liberal writings of Price and

[1] P. Oliver in *History of the Rebellion*, British Museum, *Egerton MSS.*, 2671 F 22.

Priestley, Thomas Paine's "Common Sense," and the "Declaration of Rights" of the Congress of 1774. This pamphlet, though it was whimsical and even uncouth at times, and like most of his work hasty and unrevised, showing the impatience of a strong, turbulent mind, was filled with phrases prophetic of the ideas soon to dominate in American political thinking. "God made all men naturally equal," he asserted. "Kings were . . . made for the good of the people and not the people for them," he stoutly held, and he found most governments arbitrary, and therefore the "curse and scandal of human nature." He believed that "jealousy of political privilege is a godly jealousy," [1] and he gloried in it. The ideas were not new, but Otis gave them new currency. In the "Sodalitas," a lawyers' club in which he and Adams were colleagues, the members read and discussed the great English law writers, and we know that Otis was also fully acquainted with Pufendorf, Grotius, Burlamaqui, and Vattel. The club members had great familiarity with Locke and Coke, and, as early as 1765, even dabbled in Rousseau.[2] The free life in America created in its intelligent citizens a natural affinity for the writings of the liberal political philosophers of all ages. In knowledge of the history, common law and statute laws of England, Adams believed Otis had no superior — "at least in Boston," and he thought him well versed in Greek and Roman history, philosophy, and poetry. A treatise of his on

---

[1] Tudor, *James Otis*, 125, 132.
[2] John Adams, *Works*, x, 275; ii, 148.

Latin prosody is still in existence, and he was always ready with classical allusions. It is, perhaps, not wholly fanciful to attribute Otis' eloquence in part to his passionate admiration for Homer.

Though Otis came of an old family of high rank in Massachusetts, and though he was the head of his profession, "designed by nature for a genius," as even an enemy admitted,[1] his great fame began with his speech (1761) against "Writs of Assistance." In the effort to enforce the Trade Acts the customs officials had found themselves helpless in the face of the almost universal sympathy with the smugglers. Juries refused to convict on the plainest evidence, and the British Government resorted to admiralty courts where the trial was without jury, but there still remained the difficulty of detecting the smugglers, where every neighbor sheltered them and informers feared for their lives. To overcome this impediment to justice, "Writs of Assistance" were issued authorizing the officers holding them to board ships lying in port or to enter warehouses, cellars, or garrets, by day or night, and search for dutiable goods. No special writ of search, issued on sworn testimony that the smuggled goods were concealed in a definite place, was needed. These general writs were offensive, because, as Pitt declared, they interfered with "the immunity of an English home where the wind might blow through every cranny but the King's writ could not enter." They had been used in England since the days of Charles II, and the colonists had sullenly submitted to them until six

[1] British Museum, *Egerton MSS.*, 2671 F 17, 22.

months after the death of George II (1760) when
the validity of old writs would cease, according to
law, and new must be issued. In Massachusetts
the application for them would be before the superior courts presided over by the new chief justice,
Thomas Hutchinson, recently commissioned in spite
of the fact that the father of James Otis had
been promised the place. James Otis, senior, pleaded
the merit of age and long legal practice, while
Hutchinson frankly admits in his diary that it was
"an eyesore to some of the bar" that he was not
bred to the law, but explains that after becoming
chief justice he "applied his intervals to reading"
it.[1] This was not quite so serious as though a
would-be physician should begin reading medicine
after he was in attendance upon a patient, but there
was a similitude. As Hutchinson already had three
other colonial offices, there might well have been
criticism. Peter Oliver asserts that James Otis
swore "if his father was not appointed a justice of
the supreme court, he would set the province in a
flame if he died in the attempt"; and Hutchinson
sadly reflects that at this point Otis "veered his
sails and steered into the troubled waters of republicanism." [2] Both charges are fancies of bitter enemies and rather dubious as the springs of actions
extending over at least a decade. Whatever his motives, however, Otis, "the favorite lawyer of smug-

[1] *Diary and Letters of Hutchinson*, 66.
[2] *Ibid.*, British Museum, *Egerton MSS.*, 2671 F 17. Oliver says
of Otis, senior, that he was "originally a cordwainer," but "worked
himself into a pettifogger" with a "certain adroitness to captivate the
ear of country jurors," drovers, horse jockeys, etc.

glers," as an enemy dubbed him, and Oxenbridge
Thatcher did appear before the court to represent
the Boston merchants in the hearing against the
writs.

The court scene set in the Council Chamber of
the Town House is described by John Adams writing
more than half a century after the event. "That
council chamber [1] was as respectable an apartment
as the House of Commons or the House of Lords in
Great Britain, in proportion, or that in the State
House in Philadelphia. In this chamber, round a
great fire, were seated five judges, with Lieutenant
Governor Hutchinson at their head, as Chief Justice, all arrayed in their new, fresh, rich robes of
scarlet English broadcloth; in their large cambric
bands, and immense judicial wigs. In this chamber
were seated at a long table all the barristers at law
of Boston, and of the neighboring county of Middlesex, in gowns, bands, and tie wigs. They were not
seated on ivory chairs, but their dress was more
solemn and more pompous than that of the Roman
Senate, when the Gauls broke in upon them. Two
portraits, at more than full length, of King Charles
the Second and of King James the Second, in
splendid golden frames, were hung up on the most
conspicuous sides of the apartment. If my young
eyes or old memory have not deceived me, these
were as fine pictures as I ever saw; the colors of the
royal ermines and long flowing robes were the most

---

[1] John Adams, *Works*, x, 244–45. Other contemporary pictures
of like scenes agree in the main with this memory picture of an old
man.

glowing, the figures the most noble and graceful, the features the most distinct and characteristic, far superior to those of the King and Queen of France in the Senate Chamber of Congress — these were worthy of the pencils of Rubens and Vandyke. There was no painter in England capable of them at that time. They had been sent over without frames in Governor Pownall's time, but he was no admirer of Charles or James. The pictures were stowed away in a garret, among rubbish, till Governor Bernard came, who had them cleaned, superbly framed, and placed in council for the admiration and imitation of all men — no doubt with the advice and concurrence of Hutchinson and all his nebula of stars and satellites."

Before this august body James Otis, with "a torrent of impetuous eloquence, hurried away everything before him." He had resigned the lucrative office of advocate general in order to oppose the Government, and he declared he took pleasure in arguing the cause, because it was in "opposition to a kind of power, the exercise of which, in former periods of English history, cost one king of England his head, and another his throne." If Patrick Henry uttered treason in 1765, he at least had an excellent model in this speech of 1761. Adams declares that Otis on this occasion was "a flame of fire." His own fever was contagious. Every hearer went away to take up arms against the writs. Then and there he sowed the seeds of patriots and heroes, and in that hour John Adams believed "the child of Independence was born." This oration against the writs "breathed into this nation the breath of life," declared Adams,[1] and added that thereafter Otis was forever dedicated to the cause of American liberty. It was "like the oath of Hamilcar administered to Hannibal." [2] Such a theory of individual responsibility for the Revolution is very pleasing to the eulogist, but in the larger view it is plain that James Otis was only the embodiment of New England's indomitable will to have its own way; just as Patrick Henry was only the frontier product of Virginia's high-strung spirit of liberty.

Despite John Adams' lifelong hero-worship of Otis, one must accept as true some part of his eulogy. His hero's articles, under the pseudonym of "Hampden," though in a style rugged and not elegant, are courageous, telling arguments for civil liberty and equality. There were curious seeming contradictions in his thinking which brought him much criticism, and even obloquy. Men thought him mad because being a champion of the popular cause he did not go the whole way. When in 1764 he held that it was the colonial duty to submit to the Sugar Act, and in 1765 said that it was the duty of all humbly and silently to acquiesce in all decisions of the supreme legislature, and when he admitted the Parliament

[1] John Adams, *Works*, x, 247, 276; *Memorial History of Boston*, III, 7. In a more extravagant moment Adams declared that "no harangue of Demosthenes or Cicero ever had such effect." *Works*, x, 233, 272. And again he declares him "Isaiah and Ezekiel united."

[2] Popular feeling ran so high as a result of Otis' speech that Hutchinson did not dare issue the writs, but referred the matter to England, where the law officers decided in favor of the issuing them. They were used throughout the colonies up to the outbreak of war. Gray, in Quincy, *Reports*, etc., 409–41, 540.

had the "right to levy internal taxes on the colonies," he was frowned upon even by his friends.
Yet, as the British Empire was then constituted, he
was right, for, as he said, "there would be an end
of all government if one or a number of subjects or
subordinate provinces should take upon them so far
to judge of the justice of an act of Parliament as to
refuse obedience to it." [1] That was but a forecast
of the logic of the later opponents of "nullification."
Besides, loyal as Otis was to the American cause, he
was intelligent enough to realize the danger of opposition to Great Britain. Perhaps he reflected that the
sword devours one as well as another. Moreover, he
saw America's lack of unity. Independent America
at that time (1765) would, he thought, become "a
mere shambles of blood and confusion," a scene of
mere "anarchy." Independence, he declared, "none
but rebels, fools, or madmen will contend for." He
was demanding justice, not revolution; he was urging the Government not to abuse its vast powers.
If he believed that Parliament had "supreme, sovereign power," it was a "perfect Parliament" in which
America would be represented. When his friends
put before him the danger of such representation,
he made it clear that the only kind he would accept
implied "a thorough, beneficial union of these
colonies to the realm . . . so that all parts of the
empire may be compacted and consolidated," and
the representation was to be real, not virtual.[2]

[1] Wells, *Samuel Adams*, I, 94. It is noteworthy that John Dickinson was a great admirer of Otis, and like him moderate and constitutional in his opposition. *Warren-Adams Letters*, I, 3–7.

[2] Tudor, *James Otis*, 195–99.

In truth, he was thinking of the best interests of the
empire, not of a mere American province. It was a
noble idea, too vast to be conceived by the ordinary
mind, and not unlike that greater vision of a universal confederation among civilized nations.

It was not alone these views, however, which explain why his life " seemed all eccentricity." His
rashness and excess of zeal made him enemies who
watched him maliciously. When he opposed the
Government, he estranged his aristocratic friends,
who ascribed his action to ambition, and said he had
adopted Satan's maxim, "better to reign in Hell
than serve in Heaven." [1] Moreover, he was not
well balanced, but "fiery and feverous, . . . liable to
great inequalities of temper"; obstacles, either men
or facts, enraged him. The human vices of servil-
ity or venality chafed him, made him indignant.
Though frank and arduous, he was irascible and
lacked a saving sense of humor. His passionate
spirit wore out his body, for, as a friend expressed it,
"his imagination flames, his passions blaze; sometimes in despondency, sometimes in a rage." [2] After
the cowardly assault upon him (1769) in the British
coffee-house by John Robinson and other enemies,
his eccentricities greatly augmented.[3] John Adams,
who was much in his company, confided to his
diary that Otis "grows the most talkative man

[1] British Museum, *Egerton MSS.*, 2671 F 22.
[2] John Adams, *Works*, II, 163–226.
[3] Otis sued Robinson for assault and got a verdict for £2000, which
he then generously forgave his opponent. Tudor, *James Otis*, 362–65.
Ten years later Robinson petitioned the British Government for
£236 which the suit cost him. Public Records Office, *Treasury Papers*
(*In-Letters*), 549 F 88.

alive: no other gentleman in company can find a space to put in a word." "He rambles and wanders like a ship without a helm." He feared Otis would "spoil the club." At the last, as an enemy wrote, he "became so frantic that he was frequently under the guardianship of the law." His noble mind, "overplied in libertys defense," had been overthrown. His death by a stroke of lightning was as tragic as his life. No doubt John Adams and others exaggerated his effect on the nascent revolution, but to the extent that any individual furthered that spirit, James Otis, second to none, fired New England with the resolve to retain all of its liberties. It is significant that in the Stamp Act debates in Parliament both Lord Lyttleton and Lord Mansfield mention Otis by name as the preëminent champion of the American cause.

When the Stamp Act Congress, born in Otis' fertile mind, met (October, 1765) in the City Hall, New York, it was found that "ministerial monkery" had been practiced in New Hampshire, Virginia, North Carolina, and Georgia to prevent them sending delegates.[1] A significant thing about the Congress is that the initiative came for the first time in colonial history, not from Crown officers, but from concerted action of provincial assemblies. Nevertheless, it is a curious fact that there is scarcely any mention of the Congress in the newspapers of that day, not even in the city of New York where it met. When differences began to appear among the twenty-seven men from nine colonies with varying interests

---

[1] John Adams, *Works*, x, 190.

and diverse charter rights, Christopher Gadsden urged all sections to harmonize by protesting on the broad common grounds of natural rights. As he expressed the idea in a letter, "a confirmation of our essential and common rights as Englishmen may be pleaded from charters safely enough; but any further dependence upon them may be fatal. We should stand upon the broad common ground of those natural rights that we all feel and know as men and as descendants of Englishmen." [1] In the course of eleven days, the views and interests which jangled out of tune were harmonized, and though the chairman, Timothy Ruggles, of Massachusetts, would not sign the moderate and loyal "Declarations of Rights and Grievances" agreed upon, the delegates as a whole were content. A few days more sufficed to concur upon petitions to the King, the Lords and the Commons. [2] With conscious purpose the several colonies had united for common interests and had given the world a united expression of American sentiment. It was the beginning of that union for which Otis hoped, a union that "should knit and work into the very blood and bones of the original system every region, as fast as settled." American conviction was expressed in the assertion that they were entitled to all the inherent rights and liberties of natural-born subjects, born within the realm, and like them enjoyed the right to have no taxes imposed upon them but by their own consent, which could

---

[1] Bancroft, *Hist. of U.S.* (ed. of 1884), III, 150.
[2] Niles, *Principles and Acts of the Revolution*, 155–68; Macdonald, *Documentary Source Book*, 137.

be given only in their own legislatures wherein alone
they were or could be represented. Meaningless as
the pet colonial phrases about "rights of Englishmen" [1] and "taxation without representation"
might be to a British constitutional lawyer, they expressed beliefs for which Americans would die. On
those phrases hung all the colonial law and the
prophets.

In England, meanwhile, political changes, little
if any affected by American truculence, were taking
place. Grenville's curtain lectures to George III
upon his duties were not welcome, nor did the King
relish his minister's habit of looking to Parliament
rather than to him as the source of authority. Conflict over the Regency Bill, which aimed at excluding
the King's mother from the list of regents, brought
the climax. The King decided to be rid of Grenville
even at the price of submission to the Old Whigs who
had put the yoke upon his grandfather, which it was
the life aim of George III to shake off. Failing to
secure Pitt's leadership in forming a new ministry,
the King's agent, the Duke of Cumberland, turned
to the Marquis of Rockingham. English political
parties in that day seem to have deserved Soame
Jenyns' slur that principles did not divide them, but
factions, which under name of Whig or Tory were
ready to support the Government if they enjoyed
the administration of it, or to subvert it if they
were excluded. A faction must have all power

---

[1] The English too talked of " rights of Englishmen," but the phrase
brought up in their minds Magna Charta and the Bill of Rights, while
the colonists not only thought of these, but certain "natural" rights
and colonial charter rights.

or no power, all posts or no posts. They did not
worry about noble principles.[1] During the reign of
George III, true party government can hardly be
said to have existed. Rockingham was the new leader
of the Old Whigs, lately headed by the crafty Duke
of Newcastle, whose aim was control of government
by the aristocratic Revolutionary families like those
of Robert Walpole's time. Pitt distrusted them, not
merely because of an intense personal dislike of
Newcastle, who was a member of the new ministry,
but because they wished to conserve existing conditions while he wished to destroy parties and factions,
shear special interests of their power, and keep no
man of ability out of office; but, with a united
country under "a patriot king," enter upon reform
in every direction. His vision was a world empire
on modern lines — an empire in all parts of the
world bringing peace and good rule to mankind.
To these effulgent visions Rockingham with his
small talents could not rise. Though he had what
Junius called "a mild but determined integrity,"
and had good ideals, he was a better horseman than
politician. He believed in a predominant Parliament, but one guided by the Whig nobles. Lacking
Pitt's hearty support, he could not command the
best of Whig talent. Two reputed friends of America
were included in the Ministry; one, General Conway,
was a young man of good ideals and generous im-
pulses, but without originality enough to give up the
evil political practices of the past. Another was Lord
Dartmouth, pious, mild, and honest, but wanting

[1] S. Jenyns, *Works*, ii, 251.

in force, "one who wears a coronet and prays," a Methodist Sir Charles Grandison, as Richardson dubbed him.[1] Though the Ministry lacked in ability and cohesion, it was forced to carry out Pitt's strong policies by its very eagerness to place him at its head. Moreover, it was under pressure to repeal the Stamp Act, because in ports and factory towns, as a result of American non-importation measures, thousands were idle, exports had fallen to three fourths their normal values, and petitions from the sufferers flooded Parliament.[2] It was of no use to denounce, as did some haughty members of the House of Lords, the American non-importation acts as "illegal and hostile combinations . . . to distress and starve our manufacturers and to withhold from our merchants the payment of their just debts." It did not comfort the manufacturers and traders that the former "measure had only been practiced in open warfare between two states, and the latter . . . not even in that situation . . . among civilized nations" of Europe in "modern times."[3] Ruin faced these men, and they demanded relief, not moral precepts.

Early in 1766, Parliament took up the matter of enforcement or repeal of the Stamp Act. The first step was an examination of Benjamin Franklin before the bar of the House of Commons. No one can read in full that calm and dignified revelation of the colonial spirit without reaching the conviction that it must have profoundly moved all who were

---

[1] Alvord, *The Mississippi Valley in British Politics*, I, 231–35.
[2] Hansard, *Parliamentary History*, XVI, 133–35.   [3] *Ibid.*, 186.

present.[1] With an art of argumentation which he was pleased to think he had learned from Socrates, he persuaded his hearers that even an army could not enforce the act, though it might, he admitted, cause a rebellion. Having answered with great simplicity and clarity a hundred questions about American political views and economic life, he closed with the subtle appeal to the English passion for trade, declaring that the American pride used to be "to indulge in the fashions and manufactures of Great Britain," but now it was their pride "to wear their old clothes over again, till they can make new ones."

Few more eloquent debates are recorded than that which followed in both houses of Parliament. Pitt, though feeling that he was "more fit for a lonely hill in Somersetshire than for the affairs of state," took up the American cause with spirit. He rejoiced that the Americans had resisted. For the welfare of the empire he would not have them so dead to the feelings of liberty as to become fit instruments to make slaves of the rest. Grenville was enraged that rebellion should be pronounced a virtue, that "even in this house, in this sanctuary of laws, sedition had found its defenders." He argued for the legal right to tax Americans, that the nation had run itself into immense debt to give them protection, that protection and obedience were reciprocal, Great Britain had protected, America owed obedience.[2] It was this emphasis on legal right that did the mischief.

---

[1] Hansard, 137–60; also in any edition of Franklin's *Writings*.
[2] Hansard, *Parliamentary History*, xvi, 102.

England was in an age of strict legalism. Lawyers, dominated by a rigid legalism, were most influential in guiding the administration officers in their rule of the colonies. It was they who passed on the form and legality of the colonial charters and of instructions to governors, and as to the propriety of laws made in the American provinces.

Supporters of Grenville explained that the stamp tax would not pay a third of the expense of the troops stationed in America, but that "a pepper-corn in acknowledgment of right is of more value than millions without." [1] Against this abstract right, which Burke later characterized as the "great Serbonian bog" into which whole armies had sunk, Pitt set himself. Legal right the Government might have, but a statesman would not use it. He intimated that Parliament might well take thought of the words of St. Paul, "All things are lawful unto me, but all things are not expedient." "The most magnanimous Exertion of Power is often the Non-Exertion of it." He meant to waive it by silence. [2] With a logic hard to follow, Pitt asserted British sovereignty over Americans; "we may bind their trade, confine their manufactures, and exercise every power, except that of taking their money out of their pockets without their consent." Having made that distinction, which was at least antiquated, Pitt went

---

[1] C. M. Andrews, *Guide*, etc. (1914), II, 102, gives the Comptroller General's Declaration showing the Amount received for the stamped paper was £224,119. The Government paid out, salaries, etc., £160,043. "Unaccounted for," probably destroyed, £64,155. There is a list of colonial receivers and their arrears. J. Ingersoll, 1909.

[2] *American Historical Review* (April, 1912), 573.

on to declare that America was right in her contention, and "if she fell would fall like a strong man. She would embrace the pillars of the state and pull down the Constitution along with her." Pitt was, as Grattan said, "very great and very odd," a mountebank, perhaps, but "a great mountebank, . . . a man of great genius and great flights of mind," but his logic would have carried him into embarrassing situations. In the House of Lords the American cause did not fare so well, perhaps because they had not heard Franklin's examination. Though opposed to the repeal, Lord Mansfield, one of the greatest lawyers of his age, who when he spoke was "dignity and reason itself," agreed that the colonial radicals were not to be disregarded, for many persons, like Otis, "who have entertained silly and mad ideas, have led people to rebellion and overturned empires." [1] He was most fervent in hoping that it might "please God to open the understandings and better inform the minds of this poor, innocent, loyal, brave, but wickedly misled and deluded people." [2] Though he had for them only the "greatest tenderness," he came "armed at all points" with legal precedents to prove that there was no difference between internal and external taxation,[3] that there was no distinction between the authority of Parliament within or without the realm, that if it now abdicated its supreme power in this matter, the Government would be dissolved. In mere legal

[1] Hansard, *Parliamentary History*, XVI, 172.
[2] *The Francis Letters*, I, 74.
[3] Franklin made the best point in favor of the contrary contention. See Examination.

logic he was probably right. Precedent was with
him, but he seemed to forget that the Constitution
of England had come to its present state as the result of yielding to the changing needs of the people
whose destinies it controlled. With him stood the
profligate Earl of Sandwich, the Duke of Bedford,
head of the "Bloomsbury Gang," and the Tory
aristocracy in general.

In support of the repeal, Lord Shelburne, Lord
Camden, and the Duke of Grafton bore the burden
and heat of the debate. Lord Rockingham sat by
"dumb and speechless." Though Rockingham was
the head of the Ministry, the effort at repeal was a
Pitt victory, for the eagerness of the Ministry to
place Pitt at their head led them to yield to his
policy.[1] Rockingham wanted repeal with a declaratory act, but without Pitt's backing might not have
ventured even that, faced as he was by Grenville's
threat to regard any one who did that as " a criminal
and a betrayer of his country." "He was bullied
into it by Lord Chatham," his enemies declared, but
Burke brilliantly defended his patron against that
charge.[2] None of the speakers in the Lords, if we
may judge from the little that has come down to us
in the " Parliamentary History," were very positive,
but Camden, at least, did hold clearly that taxation
and representation were inseparable, and therefore
the British Parliament, as then constituted, had not
the right to tax the colonies.

When the matter of repeal came to a vote, it is

---

[1] Alvord, *The Mississippi Valley in British Politics*, i, 238–39.
[2] Burke, *Works* (ed. 1829), ii, 50.

dubious whether it would have carried but for the Declaratory Act joined with it which asserted Parliament's right to make laws to bind the colonies in all cases whatsoever.[1] In fact, the Lords at first resolved, fifty-nine to fifty-four, in favor of executing the Stamp Act, but after two formal protests against repeal they too joined the Commons, resolved to be content with the "Declaration" — "the peppercorn in acknowledgment of right." Pitt, ill with gout, was barely able to remain through the debate and "cry aye! to the repeal in no sickly voice." Though opposed to the Declaratory Act, "that barren tree, which cast a shade over the land but yielded no fruit," he quieted the fears of some by his own insistence upon Parliament's right to subordinate the colonists to all other legislation except that which took "money out of their pockets without their consent." The victory won, Pitt "hobbled out on crutches, gaunt, alone." The crowds, at first hushed and with hats in hand, then shouted in triumph. As for the hero, the joy of thousands was his, as Lady Chatham wrote. He found the scene of that glorious morning happy "when the sun of liberty shone once more upon a country too long benighted." [2] He solemnly declared that he "never had greater satisfaction than in the repeal of this Act."

In spite of Pitt's doubt that "there would have been a minister to be found who would have dared to dip the royal ermines in the blood of the Ameri-

[1] Macdonald, *Documentary Source Book*, 140.
[2] Basil Williams, *William Pitt*, II, 200–01.

cans," it was for military enforcement, if necessary, that Grenville and his followers had stood. There were two strong reasons for their eager defense of the act. The act had been originally approved by the King, and a repeal would weaken his prestige which it was Grenville's policy to build up. George III had preferred a mere modification of the act, but when that was out of the question, and the only issue was enforcement or repeal, he consented to Rockingham's demand that he support the repealers. The King was even forced to put his acquiescence in writing.[1] Furthermore, an indirect result of the repeal of the Stamp Act was that the Imperial Government, by bending before the storm, had given up the source of money proposed to be expended in opening the Great Valley in America to settlement. A revision of the whole Grenville-Bedford imperial policy of expansion became necessary, and that faction, with whom the repeal went down heavily, became the supporters of all measures for subduing the colonists to obedience.[2] Naturally, Rockingham did not wish to push a plan cursed with the brand of the Grenville Ministry, especially an expensive one for which they had not the funds. They must retrench, and this meant indifference to western expansion in the Mississippi Valley. Moreover, they had never understood the Proclamation of 1763, and thought it only a temporary measure to be followed by gradual opening of the West, and therefore had no idea except en-

---

[1] Alvord, *The Mississippi Valley in British Politics*, I, 240.
[2] *Ibid.* 241.

forcement of the law at face value. Led by Barring‹
ton, they substituted a plan for maintaining "for
ages" extensive Indian reservations in the heart of
America.[1] Such a programme, if successful, would
stop settlement at the Appalachians.

To these ill-boding consequences America was
blind. The universal joy over the repeal "composed
every wave of popular disorder." America justified
Pitt's noble tribute. "This country, like a fine horse,
to use a beautiful expression of Job, whose neck is
clothed in thunder — if you soothe and stroke it you
may do anything; but if an unskilful rider takes it
in hand, he will find that, though not vicious, yet
it has tricks." [2] An address of the Massachusetts
House of Representatives attested the "general joy
diffused among all his Majestie's loyal and faithful
subjects throughout this extensive continent." They
found the repeal a striking instance of their "most
gracious sovereign's paternal regard," and because
his royal ear was always open to the distresses of his
people, they felt "the deepest sense of loyalty and
gratitude." All of this might have revealed to a keen
British statesman, that, though a colonist drank a
health to George III "five fathoms deep," the act
pledged him to nothing but loyalty as long as the
King was not a tyrant. The grateful colonists even
found in the repeal the proof that they were the
objects of the patronage and justice of Parliament.[2]

---

[1] Alvord, *The Mississippi Valley in British Politics*, I, 243, 248, 251.

[2] B. Williams, *William Pitt*, II, 201.

[3] Samuel Adams, *Writings*, I, 74, 81. True they went on to scold
the Governor for his manner of asking for compensation for recent
mob violence.

On a Day of Thanksgiving in Boston, Jonathan Mayhew preached from the text, "As cold waters to a thirsty soul, so is good news from a far country."

As late as 1774, the 18th of March, the anniversary of the repeal of the Stamp Act, was being celebrated by the ringing of bells, the discharge of cannon, and the display of colors on the liberty tree, but the next year (1775) it was "designedly neglected" because the colonists had learned that the repeal was not "done on generous fraternal principles." [1] These celebrations were usually directed by the "Sons of Liberty," who seemed to assume that the repeal had been due to their activities. John Adams describes their plans for "illuminations, bonfires, pyramids, obelisks, such grand exhibitions and such fireworks as were never before seen in America." [2]

One of the economic results of the repeal is suggested by Dr. Franklin's first letter from London to his wife Deborah whom he never could persuade to cross the sea. He was sending her "a fine Piece of Pompadour Sattin . . . A silk Negligee and Petticoat of Brocaded Lutestring," which he had not sent sooner, "as I knew you would not like to be finer than your Neighbors, unless in a Gown of your own spinning." It was a comfort to him to recollect, he declared, "that I had once been cloth'd from Head to Foot in Woollen and Linnen of my Wife's Manufacture." [3] In general, commerce flowed again, nonimportation ceased, plans for American manufac-

---

[1] *Literary Diary of Ezra Stiles*, I, 437, 527.

[2] John Adams, *Works*, II, 178, 179. The celebration itself is described in *The Boston Evening Post*, May 26, 1766.

[3] Franklin, *Writings* (Smyth, *ed.*), IV, 449.

tures vanished, the custom of expensive funerals and lavish mourning was resumed, homespun was given to the poor, and men once more wore suits ordered in London. Yet the merchants were not wholly content, and trade was not restored to the old basis before the trade laws of 1764 and 1765. Parliament proceeded, after the Declaratory Act and the repeal of the Stamp Act, to take off the three penny duty on foreign molasses, but replaced this with a duty of one penny per gallon on *all* molasses imported, British as well as foreign. It now gave no protection to the British sugar planters and was plainly a tariff for revenue, a taxation without representation, just as surely as was the Stamp Act.[1] A new law arranged to collect the duty on foreign textiles at the English port rather than the American, but that was a mere disguising of the fact of taxation. In all this, and more which undid the concessions of the repeal, the followers of Rockingham and Pitt, believing fully in the legislative power of Parliament, heartily joined. Moreover, to the grievance of the paper money regulation, so warmly protested as a reason why the colonists could not pay the stamp tax, Parliament gave not the cold respect of a passing glance.

Nevertheless, America rejoiced and gave herself up to generous enthusiasms for her friends in Parliament. The Boston town meeting had already thanked Conway and Barré for their "noble and generous speeches," and ordered their portraits for Faneuil Hall. A group of Virginians subscribed

[1] Schlesinger, *The Colonial Merchants*, 85–87.

nearly a hundred pounds to have Lord Camden's picture "limned," at full length in judge's robes, by either Reynolds or West, for a place of honor in Westmoreland County Court-House.[1] New York voted a statue to Pitt in a toga, while George III, for no explicable reason except colonial ignorance, was cast in lead and brass on horseback and gilded. Lord Shelburne, too, was praised, and Lord Dartmouth who, all his life, was regarded as a friend of the colonies. On the other hand, the colonial heart hardened against Lord Mansfield, Lord Sandwich, and the Duke of Bedford. The Earl of Halifax was also in their bad graces, but among them all Grenville stood alone in his bad eminence. The whole group were reputed to wish to take away every charter and to unite all colonies under governors and councils appointed by the King and burdened with no assemblies.[2] The ministerial mind was dumbfounded by the vast spaces of the earth which fate obligated it to rule; to centralize and unify seemed the only hope. Against these aims, as, indeed, against any loss of liberties already won, America had shown her spirit to be fixed. No wise statesman could thereafter ignore that fact, and yet some solution of Great Britain's imperial problem must be found. The truth now appeared that a constitution for the empire as distinguished from the realm had never been worked out. The imperial constitution

---

[1] Wells, *Samuel Adams*, 68.   For a list of Virginian subscribers see Ballagh, *Letters of R. H. Lee*, i, 23–24. James Monroe subscribed, but "never paid." Camden promised to sit, and then apparently forgot it. *Ibid.*, 26.

[2] Trumbull, *Jonathan Trumbull*, 74.

was still a thing of shreds and patches. England had her constitution and it provided for the supreme power of Parliament. But, while this was being evolved, the East and West Indies had been added, continental American colonies founded, and finally an empire conquered from France. For all these world-wide dominions no settled constitution existed; all was fluid. Pitt, the materials for whose speeches were "great subjects, great empires, great characters, effulgent ideas and classical illustrations," declared he wished "this to be an Empire of Freemen; it will be stronger for it, and it will be the more easily governed." A very noble idea it was, but did he, did any one, in that trying hour have a definite plan by which the splendid vision could be realized?

CHAPTER VIII

CONFLICTING THEORIES OF REPRESENTATION AND IMPERIAL ORGANIZATION

AT the close of the struggle over the Stamp Act, any traveler in America might, like Gulliver among the immortals in Glubbdubdrib, have fed his eyes with beholding men reputed to be the destroyers of tyrants and usurpers, and the restorers of liberty to an oppressed and injured nation. In that time of stress America had acquired leaders as well as convictions. James Otis, Patrick Henry, Christopher Gadsden, and John Dickinson had gained more than provincial fame, and their political ideas had been burned into the souls of thousands who had never before been profoundly moved. We are told that in 1765 "the principles, the objects and the ends of government, became the topics of discussion in all companies and at the firesides of private families." [1] Moreover, the colonists' controversies with their provincial governments were no longer conceived as bickerings with a royal governor abusing his little brief authority, but as a great struggle with the British Government over fundamental principles. Between Parliament's "one slight day on the American taxes," and that very momentous day more than a decade later when the Continental Congress drew up a Declaration of Independence, there was hardly a dispute between the British Govern-

[1] John Adams, *Works*, x, 191.

ment and its colonies which involved new issues, not already fought over in each individual colony between its royal governor and its assembly. On these issues the colonial mind was made up, but now the true magnitude of the involved principles was seen, and the real menace to the enjoyment of perfect liberty perceived. Furthermore, up to the time of the Stamp Act it had been for the most part the custom to abuse freely the governor and local officers, under the pleasing fiction that they misrepresented the benign and freedom-breathing spirit of the King and his enlightened ministers. That figment of the imagination was now laid aside, and the luxury of open attack on the British Government was a new sensation not easily forgotten once the colonial animal had tasted. It was an appetite much indulged as the tide of feeling rose. In the meager colonial newspapers, or in pamphlets, which in that day outrivaled the journal as a means of access to the public mind, many writers strove to show just how the times were out of joint. It was fairly easy for some smart young lawyer to clamber up to the judgment seat, and tell the British Ministry how to solve the problems of the greatest empire since that of the Romans.

In the great mass of polemical literature of the period there was much mere abuse and ill-temper, and many wrote in complete ignorance of the great questions whose solution they offered so lightly. Yet even the wisest and most sincere writers found depths beyond the reaches of their logic or knowledge. Besides the fact that "an Englishman is the unfittest man on earth to argue another Englishman into slavery," there were certain fundamental questions upon which the average American and the average Englishman could not argue to any good result, because each soon came to doubt the honesty of the other. In one sense the English orator's assertion was true that the Americans take up their rights and liberties "from the same origin and fountain, from whence they flow to all Englishmen, from Magna Charta and the natural right of the subject," [1] but new experiences and different needs had created divergences of which even the colonist was unaware, and which led him to defend his passion for self-determination with arguments that seemed to an Englishman silly or insincere. After Pitt had expressed his doubt as to how many living members of Parliament he could get to join him in maintaining with their blood the American doctrines, he asserted that "among the dead he could raise an host innumerable," [2] he was betraying his own ignorance of what doctrines the colonists really held. John Adams, who was flattered and hypnotized as most Americans were at the time of Pitt's heroic stand against the Stamp Act, realized long after that the "Great Commoner" was not so wholly sympathetic with the colonies as contemporaries thought him. Adams admitted even then that Pitt was "a great national minister because he always flattered and gratified the national passion for war, victory and conquest but he was not a wise

---

[1] Hansard, *Parliamentary History*, xvi, 196.
[2] Gordon, *The American Revolution*, i, 444.

minister. . . . He died a martyr to his idol. He fell
in the House of Lords with the sovereignty of parliament in his mouth." [1] It was thus that Adams
came at last to reject even the greatest friend of
America in Parliament.

When we analyze to-day the state papers,
speeches, and pamphlets on both sides of the controversy, we perceive that some of the terms they
used conveyed different ideas to the Englishman
than to the American. They could not discuss representation to any good end, because, regarding this
political institution, each had a different theory and
practice. They could not profitably debate the
proper extent and character of local self-government
or agree as to the distribution of authority between
Parliament and the colonial legislatures, because
clashing interests led them to different conclusions.
If they entered upon a discussion as to the extent
to which government could constitutionally interfere with the liberty of the individual, as to whether
Parliament was in that respect all-powerful or was
limited by certain unchanging laws of right and
wrong, in this argument, too, they found the path
of logic set with obstacles due to different ideals,
varied experiences. From the colonist's conception
of these matters evolved in time those principles
which moulded the American governmental system. From the dominant English ideas sprang
that system which holds in the British Empire of
to-day.

If one examines closely the meaning given to the

[1] John Adams, *Works*, x, 192, 193.

word "representation" in the two countries, one finds the prevailing ideas in each to be very different. Omitting for the moment necessary qualifications of a general statement, the variance may be briefly stated. In England the representative of a district might come from any part of the realm; in America there was a strong prejudice in favor of a representative resident in the district he represented. In England the right to vote for a representative was greatly limited by custom and precedent, while in America the franchise had no limitations which were not easily overcome. The English theory and practice did not recognize the right of a district to proportional representation, and there was little contention for it. In America any deprivation of proportional representation was hotly resented. A multitude of varying conditions and of historical developments caused these differences to emerge out of the past of each people. Representation in America grew under the care of the communities represented, not, as in its infancy in England, guided by the King's necessities, and so fixed in custom that it did not change with the changing conditions.

Though the colonists had imitated England in some of their institutions, they did not in others. English local government was reproduced in America, and the method of dealing with crime, but in the matters of representation the colonists had evolved a plan of their own. The American preference for a representative known and voted for by the people of the district which he represented was a natural development in a land whose people were pressing onward into new, unsettled regions. The frontiersman always clamored for it, not only because of his individualism, but because he felt that the representatives of the older settled district could not understand frontier needs. Yet the English custom did not wholly die out, and it was possible for a representative to live outside his district, as in the case of Patrick Henry who sat for Louisa County rather than his county of residence.[1] Indeed, the theory that a member of the House of Burgesses represented Virginia as a whole and not the county electing him was not unpopular in colonial Virginia.[2] There is much to be said for that theory wherever it is held, because it breeds statesmen more intent upon the welfare of the whole state than upon securing by "log-rolling" the interest of some part at the expense of the whole. It was the sense of that freedom, in addition to their talent, that helped Pitt and Burke and Barré to look beyond the petty concerns of their actual electors to the vast interests of the empire. Burke, born and educated in Ireland, dwelling thereafter mainly in London, could get his seat in Parliament through the favor of the voters in Wendover Borough or Bristol City,[3] but his splendid mind was free to grapple with the problems of a world dominion rather than keeping up his "fences" by urging legislation that would put money in the

[1] It was true that the London agent of a colony might also be the agent of another colony, but that came about in the interest of economy. and, moreover, the agent was not looked upon as a representative

[2] Grigsby, *Virginia Constitutional Convention*, 67, 76.

[3] *Members of Parliament*, pt. II, 137.

pockets of his constituents. William Pitt, returned to Parliament as member of the most notorious of "rotten boroughs," "Old Sarum," some sixty acres of ploughed land on which no man lived and no house stood, enjoyed a similar freedom. When Old Sarum was no longer tenable, the ministerial borough of Seaford returned him, then Oldborough and again Okehampton, but however his constituency might be hustled about the realm frɔm place to place, Pitt kept the "strength of his thunder and the splendor of his lightning" for the great affairs of the empire. Yet much as may be said for this English custom, it differed from the prevailing American ideas of representation, and helped to create misunderstanding and suspicion when the meaning of "taxation without representation" was in question.

The differing nature of the franchise in each country also affected the real meaning of representation. There had been from the first a natural adherence by the colonists to those methods of granting suffrage with which they were familiar in England. Moreover, the English Government made every effort to place colonial suffrage on the same basis as in the mother country.[1] Yet with all the imitation by the colonies and coercion by the British Government, differences arose which had to do chiefly with the ease of acquiring the right to vote. In the colonies there were qualifications which had to do with race and nationality, with religion and good character, with residence and property qualifications,[2] but

[1] McKinley, *The Suffrage Franchise in the English Colonies*, 484.
[2] *Ibid.*, chap. xv.

except the race restriction all others were easily set aside by complaisance in religion or morality, by industry in the acquisition of property, or by taking proper measures to attain residence. In England these accessible terms did not suffice. In the counties all forty-shilling freeholders could vote, but many were mere puppets moved at the polls by the great landholders. The inhabitants of some great cities of recent growth could not vote for members to represent them in Parliament. In the boroughs, though resident householders had by common law the right to vote, yet there were in places irregular provisions which conferred suffrage upon a few persons who monopolized it. At Bath it was the privilege only of the mayor, twenty-four common councillors, and ten aldermen; at Buckingham the bailiff and twelve burgesses.[1] In some cases the franchise could only be acquired by inheritance from a "freeman" ancestor. Yet there was little discontent with this limited suffrage, and only a small minority asserted with the contemporary reformer John Cartwright, "I ought to have a vote because I am a man."[2] In general, it may be said that franchise in England was an historical accident; in America it grew in accord with a system. In England one must in many cases be born to it as to the purple: in America the attainment was in the reach of all. Colonial electors were not so much greater in numbers, but were evenly distributed both as to region

[1] May, *Constitutional History of England* (ed. 1862), i, 266. See excellent summary in Cross, *England and Greater Britain*, 910.
[2] Kent, *The English Radicals*, 70.

and social position.[1] Even the American colonists were a long way from the liberal franchise Cartwright demanded. In Virginia about nine per cent of the white population voted, in Pennsylvania eight per cent, while in Massachusetts and in Connecticut only about one person in fifty took part in elections. In Rhode Island nine per cent of the people were potential voters.[2] An English pamphleteer asserted that in England not one person in twenty-five voted for a representative.

It was in the theory and practice as to proportional representation that the greatest difference lay. In England there had never been any attempt to apportion representation to the number of inhabitants; in America there was at least a predominant belief in such an apportionment. Before there was reform in England, it came to pass that ten counties in the south with scarcely three million people had nearly as many members in Parliament as thirty counties to the north with over eight millions of people. But the borough representation was "the rotten part" of the Constitution, as Chatham said, and just before the American Revolution four hundred and seventeen out of the five hundred and fifty-eight members of Parliament were borough members. Originally it had been the King's prerogative to select boroughs that might send burgesses to Parliament, and various reasons good or bad had been the grounds of his choice. Since the Restora-

---

[1] Hart, "Exercise of the Suffrage," in *Political Science Quarterly*, VII, 316.

[2] McKinley, *The Suffrage Franchise in the English Colonies*, 487· Jameson in *Nation*, April 27, 1893.

tion no new boroughs had been chosen, but that period had been one of vast industrial changes, reducing old borough towns to hamlets and raising up great manufacturing centers like Birmingham, Leeds, and Manchester, to whom the privilege of representation had not been given. The boroughs whose dwindling population no longer entitled them on any equitable basis to representation, though they still retained it, were known as "rotten boroughs." Cornwall was full of decayed boroughs, sending forty-four representatives to Parliament, though Middlesex and Westminster sent only eight. Many boroughs of this type were not only bought and sold, but advertised themselves for sale. Their owners were members of the nobility who made them a source of revenue. The King and his Ministry did not hesitate to use the nation's money to buy seats for men who would be obedient servants in the House of Commons. Lord Lonsdale sent nine members, the Duke of Rutland six, and the Duke of Norfolk eleven,[1] and all were for sale for a consideration, either money or votes. The Ministry, the would-be members of Parliament, and the noble owners haggled and chaffered like market-women over their wares. The Prime Minister wrote to an agent: "Let Cooper know whether you promised Masterman two thousand five hundred pounds or three thousand pounds for each of Lord Edgecombe's seats. I was going to pay him twelve thousand five hundred pounds, but he demanded fifteen thousand pounds." Again he wrote: "Mr. Legge can only afford four

[1] May, *Const. Hist. of England* (ed. 1862). I. 287.

hundred pounds. If he comes in for Lostwithiel he will cost the public two thousand guineas. Gascoign should have the refusal of Tregony [in the infamous Cornwall district] if he will pay a thousand pounds, but I do not see why we should bring him in any cheaper than any other servant of the Crown. If he will not pay, he must give way to Mr. Best." [1]

Lord Sandwich sold John Robinson a seat, the consideration being two thousand pounds loan, three hundred pounds election costs, and the agreement to think and act " as I do in all American points and supporting the present administration in all matters." [2] In the picture which Thackeray draws, in "The Newcomes," of the cold-blooded sale of a seat in Parliament, the novelist does not dare give the amazing details which history demands. In 1768 Lord Chesterfield, in one of his famous ethical epistles to his son, wrote, "Elections here have been carried to a degree of frenzy hitherto unheard of, that for the town of Northampton has cost the contending parties at least thirty thousand pounds a side, and George Selwyn has sold the borough of Luggershall to two members for nine thousand pounds." [3] The return of the "nabobs," fabulously enriched in India, and eager for political display, had much increased the amounts bid for parliamentary seats. It was little wonder, as a contemporary lamented,[4] that "prudent and proper persons" were deterred from attempting to come to

---

[1] Trevelyan, *The American Revolution*, I, 202.
[2] *Abergavenny MSS.*, 11; Channing, *Hist. of the U.S.*, III, 73.
[3] Chesterfield, *Letters*, 3, 1375-76.
[4] Winstanley, *Lord Chatham*, 213, note.

Parliament. As a result of this English system it became true that a majority of all the members of the House of Commons was elected by less than fifteen thousand voters, most unevenly distributed over Great Britain, and that one hundred and fifty individuals, among whom were the Lords and the King, named three hundred and seven members of the Commons.[1] Toward this political iniquity of "rotten boroughs" and unrepresented manufacturing towns with large populations the ignorant masses were indifferent, and the only protest came from the great manufacturers who were deprived of their proper influence in the state. The evil was being brought to notice, however, for there were Englishmen as well as critical colonists who saw that the House of Commons did not in the American sense represent the people of England, but only in a technical, constitutional sense. Soon the evil was discussed even in Parliament.[2] There, however, the plea for more adequate representation was answered by humdrum Medes and Persians who solemnly reiterated that the object of the prevailing English system was to secure representation of the commercial classes, the landed gentry, and the several professional classes, lawyers, doctors, and other middle-class Englishmen. Parliament represented

[1] Hansard, *Parliamentary History*, xxx, 787–925; May, *Const. Hist. of England*, i, 288.   See also Thomas Oldfield's published analysis of the electoral condition of England (1794) in Trevelyan, *George III and C. J. Fox*, ii, 178.   He asserts that 99 peers, 104 commoners, and the existing ministry returned 387 members. Only 171 represented free and independent communities.

[2] *Ibid.*, xviii, 1287. Americans were fully aware of it. Bancroft, *Hist. of U.S.*, iii, 114, 119.

not individuals, but estates. The people of Bristol could as well elect representatives of commerce as the people of Birmingham, could they not? Nothing was gained, was there, by increasing the number of voters or the number of commercial towns sending representatives?

The American theory and practice presented a sharp contrast to this. In New England practically every town was represented, to the south every county.[1] When the British Government tried, by vetoing grants of representation to new counties and towns, to put a stop to the process of making colonial legislatures more popular and more representative, the very fact of opposition stiffened the colonial will to have its own system, and it fixed the colonial ideal.[2] Nevertheless, apportionment in America was not always fair nor in keeping with the ideal; in fact, it was bad in Pennsylvania, New York, and South Carolina, but there was no injustice equal to that of the "rotten borough."[3] Perhaps the worst sufferers in the colonies were the Scotch-Irish in the western part of Pennsylvania, who, deprived of proper representation in that legislature, pushed up the Great Valley and out into the Piedmont region of western South Carolina, where again they were deprived of proportional representation by the sea-

[1] Of fifty-nine towns incorporated in Massachusetts (1691–1761) only one was not given representation in the General Court. Statement accredited to W. G. Leland by Channing, *Hist. of the U.S.*, III, 75.

[2] H. A. Cushing, *From Province to Commonwealth Government*, 19–27.

[3] Like the British Government, that of Virginia was based on a representation of local units and not a representation of numbers. Grigsby, *Virginia Constitutional Convention*, 67, 76.

board planters.[1] But the significant fact here and
in other cases is that the refusal of proportional representation was resented. "As freemen and English
subjects" the Scotch-Irish and Germans of the
interior protested against three Quaker counties of
Pennsylvania having twenty-four out of thirty-six
deputies in the colonial assembly, though they had
less than half the population. They would admit
no divine right in the counties of Philadelphia,
Bucks, and Chester to enjoy such an unjust privilege.
An American was not content with the kind of representation which seemed to satisfy the people of
England. Yet the defenders of the Ministry made
the mistake of imputing to the whole empire, America and all, that system of representation which
was of purely insular origin and adaptability. The
American, on the other hand, was asking more than
was enjoyed in England, and had no conception of
the limits of the "liberty" enjoyed by the mass
of Englishmen whose rights he coveted and claimed
as his own.

When John Adams defended his client John Hancock against the charge of smuggling, he argued
that the Boston merchant had never consented to
the law which made his act a crime, "he never voted
for it himself and he never voted for any man to
make such a law for him."[2] Adams was not expressing a new idea; the New England fathers had held
that idea for four generations. As early as 1693, a
contemporary reported that the people of Hartford

[1] H. B. Grigsby, in Washington and Lee, *Historical Papers*, no. 2, p. 9.
[2] John Adams, *Works*, ii, 215.

"Have separated not only from the Church, But Crowne of England, and allowe of noe appeale from theire Courts nor the Lawes of England to have any force amongst them, some of the wissest have saide, wee are not permitted to vote for any member of Parliam^t, and therefore not lyable to theire lawes." [1] Men like Adams, with ideas rooted so deep in the past, listened with impatience to the words of even a great legal authority like Lord Mansfield, when he assured them, with perfect correctness as far as the law was concerned, that they had "virtual representation." Such an assertion, wrote Adams, in a burst of rhetorical frenzy, takes one from truth and fact into the "wild regions of imagination and possibility where arbitrary power sits upon her brazen throne, and governs with an iron sceptre." [2] Pitt too found it the "most contemptible idea that has ever entered into the head of man," and yet the British argument, that Americans were as much represented in Parliament as the greater part of the people of England, seemed to find proof in the very fact that Pitt there defended American rights, together with Burke and Camden and Barré and Fox, a group possessing the best political talent in England. On the other hand, the situation in England was different where the interests of the electors and non-electors were the same. Although, as was asserted, among nine million inhabitants of Great Britain there were eight million who had no votes in electing members to Parliament,[3] the security

[1] *Documents Relating to the Colonial History of New York*, iv, 71.
[2] John Adams, *Works*, ii, 215.
[3] Mansfield, in Hansard, *Parliamentary History*, xvi, 201.

of the non-electors against oppression was, as Daniel
Dulany, of Maryland, explained, "that their oppression would fall also upon the electors and the
representatives." [1] Wearied by the comparison of
America's case with that of Manchester, Birmingham, and Sheffield, Otis pointed out that "the counties in which those respectable abodes of tinkers,
tinners and pedlars lie, return members; so do all the
neighboring cities and boroughs. In the choice of
the former, if they have no vote, they must naturally and necessarily have a great influence. I believe
every gentleman of a landed estate near a flourish-
ing manufactory will be careful enough of its interest." [2] Americans were not so secure, because
acts oppressive to them might be popular with the
English electors. "Should the British empire some
day be extended round the whole world," cried Otis,
"Would it be reasonable that all mankind should
have their concerns managed by the electors of Old
Sarum, and the occupants of the Cornish barns and
ale houses?" [3] As for Sheffield and Manchester, if
they were not represented, "they ought to be."

It was precisely in that expression "ought to be"
that the most dangerous difference in American and
English ideals was to be found. In England certain
constitutional principles had been dominant for
hundreds of years. Mansfield, of course, pointed out
that to change the representative system would be
to change the British Constitution, and he asked

[1] D. Dulany, *Considerations on the Propriety of Taxing the Colonies*,
3–8.

[2] *Ibid.*, 6–10, 51.

[3] Tudor, *James Otis*, 191.

with a sneer if that "was to be new-modeled too." There were other Englishmen like Pitt and Burke who as a matter of expediency would let the Americans have their own way, even in so grave a matter as the interpretation of the Constitution, but even they were not ready to reform Parliament in order to make it morally defensible nor to concede that it did not have sovereign powers if it chose to exercise them. Soame Jenyns, the popular English pamphleteer, waxed very facetious over the idea of American representatives in Parliament. Having seen specimens of colonial powers of speech, he feared that "the sudden importation of so much eloquence at once would greatly endanger the safety of the government of this country." Adam Smith had, however, favored having the colonies send representatives as "a new and dazzling object of ambition" to colonial leaders,[1] and even Grenville had looked upon the plan favorably; but Burke poured the vials of his scorn upon such a "visionary union" whose author seemed to have "dropped down from the moon without any knowledge of the general nature of this globe." Through six pages of almost boisterous ridicule Burke played with the folly of such an idea.[2] He pictured many fancied difficulties, writs going astray, vessels lost, American members delayed by storm and arriving too late, the King's death and a new Parliament, voyages of six thousand miles to no purpose, and finally the in-

[1] Adam Smith, *Wealth of Nations*, chapter on "Colonies," pt. III, 290-91.
[2] Burke, *Works*, II, 136-43.

finite difficulty of settling that representation on a fair balance of wealth and numbers through the several provinces of America. It costs the author of the idea nothing, Burke sneered, "to fight with nature and to conquer the order of Providence" which plainly opposes such a union. "Has he well considered what an immense operation any change in our constitution is? How many discussions, parties and passions, it will necessarily excite?" When one comes to the end of all his ridicule and objections, we find that he might have put all in the simple admission that he dreaded the reform of Parliament, a reform which the younger Pitt barely missed carrying before the end of the century.

Yet Burke might have saved his sarcasm, for, as Samuel Adams declared, "there is nothing that the colonies would more dread" than a representation in Parliament. By that arrangement it was feared the supreme power of Parliament over the colonies would have been established, annihilating their provincial assemblies, and destroying the power of their charters.[1] The idea was not made more popular in America, by the fact that it was favored by Governor Bernard, of Massachusetts.[2] Otis, who thought in imperial terms, and not as a disgruntled colonist who favored such a representation, wished all parts of the empire "compacted and consolidated" so that the national strength and power would shine with greater splendor than had ever yet been seen by the sons of man. He intended no mere return of

---

[1] Wells, *Samuel Adams*, i, 91–93.
[2] *Barrington-Bernard Correspondence*, 138, 139.

a half-score ignorant, worthless persons "who might be induced to sell their country and their God for a golden calf." This was his answer to the merchant who offered to carry American representatives to London for half they would sell for when they got there. Nevertheless, Otis admitted that the idea was much disliked among his fellow countrymen. The famous resolutions of the Massachusetts legislature (October, 1765), which Hutchinson said seemed "to be designed as a sort of Magna Charta, or rather a declaration of the fundamentals of the Constitution," expressed opposition to such a plan.[1] It was because such a representation was impracticable, the resolutions held, that the several legislatures in America were constituted.[2] The Stamp Act Congress, too, declared the colonies "are not" and "cannot be" represented in Parliament. Franklin had thought well of such a representation, but as early as 1766 he had lost hope. "The Parliament here do at present think too highly of themselves to admit representatives from us, if we should ask it; and, when they will be desirous of granting it, we shall think too highly of ourselves to accept it." Representation ought to have been thought of earlier; the project is now "in the situation of Friar Bacon's project of making a brazen wall round England for its eternal security." The time was past.[3]

[1] Hutchinson, *History of Massachusetts*, III, 133, 447.

[2] *Ibid.*, 76, 92; Tudor, *James Otis*, 195, 197; Niles, *Principles and Acts of the Revolution*, 163.

[3] Franklin, *Writings* (Smyth, *ed.*), IV, 456. Lord Barrington declared that "no Influence could make ten Members of either House of Parliament agree to such a Remedy." *Barrington-Bernard Correspondence*, 140.

One comes, therefore, at last to see that at a time when the prevailing American and the English ideals of representation differed radically, and when the American refused to entertain the idea of sending his own representatives to Parliament, there was every element present to embitter the minds of practical politicians who sought through argument a solution of Great Britain's imperial problem. Lord Camden asserted that "Taxation and representation are inseparably united; God hath joined them, no British parliament can separate them," but if these governmental attributes were so married there must be an agreement as to what the union signified. In England the only meaning attached to the phrase "no taxation without representation," was that neither the King nor his Ministers could lay a tax without getting the consent of Parliament. In America the theory was that none had power to tax except an assembly containing representatives of those taxed, men actually elected by the persons who were to pay the tax. There was a great gulf fixed between the two principles, and nothing but the magic of time could close the gap.

It might have been possible, nevertheless, for each country to enjoy the practice and principle to which it was bred but for another fundamental difference of opinion concerning the nature of the respective powers of Parliament and of the colonial legislatures. "In Britain," wrote Governor Bernard (1765), "the American Governments are considered as Corporations empowered to make by-Laws, existing only during the Pleasure of Parliament. . .

In America they claim . . . to be perfect States, no otherwise dependent upon Great Britain than by having the same King." [1] Lord Mansfield declared the American governments were "all on the same footing as our great corporations in London," and pointed out that such colonial governments had been destroyed simply by a process in the Courts of Chancery or King's Bench. How could such a legislature, at the mercy of the very courts of England, have the sole power of laying taxes? [2] Burke endorsed this and added, "It is extremely absurd that the Colonies should be subject to the *judicial* but free from the *legislative* authority of their mother country." The unity of legislation in the empire, declared a member of Parliament, is "as essential to the body politic as the Deity to religion." [3] The colonial legislatures, thought Mansfield, existed on sufferance; they might be scolded, prorogued, or dissolved at the whim of a governor directed by the Ministry. But that was not the colonial conception of their legislatures, not even in Pennsylvania in whose charter the legislative supremacy of Parliament was expressly recognized. [4] As early as 1700 Sir William Beeston wrote that the Jamaica assembly were "stirred up to believe that what the House of Commons could do in England they could

---

[1] *Barrington-Bernard Correspondence*, 96; Soame Jenyns, *Works*, 425.

[2] Hansard, *Parliamentary Debates*, xvi, 175–76. The supremacy of Parliament was best stated by Lord Mansfield in the case of Campbell *vs.* Hall. Thayer, *Cases on Constitutional Law*.

[3] Pownall, *Thomas Pownall*, 205; Almon, *Debates of Commons*, ix, 96.

[4] Macdonald, *Documentary Source Book*, 81.

do here, and that during their sitting, all power and authority was only in their hands." [1] And thirty-five years later the Commons House of Assembly in South Carolina resolved that they had "the same Rights, Powers, and Privileges in regard to introducing and passing Laws for the imposing of Taxes on the People of this Province as the House of Commons of Great Britain have in introducing and passing Laws on the People of England." [2] In 1771 Samuel Cooper, writing to Thomas Pownall from Boston, declared "the greater Part [of the people] have a settled persuasion . . . that our Parliament here ought to come between the sovereign and the American subject, just in the same Manner that the British Parliament does with respect to the British subject, and that whatever takes place contrary to this is . . . the Meer effect of Pow'r and not the result of reason or [of] the Constitution." [3] To that idea of their powers they were to cling until the day when the empire was rent in twain. It was the prevailing colonial belief that each part of the empire to which Englishmen had removed had the sole right to tax itself. In England the view dominated that political power, sovereignty, resided at the center. It gave a member of Parliament no little sense of pride to regard himself as an actor in "a senate regulating the eastern and western worlds at once." As Walpole expressed it, "The Romans were triflers to us." As the empire grew, no other method of rule

[1] *Calendar of State Papers*, Colonial Series (*America and West Indies*, 1700), 424.
[2] Wallace, *Henry Laurens*, 39, 172.
[3] *American Historical Review*, VIII, 325.

than that so long used for the British Isles had been even considered. Governor Bernard was perfectly right when he wrote to Lord Barrington (1765) that "all the Political Evils in America arise from the Want of Ascertaining the Relations between Great Britain and the American Colonies. . . . The Patch-work Government of America will last no longer." [1] Some one must decide how to distribute the authority between the center and the parts in that vast empire. Britain, growing and expanding, had forced the governing mind to dwell upon problems of empire; provincial America, bound up in the interests of an isolated community, became absorbed in intensive self-government.

Had the men who held in their hands the fate of the King's dominions looked less to theories of the imperial law and more to what was actually going on within the empire, a federal solution would have been all but in their grasp. [2] It had long been the custom for the Crown, the active instrument of imperial government, to control through instructed officers many colonial affairs. Its charge through-out the empire of the navy and army, of war and peace, of all foreign affairs was scarcely opposed. The colonial post-office was in its charge, Indian trade and affairs were being taken over, as was the regulation of the back-lands and the building of new colonies. Imperial trade and navigation laws were enforced by the Crown, and though offensive

---

[1] *Barrington-Bernard Correspondence*, 96, 97.
[2] A. C. McLaughlin, "Background of American Federalism," in *American Political Science Review*, XII, no. 2, 215–40.

in a degree to the colonist the right was little questioned. On the other hand, the colonies levied their own local taxes and looked after their own internal police. They even contributed in a niggardly way, but of their own will, to the defense of the empire. They managed a multitude of the concerns of the colonists' daily life with only a little nagging from the royal governor. Laws of Parliament like those against the land bank and paper money, and a few others that seemed to thwart local legislative activity, were after all imperial in their nature. Even obnoxious trade acts were in keeping with the theories which in that age dominated the thinking of colonizing peoples, and a grumbling colonist himself would admit that the control of imperial trade was one of the main duties of Parliament. Great Britain had, in a word, by 1760, a working plan that was federal, a political system in which the usual powers of government, separated and distinguished, were distributed between governments accustomed to keep within their own spheres and to exercise only their proper quotas of authority.[1] Except for the disputed right of Parliament, the central authority, to exact money directly from the colonists for imperial use, the scheme of distribution of powers which, a generation later, was to be embodied in the American Federal Constitution was already the practice of the British Empire. The men who moulded British destinies — and there were great and good men, too, with not the least disposition to

[1] A. C. McLaughlin, "Background of American Federalism," in *American Political Science Review*, XII, no. 2, 215, 219.

tyranny — failed to see what time had wrought, and that they needed only to furnish a working legal basis for the empire they already had if they would solve their problem of imperial organization. Instead of that, they insisted on the principle of centralization of power, the indivisible nature of Parliament's sovereignty, and they ridiculed the idea of distribution of powers. Lord Mansfield, in an argument which an admirer described as "so full, so learned, so logical, and in every respect so true that not an atom of doubt remained in the breasts of his hearers," proved by a "multitude of examples" that it was impossible to suppose two supreme legislatures, "impracticable to draw a line for bounding the authority of the British legislature," and absurd to attempt "to distinguish between one act of legislation and another, as if a greater degree of power were required to lay taxes than to make any other kind of Law." [1]

Such a position left the colonists to accept subordination to an absolute government, or to deny the authority of Parliament altogether.[2] As Burke warned the Ministry in 1774, if you "poison the very source of government by urging subtle deductions and consequences odious to those you govern, from the unlimited and illimitable nature of supreme sovereignty you will teach them by these means to call that sovereignty itself in question. . . . They will cast your sovereignty in your face. Nobody will be argued into slavery." [3] That was the kernel of

[1] *The Francis Letters*, I, 74.
[2] *American Political Science Review*, XII, no. 2, 228.
[3] Burke, *Works*, II, 73.

the difficulty in solving England's problem of empire. Logic and legal precedents would beat in vain against the wall of American convictions, formed as we have seen them formed by frontier experiences in a new land a thousand leagues from Westminster Hall, redolent with the sanctity of law and precedent.

CHAPTER IX

AMERICAN VERSUS ENGLISH IDEAS OF THE BRITISH CONSTITUTION

HAD it been possible to please both radical colonist and conservative Englishman with some happy solution of the proper extent and character of local self-government, and had that solution included some mode of permitting each integral part of the empire to enjoy what theory and practice of representation it preferred, harmony might have reigned within the British dominions. But if Parliament was to exercise the supremacy to which it made claim, there still remained between the colonial liberal and the British conservative a differing conception of the extent of Parliament's power over the individual citizen which boded ill for any real restoration of good understanding.

Whenever the colonial orator or pamphleteer failed to sustain his argument against an offensive act of Parliament by appeal to charter rights, or to the rights of Englishmen as found in Magna Charta and the Bill of Rights, he took refuge in natural rights, or in his own conception of the British Constitution. It was this dangerous doctrine, "destructive to all government," which the Lords, in their protest against the repeal of the Stamp Act, declared "has spread itself over all our North American colonies, that the obedience of the subject is not due to the laws and legislature of the realm

farther than he, in his private judgment, shall think
it conformable to the ideas he has formed of a free
constitution." [1] Otis resorted to this doctrine in his
attack on "Writs of Assistance." That an act of
Parliament had made them legal did not pose him.
He declared, "no act of Parliament can establish
such a writ"; for "an act against the Constitution
is void," the courts must pass it into disuse. He
implied that the Constitution as he conceived it contained pledges of protection to the rights of the individual which even Parliament could not gainsay.
Those pledges were its bounds "which by God and
nature are fixed," he declared in his "Rights of the
British Colonies." "Hitherto have they a right to
come, and no farther." Some seven years later
Samuel Adams, expressing the ideas of the Massachusetts House of Representatives, wrote, "It is the
glory of the British Prince and the happiness of all
his subjects, that their constitution hath its foundations in the immutable laws of nature, and as the
supreme legislature as well as the supreme executive
derives its authority from that constitution, it
should seem that no laws can be made or executed
that are repugnant to any essential law in nature." [2]
To Adams's mind this "law in nature" was his own
idea of right and wrong. From the days when young
Alcibiades asked Pericles the meaning of the word

---

[1] Hansard, *Parliamentary History*, xvi, 186.

[2] Samuel Adams, *Writings*, i, 190 (writing to Conway. Secretary
of State, who had resigned a month earlier, though the colonists did
not know it). John Adams wrote (1762), "an act of Parliament
against natural equity . . . would be void." John Adams, *Works*,
ii, 139.

law, learned men have disagreed as to its exact meaning, but Samuel Adams, always in intimate converse with the Oracle of politics, never allowed the shadow of dubiety to rest upon his assumptions. He was always sure that what seemed wrong to him could not be sanctioned by the British Constitution. In fact, he and other Americans were but imitating Pym and Hampden of the older British revolution, in claiming to be already vested with rights, which in reality they were at that moment endeavoring to achieve.[1] His idea of the limitations of Parliament was the prevailing American view, but Lord Mansfield and conservative Englishmen in general rejected it utterly. The British Constitution, they informed him, was the Magna Charta and Bill of Rights and the common law as the British courts throughout the centuries had left it, but in addition to all these elements it was the changing law of Parliament. Even William Pitt, the greatest defender of the colonists' cause, after holding that he thought them "deprived of a right," added, "but by an authority they ought not to question."[2] He merely confessed his faith in the absolute power of Parliament. "What Parliament doth no power on earth can undo" Blackstone had put it (1758) in his lectures at Oxford.[3] Any act of Parliament might any day change even the Constitution of England.[4] Such an idea seemed preposterous to one who drew

[1] McLaughlin, *The Courts, the Constitution and Parties*, 69, 72.
[2] *American Historical Review* (April, 1912), 573.
[3] Blackstone, *Commentaries* (1768 ed.), i, 91, 161.
[4] Perhaps the most striking example of that was the Act of 1911 which destroyed the power of the House of Lords.

his political philosophy from colonial experience and the political writers of the seventeenth century. Of a pamphleteer who inferred that Parliament had a right to tax because it resolved that it had, Samuel Adams wrote, with a sneer, "I shall only say that his reasoning is much like that of a late letter writer from London, whose wonderful performance, if I mistake not, was inserted in all newspapers, who says that 'when an Act of Parliament is once passed, it becomes a part of the Constitution.'" [1] The acceptance in England of the supremacy of Parliament was a political habit only lately acquired, while the colonists, who had really broken their British ties in the seventeenth century, were carrying on old English doctrines still in favor when the "Fathers" left the homeland and first set foot in America. [2] As Governor Hutchinson explained to the English agent of his colony, "Our friends to liberty take advantage of a maxim they find in Lord Coke that an act of Parliament against Magna Charta or the peculiar rights of Englishmen is *ipso facto* void." In a word, they were depending on an obsolete law writer whom the British Constitution had outgrown.

The colonial idea as expressed by Otis and Adams was not new in America, for it will be recalled that, when the Puritan magistrates of Massachusetts Bay were asked (1683) to give up their charter which it was argued they had legally forfeited, the ministers who were consulted said that though according to some corrupt and unrighteous laws they might have

[1] Wells, *Samuel Adams*, I, 59.
[2] McLaughlin, *The Courts, the Constitution and Parties*, 81, 91.

done so, yet according to laws of righteousness and equity they had not done so.[1] These were the laws to which Jonathan Mayhew had appealed when in 1750 he held that the King was limited, not merely by acts of Parliament, "but by eternal laws of truth, wisdom, and equity and the everlasting tables of right reason — tables that cannot be repealed, or thrown down and broken like those of Moses."[2] Indeed, long before any American had appealed to natural law, Sophocles expressed the idea in Antigone's defense of her illegal burial of her brother. She acted, she pleaded, in free obedience to the "unwritten and unchanging laws of heaven — laws that are not of to-day or yesterday but abide for ever, and of their creation knoweth no man." The colonists, however, had not drawn their ideas of natural law directly from antiquity, but from writers on political theory in the time of the Stuarts. Locke had said, "A government is not free to do as it pleases . . . the law of nature stands as an eternal rule to all men, legislators as well as others." We find in the debates in Parliament in the ten years preceding the Revolution, nearly as much use of Locke's philosophy as in America, but in England the fixed traditions, the settled customs, the old environment, the established classes determined to resist change, prevented the practical application of the doctrines; while in America the frontier favored experiment and the seed fell on good ground. Contemporaries of Samuel Adams saw reason to

[1] Hutchinson Papers in Mass. Hist. Soc., *Collections* (3d Ser.), I, 80.

[2] Thornton, *The Pulpit of the Revolution*, 95.

lament the "evil Consequences arising from the Propagation of Mr. Locke's democratical Principles," [1] but before Locke it had been held by Thomas Edwards that, in spite of past laws and agreements, men of the new age ought to enjoy "their natural and just liberties agreeable to right reason." [2] And these writers of the Stuart period were but elaborating the idea of Melanchthon a century earlier who, in defending natural law, said that he relied on the saying of St. Paul that the law is written in the human heart.[3]

Though colonial political literature in the decade before the Declaration of Independence abounds with appeals to this natural law, it had its exponents also in England. Even Blackstone, after declaring that "if Parliament will positively enact a thing to be done which is unreasonable, I know of no power that can control it," goes on to say that in a conflict between legislation and natural law, the latter must prevail. "This law of nature," he explains, "is of course superior in obligation to any other. It is binding all over the globe in all countries and at all times, no human laws are of any validity, if contrary to this." [4]

Both the prevailing colonial mind and that of the

---

[1] Dean Tucker, *Four Letters on Important National Subjects*, **89.**

[2] Thomas Edwards, *The Third Part of Gangræna*, etc., 16–17.

[3] Höffding, *History of Philosophy*, I, 40.

[4] Blackstone, *Commentaries* (ed., 1768), I, 41, 91. This seeming contradiction Roscoe Pound (*Yale Law Review*, Dec., 1912, pp. 17–19) explains by the historical fact that although after the Revolution of 1688 the absolute supremacy of Parliament was established, yet in fact the great bulk of English law was traditional (formed in theory under the laws of nature), not made by Parliament.

English radicals drew from this idea of natural laws, which put bounds to the power of Parliament, a deduction which was to become a fundamental principle in American constitutional law. John Dickinson, after propounding the question, "who are a free people?" answered with assurance, "Not those over whom Government is reasonably and equitably exercised, but those, who live under Government, so constitutionally checked and controlled that proper provision is made against its being otherwise exercised." [1] "There are," wrote Samuel Adams, "fundamental rules of the Constitution, which it is humbly presumed neither the supreme legislature nor the supreme executive can alter. In all free states the Constitution is fixed." [2] Adams here expressed the idea which underlies a written constitution, which can be changed solely by the people and only with great difficulty, and which places definite bounds to the power of the legislative and the executive branch of government. It was an idea which grew naturally out of the colonial experience with written charters. They had been used for generations to seeing their legislatures hedged about by fixed law. Their experience was bolstered by the philosophy of great political thinkers whom they reverenced. Both Adams and Otis were acquainted with Vattel, the latest and most popular of continental writers. Indeed, Otis in his "Rights of the Colonists" quotes from Vattel's "Law of Nature

[1] John Dickinson, *Memoirs*, Pa. Hist. Soc., XIV, 356; Macdonald, *Documentary Source Book*, 148.

[2] The same idea in the "Circular Letter"; also in Samuel Adams, *Writings*, I, 134, 156, 170, 175, 180, 185, 190, 196; II, 325, 350, 452.

and Nations" wherein he asserts that the authority
of the legislature does not extend so far as to change
the constitution of the state. "It is from the constitution that these legislators derive their power;
how can they change it without destroying the
foundation of their own authority?" asks Vattel.
"They ought to consider the fundamental laws as
sacred," he continues, "for the Constitution of the
state ought to be *fixed*."[1] It was an idea full of
promise to men faced with a threat of absolute rule
by a parliament three thousand miles away in which
they had no voice. Against a conception that the
British Constitution was from day to day what
Parliament made it was now set the dictum that
every free government is bound by fixed law. If a
government is bound to regard the unchanging laws
of nature, reasoned the American mind, then it is
restrained by fixed law and is a free government,
and that was what the colonist insisted the British
Government would be if not distorted by such
"enemies of liberty" as Lord Mansfield.

Americans were not unaware of their inheritance
from English history of traditions of freedom growing from precedent to precedent, from Magna Charta
to and beyond the Bill of Rights, until English liberty was second to none in all the world. "Here
lies the difference between the British Constitution
and other forms of government," wrote John Adams
in 1766, "that liberty is its end, its use, its designa-
tion, drift and scope, as much as grinding corn is the

[1] James Otis, *Rights of the Colonists*, 109; Samuel Adams, *Writings*,
II, 325.

use of a mill." [1] Samuel Adams, too, had paid his
tribute (1750). "There is," he wrote, "no form of
civil government . . . appears to me so well calculated to preserve this blessing [of liberty] or to secure to its subjects all the most valuable advantages
of civil society, as the English." [2] Otis found the
British "the most perfect form of government, that
in the present depraved state, human nature is
capable of." [3] It was long before Otis or the "brace
of Adams" realized that what they loved was not
the British Government, but their idea of it.

American thought and English thought had come
to the parting of the ways. A section of the Anglo-
Saxon world was entering on a new stage of the
development of free government. Through the
efforts of courageous Englishmen the power of the
King to rule in an arbitrary manner (except by corruption) had been destroyed, but it was still possible
for Parliament to govern in an arbitrary way, and
America was to lead in the struggle to establish, at
least in the Anglo-Saxon world, a government of
law and not of men, of written basic law and not of
men raised by their fellows to a little brief authority.
For the moment Americans had outstripped Englishmen in the race for political freedom. The absolutism of Parliament was to Otis and Adams as
hateful as the absolutism of the King, but for the
ruling class in England there was no such fear.
From the days of Charles I, the English political

[1] Lord Acton, *Essays on the French Revolution*, 23.
[2] Wells, *Samuel Adams*, I, 21.
[3] Tudor, *James Otis*, 105.

development had been in the direction of absorption
of power by Parliament, a tendency to concentrate
all power legislative and executive in that body.
Once it was elected all sovereignty was vested in it,
and the English people, or merely that small part
which enjoyed the franchise, was sovereign only
during an election. Forms still obscured that concentration of power to such a degree that even so
profound a student as Montesquieu thought the
English political system was a nicely balanced one
with the legislative branch carefully set over against
the executive and each checking the other. The
omnipotence of Parliament, its power to alter the
very Constitution of England through its changing
laws, was a fact not fully grasped even by Englishmen. However, there were some forward-looking
Englishmen who did see it, and who were demanding
reform. One must not miss the important fact that
the American Revolution was politically not merely
a clash between England and America, but a civil
war, a factional war within the British Empire. It
must be noted that not only were there Americans
who defended the views of the British official middle-
class mind, as typified in Mansfield,[1] and Englishmen
who were liberal enough, like Pitt and Burke, to let
the colonists have their own way because that was
expedient, but other Englishmen who truly looked
at the British Constitution as did Americans. Lord
Camden, appealing to "that consummate reasoner

---

[1] Like Martin Howard, of Rhode Island, in "A Letter from a
Gentleman at Halifax" (1765), who held that a colonist might question the justice of a measure of Parliament, but not its jurisdiction.

and politician Mr. Locke, whose principles were drawn from the heart of our constitution," declared "as a lawyer" that the Constitution was against taxing the Americans, intimating that a mere act of Parliament would not change the Constitution and thus make such taxation legal. He asserted that the British Constitution was "grounded on the eternal and immutable laws of nature." It was a constitution "whose foundation and centre is liberty which sends liberty to every subject" within "its ample circumference." [1] Lord Camden took this kindly view of the Constitution as it stood, but others, radical reformers, like John Cartwright, recognized Parliament's absolutism and demanded reform. He held that the Constitution ought not to be easily changed from day to day, but "should be written and taught to children with the Lord's Prayer and the ten commandments." [2] In that way the limits of Parliament's power over the individual would be known and every man could stoutly assert his own rights.

Men who thought with Lord Camden and John Cartwright were in the minority in England, while those who agreed with Adams and Otis were in the majority in America. Such a state of affairs menaced the unity of the empire. Though America and England had political principles and traditions springing from a common source, though they were wonderfully alike in their ideals of political liberty, and though they used common measures of social

---

[1] Hansard, *Parliamentary History*, xvi, 178.
[2] Kent, *The English Radicals*, 70.

justice, yet historical chance and varied environment created differences in methods of attaining and enjoying political liberty which proved fatal to union. The contrast cannot be too strongly insisted upon. Samuel Adams and many of his fellow countrymen, on the one hand, believed that the British Constitution was fixed by " the law of God and nature," and founded in the principles of law and reason so that Parliament could not alter it,[1] but Lord Mansfield and his followers, on the other hand, asserted rightly that " the constitution of this country has been always in a moving state, either gaining or losing something," and "there are things even in Magna Charta which are not constitutional now" and others which an act of Parliament might change.[2] Between two such conceptions of the powers of government compromise was difficult to attain. It was best, doubtless, for the highest good of free institutions in the world that each idea should freely work out its logical destiny. Both had splendid possibilities in their ultimate forms. In these two concepts one detects the main difference between English governmental ideas and those underlying principles which furnish the basis of the Constitution of the United States. In England all political power is in the hands of government, though the ministry which wields that power is easily overthrown by a dissatisfied people. In America, with its written constitutions and judicial review, all government is of limited authority, though its agents are not so quickly or

---

[1] Wells, *Samuel Adams*, I, 75–97.
[2] Hansard, *Parliamentary Debates*, XVI, 197.

easily displaced when not obedient to the will of the people. Each system has its merits, each its disadvantages. These were the ultimate ends to which differing ideals were carrying two great peoples, but the immediate result of these diverging opinions was alienation and war. These fundamental differences in political thinking made the colonists and the rulers of the mother country impatient and suspicious of each other when they began to dispute over questions like the Navigation Acts and the Stamp Act. Men who believed that Parliament had succeeded to the King's "divine right" could see only hysterical nonsense in the Massachusetts confession of faith of 1767. "The natural rights of the colonists," it ran, "we humbly conceive to be the same with those of all other British subjects and indeed of all mankind. The principal of these rights is to be 'free from any superior power on earth and not to be under the will or legislative authority of man, but to have only the law of nature for his rule.' In general, freedom of men under government is to have standing fundamental rules to live by, common to every one of that society and made by the legislative power erected in it, a liberty to follow my own will in all things where that rule prescribes not, and not to be subject to the inconstant, uncertain, unknown, arbitrary will of another man." Such talk was a mere flight of fancy the legal advisers of the Crown would say, alarming even in a speculative book, but full of menace if indulged in by men who were responsible for the government of British subjects in an American province. And what did Christopher Gadsden mean by allusion to those "latent though inherent rights of society, which no climate, no time, no constitution, no contract can ever destroy or diminish"? To a mind that venerated the Constitution such ideas were poisonous, and pointed plainly to anarchy. Colony and mother country had drifted far apart when representative men from Massachusetts and South Carolina could give serious expression to ideas so shocking to typical members of Parliament. Such differences in ideals were as important causes of a breaking-up of the empire as more concrete matters like oppressive taxation. Daniel Webster only exaggerated the truth when he declared that the American colonists took arms against a preamble and fought eight years against a declaration. There was no ruinous material damage to America in the attempted taxation, but as John Dickinson said, "A free people can never be too quick in observing nor too firm in opposing the beginnings of alteration either in form or reality, respecting institutions formed for their security. The first kind of alteration leads to the last." [1] The Americans did not regard liberty as a mere comparative release from tyranny; but possessed, as Burke said, "a fierce spirit of liberty" stronger than in any other people of the earth, and yet it was a spirit that accorded with English principles and English ideas. On that very subject of taxes — in England too — the greatest spirits, Burke reminded Parliament, had acted and suffered,[2] and yet the

[1] Lord Acton, *Essays on the French Revolution*, 25.
[2] Burke, *Works*, ii, 120.

people of England had but gained the right to be taxed only by Parliament, while James Otis implied something more when he cried — " By the laws of God and nature, government must not raise taxes on the property of the people without the consent of the people or their deputies. There can be no prescription old enough to supercede the law of Nature and the grant of God Almighty, who has given all men a right to be free." [1] It was because British statesmen could not grasp the true meaning of such words that their colonists in America, who at one time, in Franklin's words, "had been led by a thread, governed at the expense of only a little pen, ink and paper," were before long to be " kept in subjection only by forts, citadels, garrisons and armies."

[1] Lord Acton, *Essays on the French Revolution*, 24.

CHAPTER X

THE "GENIUS" OF TOWNSHEND THREATENS
TO WRECK THE EMPIRE

WHEN the news of the Stamp Act repeal came to America, the populace would have extracted less joy from the kegs of beer at the "King's Arms" or from John Hancock's "pipe of Madeira," flowing for all comers, if it could have known how little the ministerial heart had changed. The people might have feasted on the ox roasted in the fields, and have drunk the toasts to King George "of glorious memory," but they would have been merry with reservations had they understood that not even their friends in Parliament, not even Pitt and Burke, opposed as they were to offensive taxation and the use of force in America, were willing to consider seriously any reform of the British Constitution, nor inclined to change the commercial policy which aimed at making the colonies profitable to England. Unfriendly to reform, the privileged class, which then had all political power in England, believed with some reason that the British governmental system was without a rival in the present or the past of the world. Except for the quarrels of the factions all went smoothly, and the holders of political power had a complacent sense that no reform was needed, no change desirable. How far even the most enlightened were from sympathy with democratic ideas of government is revealed in a letter of Edmund Burke to the Duke of Richmond: "You, if you are what you ought to be, are in my eyes the great oaks that shade a country and perpetuate your benefits from generation to generation. The immediate power of a Duke of Richmond, or a Marquis of Rockingham, is not so much of moment; but if their conduct and example hand down their principles to their successors, then their houses become the public repositories and offices of record for the Constitution: not like the Tower or Rolls Chapel, where it is searched for, and sometimes in vain, in rotten parchments under dripping perishing walls; but in full vigor, and acting with vital energy and power, in the character of the leading men and natural interests of the country." [1] This was government under aristocratic leadership, but certainly not by the will of the people.

The lower classes in England were helpless in the grasp of this privileged class, which was made up of lawyers, wealthy landholders, merchants, and a nobility whose ranks the other privileged classes strove to enter. The whole enfranchised body of citizens was a small group, and, therefore, all the more jealous of its monopoly of the places in Parliament and the lucrative offices of the realm. How little sympathy some of its more aristocratic members had with any democratic ideas is shown in the comment of the Duchess of Buckingham upon the doctrines of Methodism. She found them " most repulsive, and strongly tinctured with impertinence and disrespect toward their superiors, in perpetually

[1] Trevelyan, *The American Revolution.* I. 122.

endeavouring to level all ranks and do away with all distinctions. It is monstrous to be told that you have a heart as sinful as the common wretches that crawl the earth." [1] The lower class, "the common wretches," was inarticulate except for a few radical champions, and so little enlightened or politically experienced as to be of no value in upholding the American cause, had they understood it. The colonists could, therefore, look for little helpful sympathy from that British democracy which, in after years, was to become America's chief ally in the struggle for the dominance of free political institutions in the world.

The leadership of the privileged class in English politics fell, soon after the repeal of the Stamp Act, into the hands of a brilliant trifler, Charles Townshend. This came about through one of those strange series of events which have led the unskeptical of all ages to see the intervention of some Providence in human affairs. The members of the Rockingham Ministry had realized from the first that only if they could include Pitt in their councils could they hope to gain the confidence of the nation. As the time went on, it became clear that this indispensable member would not come to their aid. From the moment that was clear, the "administration was dead, only lying in state." To expect the King's hearty support was a castle in the air, since he had turned to them only as the last hope of escape from the assiduous moralizing of Grenville. Between them and him, a great gulf was fixed. George III founded

[1] Barbeau, *Life and Letters at Bath*, 164.

his reign on the principle that it was the King's duty to lead rather than to follow. George II, having discovered in bitterness that "ministers were kings in this country," his grandson, George III, had tried, from the first boyish days when he began to rule, to remove that stigma from the British Constitution. He would no longer be the puppet of the party dominating in Parliament.

At first he was successful in his efforts to overthrow the power of the Old Whigs, who had so plagued his revered grandsire. Parliament, once utterly subservient to the Whig nobility, became for the moment the obedient servant of the court. There was formed, however, an opposition party to the court, founded by the Duke of Newcastle, but known as the Rockingham Whigs. In their conception, government ought to be the representative of one political party in the State, not dominated by the Crown, but upheld by its own adherents in Parliament. They did, it is true, try to strip power from the King, in order to secure it for themselves, but in this process they were aiming at that system of government which time has made the dominant one in democratic countries, parliamentary government.

This faction and George III were each fighting for a principle, and William Pitt would not be drawn into the Rockingham Ministry because he sympathized with the King, and opposed strong party organization. Pitt still hugged the delusive phantom of a ministry from which no man of ability and integrity would be excluded, the members of which would not be listed under any factional banner. Fired again by his youthful reading of Bolingbroke, he yearned for a united country under a " Patriot King." These he would lead to the fulfillment of noble plans at home and abroad.

When the King's loan of the votes of his henchmen to the Opposition had made the existence of the Rockingham Ministry no longer possible, Pitt joined with George III to put an end to party government. He accepted the peerage, and set about forming a ministry in which he held only the office of Lord Privy Seal, and into which he brought a motley group made up of members of several political factions. Among his own friends Lord Camden became the Lord Chancellor, Lord Shelburne took charge of the colonial affairs, and the Duke of Grafton became the nominal head of the Ministry, though Chatham said in later years that he never "thought of that boy as the first minister of a great nation." Of Rockingham's followers, Conway retained his place as Secretary of State, and against Chatham's judgment, Charles Townshend, who had been constant to no faction, became Chancellor of the Exchequer. The Secretary of War was Lord Barrington, who also had no strong political ties. This curious assembly drew Burke's best invective. It was "an administration so checkered, . . . so crossly indented and so whimsically dovetailed . . . so variously inlaid, such a piece of diversified mosaic . . . here a bit of black stone and there a bit of white, patriots and courtiers, . . . Whigs and Tories, treacherous friends and open enemies.— that it was indeed a very curious show, but utterly unsafe to touch and unsafe to stand on." [1] This Cabinet was actually gathered at St. James's to kiss hands in token of their loyalty, before they learned, to their consternation, that their chief was now the Earl of Chatham. It was a blow at his prestige with the English people, and it took him from the House of Commons, where his presence was absolutely necessary for the success of the Ministry. He was Samson with his locks shorn, wrote Choiseul; only the twilight of his popularity seemed to remain. Men could not foresee that the Earl of Chatham was to rival the people's idol, Pitt, "the Great Commoner."

Hardly was this strange administrative contrivance created, when Chatham, half of whose life was spent in sickness and seclusion, was seized with one of the strange fits of despondency, the penalty which his high-strung nervous system paid for occasional powers beyond the reach of common men. That and gout, and a mediæval medical adviser, whose every remedy probably made his patient worse, kept him in bed when the fate of an empire was to be decided. [2] Such a ministry as Chatham had formed, even though made up of persons "whose imaginations he had subjugated," could have unity only in his presence. No one dared face him, and when he was in any group he stood alone. Burke, in a burst of raillery, described him as "one so immeasurably high . . . a being before whom thrones,

---

[1] Burke, *Works* (ed. 1869), II, 620.
[2] Winstanley *Lord Chatham and the Whig Opposition*, chap. I·
B. Williams, *William Pitt*, II, 241–43.

dominations, princedoms, virtues, powers, [waving his hand over the Ministry's bench] all veil their faces with their wings." [1]

When illness had eliminated Chatham, the nominal leader of the Ministry was the Duke of Grafton, who embraced Pitt's ideas with religious fervor. His early political studies, based on "the sound system of Mr. Locke" and his true friendliness toward America, promised a sympathetic conduct of their affairs. His own need of a leader, however, was shown in his words when, lately, he resigned from the Rockingham Ministry. Under Pitt, he said, he was "ready to take up a mattock or a spade." It was this man who should have shouldered the burden of responsibility; but when Lord Chatham could no longer leave his room, indeed, "before this splendid orb was entirely set," to borrow Burke's imagery, and "while the western horizon was in a blaze with his descending glory, on the opposite quarter of the heavens rose another luminary," Charles Townshend, "who for his hour became lord of the ascendant." This man, whom Horace Walpole thought "inferior to no man in any age" if his faults could have been moderated, whose ready wit, "boundless facility of repartee" and a gift of mimicry, compared to that of Garrick, caused him to be courted in every society, and to be the "spoilt child" of the House of Commons; this man who had neither consistency nor stability of character, in whose assertions one could have no faith, in his promises no trust, began to assume

[1] Pitt, *Correspondence*, III, 145 (note).

authority and to undo all of Chatham's work in two great branches of the government — in America and the East Indies.[1] Betraying his chief every hour, opposing his stand in the effort to reform the East India Company's affairs, he suddenly defied the whole Ministry with a proposal, as Chancellor of the Exchequer, of a "mode by which a revenue may be drawn from America without offence." He was, it is true, forced to do something to raise more money, because Dowdeswell and Grenville of the Opposition had pleased the country squires by forcing a deduction of one shilling from the four shilling land tax. The Ministry had opposed that reduction, had been beaten,[2] and ought to have resigned, but did not, and Townshend, "warm in the sunshine of majesty," seized the opportunity to declare before a delighted house, "I laugh at the absurd distinction between internal and external taxes"; and, forgetting the ringing assertion of that distinction by his absent chief, he declared the idea ridiculous to everybody except an American. He seemed to think that by overthrowing the logic of the colonists he could conquer their passion for freedom. He had estimated four hundred thousand pounds as the amount necessary to care for the colonial military expenses in the coming year, and

[1] B. Williams, *William Pitt*, II, 230. One looks in vain for surviving proofs of Townshend's brilliant wit. Neither the meager reports of his famous "Champagne Speech" nor reported conversations with him bear out in the least his repute as a superman. Historical MSS. Commission, *Reports (Various Collections)*, VI, 279–81.

[2] Four shillings on every pound of valuation, the total income from that source being over two million pounds.

the Opposition had demanded that it be cut in two and paid entire by America.

Being now "master of the revels," he recklessly proposed a tax — an external one, of course, since that pleased the meticulous Americans — and a reorganization of the customs service to make it effective; as the plan was worked out, the duties fell on red and white lead, on certain varieties of glass and paper, and on teas.[1] With the funds to be gained by this device, estimated at forty thousand pounds, Townshend proposed paying the salaries of royal officers in the colonies, thus setting free the colonial governors and judges from the control of American legislatures. Troublesome assemblies would thus become superfluous, and the administration of the colonies be simplified and centralized. Whatever remained out of this revenue would be used to pay for the defense of the colonies.

Besides the new duties, the regulations of the long-established colonial system were to remain for the protection of English manufacturers and merchants, but their high profits on what they sold in the protected American markets would be tapped for the benefit of the British treasury. All of this programme was carried through, including a board of commissioners to be stationed in America for the more effective execution of the Trade Acts, and so much more efficient were the new measures for en-

[1] Macdonald, *Select Charters*, 1606–1775, p. 323. There was a three penny duty on tea, but at the same time a remission of the duty paid by the East India Company at the English port to which it was brought before being shipped to America. Thus the dutied tea undersold smuggled tea in American markets.

forcement of the long-established Navigation Laws that the old colonial system was reëstablished, and Townshend might be said to have reënacted all the navigation and trade laws, which from 1660 on had been endured, chiefly because they were not obeyed.[1]

Before the last of the acts necessary to carry out these plans was actually enacted, Townshend died (September, 1767), leaving the Duke of Grafton to continue as best he could to ride the whirlwind which had been conjured up by his reckless colleague.

Long afterwards, Lord Lyttleton pointed out in the House of Lords (March 5, 1776) that it was under Grafton's Ministry that the act giving the first offense to the Americans was made; that his own hands had fired America, and that he presided over the treasury and urged Parliament to vote for these offensive measures. "He forgets the grand edifice which he has built and tries now to destroy his own work." To this Grafton answered: "This young lord was only yesterday admitted to the mysteries of this chamber, and he does not know the secrets of the cabinet. It was under my administration that the bill received the sanction of Parliament. But it was deception, and fraud which threw me blindly into this mistaken undertaking. It was represented in the cabinet that this tax was the least onerous for the Americans to make their public contributions. It was their choice, and to their taste. As soon as my eyes were opened, I urged the king to revoke it; but the majority silenced me, and stopped all my efforts to suppress this evil." [2]

[1] Channing, *Hist. of the U.S.*, III, 91.
[2] *Archives des Affaires Étrangères, Angleterre*, vol. 515, no. 4.

Nevertheless, it was, perhaps, now within Grafton's power to have reorganized the Ministry on liberal lines, and to have reversed the fatal policy left in Townshend's legacy. But he was too timid, and so eager to please that he would do wrong rather than offend. His frequent threats to resign suggest, however, that he would gladly have run away from political dangers. It was at this time, too, that he began to "postpone the world" for his hounds, a horse-race, or Nancy Parsons, whose attractions Gainsborough has made it quite possible for posterity to understand. Instead of increasing the Ministry's liberal character after it passed under his direction (September, 1767), he permitted changes which constantly tended to weaken that character.

Lord North succeeded to Townshend's place, and Shelburne's office was divided, leaving the fate of colonial affairs to Lord Hillsborough. Before the end of 1768, both Chatham and Shelburne had resigned, leaving Grafton the nominal as well as actual head.

All this tended to swell the influence of those who, descanting "upon the folly and wickedness of the American incendiaries," would force American subordination to Parliament. Moreover, the turn of affairs having revealed to George III the failure of his experiment with a powerful prime minister, who was expected to unite all factions under a "Patriot King," he now tried seizing the reins of power himself. His personal following was growing, and with its aid George III began to direct the march of political affairs until the influence of the Crown assumed alarming proportions. George III and his minister, using pensioners and placemen, bought with the nation's money and offices, bent the House of Commons to the royal will for some fifteen years. Given an honest Parliament, whose vote was not determined by "a band of hired men," paid to support the King, the truckling ministers who stood by George III might have found obedient majorities hard to maintain.[1]

When the news of the Townshend Acts reached America, it was revealed to the over-sanguine colonial mind that the repeal of the Stamp Act had implied no concessions to American political philosophy, no acknowledgment of the principle that taxation of the colonies was even inexpedient. It had meant nothing else to the official British mind but that the Stamp Act itself was a mistake. The accompanying modifications of the Sugar Act implied only a conviction that the Government had gone a little too far into trade regulations. Of course there would be new taxes not so objectionable, and efforts would be made to render more effective the old trade restrictions, so profitable to British traders and manufacturers. It was now clear that the British Parliament meant every word of its Declaratory Act, which asserted Parliament's right to pass laws to bind the colonies "in all cases whatsoever."

Not only was the American's purse touched, but his pride and his passion for self-government, now

---

[1] Hansard, *Parliamentary History*, xxx, 789. Grey's defense of a petition to reform Representation. *Parl. Reg.*, xxii, 147.

struggled for, and on the whole enjoyed, during nearly one hundred and fifty years. John Dickinson wrote to Mr. James Otis (December 5, 1767) that "Massachusetts must first kindle the Sacred Flame, that on such occasions must warm and illuminate the Continent." The colonies, he urged, "must instantly, vigorously and unanimously unite themselves . . . to maintain the Liberty with which Heaven itself hath made us free."[1] Men in those days wrote in exalted phrases that betokened their high spirit.

Dickinson himself, the first of whose famous "Farmer's Letters" had appeared three days before writing the above letter, did as much to kindle that flame as any one individual in America. His legal training in the Middle Temple, one of the Inns of Court in London, had given him a firm foundation in English common and statute law.[2] It was there, and not so much on natural law, that he and similarly trained Americans based their arguments against the British right to tax without their consent.[3] Charles Cotesworth Pinckney, who though constant for American liberty was a conservative, Edward Rutledge, who opposed independence to the last, and Daniel Dulany, who became a Loyalist after being the greatest opponent of the Stamp Act,

[1] *Warren-Adams Letters* (Mass. Hist. Soc. *Collections*), LXXII, 3–4.
[2] C. J. Stillé, *Life and Times of John Dickinson*, 21–30.
[3] *Ibid.*, 26. There were between 1760 and the close of the Revolution forty-seven from South Carolina, twenty-one from Virginia, sixteen from Maryland, eleven from Pennsylvania, five from New York, and only one or two from the New England States who were trained in the Middle Temple.

were, like Dickinson, trained in the Middle Temple. These men, while shy of revolution and of glittering generalities about immutable laws of nature, were vigorous advocates of constitutional resistance within the lines of English law. Dickinson, having written some able and convincing pamphlets at the time of the Stamp Act, began now to issue a series of "Letters from a Farmer." With an Arcadian simplicity, sure to appeal to a population which was over ninety per cent rural in its character, he descanted upon his modest prosperity, his library, his two or three friends of "ability and learning," and the knowledge of history and "the laws and constitution" of his country which he gained therefrom. Assured that the "sacred cause" of liberty "ought to be espoused by every man on every occasion, to the utmost of his power," he submitted arguments, not always consistent, at times even contradictory, but based on English law and English traditions, and always good enough to convince the colonial mind that Parliament's imposition of duties, not merely for the regulation of trade, but for raising money for imperial purposes, was "an innovation" and ought to be resisted. If Parliament could tax American imports, he warned the colonists it could overtax any colonial articles, which for selfish reasons England did not wish manufactured in America, and that done "the tragedy of American liberty is finished." He reminded his fellow countrymen that the colonies were "separated from the rest of the world, and firmly bound together by the same rights, interests and dangers. . . . They form one

political body of which each colony is a member."
This expressed an idea of which the colonists were
daily becoming more conscious, the inherent unity
of interest which distance from Europe, common
political institutions, contiguous territory, and not
wholly dissimilar conditions had created. Moreover,
he asserted, and was believed, "we are only as much
dependent on Great Britain as one perfectly free
people can be on another." These ideas were read
from Maine to Georgia and warmly approved by
nearly everybody except royal officers and their
henchmen.

Legislative protest and literary argument there
was in plenty, but also actual measures taken to
awaken the British Ministry to a sense of the harm
they had done to American interests. Such action
against the Townshend measures appeared earliest
in New England where the cumulative effects of all
the trade restrictions and burdens on commerce
were first felt. New York was not far behind in re-
taliatory measures; Philadelphia followed at the
Quaker City's well-known leisurely pace; while the
South did not give support until 1769. The planters
of that section were less seriously affected than the
northern merchants. It was these merchants who
were most vitally touched, and who were in a position to do something that would tell. As practical
men they did not stake much on appeals to British
reason. The best argument, they were sure from
past experience, was that of profit or loss. Take
away the money made in English trade with America, and make it clear that the loss was the con-

sequence of unwise acts of Parliament, and true penitence would follow. A hurt to English trade was a spur to English reason. Non-importation of British goods was a means of awakening the English conscience. Power to starve meant power to convince. Therefore, the effort to use the boycott is the big fact in the Revolutionary movement before the Continental Congress.[1]

The first move to this end was not taken by the merchants, but by the town meetings in Massachusetts. In the fall of 1767 hard times had come, men talked of high war taxes and "unfavorable balance of trade." "Deluges of bankruptcies"; "alarming scarcity of money"; "stagnation of trade" which was loaded with restrictions, and general distress called for efforts to reduce the cost of living.[2]

In the town meetings, Boston leading, agreements not to purchase stated lists of imported goods were made and signed. Home manufactures, especially of glass and paper, were to be patronized by the signers, and all agreed to be frugal as to mourning. Though tea was not included, the ladies were urged in the press to give up luxurious and enervating Bohea, which they were assured was the source of many modern complaints; "tremblings, apoplexies and consumptions." This they later agreed to do, though the men, they hoped the public would notice, did not give up their wine and rum in the taverns.[3] Ultimately fifteen hundred families

---

[1] Schlesinger, *The Colonial Merchants*, 105.
[2] *Ibid.*, 106.   [3] *Ibid.*, 107–10.

in Boston had given up tea, and Harvard students
also gave up that form of stimulant. Soon the press
began to tell of the saving of rags and the making of
paper, and of theses at Harvard printed on the
domestic product. Efforts were made to revive the
linen industry, and the Boston town meeting subsidized free spinning schools to help the poor. Spinning became such a social diversion that Peter Oliver
sourly commented, "the female spinners kept on
spinning six days of the week, and on the seventh
the Parsons took their turns and spun out their
prayers and sermons to a long thread of Politics."
Some progress was actually made toward industrial
independence, but complete success could not be
reached because capital was shy, fearing lest such
enterprises should collapse when trade should be
renewed.[1] The Boston plan spread to Rhode Island
and Connecticut, but stopped there, and had no
vogue outside of New England, where, indeed, it
failed to relieve hard times.

The next effort was aimed more at coercing England than cutting the high cost of living. It was an
effort of the northern merchants at a non-importation league. These merchants were concerned not
merely with the Townshend Acts, but they hoped
to restore the old conditions of trade before 1764.
This aim they never abandoned, until by 1770 they
became alarmed by the violence of the mob, an
awakened self-conscious group of radicals, whose
fires of discontent had been fanned by the agitation
against the offensive acts of Parliament.[2] Even

---

[1] Schlesinger, *The Colonial Merchants*, 122-23.   [2] *Ibid.*, 91.

strong men, if they feared the tyranny of mob rule more than the tyranny of Parliament, were soon cured of disorderly methods. The gentle memorial and the insinuating boycott would do, if it did not lead to the riot; when that began, the merchants realized that they had overreached themselves in summoning up a genius of sedition, the unprivileged classes, that could not be conjured back again. The merchant differed from the other groups of malcontents, in that he valued the empire and did not desire to disturb its foundations. Reform and not rebellion was his aim.

At first, however, they did not foresee such an outcome, and the Boston merchants hesitated about a boycott of English goods only because they feared that New York and Philadelphia would not join them. Spurred by the "Letters of a Farmer," who reminded them of the success of non-importation in the time of the Stamp Act, an effort was made (March, 1768) to create a non-importation league. At the "British Coffee House" in Boston, they drew up, and a big majority signed, an agreement not to import from England for one year, if New York and Philadelphia would make a like agreement.[1]

It was easier to get the merchants to sign such promises, because they were made desperate by the hardship to trade, legal or illegal, introduced by the new "American Board of Commissioners of the Customs" whose jurisdiction ranged from Florida to Davis Straits. The whole customs service was remodeled and furbished up with new and more

---

[1] Schlesinger, *The Colonial Merchants*, 114–15.

modern business methods. There was a horde of new employees, mostly Britishers and not colonists, who were looked upon as a swarm of office-holders fattening upon the fruits of colonial toil. Peculation and laziness were reduced and a unity brought into the whole customs machine. Smuggling was much reduced, but at a cost of putting colonial commerce to great expense and trouble. There were new fees, new bonds, new certificates. Every master of a vessel must have a list or "Cocket" accounting for every item in the cargo. "Writs of Assistance" were more generally used, the coast patrol was improved, and smaller vessels than were used in the past pried into every creek or inlet. The burdens were so increased that trade of certain kinds was stopped altogether. By this pestiferous efficiency, however, thirty thousand pounds yearly was collected for six years, at an annual cost of thirteen thousand pounds.[1]

Impelled by like experiences, and by the recent action of the Boston merchants, the traders of New York met in April, 1768, and signed an agreement not to import British goods after October 1st, if Boston would abide by its late action, and Philadelphia would join the league. Boston did not like the delay of six months, but remained firm for non-importation. Philadelphia merchants, however, not suffering the trade embarrassments to a like extent, and unmoved by the pleas of their fellow townsman, Dickinson, did not take the proposed league seriously. From this indifference to the Continental

[1] Channing, *Hist. of the U.S.*, III, 90–91.

cause, they could not be moved and the projected league collapsed.[1]

The Boston merchants now took up the question of independent action, not contingent on agreement by other ports. A new covenant (August 1, 1768) bound the signers, all but sixteen merchants, to cease ordering goods, and to discontinue all imports with certain needful exceptions for one year after January 1, 1769.[2] Other trading towns in Massachusetts emulated this action. The New York merchants on August 27th signed a compact with the same general aim, and the retailers signed a separate agreement, neither to buy nor sell goods brought in contrary to the merchants' covenant. Even the smugglers promised not to bring in goods from Hamburg or Holland.[3] On September 1st, the New York merchants sent a copy of their agreements to the Philadelphia importers. There the great Quaker merchants were masters of the situation, and were resolved not to suspend trade until petitions and prayers to the King and Parliament, lately sent by the provincial assembly, were proven vain. When for their tameness they were denounced in the public press as "selfish, dastardly merchants," a few of them were stung to action which, however, came to nothing but a new and mild memorial to the merchants and manufacturers of Great Britain, merely warning them that importations must be

[1] Schlesinger, *The Colonial Merchants*, 116–19.

[2] *Ibid.*, 120. Later changed to such a time as there should be a repeal of the Townshend duties.

[3] *Ibid.*, 124; Becker, *Political Parties in the Province of New York,* 163.

curtailed if relief did not soon come.[1] Again they
waited, only to learn that the London merchants
could do nothing, and not until February, 1769, did
public opinion drive them to action. Then there
was merely a cancellation of orders under certain
conditions, but, March 10th, a great majority of the
merchants agreed to accept no goods shipped after
April 1st until the Townshend Acts should be repealed.[2] All who refused to sign were to be "dis-
countenanced by all lawful and prudent measures,"
a threat well within the proprieties in the "City of
Brotherly Love." Gathering spirit with momentum,
they later extended the principle of the boycott and
stigmatized all violators as "enemies of the Liberties
of America." By the spring of 1769, therefore, the
three great northern ports had non-importation
agreements, Philadelphia limping into the arrangement some six months later.

It would have been easy for these agreements to
become a mere "scrap of paper." So much depended upon good faith that opponents had only to
whisper suspicions, and rumor, with its thousand
tongues, would spread them. There was the sneer
that the plan only enabled the merchant to oblige
one "to take old moth-eaten clothes that had been
rotting in the shop for years, and to pay a monstrous
price for them." Was it not better to pay the
Townshend duties forever than to pay the shameful
prices thus exacted? The merchants with empty

[1] Schlesinger, *The Colonial Merchants*, 126–27.
[2] *Ibid.*, 128. Some twenty-two articles were excepted for good
reasons.

warehouses questioned the honesty of those who still had goods to sell. Boston suspected New York of taking advantage by delay. New York retorted that Boston was more active in "resolving what it ought to do than in doing what it had resolved." In Boston the Governor and customs officers were suspected of exerting "every nerve to render abortive the non-importation agreement."[1] They certainly had in their service a veritable marplot in the person of John Mein of the "Boston Chronicle." Having access apparently to the customs records, he published from time to time very meticulous accounts of large quantities of goods imported by signers of the agreements. Though the committee appointed by the merchant body to inspect the official cargo lists assured the public that Mein was twisting the facts to suit his purpose, yet he created an atmosphere of suspicion which was hard to dispel. It did no good to call him a "conceited empty Noddle of a most profound Blockhead" if he made some people believe that even John Hancock kept "a number of vessels running to London and back, full freighted, getting rich by receiving freight on goods made contraband by the colonies."[2] The merchants' committees spread broadcast certain handbills urging all to boycott the stores of a small group, including the sons of the Lieutenant-Governor, who had refused to sign the agreements, but John Mein published a list of signers, "a few grave, well disposed Dons," whom he accused with great

---

[1] Schlesinger, *The Colonial Merchants*, 157.   [2] *Ibid.*, 168.

circumstance of clandestine importation of the very
goods they were sworn to boycott. His columns were
open also to foes of the merchants' committees.
Should we not blush to talk of liberty? cried one.
"Have we not established courts of inquisition in
the colonies unparalleled in any age or nation?
Where . . . was there ever an instance of men, free
men, being summoned by illegal and mock authority
to answer for actions as offences which are war-
ranted by the laws of the land, the law of nations
and the law of God?" [1]

Maddened by such opposition, it was finally voted
by the "patriotic" merchants that the offensive
editor, John Mein, and the merchants who refused
to join in the boycott of English merchants, "deserve to be driven to the obscurity from which they
originated, and to the Hole of the Pit from whence
they were digged." This condemnation was printed
on handbills and pasted over mercantile chimney
places and sent far and wide through the province. [2]
Mein was at last mobbed and his life endangered as
the best answer to his stubborn arguments.

When at last the whole body of Boston merchants,
more than a thousand persons, marched in solemn
and orderly array to the stores of those who refused
to join the boycott, the Lieutenant-Governor denounced their house-to-house marchings *en masse*,
as conducive to terror, and dangerous in tendency.
His council, by a bare majority agreed. [3] As a result
of the boycott, Hutchinson wrote that contraband

---

[1] Schlesinger, *The Colonial Merchants*, 170–71.
[2] *Ibid.*, 177. [3] *Ibid.*, 176–77.

tea from Holland may be lawfully sold, while "it's a high crime to sell any from England." It was clear that the merchants alone dominated public opinion. In general, it may be said that they were earnest, and against heavy odds got good results.[1]

Customs records do not differentiate prohibited articles from those allowed, but available figures show a decrease of British imports of almost fifty per cent. They dropped from £430,806 to £223,694. Hutchinson admitted that the boycott was well enforced; Samuel Adams declared that the merchants "have punctually abode by their Agreement." [2]

Non-importation in New York differed little from that in Boston, except that the merchants' committee had the most trouble to prevent clandestine importation from Pennsylvania. The prohibition was very well enforced in New York. The radical element there was impatient with the deliberate measures of the merchants. Mass meetings threatened personal injury to violators, and one was made to repent on a scaffold erected near Liberty Pole. Though the merchants grew fearful of violence and "mobbish proceedings," nevertheless mob action made dubious traders beware.

In Philadelphia the opposition to non-importation, when once adopted, was very mild. Alexander Mackrabie, a visitor there in 1769, amusingly describes one effort to evade the vigilance of the committee: "a discontented Gentleman made a Purchase of a Cheshire Cheese last week; and another Mal-

[1] Schlesinger, *The Colonial Merchants*, 157, 178–79. [2] *Ibid.*, 182–83.

content thought to drown his Resentments in a
Hogshead of English Entire Butt. These Delicacies
happened misfortunately to be shipt from Europe
after the Resolutions on this side had transpired, and
of consequence Messrs. of the Committee took the
liberty to interfere. The Purchasers made a gallant
stand in defence of their bellies, but their Opposition
was vain. Hard words and bad Names flew about
in support of Liberty. They cursed and swore,
kicked and cuffed and pulled Noses; but the Catastrophe was, that the prisoners were regaled with
one and t'other — I mean the cheese and porter
— qualified with two dollars' worth of Bread. They
have sent away a ship loaded with Malt today.
Nobody would either buy or store it." [1] Besides
this and a few other serio-comic efforts at evasion,
there was little antagonism. Objection was made to
West Indian traders keeping up a profitable business, but the dissatisfaction took the form of efforts
to modify the boycott or repeal it. Though the
monthly Quaker meeting advised Friends to have
nothing to do with non-importation measures, many
prominent Quakers did not heed the advice.[2] There
was no mob violence in Philadelphia and none was
needed. British imports to Pennsylvania fell in
value from £441,829 in 1768 to £134,881 in 1770,
which is the best record in any of the continental
colonies.[3]

[1] *The Francis Letters*, I, 107.
[2] Schlesinger, *The Colonial Merchants*, 187–88; 191–92.
[3] *Ibid.*, 149–55; 193. The minor colonies, New Hampshire and
Rhode Island, observed the non-importation agreement indifferently,
but New Jersey, Delaware, and Connecticut did well in that matter.
Ibid., 194–96.

In the South the economic unrest was not so plainly a result of the Townshend Acts, and non-importation movements were slower and different in character. It was the planters there who were in trouble. Their habit of ordering goods from England, through a merchant who gave credit and took paper promises to pay with next year's crops, had left them, in these times, deeply in debt. The merchants, Scotchmen or Englishmen who marketed at home these southern staples, tobacco, rice, or indigo, had been little affected by the new duties, and it was the planters who finally grew desperate over their losing struggle to pay their debts. Their non-importation associations, aimed at cutting expenses and giving a blow to these creditors, came tardily, in 1769, and were resisted by the merchant class.[1] In Virginia the movement was initiated by George Washington, and in May, 1769, he and other members of the legislature, just dissolved by the Governor for questioning Parliament's right to tax them, met in a private house and formed an association. They pledged themselves not to use the dutied goods except cheap paper, and not to import a long list of luxuries, nor to buy slaves brought in after November 1st.[2] It was estimated that Great Britain lost not less than £300,000 by a like provision as to slaves in South Carolina. This agreement nearly all but the merchant class signed. In Maryland such a movement had already partly succeeded, and shortly after was crowned with success.

[1] Schlesinger, *The Colonial Merchants*, 135.
[2] *Ibid.*, 136–37, 207. C. R. Lingley, *The Transition in Virginia*, 56–57; Rowland, *Life of George Mason*, I, 143

In South Carolina the strong mercantile class, with its face set against non-importation, was met and vanquished by the workingmen led by Christopher Gadsden, a merchant and planter, but a born radical. The associations in the northern provinces, and urgent letters from the merchants there, pleading for united action, had not moved the merchants of Charleston, but early in 1769, agitation for use of economic pressure began in the local press. Gadsden pointed out that the importers of European goods were strangers in the provinces, many having only a few years' residence. To expect them to act was folly; let the freeholders and fixed settlers take the lead.[1] A non-importation agreement was offered, which the mechanics of Charleston approved at a meeting under the Liberty Tree, July 4, 1769, and it was signed by two hundred and thirty persons. The body of merchants frowned on this affair, and denounced the burden laid upon them as "more grievous than ever was conceived by the most arbitrary minister of the most despotic King." At a meeting they adopted less rigorous regulations, hoping to moderate the mechanics' demands, but class feeling rose daily until the merchants agreed to a joint committee, which arranged terms satisfactory to all, but which represented a victory for Gadsden's followers.[2] The agreement was to remain in force until all the Parliamentary Acts of regulation were repealed. In Georgia, where there was a like situation, the merchants made a determined effort to head off the popular movement; but in

---

[1] Schlesinger, *The Colonial Merchants*, 141–43.   [2] *Ibid.*, 144–46.

vain, for the terms finally agreed upon were little different from those adopted in South Carolina two months earlier. North Carolina came at a snail's pace behind them all, but at last under the leadership of Cornelius Harnett the "Sons of Liberty" defied Governor Tryon, and adopted a non-importation association well in keeping with that of her neighbors.

In spite of the success on paper in the southern colonies, imports from England actually increased in the years 1769 and 1770, Virginia importing most of all. There were no trading centers wherein prying committees could discipline unfaithful merchants. The dispersion of population in a planting province made it impossible for even the eyes of Argus to detect evasions of the covenants. Enforcement could not be made a part of the daily routine, as in Boston, New York, or Philadelphia. Even George Washington was lax when it came to literal obedience.[1] It was futile anywhere in the South unless merchants and factors had their hearts in the undertaking. Georgia's agreement, once made, was speedily ignored. In North Carolina, too, it seems to have been disregarded.[2] In South Carolina the greatest opponent of non-importation was Henry Drayton who later went over wholly to the revolutionary cause. He opposed on legal and constitutional grounds, denouncing the threats against non-signers as "Popish methods of gaining converts to their religion by fire and faggot. To stigmatize a man . . . with the infamous name of *an enemy to his country*

---

[1] Schlesinger, *The Colonial Merchants*, 197–98.   [2] *Ibid.*, 208–09.

can be *legally* done," he declared, "by no *authority*
but by *that* of the *voice* of the Legislature." Gadsden,
who was denounced by Drayton as a "Cromwell,"
replied that whenever the people's rights are shame-
fully invaded by a corrupt Parliament, mankind
exerts "those *latent*, though *inherent* rights of SOCIETY
which *no climate, no time, no constitution, no contract*
can ever destroy or diminish." Gadsden had the
backing of the community, and Drayton's opposition came to naught.[1] Besides the fact that two
thirds of the committee of enforcement were mechanics and planters,[2] the success of non-importation in Charleston was assured by the bitter resentment aroused by the local agents of the British
Government, both in the customs house and in the
Court of Vice-Admiralty created by the Townshend
Acts. Henry Laurens, conservative as nature had
made him, was won to the side of opposition to
England by his maddening experiences (1767–68)
with these men, whom he likened to the "miscreants
who were driven out of the Temple by Jesus with
a scourge of small cords." One collector, Laurens
declared, "had caused more vexation to the merchants in six months . . . than all of the king's
officers since the beginning of the colony." Such
officers, he added, "are the most likely instruments
to affect disunion between the mother country and
her American offspring." [3] Unfortunately for the

---

[1] Schlesinger, *The Colonial Merchants*, 204–05.

[2] There were thirteen planters, thirteen merchants, and thirteen
mechanics on the committee to execute the non-importation association. Wallace, *Henry Laurens*, 124.

[3] Wallace, *Henry Laurens*, 138, 141, 143, 148, 149.

British Empire, there were too many such insects stinging the colonists to madness. It is noteworthy that South Carolina's boycott was to remain in force until the customs board should be abolished and the vice-admiralty jurisdiction in cases of violation of the customs laws be annulled.

Hardly had the South swung into the non-importation ranks when a number of conditions began to threaten the whole organization. First of all, the merchants who were warm enough for economic reform when their pockets were touched, cooled rapidly when they discovered that the "Sons of Liberty" were looking upon them as standard-bearers leading into battle for constitutional rights.[1] Repeal of irritant trade acts was all very well, but the rights of man and a reform of the imperial system, won by mob action or even, perhaps, at the cannon's mouth, did not make so great an appeal to men of property. Moreover, the real burden of non-importation, after the first advantage reaped in high prices, fell upon the merchants of the commercial provinces, who were nevertheless denounced as "extortioners" if they raised prices to offset declining business. Alexander Mackrabie wrote from Philadelphia, in January of 1770, that the Americans had overshot the mark. "The Stores are empty; those Persons who have Goods lately imported, and in the Possession of the Committees are discontented, and will soon grow clamorous. Rogues are making their advantage, and the Quakers grow cold and plead Conscience. Here are few Manufacturers

[1] Schlesinger, *The Colonial Merchants*, 210.

to supply the deficiency of Goods from Europe."[1]
They were further afflicted by a decrease in the export trade to England which began to be felt in
1769.[2] Finally in May, 1770, came the news,
presaged nearly a year before, that Parliament had
repealed the Townshend duties except the tax on
tea, which was kept because George III held that
"there must always be one tax to keep up the right."
The Massachusetts merchants, with their prosperity bound up with unrestricted foreign commerce,
alone remained firm for the principle. They had,
indeed, been pushing (1769) for more radical
measures which should be aimed at the whole restrictive system, but had received no encouragement
from New York or Philadelphia.[3]

Albany, Providence, Portsmouth, and Newport
now made a premature break from the agreement
into which they had been dragged "like an ox to the
slaughter." Threatened with boycott by the great
trading centers, they wavered back and forth for a
time, and the fate of non-importation was left with
Boston, New York, and Philadelphia. Boston stood
like a rock, but in the other great cities there were
conflicting views. The great merchants believed
half a loaf better than none, and would accept the
remedial act. The other classes, workingmen and
tradesmen, with little property to lose, and animated
by their radical leaders with visions of a new heaven

---

[1] *The Francis Letters*, i, 110.

[2] Schlesinger, *The Colonial Merchants*, 211–12. There is an excellent
table of statistics for the exports from the colonies in 1771 in Channing, *Hist. of the U.S.*, iii, 116.

[3] Schlesinger, *The Colonial Merchants*, 132–33.

and a new earth in the political world, were for insistence on principle and a complete repeal of the
Townshend duties.

Philadelphia, supported by Franklin's advice to
hold on, might have stood firm, but New York, the
real pillar of the mercantile edifice, fell under the
assaults of Mammon, the interests of the great
merchants. The two factions struggling for mastery
there resorted at last to a house-to-house canvass
which on the face of the results seemed to indicate
a desire to resume trade with England. While the
decision was still in doubt came the report that Parliament, to relieve New York's money stringency,
had authorized the issue of £120,000 legal tender
paper money. Against that good news and the
rumor that Boston was importing on the sly, the
utmost efforts of Isaac Sears, the ultra-radical
leader of the mechanics, were in vain. Even his
rioting followers could not frighten the merchants,
and importation, except for tea, was resumed.[1]
It was of no use for James Madison and his fellow
students at Princeton to assemble in black gowns
and witness the burning by the hangman of the
letter that brought the news, or for the Philadelphia
mass meeting to condemn this "sordid and wanton
Defection," or for the meeting in Faneuil Hall to
declare "its abhorrence and detestation." The patriotic indignation of all the other provinces could
not change the fact that the great pillar of non-
importation was prone. Even Boston could not
preserve the Spartan spirit. "Persons in trade,"

[1] Schlesinger, *The Colonial Merchants*, 222-27.

wrote Andrew Eliot, "were weary, and, as interest is generally their god, began to be furious." A last hope lay in an effort to get an inter-colonial congress of merchants, but the Boston invitation to Philadelphia arrived after the Quaker City merchants had joined the general rout.[1] After that defection in the commercial provinces the associations in the southern provinces crumbled. In South Carolina, the boycott had caused the price of rice to decline, and this loss hastened the decision to follow the North in resuming importations except tea and any other dutied articles. In Virginia, too, the feeble non-importation spirit flickered out.

Though the English merchants and manufacturers suffered loss of trade, there was little real distress caused by the American boycott. The Bishop of St. Asaph must have exaggerated when he declared that during the non-importation measures "We suffered more by our loss of trade with them, than the wealth flowing in from India was able to recompense." War in Europe, coincident with falling of exports to the colonies, increased the demand for wool goods in Germany. Bountiful crops in England lowered the price of foodstuffs to the workingman. Though the British merchants presented a petition to Parliament to repeal the Townshend Acts, Franklin thought they did it reluctantly, and their action seems to have "furnished merely the occasion, not the cause, for Lord North's motion to repeal all the Townshend duties save the tea tax."[2] The partial

---

[1] Schlesinger, *The Colonial Merchants*, 228–32.

[2] Force, *American Archives* (4th Ser.), I, 99; Schlesinger, *The Colonial Merchants*, 237–39.

repeal came only in consequence of a wish to correct a law founded upon a principle which had proved harmful to British commercial interests.

North had come to the head of the Ministry as a result of the resignation of Lord Chatham late in 1768, and of the Duke of Grafton, early in 1770. Chatham had slowly fought his way back to health, while sadly watching his subordinates betray, as it seemed to him, the trust he had put in them. Besides permitting the colonial dispute to be revived, Grafton was in the act of intriguing to compel the resignation from the Ministry of Lord Shelburne, one of the only two men there who still possessed Chatham's confidence, when that greatest and most popular statesman of his generation resigned and was accompanied by Lord Shelburne.[1] From that moment Grafton's position was precarious; he never knew when Chatham would use all his splendid powers to overthrow the strangely metamorphosed ministry that had once been his own. Not until January of 1770 did the bolt strike, when Chatham, who had not attended Parliamentary debates for three years, rose to answer the Speech from the Throne, and called upon the "descendants of the Barons of Runnymede to emulate their predecessors and right the wrongs of a distressed nation." [2] Pointing out the evils of the time, and the universal discontent, he moved a resolution which was an indictment of the Ministry, and he was supported

---

[1] Alvord, *The Mississippi Valley in British Politics*, II, 14–16. Winstanley, *Chatham and the Whig Opposition*, 235–36.

[2] *Chatham and the Whig Opposition*, 293–94.

by Lord Camden, who had reluctantly remained with Grafton. That act doomed Camden, and the effort to replace him ending in the tragedy which closed the life of Charles Yorke, who had been chosen for the place, Grafton himself resigned. Drubbed as he had been for months by Junius, "the Mars of Malcontents," about whom everybody was asking with Mackrabie, "Who the devil can he be?" Grafton slunk with relief out of the light that beats upon a prime minister. With Grafton's fall, the Ministry should have fallen and Parliament been dissolved, but George III, in his hate of the men who had sought to thwart his will, refusing to turn to Chatham or Rockingham, upheld his Ministry against the attacks of the Opposition and appealed to Lord North to rescue him from his peril by becoming the head of the Ministry. He did his master's bidding, not only then, but for a dozen years thereafter, at the cost of dismembering the British Empire, and the eternal blackening of his own reputation.

CHAPTER XI

MEASURES THAT RAISED REBELLION BUT DID
NOT QUELL IT

THE Acts for which Townshend was responsible had not been solely concerned with matters of commerce nor was the reaction against them confined to a merchants' boycott. One of the most offensive provisions of the Act which laid duties on certain articles was that the revenue derived was to defray "the charge of the administration of justice, and the support of civil government, in such provinces where it shall be found necessary" and to pay the expenses of defending the colonies.[1] So sure were the Ministry of success of their plan for taxing America to pay its own officers that Pownall, explaining the Duke of Grafton's purpose, wrote Hutchinson, "It is meant that you shall have a handsome salary fixed as Chief Justice, as soon as the American revenue shall create a fund." This purpose Governor Bernard says became known to Otis and Adams who informed the Massachusetts Legislature that Hutchinson was a pensioner of Great Britain and that he actually had a warrant from the Lords of the Treasury for £200 a year out of the new duties.[2] There is, wrote a Loyalist, "no absurdity in politics however gross or impossible to be true, but meets with entire assent" as soon as published.[3] If judges,

[1] Pickering, *Statutes at Large*, XXVII, 505–12.
[2] *Warren-Adams Letters*, p. 7.
[3] British Museum, *Egerton MSS.*, 2659 F 141.

and perhaps governors too, asked the radicals, were to be paid out of funds extorted from the colonies by Parliament, where was their self-government? Josiah Quincy reminded his readers of the words of that silly tyrant, King James, "Let me make the judges, I care not who makes the laws"—and asked, "Could Nero wish more?" The fear of thus being robbed of the control of the officers appointed over them aroused that eternal vigilance which had marked the long colonial struggle to attain self-rule. Having learned from the English Parliament how to starve an executive into obedience, they had no mind to be deprived by Parliament of that useful weapon. If a governor should come not to have to "begg his daily bread from a hard hearted assembly," he might become a mere tool of the British Ministry, and that, as Samuel Adams expressed it in the Massachusetts "Circular Letter," would tend to subvert the principles of equity, and endanger the happiness and security of the subject.[1] In the "Letters of a Farmer" John Dickinson pointed out that the power to withdraw supplies was "one of the foundations of liberty," and he quoted Hume, "whose political reflections are so much admired," as to the use made of that power by Englishmen in the past. Dry remonstrances are of no use with kings and governors, he asserted, because "*They* CANNOT understand the reasoning that opposes *their* power and desires. But let it be made *their interest* to understand such reasoning — and a *wonderful light* is instantly thrown upon the matter; and then,

[1] Massachusetts, *State Papers*, 134–36.

rejected remonstrance becomes as clear as proofs of holy writ." [1]

Another phrase which disturbed the serenity of the colonial mind was the one explaining that the proceeds of the tax were to pay the expense of protecting "the British colonies and plantations in America." Dickinson regarded that intent as "more dreadful than the Stamp Act" because that measure proposed to pay the expense of defending the thirteen British colonies only, while this applied to Florida and Canada, lately Spanish and French colonies. "So that the *British colonies* are to be drained of the rewards of their labor, to cherish the scorching sands of *Florida*, and the icy rocks of *Canada* and *Nova Scotia*, which never will return to us one farthing that we send to them." [2] Moreover, on the whole subject of the support of soldiers for colonial defense the provincial mind was already in a state of irritation. The Quartering Act, which had been passed in April, 1765, at the solicitation of General Gage, commander-in-chief of the British armies in America, laid considerable burdens upon any colonial community where a large proportion of the proposed army of ten thousand men might be stationed. New York was selected by Gage as his headquarters not by reason of the need of troops there, but because of its strategic advantages. As a result a large part of the burden fell upon that province, which did not at first object to the presence of the troops, but did object to an act of Parliament commanding them to do a thing which actually

---

[1] John Dickinson, *Political Writings*, I, 225–26.   [2] *Ibid.*, I, 221.

laid a tax upon them because of the expense that
accrued in complying with the act. Two weeks
after the arrival of the troops, the New York Assembly, pressed by the Governor, passed an act
complying in part, but omitting the salt, vinegar,
"beer or cyder" for which the Quartering Act provided.[1] The conduct of New York in other respects
also was such as to draw from Chatham, the "great
advocate of the colonies," confessions of irritation.
"New York has drunk deepest of the baneful cup
of infatuation," he wrote to Shelburne. He admitted
that their disobedience to the Mutiny Act would
"*justly* create a great ferment" in Parliament, and
leave "no room to say any word in their defense."
As a result of the refractory conduct of the New
York Assembly, one of the Townshend Acts suspended the legislative privileges of that body until
complete provision in accord with the law was made
for the King's troops.[2] There was no difficulty in
getting such a law through Parliament, because
many had come to believe that the leniency at the
time of the Stamp Act was a blunder. The landed
aristocracy of England, unaffected by economic
loss, had thought all the time that the colonists were
rebels and ought to be quelled by military force.
It was an age of blood and iron in England among
the governing classes. The critics of the conciliatory
policy were confirmed by American observers like
Governor Bernard, who informed Lord Barrington
that, "since the Insurrections against the Stamp-

[1] Becker, *Political Parties in the Province of New York*, 54.
[2] Pickering, *Statutes at Large*, xxvii, 609, 610.

Act, The Americans have found the Governments
so contemptibly weak & the People so superior to the
Royal Authority that they are not a little elated
upon their Triumphs over the defenceless Officers
of the Crown. . . . It will cost much time & Treasure
to bring America to that Degree of submission Parliament would desire." [1] No doubt Shelburne's secretary was right when he wrote that by the Stamp
Act revolt the American habits of obedience were
broken. Even riots in England were attributed to
the "indulgence shown to America." They had
"imported rebellion from America," cried the
Tory Jeremiahs. There must be no more of that
"extraordinary indulgence" with which Parliament
had treated "these undutiful children." The restraining act was passed, therefore, with little opposition.[2] A serious clash was avoided, however, by
the fact that the New York Assembly, even before
the news of the measure reached them, had voted
the money necessary to meet all provisions of the
Quartering Act, saving its face by not itemizing the
"salt, vinegar, beer or cyder" which were in dispute.
Governor Moore interpreted that action as rendering
the restraining act of no effect and the assembly was
allowed to function as usual.[3] The principle involved
was not allowed to escape the colonial mind, however, for the first of the "Letters of a Farmer," read
throughout America, made clear that New York had

[1] *Barrington-Bernard Correspondence*, 95.
[2] Pownall, *Thomas Pownall*, 194–98. Pownall, who had been
governor of Massachusetts and who understood the provincial mind,
opposed in a strong speech that went to the heart of the whole matter
[3] Becker, *Political Parties in the Province of New York*, 57.

been "punished in a manner pernicious to American freedom and justly alarming to all of the colonies." [1] As all the people of England were interested in Hampden's ship-money cause, so must all give attention to this "dreadful stroke aimed at the liberties of these colonies." He is "not a wise man who folds his arms, and reposes himself at home, viewing with unconcern the flames that have invaded his neighbors house." The Massachusetts House of Representatives wrote to Dennys De Berdt, its agent in London, urging him to protest against the restraining act. "A legislative body," ran a passage of the letter, "without the free exercise of the powers of legislation, is to us incomprehensible. There can be no material difference between such a legislative and none at all." The New York Legislature has no "free exercise of legislative power, while their very existence is suspended upon their acting in conformity to the will of another body. Such a restriction throughout the colonies, would be a short and easy method of annihilating the legislative powers of America." [2] The New York Legislature itself sent to Parliament (December 17, 1767) a series of resolutions one of which declared that the restraining act (which in fact had never operated for a day) was "destructive of the very end of representation." [3]

The same principle was involved when the House

---

[1] John Dickinson, *Political Writings*, I, 143–50.

[2] Samuel Adams, *Writings*, I, 147. Massachusetts had its own quarrel with the royal governor (January, 1767), over the lodging of a company of artillery and therefore felt strongly in the matter. *Ibid.*, 133.

[3] Hansard, *Parliamentary Debates*, XVI, 604.

of Lords voted an address to His Majesty, "to be presented by the Lords with the White Staves," that he should give instructions to the governors of the colonies to "require the several assemblies to vote a compensation for the owners of property destroyed during the Stamp Act tumults." The House of Commons used the expression "ought to have" compensation,[1] and whatever the King's Minister intended Samuel Adams declared that "His Majesty's most gracious & mild Recommendation, a Term which his Lordship & our noble and generous Patrons took so much Pains to use, was construed by the Govr of this Province into a Requisition precluding all Deliberation."[2] Such language Adams explained was "very displeasing" to the representatives of a free people. After a long wrangle with the Governor over the question as to whether the granting of compensation was an act of "justice" or of "generosity," and as to whether the reputation of the town of Boston was implicated or not, the Massachusetts Assembly passed a compensation act (December, 1766) which was later disallowed by the Privy Council because it also granted an amnesty to the members of the mob.[3] In New York there was a similar reluctance, but an ultimate partial obedience.

[1] *Journals of the House of Lords*, xxxi, 262 (February 10, 1766). The word "recommend" was originally proposed, but by a vote of 63 to 60 was changed to "require." *Grenville Papers*, iii, 358; Hansard, *Parliamentary History*, xvi, 161–62.

[2] Samuel Adams, *Writings*, i, 97.

[3] Palfrey, *History of New England*, v, 366–67. The money had been paid by the time the veto was made known and the matter ended there.

Governor Bernard of Massachusetts had the fatal gifts of a wrangler, and his irritating disputations with the colonial assembly led him and his government ever farther afield from the straight and narrow path which might have been the guide to a state of peace and harmony. He chopped logic with the assembly over its choice of speaker, over his right to negative its election of a council, and concerning the use of the word "requisition" rather than "recommendation." With such unseemly bickerings, he lost his own influence and nagged his people into a state of passion in spite of the best of intentions on his part.[1] One of the great sources of friction between England and her colonies was that which no human ingenuity could prevent as long as the Government of the country sent its citizens, imperfect human beings, necessarily not the best, but only the most available, to rule three thousand miles from home a people whose inferior cultural development the imported rulers were sure to misunderstand and with whose love of self-government they would have no sympathy. Bernard became at last (1769) so plainly incapable of managing the situation in his province that he was pensioned and recalled to England. It was none too soon, for public opinion of him, whether justified or not, was shown in an indictment against him by a grand jury of Suffolk County which found that in many letters to the British Ministry he had "maliciously, willfully and falsely . . . libeled slandered and defamed" the Council of Massachusetts Bay and tried to intro-

[1] *Barrington-Bernard Correspondence*, xvi–xxi.

duce an arbitrary government there.[1] There is an eloquent entry in the diary of John Rowe (August 1, 1769), "the Rippon, Man of War — for England and Gov'r. Bernard went home in him. The flag hoisted on the Liberty Tree the Bells Ringing — Great Joy to the People. A great Bonfire in King St. and on Fort Hill." Such was Boston's delight in speeding the parting guest.

Long before the departure of this unpopular governor, things were going from bad to worse, not only in New England, but throughout the colonies, owing to the gradual rise of the tempest over the Townshend Acts. The efficient service of the new customs commissioners broke the power of the smugglers and made the evasion of the old trade regulations or of the new Townshend duties very difficult. The modification of the Sugar Act had removed the incentive to smuggle the incredible quantities of rum which were imbibed by the mechanics of that bibulous age, but the heavy duties — seven pounds sterling per tun on the rich man's Madeira wines — offered a dazzling premium to the successful smuggler. The passion of that generation for alcoholic stimulation passed beyond the imagination of this somber age, following the Eighteenth Amendment. That reigning thirst had to be satisfied and public sympathy was all with the benevolent gentlemen who tried to import wine without paying the duty. At Boston so ominous was the conduct of the populace toward the commissioners who would enforce the law that those officers

[1] Palfrey, *History of New England*, v, 415.

repeatedly requested a public vessel to protect them, and in the spring of 1768 secured the presence of the man-of-war Romney. They were pressing Hillsborough for a regiment of soldiers in addition when events occurred which convinced the Ministry of the wisdom of the request. John Adams wrote that "a great uproar was raised in Boston on account of the unlading in the night of a cargo of wines from the sloop Liberty from Madeira, belonging to Mr. Hancock, without paying the customs."[1] He did not explain that Kirk, the tidesman, was "hoved down" into the cabin where for three hours he listened to men "a-hoisting out of goods" some of which were "good saleable Madeira." Later when Kirk had informed the proper officers the Liberty was seized and towed away under the guns of the Romney. The mob that watched this action flew into a passion, assaulted the customs officers, broke the windows in their homes, and so frightened the commissioners that they retired to Castle William where they remained until the Ministry listened to their prayers, and October, 1768, some four months later, sent two regiments to protect the King's officers in Boston.[2] In other places informers were tarred and feathered; the revenue sloop Liberty was burnt at Newport; wine seized at Philadelphia was stolen by the mob under the very noses of the

[1] John Adams, *Works*, II, 215. Adams goes on to say that "Mr. Hancock was prosecuted on great number of libels for penalties upon acts of Parliament amounting to 90 or 100 thousand pounds sterling." Adams was his counsel and the case ended only with the battle of Lexington.

[2] Hutchinson, *History of Massachusetts Bay*, III, 190–95.

King's officers, and one of them who was beaten
went away swearing he would not tarry among such
a "sett of People" whose greatest pleasure would
be the opportunity of burying him.[1] It was not
strange that Loyalists wrote of the existence of a
"strange infatuation" never paralleled, and that
"rebellion hath reared its head high above the dic-
tates of reason, gratitude and interest."[2] There
was little popular response to John Dickinson's
pious exhortation, "Let us behave like dutiful
children who have received unmerited blows from a
beloved parent." The mob understood "turbulence
and tumult," better than "constitutional modes"
of protest.

We of this age, standing outside the turmoil of
rising rebellion, may smartly criticize the British
Government for sending soldiers to Boston. The
standing army which wise statesmanship had provided to protect the empire had fallen to a mere
military police to enforce hated laws on unwilling
subjects. Yet what other device had the world
known or used for securing obedience from deluded
citizens? England was peculiarly blessed to have
among her statesmen a Pitt, a Burke, a Camden,
or a Barré, even a few enlightened men, apostles of
a new era, who could see that "It is not by votes
and angry resolutions of this house [of Commons]
but by a slow and steady conduct that the Americans
are to be reconciled to us." It was not the spirit of

[1] *Rhode Island Colonial Records*, vi, 593–96; Mass. Hist. Soc., *Collections* (4th Ser.), x, 611–17.
[2] British Museum, *Egerton MSS.*, 2659 F 141.

the age to deal gently with far-away peoples, little understood, and for whom, indeed, the ruling class in England had a quiet contempt. It is plain to this sophisticated age that Secretary Conway, writing to Gage and to the colonial governors, talked too much about "handling public violence with severity and chastisement," about the "timely exertion of force" and "the dreadful consequences that will attend resistance to acts of Parliament."[1] He was perhaps too free with advice to "use the utmost power after trying persuasive measures"; yet he was the man, "his face as the face of an angel," in Burke's words, who moved the repeal of the Stamp Act and who always favored lenient measures toward the Americans. This handsome, gracious, "sweet-voiced" liberal, who was the friend of Hume, and who secured a pension for the exiled Rousseau, was famed as the advocate of the colonial cause, yet when in a position of responsibility neither history nor reason taught him any other mode of dealing with rebellion than the threat of the use of force. Therefore, he and his successors "put their faith in pike and gun"; and when the validity of an act of Parliament was denied, troops were sent to make it valid.

When the soldiers arrived in Boston "to rescue the Government out of the hands of a trained mob, and to restore the Activity of the Civil Power," as Bernard expressed it, the provincial council and the selectmen of Boston refused, in spite of the Quartering Act renewed in 1767, to provide subsistence

[1] Hansard, *Parliamentary Debates*, xvi, 112–19.

within the town of Boston. They argued that the wording of the law made it clear that the troops should go to the barracks on a distant island in the harbor.[1] To lodge them there was to defeat the very purpose for which they were sent, and Colonel Dalrymple, the commander, lodged them in the town house, in Faneuil Hall, and on Boston Common. It was later asserted that many of the troops died for want of proper barracks, but again that it was from "too free use of rum."[2] Gage later hired houses for them at the expense of the Government. The Governor provided subsistence and risked reimbursement.

It mattered not how justly Boston suffered this ignominy of these unwelcome guests, their presence was an "intolerable grievance." Into the drab Puritan Sabbath came the red coats, the drum and fife drill, the marching and counter-marching during divine worship, all very disturbing to the selectmen and the deacons as well as demoralizing to the people. "Our City," wrote a group of citizens, among whom were John and Samuel Adams, Otis and Hancock, "is yet a Garrison filled with armed men, as our harbor is with Cutters, Cruizers, and other armed vessels." The Exchange is "turned into a guarded den of — Revenue Officers to plunder our trade and drain the country of its money."[3] This was written to "that intrepid patriot, John Wilkes," who, though in many minds a vulgar demagogue, was

---

[1] *Barrington-Bernard Correspondence*, 167, 179; Hutchinson, *History of Massachusetts Bay*, iii, 207–08.

[2] British Museum, *Egerton MSS.*, 2659 F 141.

[3] Palfrey, *History of New England*, v, 415.

at this moment a hero in American eyes. To the colony's agent in London, Dennys De Berdt, the House of Representatives wrote that "as Englishmen, as well as British subjects," the colonists "have an aversion to an unnecessary standing army, which they look upon as dangerous to their civil liberties; and considering the examples of ancient times, it seems a little surprising, that a mother state should trust large bodies of mercenary troops in her colonies, at so great a distance from her lest, in process of time, when the spirits of the people shall be depressed by the military power, another Cæsar should arise and usurp the authority of his master." [1] Being there, the troops behaved as well perhaps as troops in a hostile city ever did, but there was a nagging spirit in both citizens and soldiers which boded ill for peace. Captain Dundas at the Coffee House smartly upbraided the worthy merchant John Rowe with "you are a Damn Incendiary and I shall see you hanged in your shoes." The dignified Rowe mildly protested, but looked about for witnesses, and noted that "it was spoke about Twelve of Clock at Noon." [2] When, however, sentries were "treated more like dogs than men," pelted with oyster shells and snowballs, and an informer, a sailor, was tarred and feathered and carried through all the main streets, we are justified in wondering where were the twelve constables, the selectmen, John Hancock and his Cadets, and the principal citizens who were so instant in action at a fire or patriotic celebration.

[1] Samuel Adams, *Writings* (Cushing, *ed.*), I, 145–46.
[2] *Letters and Diary of John Rowe*, 176.

If there was trouble, we are told it was the red-coated soldiers, "Lobsters" and "Bloody Backs" as the mob called them, who were thrown into jail by some popular magistrate.[1] With such conditions trouble would come without efforts by "certain busy characters," whom John Adams suspected of seeking "to kindle immortal hatred between the inhabitants of the lower class and the soldiers" by exciting "quarrels, rencounters and combats."[2] The outcome of this state of affairs was an event which, compared with the Cawnpore tragedy or the Sicilian Vespers, seems trifling enough, but in the little frontier town of Boston it took the dignity of a massacre. John Rowe set down the essentials in his diary: "March 5. This night the 29th Regim^t on Duty. A Quarrel between the soldiers & Inhabitants. The Bells Rang — A Great Number Assembled in King Street. A Party of the 29th under the Command of Cap't. Preston fired on the People — they killed five — wounded several others . . . the inhabitants are greatly enraged & not without Reason."[3] In spite of the hot passions of the time and the bitter indignation, the soldiers were in due time tried, with John Adams and Josiah Quincy as counsel, and all found not guilty except two who were punished by branding in the hand, the penalty of manslaughter. It was shown clearly at the trial

[1] *Letters and Diary of John Rowe*, 60, 194; *Maryland Historical Magazine*, iv, 284.

[2] John Adams, *Works*, ii, 229.

[3] *Letters and Diary of John Rowe*, 197–98. For good accounts see Frothingham, *Life and Times of Joseph Warren;* American Antiquarian Society, *Proceedings*, xiv, 40–51; Goodell, *The Boston Massacre; Deacon Tudor's Diary* (Wm. Tudor, *ed.*).

that the soldiers had endured threats, gibes, insults, and actual violence before they had fired in what they believed was self-defense. Historical scholars of distinction have not hesitated to say that some of the rioters "died as the fool dieth," that to make heroes of these undesirable citizens was to put the martyr's crown on the brow of vulgar ruffians.[1] There was futility in any argument either at the time or since, because if one held that the citizens were maddened by the soldiery, the answer was that the soldiers were nagged to desperation by the citizens. If against that rejoinder it was argued that the soldiers never ought to have been sent there, the reasonable reply was that the growing ascendancy of mob-law had made military force necessary. Following that chain one comes ultimately to ethical questions of right and wrong upon which none may speak with finality.

On the day following the "massacre" there was a town-meeting in Faneuil Hall and a committee of fifteen chosen to inform Hutchinson, the Lieutenant-Governor, that the soldiers must be removed. Samuel Adams headed this committee which intimated to Hutchinson that the people of Boston were in a dangerous mood, the soldiers must go. The Governor warned them that an attack on the King's troops was treason; that only General Gage at New York could order their removal. One regi-

---

[1] When in 1887 the Massachusetts Legislature proposed for political purposes to erect a monument to the victims of this affair the Massachusetts Historical Society voted that it "heard with regret" of this intent to give these victims "grateful recognition at the public expense." Mass. Hist. Soc., *Proceedings*, (2d Ser.), III, 314–18.

ment, the 29th, he would place in the Castle at once because of its offense. The committee returned to the people, now in such a throng that Faneuil Hall could not contain them and all moved to the Old South Meeting-House. Adams, "his gray locks flowing in the wind," led the committee through the masses of people and in their midst read the reply of the Lieutenant-Governor, declaring it unsatisfactory, an opinion backed by three thousand eager voices. A new committee, again headed by Adams, was sent to confront Hutchinson with some military officers and his council seated with all the formality and majesty of government in the Council Chamber, hoping their great white wigs and English scarlet-cloth coats would overawe the committee. When the former reply was repeated, Adams, stretching his arm, "which slightly shook with the energy of his soul," toward Hutchinson, said: "If you have the power to remove one regiment you have power to remove both. It is at your peril if you refuse. The meeting is composed of three thousand people. They are become impatient. A thousand men are already arrived from the neighborhood, and the whole country is in motion. Night is approaching. An Immediate answer is expected. Both regiments or none!" [1] The hesitating Lieutenant-Governor and Council saw the light and yielded to the demand, believing that otherwise they would have been "in a perfect convulsion." Lord North later referred to the troops concerned as "Sam Adams' Regiments."

[1] Wells, *Samuel Adams*, I, chap. XVI.

Adams' leadership in Boston had begun long before, but from this on it was supreme. An admiring biographer of Adams asserts that "the principles that became fixed in his mind, as soon as he was capable of understanding political subjects, were never changed."[1] During forty years there was no instance of inconsistency. No wonder the twilight of dubiety never rested upon views so long matured. It is significant that for his master's thesis at Harvard (1743) he chose for his subject the postulate "Whether it be lawful to resist the Supreme Magistrate, if the Commonwealth cannot otherwise be preserved." He took the affirmative, being not at all abashed by the presence of the Governor and Council in his audience.[2] Indeed, all his life he would have "stood upright before the Cham of Tartary." Over thirty years later he was arguing the same theme, doubtless in much the same way before the Continental Congress. With such a beginning, and with his compass set for such a course, it was not strange that his admiring kinsman could write of him in 1765: "Adams, I believe, has the most thorough understanding of liberty and her resources in the temper and character of the people, though not in law and constitution; as well as the most habitual, radical love of it, of any of them, as well as the most correct, genteel, and artful pen. He is a man of refined policy, steadfast integrity, exquisite humanity, genteel erudition, obliging, engaging manners, real as well as professed piety, and a universal good character, unless it should be

[1] Welis, *Samuel Adams*, I, 18.　　　[2] *Ibid.*, 10–11.

admitted that he is too attentive to the public, and not enough so to himself and his family." [1] Indeed, Adams was poor in the things of this world, and had no talent for business, no desire for pecuniary gain He was therefore looked upon as thriftless and wanting in wisdom to estimate riches at their just value. Loyalist enemies nevertheless attributed Adams' political opposition to rancor because his father, once rich, had been financially ruined by the interference of Parliament with a paper-money venture of his, known as a "Land Bank Scheme." Adams' father, a deacon in the Old South Church, justice of the peace, selectman, and a representative in the Massachusetts Legislature, had been one of the principal shareholders in this enterprise, which, though frowned upon in conservative money centers, was considered highly respectable in this frontier community ignorant of the principles of high finance. As late as 1758 Samuel Adams' property was attached by the sheriff on account of the old "Land Bank" affairs of his father. He successfully resisted this effort to seize his property, and, no doubt, thought of himself as a defender of colonial supremacy against an act of Parliament meant to overrule the laws of the colony. [2] His failure as a tax collector (1763–65) in very troublous times to force the payment of all arrearages was twisted into a "defalcation" by Governor Hutchinson and other Loyalist enemies. [3] They, doubtless, honestly be-

[1] John Adams, *Works*, II, 163–64.

[2] Wells, *Samuel Adams*, I, 8–10, 13, 25–27.

[3] *Ibid.*, 37–38; Hutchinson, *History of Massachusetts Bay*, III, 294–95; Mass. Hist. Soc., *Proceedings*, XX, 216–23.

lieved this, but were too prejudiced to see the truth. Nor did they ever cease to twit him about the malthouse business in which he was a partner with his father. "Sam the Maltster" was the mildest of their epithets. Peter Oliver, an exiled Loyalist, wrote that if he "wished to draw the picture of a devil" he would get Sam Adams to sit for him. "One view of his countenance, showed the malignity of his heart." He found Adams shrewd rather than solid of judgment, one who understood human nature in low life. He seduced Hancock, Oliver said, "as the devil seduced Eve by whispering in his ear." He had "a serpentine cunning" and "a religious mask always ready for occasion." [1] Another enemy speaks of his unrivaled "talent for artfully and fallaciously insinuating" malice into the public mind,[2] which was only an ill-natured way of saying that he knew how to touch every chord that would sway the feelings of New England. He comprehended its antipathies and its bigotry, its hatred of "Papists" and its belief that all Episcopalians were "tools of the British government." He had unparalleled skill in gathering the discontented into the Cave of Adullam. "Sam the Publican" could express the common man's aspiration for liberty, and he knew devices for arousing it.

John Adams describes a meeting of the "Sons of Liberty," "three hundred to four hundred plates, an awning of sail cloth overhead," the diners cultivating the sensations of freedom. Forty-five toasts

[1] British Museum, *Egerton MSS.*, 2671 F 24.
[2] Hutchinson, *History of Massachusetts Bay*, III, 295.

were drunk, and it is a tribute to the mildness of the
beverages taken when Adams records that he "did
not see one person intoxicated during the festival."
The toasts called for the punishment of Governor
Bernard, "the speedy removal of all task-masters,
the redress of all grievances," and "strong halters,
firm blocks, and sharp axes to all such as deserve
either." "Otis and Samuel Adams are politic," continues the diarist, "in promoting these festivals;
for they tinge the minds of the people; they impreg-
nate them with the sentiments of liberty; they render the people fond of their leaders in the cause." [1]
Peter Oliver pictures Adams "a master of vocal
music," organizing "singing societies of mechanics
where he inculcated sedition." He was no parlor
radical, but like Socrates he had the benevolent
habit of pouring himself out to everybody, and he
thus became the natural leader of the fishermen and
shipmasters and roustabouts. Enemies called him
a demagogue, friends preferred to say "a master of
practical politics." Critics spoke of his intrigue,
friends called it "gift for organization." Being plain
of dress, of speech, and deportment, he was considered a man of the people. His Harvard degree
was forgotten and his knowledge of history, politics,
and the philosophy of Locke made his leadership
easily accepted. He was trusted by the people, if
not by the conservative few. In the canvass and
the caucus he was supreme. His short, pithy, passionate speeches, and his skill, not to say cunning,
as moderator of the town meeting made him master

[1] John Adams, *Works*, II, 218.

there, where he was a "Colossus of debate," winning every one with "a nervous simplicity of reasoning and eloquence." Though prematurely gray, trembling in voice, and palsied in hand, his mental and moral courage was beyond dispute. For the good of his colony Adams would have been stretched on a gridiron or stuck full of arrows like St. Sebastian. He was proud that he could "bear with equanimity alternate smiles and frowns." With little of fire or ornament in his speech, he roused and fortified the people, who came to trust his unbending will and cheerful, commanding spirit. He was narrow-minded enough to be a perfect politician, never torn between two opposing views, and therefore utterly intolerant of opponents, who hated him accordingly. "Damn that Adams," cried a foe, "every dip of his pen stings like a horned snake." This "Cromwell of New England" was drawn by an adversary as a "hypocrite in religion, a republican in politics, of sufficient cunning to form a consummate knave," and Adams retorted by calling his traducer a "time server and tool of government," an "enemy of Religion and Liberty." As for Adams' religion it was doubtless sincere enough. Certainly he was patient in attendance upon Puritan religious service, ever reverential in speaking of divine matters, if not of human institutions claiming to do with them. He was always sure that the hand of God was in the affairs of men. Even government — when it followed his precepts — he believed was "an ordinance of Heaven, designed by an all-benevolent Creator for the general happiness of his rational creature, man." Boston he prayed might "become a Christian Sparta." He hated all formalism, and reiterated his belief in a life of Christian conduct rather than dependence on creeds.[1] His acquaintance with the Scriptures he often proved by his likening of notable figures among the Loyalists to Biblical characters of ill repute. It was about the time of the Stamp Act that Adams first became an outstanding figure. With real literary power he wrote state papers for the Massachusetts House of Representatives, letters to newspapers, letters to the colonial agent, letters to great Englishmen who might aid the cause.[2] American of Americans, he had no thought of the good of the empire, but was a zealot for the destiny of his native land. Through debates and newspaper articles in a style cogent, clear, and with imagery suited to the masses, he centered attention on colonial ills. Though too passionate and too eager for advance, content only with perfection, he was no statesman, but a master agitator. Single-minded in his preference for the approval of the masses, and delighting to think himself indifferent to "the sunshine of power, and the flatteries of the great," he came to stand supreme in Massachusetts as the "man of the people." It was Samuel Adams, who, after one failure, had induced the Massachusetts House of Representatives (February, 1768), two years before the "massacre," to send a circular letter to the other colonial assemblies, urging the need of harmony in asserting their natural and con-

---

[1] Wells, *Samuel Adams*, I, 53, 269; II, 337–38.
[2] Samuel Adams, *Writings* (Cushing *ed.*), I, *passim.*

stitutional rights.[1] To this moderate paper over half the other colonies returned a sympathetic reply.[2] It became the classic example of the way to secure unity of action and interchange of sentiments.

When Hillsborough, for the time in charge of colonial affairs, learned of this effort to unify action, he secured the backing of the British Cabinet to a circular letter of his own, which went out to twelve colonies, berating Massachusetts for seeking to "create unwarrantable combinations" and "to excite an unjustifiable opposition to the constitutional authority of Parliament." [3] All governors were ordered to prevail upon their assemblies to take no notice of this call to sedition. In the King's name he required the Massachusetts Assembly also to rescind that "rash and hasty proceeding," the work of "a desperate faction." A dissolution was to follow a possible refusal. This action was a reckless challenge to a high-strung people. It furnished the colonists with an argument that the right of petition was being denied them, and helped to give immense publicity in the newspapers to all the colonial arguments and statements of grievances.[4] By a vote of 92 to 17, the Massachusetts Assembly refused to rescind the offending resolution, and said in its address to the Governor: "If the votes of the House are to be controlled by the direction of a

[1] Samuel Adams, *Writings*, I, 184.
[2] New Jersey, Virginia, Connecticut, Maryland, Rhode Island, and South Carolina were quick to act; the others more slow.
[3] Almon, *Prior Documents*, 203, 204, 220.
[4] Manuscript study of Massachusetts Circular Letter, by L G. Van Der Velde. (In U. of M. Library.)

minister, we have left us but a vain semblance of liberty." [1] Paul Revere made a silver punch-bowl "to the memory of the Glorious Ninety-Two Members," and that mystic number became a popular catchword recalling the courage of those who refused to rescind. Friends in England, gathered with Colonel Barré at a festive board, drank toasts to "the ninety-two patriots of Massachusetts Bay." [2] During the debate, James Otis declared that it was rather Parliament, which should recall its unwise acts. "Let Britain rescind her measures, or the colonies are lost to her forever."

Notwithstanding the thunderous threats of Hillsborough that he would dissolve any assembly which did not treat the Massachusetts letter "with the contempt it deserves," every colony flew in the face of authority and endorsed the idea of united action. [3] As the South Carolina Committee reported, the House would certainly treat any letter or paper in the least opposing the just authority of Parliament or tending to inflame the minds of the colonists against their sovereign with the contempt it deserved, but that no paper having the slightest tendency in this direction had come to their attention. The circular letter was endorsed as "replete with duty and loyalty to His Majesty, respect for the Parliament of Great Britain, sincere affection for our Mother Country, tender care for the preservation of the rights of all His Majesty's subjects, and

---

[1] *Massachusetts State Papers*, 150.
[2] Niles, *Principles and Acts*, 116.
[3] Almon, *Prior Documents*, 213–20.

founded upon undeniable Constitutional Principles." Addresses in this sense to the King, and Massachusetts, and Virginia, were recommended, whereupon the Governor indignantly dissolved the assembly.[1] Hillsborough's folly had merely spread the spirit of resistance to Government from one colony to all. American public opinion as to the Townshend measures became consolidated, and members of Parliament, who had heard the words of Nicholson Calvert, explaining his change of vote during the stamp controversy, might well have had chills of apprehension. "Sir," he had said, "it has always been my opinion [that] to lay any taxes upon a numerous people situated as the Americans are, without their consent, is impossible. It is a widely different thing, Sir, the quelling a paltry riot in Moorfields, or Bloomsbury-Square, to that of making two millions of people, distributed from one corner of the American continent to the other, all unanimous in the opinion of right on their side, submit to your decisions. It matters little to the question, whether they are in the right or not, they think themselves so." [2]

The Massachusetts Assembly, having been dissolved, a town meeting in Boston (September 12, 1768) expressed bitter resentment that a standing army was kept up in the province. The inhabitants were urged to arm, because of an apprehension "of an approaching war with France." When the Governor refused to call the assembly, which the

[1] Wallace, *Henry Laurens*, 155.
[2] Hansard, *Parliamentary History*, xvi, 109–10.

meeting hoped might preserve their rights and privileges, a convention of all the towns of the province was called. The Governor warned the delegates, gathered from ninety-six towns, that they were usurping the King's sovereignty over the province and would "repent their rashness." The usurpation was denied by the convention, but, having drawn up a list of grievances, it adjourned.

With the passions of New England at such a pitch, the British Parliament, which met in December, 1768, took another forward step in the policy of coercion. One hundred years earlier, John Evelyn wrote in his diary: "Some of our Council were for sending them [Massachusetts] a menacing letter, which those who better understood the peevish and touchy humour of that colony were utterly against." It was a pity that such counsel did not stay the hand of Parliament on this occasion. Resolutions and an address initiated by the Lords, and later passed by the Commons, 169 to 65, supported the King in the measures already taken for "inducing a due obedience" to Government, and offered to "stand by and support" him in further acts to maintain the civil authority in Massachusetts.[1] The 'riots and tumults" in Boston were frowned upon in the resolutions, and the circular letter was set down as inflaming to the colonial mind and "subversive of the constitution." The use of military force was defended, and the illegal convention of September, 1768, condemned as inciting sedition. The calling of the convention manifested, it was

---

[1] Hansard, *Parliamentary History*, xvi, 476, 510.

held, a design to set up a new authority "independent of the crown of Great Britain," and to elect deputies to it was a "daring insult" to the King and an "audacious usurpation of the powers of government." These were all expressions of the rigid and uncompromising ideas of power, common in that day to the English official class, which had grown out of that Revolution of 1688, which had left the Government, every organ of it, in the control of the property-owning middle class. The Lords and Commons simply voiced the divine right of established authority. Resistance to it was solemnly and withal conscientiously attributed to innate wickedness and lack of gratitude to those who so benignly governed. They did not understand or sympathize with their own lower classes who lived under their very eyes, and it was hardly likely that their vision would be better for a people three thousand miles distant. In this instance, the majority of the Lords and Commons went on to advise the violation of one of the principles of English law, by proposing that the King's Ministers get the names of the Boston leaders most active in committing treasons, and, reviving an old statute of Henry VIII, bring them speedily to condign punishment. This obsolete law passed "in one of the most cruel and tyrannical reigns," and when England had not a colony, enabled the King's officers to bring for trial in England men accused of treason outside the realm.[1] It is true, as Hansard says, that no measures were ever opposed with more firmness. Even

[1] Hansard, *Parliamentary History*, xvi, 479–80, 491.

Richard Grenville doubted their wisdom. "Measures such as this," cried Captain Phipps in the Commons, "are more calculated to raise the rebellion they are pretended to be pointed at, than to quell it, did it exist." Suppose, he asked, "the accused Americans, after being torn from their country and brought three thousand miles to London, are given a trial by jury. Will it be anything but a mockery, divested of all its advantages? How can they avail themselves of the right to challenge jurymen, whose character and connections are unknown to them?" Will not they and their friends suspect that the twelve men found here are of the devotion of the Ministry and capable of perjury and murder? "How are they to avail themselves of counsel, whose abilities and fame they are strangers to? By what process are they to compel the appearance of witnesses from the other side of the Atlantic?" And even suppose they are after all acquitted? "What reparation can be made to men dragged from the endearments of domestic life, brought from the land of liberty, flowing with milk and honey, to drink at the bitter fountain of oppression? Will they return less possessed of the confidence of their fellow subjects, and less inclined to abuse it?" Will they be less solicitous "to shake off the yoke from this new outrage?" Will not their fellow-countrymen come to think that "these men are brought over here to be murdered," perhaps at the instigation of a governor "heated by dispute, piqued by opposition"? Will they not think that those who support "the rights of the people, are, like Tarquin's poppies, to be cut off for overtopping the rest?" [1] For all this excellent logic, there were only deaf ears. As Walpole wrote on a like occasion, "Eloquence, reason, and argument, avail little against a compact parliamentary majority."

This new measure assailing the personal rights of the leaders in New England was quickly resented by a people gifted with "a perpetual jealousy respecting liberty." It was Virginia that first voiced the colonial protest. As if to separate her from Massachusetts, the Ministry had been more kind to Virginia and had even adopted a conciliatory attitude. It became necessary to provide for Lord Botetourt, a member of the Berkeley family, famous in Virginian annals. His bankruptcy and business dishonor had forced his retirement from British polite society; and the Ministry thought by making him governor to give him an income and at the same time through his attractive and amiable personality get back into the graces of Virginia. He summoned the legislature on May 8, 1769, and in a most gracious manner granted a number of their petitions, one against the use of writs of assistance and another asking an extension of their jurisdiction toward the west. But barely a week had flown by when the assembly's committee of correspondence received from Virginia's agent in London a copy of the "baneful resolutions" of Parliament. At once resolutions, drawn up by George Mason and introduced by George Washington, were adopted, declaring that the sole right of imposing taxes on the people of

[1] Hansard, *Parliamentary History*, xvi, 508-10.

Virginia lay with the assembly; that they had a perfect right to ask the concurrence of other colonies in addresses to the King in behalf of their violated rights; that trials for treason committed in Virginia ought to be held in that colony.[1] There was no opposition. Along with Patrick Henry, Richard Henry Lee, and Thomas Jefferson went Peyton Randolph and Pendleton, who five years before had seemed conservative. To the speakers of all colonial assemblies were sent copies to which the approving replies were most harmonious. On the following day, an address to "His Majesty" informed George III that the House of Burgesses could not "without Horror, think of the new, unusual, and permit us, with all Humility to add, unconstitutional and illegal Mode" of trial proposed for those accused of treason in America. "How truly deplorable must be the Case of a wretched American, who, having incurred the Displeasure of anyone in Power, is dragged from his native Home . . . thrown into Prison . . . Conveyed to a distant Land, where no Friend, no Relation, will alleviate his Distresses . . . where no witness can be found to testify his Innocence." To avert this, they prostrated themselves at the foot of his "Royal Throne," and loyally wishing that his reign might be long, they hoped that after death His Majesty might "taste the fullest Fruition of eternal Bliss," and his heirs reign "until Time shall be no more."[2] The Governor, under his instructions, could do nothing else, after the resolutions

[1] *Journals of the House of Burgesses, 1766–69* (Kennedy, ed.), 214.
[2] *Ibid.*, 215–16.

denying the authority of Parliament, but dissolve the assembly. As private citizens, the members at once gathered in the house of Anthony Hay and adopted resolutions for non-importation and an association to uphold it.[1] The spirit of all, perhaps, was that expressed by George Washington in a letter written to Mason a month earlier, declaring that "no man should scruple, or hesitate a moment, to use a—ms in defense of so valuable a blessing" as the liberty "which we have derived from our ancestors."[2]

Such was the state of the public mind in Virginia, and after the "Boston Massacre" Governor Hutchinson wrote: "Boston people are run mad. The frenzy was not higher when they banished my pious great-grandmother [Anne Hutchinson], when they hanged the Quakers, when they afterwards hanged the poor innocent witches."[3] Already, Henry Laurens had written from South Carolina: "The cloud is gathering thick in the North and will soon spread over America, if not dispelled by wise measures in Britain. New England is in arms; New York slumbers but will not sleep if there shall be a necessity for her appearance. Pennsylvania is divided, but the most powerful part is on the side of liberty. . . . South Carolina and Georgia, weakest sisters, will not subscribe to the right of a British Parliament to lay internal taxes upon America, and though feeble, have gathered strength among them-

---

[1] Lingley, *The Transition in Virginia*, 55–56.
[2] *Writings of George Washington* (Ford, *ed.*), II, 263.
[3] *Massachusetts Archives*, XXVI, 540.

selves — will be keen in asserting their liberty, and
sullenly and stubbornly resist against all ministerial
mandates and admonitions. Men of war and troops
are actually arrived at Boston and a few days more
will inform us how they are received by the people
of Massachusetts." [1] South Carolina itself was soon
engaged in the bitter struggle known as the "Wilkes
Fund Dispute." The lower house of the assembly
had (December, 1769) expressed its sympathy with
the English "Society of the Supporters of the Bill of
Rights" by voting a sum of £10,500 to be sent to that
Society in England "for the defense of British and
American liberty." The English Society which the
Commons sought to aid was formed to promote political changes of the most fundamental character, and
to assist John Wilkes in his struggle with George III
and his supporters. The right of the Commons thus
to vote money, without the consent of the Council and the Governor, was challenged, though there
were undoubtedly precedents for it in the long fight
which the Commons had made to gain control in
money affairs. The Ministry finally took a hand,
and even the King gave the matter attention, and
threatened to make an example of the treasurers
who lent themselves to this plan.[2] The South Carolina Commons, however, refused to bow even before
the King, and the bitter controversy dragged on for
several years. Thus the American colonies were
in ferment from Penobscot Bay to St. Mary's River.

At this crisis occurred the partial repeal, already
briefly alluded to, of the Townshend duties. They

---

[1] Wallace, *Henry Laurens*, 152–53.　　[2] *Ibid.*, chap. XIII.

were denounced by Lord North, who had succeeded
Grafton as the head of the Ministry, as "preposterous," not merely because they had given birth to
dangerous combinations and dissatisfaction among
American merchants, but because they were "un-
commercial." Like a high tariff they had stimu-
lated manufactures in the colonies, and that affected
badly "the prosperity of this kingdom." He would
keep the old duties on wine, sugar, and molasses, and
the duty on tea, which made part of the Townshend
Act. Junius scored him for doing everything except
remove the offense, for "an odius, unprofitable
exertion of a speculative right, . . . fixing a badge
of slavery upon the Americans, without service to
their masters." [1] It was necessary to keep the tea
tax, North declared, lest Americans set the abolition
down, not to goodness, but to fear. He would not
go as far as Hillsborough, granting the colonists
"nothing except what they may ask with a halter
round their necks," but America must not think Parliament terrified into concessions. "The properest
time to exert our right to taxation is," declared Lord
North, "when the right is refused." He had before
told Parliament, "America must fear you before
she can love you." He would have the colonies
prostrate at his feet. He heartily wished to repeal
the whole law, he asserted, but that he could not
do, without giving up the just right to tax the
Americans.[2] So the duty on paints, glass, and paper
was removed, leaving the tea tax, to the end that, as

[1] *Letters of Junius* (London, 1799), ii, 31.
[2] Hansard, *Parliamentary History*, xvi, 854.

Pownall sneered, "they might still keep the yoke
about the neck of the Americans." In the pompous
preamble of the Townshend Act, the purpose had
been stated to be the "defending, protecting, and
securing the said dominions" and "defraying the
charge of the administration of justice and support
of civil government." After the repeal, except for
the tax on tea, Burke taunted the Ministry with
the "precious Mockery" of such a performance —
"a preamble without an act." The revenue was
"five-sixths repealed,— abandoned,— sunk,— gone,
lost forever." "And this is," he sneered, "preserving dignity in England." [1]

To this, at last, had come the measures of that
"delight and ornament" of the House, Charles
Townshend. In the memorable words of the Pennsylvania Farmer, they had kindled "the sacred flame
that fused the continent." New England had first
been stirred to a boycott of English goods. Then, in
succession, the merchants of Boston, New York, and
Philadelphia had entered upon non-importations.
The South had followed, and though the effect upon
English manufacturers may have been small, the
colonies had learned a lesson in united action. The
American provinces had shown hostility to having
their judges and executives paid by a distant power
and thus rendered indifferent to the colonial will.
They had resented defense of the colonies by English soldiers, and had expressed their will to defend
themselves. When there was a reaction in Parliament against the "extraordinary indulgence" shown

[1] Burke, *Works* (ed. 1869), ii, 12.

in the Stamp Act repeal, and the restraining resolution was passed to force New York to obey the Quartering Act, there was a general challenge from the colonial legislatures. Like unity of sentiment was shown by the general approbation of the Massachusetts circular letter, and Lord Hillsborough's folly in commanding all provincial assemblies to reject it merely swelled the chorus of approval. When Parliament, too, took notice of the letter and of the Massachusetts "Convention," and went so far as to propose seizing the Boston "traitors" and bringing them to London for trial, they only provoked the "Virginia Resolutions" and a universal endorsement of them by the colonies. Minor clashes also embittered the relations of colonies and parent state. Massachusetts showed incensed pride and high spirit at being "required" to vote compensation for damage done by rioters. The officers of the customs at Boston met with such opposition in performing their duties, that they summoned the fifty-gun ship, the Romney, and needed every gun when the seizure of John Hancock's sloop Liberty fired the mob spirit in Boston. Riotous conduct there brought the Ministry to a policy of military coercion, and the city's irritation over the "Bloody Backs" in their midst led straight to the "Boston Massacre." Even before this climax the merchants and property-owners in general had begun to falter. The mechanics and laborers and the "lower classes" in general had joined all too vociferously the movement to reform the imperial system and to secure the rights of man. Therefore, the partial penitence in Parliament resulted in wrecking the non-importation agreements in America, and for a time put an end to this concrete evidence of colonial unity. An era, if not of good-feeling, at least of indifference, seemed to have come, but it was all on the surface of things, for certain fundamental differences between England and America were daily making their union hard to preserve.

CHAPTER XII

THE SOCIAL AND INTELLECTUAL GULF BETWEEN THE PARTS OF THE EMPIRE

FOLLOWING upon the news of the partial repeal of the Townshend Acts, there was an apparent era of good-feeling. The spirit of loyalty grew. John Adams saw a "subsidence of the patriotic spirit." The people seemed to grow weary of contention with Parliament. "The friends of the people," he sighed, were "left in the lurch" by the people themselves. Adams, having learned by experience, resolved to become "more retired and cautious." Even Hancock and Otis had cooled. But Samuel Adams, in whom Hutchinson saw one of the "sons of sedition," seized upon the least remaining grievance, the presence of soldiers in the Castle, or the removal of the General Court to Cambridge, to exercise his "black art" in the press and thus revive the spirit of opposition. He reminded men that if they tamely suffered a lawless attack upon their liberties, millions yet unborn might be the sharers in their slavery. In his Jacobin heart he believed Thomas Hutchinson, the new Governor, to be an "Egyptian tyrant," a restless adversary, "forming the most dangerous Plans for the Ruin of the Reputation of the People," in order to build his own greatness "upon the distruction of their Liberties." Nothing was, perhaps, further from the truth, for nobody can read Hutchinson's scholarly "History of Massachusetts Bay" without being sure that he loved the province as patriotically as Hancock or the Adamses. Reflecting that the independent spirit of Brutus, "to his immortal honor," had expelled the proud tyrant of Rome, Adams intimated his readiness to serve Boston in the same heroic manner. It was understood that the Governor's salary was now to be paid by the Crown, and the "tragedy of American freedom " was, Adams thought, nearly completed. Because of Adams' relentless efforts during the lull in the rising storm of American opposition, his admiring biographers have attributed to him the glory of driving New England steadily on toward the goal of independence. But we have traced certain fundamental differences and more are to be noted, which would have brought about the practical independence of the colonies without any tutelary genius of the Adams variety. Many things indicate that independence of England was foreordained before Patrick Henry scattered treason with his fiery allusions to Tarquin and Cæsar and Brutus; or Samuel Adams spread the gospel that the sacred rights of man were superior to acts of Parliament. Owing to forces working during the whole colonial period to differentiate America from England, the two countries had come to be unlike in character, ominously opposed in interests. The French traveler, Mathieu Dumas, observed that in spite of the American resemblance to England "in language, in costume, in customs, in religion, and in the principles of government, a distinct national character is forming itself."

America's predominant concern was in the farm;
England's was rapidly coming to be manufacturing
and commerce. In America, the forest environment
formed the character of a large per cent of the people, making them individualistic and democratic.
In England, the city and town moulded the social
life, throwing emphasis on the community. When
Patrick Henry and Thomas Jefferson left their back-
country homes and went for the first time to the
capital of Virginia at Williamsburg, it is doubtful
whether either had before seen more than a dozen
houses together. Probably ninety per cent of the
colonists lived what might properly be called a rural
life. Of them, the "uncouth, huge monstrous"
wilderness made hunters, woodsmen, or even farmers, in its clearings, but not conscious, social units
of a vast community, the British Empire. Almost
the reverse was true in England where the progress
of the Industrial Revolution, following the invention
of the flying shuttle, the spinning jenney, and the
growth of the factory system, had changed towns
into cities and drawn the country people into the
great centers of population. In a society of this
kind, English statesmen gained their experience in
government. Such men living in great centers of
population, where order can be preserved only by
the stern enforcement of highly developed legal
regulations, could have little understanding or sympathy with a people in a sparsely settled frontier
province where laws were few and individual liberty
was easily confused with a happy state where there
was no government. The average London-bred

member of Parliament could not even imagine life in the free spaces of America, much less legislate wisely for it. Thus a difference in environment and of methods of living worked changes in certain basic conceptions of political order which threatened the unity of two parts of the empire. Every social and intellectual difference which diverse conditions created between England and America diminished the understanding and sympathy which alone would keep harmony in the empire. The wealth and cultivation of old, dignified, and conservative England contrasted sharply with the rude American frontier conditions, where the imitations of London fashions in Philadelphia or Boston merely aroused the mirth of English observers. An English "Lady of Quality" describes a "grand ball" at Wilmington in North Carolina at which "the dresses, dancing and ceremonies were laughable enough," but she confided to her diary, nothing so ridiculous as her own figure " dressed out in all my British airs, with a high head and a hoop, and trudging through the unpaved streets in embroidered shoes by the light of a lanthorn carried by a black wench half naked. No chair, no carriage." [1] The traveler accustomed to the elegance of London and of Bath became the carping critic or condescending patron of the more unsophisticated American life. The visiting colonist in London, on the other hand, was more apt to see the corruption than the refinements of the metropolitan city. English writers betrayed their sense of superiority to the colonists in careless language

[1] British Museum, *Egerton MSS.*, 2423 F 100.

that nettled American readers. James Otis found it maddening that "Every garreteer, from the environs of Grub Street to the purlieus of St. James, has lately talked of *his* and *my* and *our* colonies, and of *rascally colonists*, and of *yoking* and *curbing* the *cattle*." Why, he asked, could not American peasants "with as much propriety speak of *their* cities of London, and Westminster and of their isles of Britain" and Ireland.[1] Franklin, too, was angered that "Every man in England seems to consider himself as a piece of a sovereign over America; seems to jostle himself into the throne with the King and talks of *our subject* in the Colonies." He objected to the common talk in London about "the *sovereignty of this nation over* the colonies."[2]

Nor did "the heir apparent of the Romans," as Walpole dubbed his fellow-Britons, stop with assumption of political superiority. Lord North's friends, said a London pamphleteer, were apt to ask, "Shall we be bearded and scoffed at by a race of dastardly cowards, sprung from our bastards, our swindlers and our convicts; fellows who will fly away and caw like crows at the smell of gunpowder?"[3] Even the immortal James Wolfe had, upon most inadequate grounds, and with no consideration for the lack of drill and discipline, declared the colonial soldiers "The dirtiest, most contemptible cowardly dogs that you can conceive. There is no depending on them in action. They fall down dead

[1] Tudor, *James Otis*, 193.
[2] Franklin, *Writings* (Smyth, *ed.*), v, 17, 21.
[3] *Serious Considerations on the Political Condition of Lord North* (London, 1783), 54.

in their own dirt and desert by battalions, officers and all." [1] Such rash words were due simply to his lack of knowledge of the backwoods method of fighting. Henry Laurens heard on every side in London, on the eve of the war, that "one British soldier would beat six Yankees." [2]

Such loose talk embittered many a colonist, and roused every rebellious sentiment in his provincial soul. Lord Clare might hug and kiss Benjamin Franklin, after they had had a bottle and a half of claret each, but the "Friend of the Human Race" put down that, and his Lordship's protestation that he had never met a man he was so much in love with, as mere "flummery." He knew he was being patronized. [3]

Both Briton and Yankee had his peculiar vanity. Defoe's thrasonical brag in "The Compleat Englishman," that "we are the greatest country in the world; our climate is the most agreeable to live in; our Englishmen are the stoutest and best men in the world," was not shocking to the typical Englishman of the time of George III. [4] On the other hand, few Americans would have rebuked Jonathan Mayhew for his vanity when he complacently proclaimed in his sermon on the repeal of the Stamp Act, "if any miserable people on the continent or isles of Europe, after being weakened by luxury, debauchery, venality . . . should . . . be driven in their extremity to seek retreat from slavery, in some distant climate;

---

[1] L. S. Mayo, *J. Amherst*, 108.   [2] Wallace, *Henry Laurens*, 197.
[3] Franklin, *Writings* (Smyth, *ed.*), v, 147.
[4] Defoe, *The Compleat Englishman*, i, 369.

let them . . . find one in America, under thy [Liberty's] brooding, sacred wings." [1] It was quite the fashion for Americans, like the Princes of Abyssinia, to pity those "slaves of misery" whom fate had excluded from their seat of tranquillity. Ten years after the Revolution began, Jefferson wrote, urging Monroe to come to France: "It will make you adore your own country, its soil, its climate, its equality, liberty, laws, people, and manners. My God, how little do my countrymen know what precious blessings they are in possession of, and which no other people on earth enjoy." [2] We shall see millions come to live in America, he prophesied, but very few Americans come to live in Europe. "I always," wrote John Adams (1765), "consider the settlement of America with reverence and wonder, as the opening of a grand scene, and design in Providence for the illumination of the ignorant and the emancipation of the slavish part of mankind all over the earth." [3] Most Americans were sure that the western continent was the fairest of created worlds, and they glowed with confidence in its future and were impatient in pursuit of its destiny. When two peoples were each so sure that they alone were the special recipients of the favor of Providence, neither was likely to yield much, if their interests clashed.

In spite of Peter Kalm's observation that "the English colonies in this part of the world have increased so much in their numbers of inhabitants, and in their riches, that they almost vie with Old Eng-

---

[1] Tudor, *James Otis*, 146.   [2] Jefferson, *Works* (Bergh, *ed.*), VI, 21.
[3] John Adams, *Works*, I, 66.

land," there was a vast difference in the wealth of the two countries and in its distribution. Mayhew spoke the truth when he said, "There is scarce a man in any of the colonies, certainly there is not in the New England ones, that would be deemed worthy of the name of a rich man in Great Britain." Here and there, he admitted, there might be one worth twenty to fifty thousand pounds sterling, but all the rest in a low condition or not greatly rising above it.[1] True, America was at least dimly aware that it possessed enormous resources; it dreamed of exploiting millions of acres of potential cornfields and mountains of iron; but, for the moment, it was poor as the European world measured wealth. As Franklin said, "America is a land of neither the very rich nor the very poor, but one in which a general happy mediocrity prevails." On returning (1772) from a tour through Ireland and Scotland where he found a small part of the society opulent landlords, gentlemen and great noblemen, living in affluence and even magnificence, but the mass of the people, poor, clothed in rags, and living wretchedly, in dirty hovels of mud and straw, he reflected with contentment upon the happiness of New England, "where every Man is a Freeholder, has a Vote in public Affairs, lives in a tidy, warm House, has plenty of good Food and Fewel, with whole clothes from Head to Foot, the Manufacture perhaps of his own Family." [2]

In England the advance of the Industrial Revolu-

---

[1] Thornton, *The Pulpit of the Revolution*, 125.
[2] Franklin, *Writings* (Smyth, *ed.*), v, 362.

tion had created greater concentration of capital in the hands of a few; and Indian nabobs came home to swell the ranks of the newly rich, and to spend in arrogant display what was often gotten by pillage and oppression. There was no outrageous exaggeration in Humphrey Clinker's "Letters from Bath," which Smollett published in 1771, describing the "general tide of luxury, which hath overpowered the nation, and swept away all even the dregs of the people . . . clerks and factors from the East Indies, loaded with the spoils of plundered provinces; planters, negro drivers, and hucksters from our American plantations, enriched they know not how; agents, commissaries, and contractors, who have fattened in two successive wars on the blood of the nation; usurers, brokers and jobbers of every kind; men of low birth and no breeding; have found themselves suddenly translated to a state of affluence unknown to former ages." [1] Less imaginative and more sober historians agreed with the novelist, Smollett. In England there were extremes of wealth and poverty; in America very moderate contrasts in income.

These variations in the amount and distribution of wealth created a moral and social gulf between Britain and her American colonies which sundered them nearly as much as the seas that rolled between. One must take with a grain of salt Franklin's comparison of "extream Corruption among all orders of Men in this old rotten State [England], and the glorious pub'ic Virtue so predominant in our rising

---

[1] Smollett, *Humphrey Clinker* (ed. 1899), i, 48; B. Saunders, *Macpherson*, 262.

Country," [1] but it is certain that there was a great antithesis.

That simple-hearted Loyalist and Puritan, Samuel Curwen, driven from Boston by the intolerance of his "Whig" neighbors in the first spasm of the rising rebellion, was much shocked to find in London a sharp contrast to the simple, sober manners of his American home. "The dissipation, self-forgetfulness, and vicious indulgence of every kind," he wrote, "which characterize this metropolis, are not to be wondered at. The temptations are too great . . . The unbounded riches of many afford the means of every species of luxury, which (thank God) our part of America is ignorant of." [2] All this had come in the train of Chatham's glorious triumphs which had laid at England's feet the treasures of two continents. Until the sounder part of her citizens should restore the balance, the ruling class, flaunting its frivolity and immorality before industrious, moral, and intelligent colonists, were sure to force the conviction upon them that it was absurd to accept rule by men so plainly unfit, by methods they despised.

The Huguenot planter, Henry Laurens, whose loyalty had stoutly withstood the strain of the fray over the Stamp Act, cooled greatly toward the England which he had cherished, when, in 1772, he traveled there and was witness of the state of morals among the ruling classes. "Oh, the wretched state of female virtue in this kingdom," he exclaimed. "Chastity is certainly out of fashion in England and

---

[1] Franklin, *Writings* (Smyth, *ed.*), vi, 312.
[2] S. Curwen, *Journal*, 33.

women talk another language than that in which
modesty was best understood twenty years ago." [1]
His puritanical soul revolted as he mingled with the
"best people" of England, and became aware of a
spiritual separation from England which he had not
known before. "The news which is now circulating,"
he wrote home, "relates to the marriage of the Duke
of Gloucester to Lady Waldgrave, which His High-
ness has at length declared to his royal brother, in
consequence of which he is forbid the King's presence. The marriage was celebrated six or seven
years ago, and it was notorious that the parties co-
habitated as man and wife, which gave his Majesty
no offense. This same King while his brothers
debauched men's wives and daughters throughout
the island winked at their amours, but as soon as
they have committed the impolitic honest act of
matrimony, or as soon as they respectively [respect-
ably?] had declared the act, he disgraced them by
banishment from court. You know it is said somewhere, Thou shalt not commit adultery, by our
King to his brothers, Thou shalt not commit matrimony. Thus policy militates against religion; but
the latter will be the hold-fast when the former fails
and is of no use." [2] He might have added that the
Duke of Grafton, in spite of the fact that he followed
the races and cultivated the society of the notorious
Nancy Parsons, was thought none the less worthy,
except by the carping Junius, to be elected Chancellor of Cambridge University, nor as Prime Minister to guide the destinies of the nation.

[1] Wallace, *Henry Laurens*, 185–86.   [2] *Ibid.*, 186.

Three years among such scenes deepened his sad conviction that the King and his Ministers and the members of Parliament were unworthy to rule over an honest and moral people, as he thought his fellow-citizens in America. Disillusionment changed his erstwhile veneration to bitter sarcasm.[1] He also came to a sound philosophy which put away any envy for the gilded aristocracy about him. "You learn from hence, good sir," he moralized to a correspondent, "that Kings and princes have troubles and perplexities and passions and crosses to contend withal as much as men have who move in a more humble sphere. Good health, a tolerable share of understanding, a sound conscience, with good rice fields are preferable to the title of Sir Toby Tribble procured by bribery, perjury and fraud." [2]

Laurens, of course, was seeing that side of life to which travelers are most likely to give attention in any great metropolis like Paris or London. In many smaller cities and towns of England and on every countryside simple and honest men with good morals were keeping the heart of English life sound and wholesome. From that stratum of society came Watt and Howard and Arkwright and Brindley. John Wesley, "that low and puny tadpole of divinity," as the author of "Rock of Ages" called him, gives in his famous diary a different view of the English people from that of Laurens, but he traveled among the middle and lower classes.

English high life was for the moment at its worst. Horace Walpole, the cultivated aristocrat with the

---

[1] Wallace, *Henry Laurens*, 185.   [2] *Ibid.*, 187.

philosophy of a Jacobin, abandoned himself to rhetorical extravagance about the morals of his time. "What is England now? — A sink of Indian wealth, filled by nabobs and emptied by Maccaronis! A senate sold and dispised . . . A gaming, robbing, wrangling, railing nation, without genius, character or allies." [1] On the eve of the war (1775) he bemoaned a condition which he but little magnified. "We are given up to profusion, extravagance and pleasure: heroism is not at all in fashion. Cincinnatus will be found at the hazard table, and Camillus at a ball." [2] "The gaming," he declared, "is worthy the decline of our Empire . . . The young men of the age, lose five, ten, fifteen thousand pounds in an evening . . . Lord S., not one and twenty, lost eleven thousand . . . last Tuesday but recovered it by one great hand at hazard . . . his cousin, Charles Fox, shines equally well (at hazard) and in the House of Commons." [3]

Little wonder that the English Juvenals compared London and Bath with Rome and Baiæ! In the memoirs and letters of the time we find numerous passages as filled with love and wine as a Bacchic ode. "Port" and "Burgundy" and "Claret" dot the pages, and fill the interstices between Hamborough beef and gooseberry tart which furnished forth the midnight feasts. Fine gentlemen, used to swaying the rod of empire, are found at three o'clock in the night, "flown with insolence and wine," and yet ready in the morning to grace a cock-fight. Such

---

[1] Horace Walpole, *Letters* (Toynbee, *ed.*), VIII, 308.
[2] *Ibid.*, IX, 171.   [3] *Ibid.*, VII, 365–66.

methods of dissipation seemed to the fashionable men of that generation to be the only way of attaining "a tolerable state of insensibility to the ills of human life."

All this was not the England of the age of King John, and of Cromwell, and of the Glorious Revolution, the "Old England" of which the colonist dreamed. When on business or on pleasure bent like Franklin or Laurens, or as an exile like Samuel Curwen, the sober provincial saw this passing phase of English life, his dream was shattered, and a loyal British subject was unconsciously made ready for a step in the direction of rebellion. He was apt like Franklin to use impatient exaggeration: "Had I never been in the American Colonies," he wrote, "but was to form my Judgment of Civil Society by what I have lately seen, I should never advise a Nation of Savages to admit of Civilization. Compared to these People every Indian is a Gentleman." [1] When such a disgruntled colonist returned to America, he led others away from their loyalty. Some not so sturdy, nor with so enduring a fiber of character, abandoned the ways of their Puritan fathers, and took up the fashions of London polite society. Laurens confided to his brother, begging him "for goodness' sake" to let it go no further, that an old South Carolina neighbor had "learnt to play at cards and makes Sunday subservient to visiting Richmond and Kew" — places of pleasure and dissipation. Laurens could have found plenty of card-playing in a few places in America which imitated

---

[1] Franklin, *Writings* (Smyth, *ed.*), v, 362.

the London fashions, for at this time Alexander
Mackrabie, a visitor in New York, was writing the
famous Sir Philip Francis, "Here are no Diversions
at all at present . . . I have gone dining about from
House to House, but meet with the same dull round
of Topics everywhere,— lands, Madeira-wine, fishing Parties, or Politics . . . They have a vile Practice
here . . . of playing Back-Gammon (a Noise I de-
test) which is going forward in the public Coffee-
House from Morning to Night, frequently ten or a
dozen Tables at a time." [1] Nevertheless Laurens
knew that among God-fearing Puritans at home it
was not done.

John Adams expressed well the Puritan hatred
of card-playing. "It gratifies none of the senses,
neither sight, hearing, taste, smelling, nor feeling.
It can entertain the mind only by hushing its clam-
ours, cards, backgammon, etc., are genteel antidotes
to reflection, to thinking — that cruel tyrant within
us. They choke the desire for knowledge," he
added. [2] In his early and intellectually priggish days,
he confided to his diary his amazement that men
could play cards, drink punch and wine, smoke tobacco and swear "while a hundred of the best books
lie on the shelves, desks, and chairs in the same
room." [3] In those callow years he coached himself
daily in the same demure diary to "study Seneca
and Cicero and all other good moral writers," praying fervently meanwhile that "foppery, folly, and
vice" in himself might be subdued. "Who can

[1] *The Francis Letters*, I, 97.
[2] John Adams, *Works*, II, 62-63.   [3] *Ibid.*, 62.

study," he lamented, "in Boston streets . . . I cannot raise my mind above this mob crowd of men,
women, beasts, and carriages, to think steadily.
My attention is solicited every moment by some new
object of sight, or some new sound. A coach, a cart,
a lady, or a priest, may at any time . . . disconcert
a whole page of excellent thoughts." [1] He was ever
calculating, too, what company would be good for
him: castigating his tendency to waste time, and
exhorting himself to read Milton, Shakespeare,
and Butler's "Analogy." In all this he was merely
revealing the New England conscience, a species of
that inward monitor found in all lands, but in certain peculiar manifestation more abounding in Massachusetts, Connecticut, and Rhode Island than any
other corner of the earth. The pulpits of those
colonies thundered against the theaters which scandalously advertised those worldly pageants, "Ham-
let" and "Othello." Laws against Sunday travel
were still enforced in Massachusetts and Connecticut, and though men mourned that only the shell of
orthodoxy was left, John Adams could still say with
truth that the New England man was "a meeting-
going animal." The gate by which Boston was
entered on the north was closed on the Lord's day,
and one might be fined for strolling on the Common.
Taverns and shops were shut, and no Boston Nello
could dress a periwig after sundown on Saturday.
The Puritan left no device untried to make of Sunday a virtuous vacuum. Peter Oliver, the banished
Loyalist, sneeringly recorded that "some of the pious

[1] John Adams, *Works*, II, 65.

zealots refused to brew their beer on Saturday lest it should *work* on Sunday in defiance of the fourth Commandment." [1] Prejudice against "Romish holidays" was softened from the early days when spruce and laurel and evergreens were forbidden emblems, and men had sat in jail for eating a Christmas mince pie. The descendants of Sewall would no longer have arranged the coffins in the family vault as "an awful but pleasing Christmas diversion," yet the curse of dullness had not yet been lifted from the observances of that holiday. In the eyes of a liberal foreigner, New England led not only a simple life, but a narrow and bigoted one, and even the natives of New England, when opportunity made them polished and cultivated gentlemen, agreed with Englishmen who found Boston, in 1769, "a noisy turbulent place inhabited by people of coarse insolent manners, not amenable to reasonable control, and like a huge recreation ground full of unruly boys, playing at politics, and aping the ways of serious citizens, and not a community of civilized creatures." [2] That criticism, which was most likely to emanate from educated Englishmen, that America was not "a community of civilized creatures," was just the opinion most certain to cut to the quick, and yet from the Old-World point of view there was ground for this comment. At a time when the old brick Independence Hall in Philadelphia, and Trinity Church in New York, and the old yellow brick Faneuil Hall in Boston were the finest speci-

[1] British Museum, *Egerton MSS.*, 2671 F 13.
[2] Belcher, *First American Civil War*, I, 105.

mens of architecture in North America, England possessed Westminster Abbey, Lincoln and Lichfield and Wells Cathedrals, Magdalen Chapel, Conway, Carnarvon and Warwick Castles, and hundreds of country homes unrivaled in the world.[1] Art galleries, libraries, every creation of civilization abounded in England, while in America little had been done to that end except to clear the forest from the land. American architecture was "bare and square"; England's gifted with every grace which the art of man had devised. Colonial churches, wherein, at the time they were built, no music rose lest it "bewitch the mind with syrenes sounds," were not likely to please the sense with æsthetic lines. It was a Puritan dictum that God's altar needed not the art of man. Colonel Barré need not have warned his American friend, Josiah Quincy, to let his countrymen beware, as of a deadly poison, of taste in their buildings. Granted that Barré's theory was correct that " 't is taste that ruins whole kingdoms, 't is taste that depopulates whole nations,"the danger to America was so far removed in that day that the most ardent patriot need not worry lest his countrymen be "ruined by a taste for fine arts." [2]

What was true of architecture was true of other forms of art. America could boast no rivals to Gainsborough, Romney, or Reynolds. Products of Flaxman or Wedgwood might be found here and there in luxurious American homes, but the makers

---

[1] Walpole, *Letters*, III, 119, 186.
[2] Mass. Hist. Soc., *Proceedings*, L, 452.

had no rivals, not even imitators in the colonies. Franklin would go no further in 1763 than to claim that "some of our young Geniuses begin to lisp attempts at Painting, Poetry, and Music." [1] England was amply supplied with cultivated men and women who would give appreciation and patronage to talent or genius in art, but if America produced a West or a Copley, he must go to live in England, that the sensitive growth of his genius might not be chilled. Benjamin Franklin (1763), before his heart was seared by what he believed to be the wrongs of his country, wrote of England: "Of all the enviable Things I envy it most its People. Why should that petty Island, which . . . is but like a stepping Stone in a Brook, scarce enough of it above Water, to keep one's Shoes dry . . . enjoy in almost every Neighborhood more sensible, virtuous and elegant Minds than we can collect in ranging a hundred Leagues of our vast Forests?" [2] The answer was, of course, simple, for in America the fortunes were not yet made which were to give leisure for the refinements and amenities of life. Human time and human energy were too much absorbed in the mere struggle for existence. The wilderness had attracted the robust and strong, and the land-hungry, but not the neurotic, nor the weak, nor the intellectual and artistic. The latter had been left behind, and America would have to develop those types with the passing of generations, or bide her time until her evolving civilization should create conditions attractive to the European artists and intellectuals.

[1] Franklin, *Writings* (Smyth, *ed.*), IV, 194.   [2] *Ibid.*

For the present the refinement of England was exhibited in the noble political philosophy of Burke, the lofty eloquence of Pitt, and Horace Walpole's cultivation as seen in his charming letters, while the ruder culture of the American frontier of the British Empire was shown in Patrick Henry's stump oratory, Thomas Jefferson's amateur philosophy, and the homely wisdom of "Poor Richard." A Horace Walpole was unthinkable in the American colonies, and even Benjamin Franklin was a phenomenon sufficient to be the pride of a continent. Great as was the latter's reputation in science, his observations in that field would not always bear inspection, as for example his flies, which, after being embalmed in a bottle of Madeira, came to life months later! [1]

In every manifestation of artistic appreciation there was the same sharp contrast. At a time when Handel was moving England with his choral music, psalmody was in America, Jonathan Boucher wrote, "everywhere ordinary and mean." Boucher's criticism referred to a time long after it was proposed to permit singing only to godly men regardless of their voices, and to bar "carnall men and Pagans." [2] At a time when some of the world's greatest musicians were rising to fame on the European continent, and when they enjoyed a great, appreciative audience in England, the colonists had attained only the rudest stages of that art. Not that "music, heavenly maid," had fled the colonies, but she had never been warmly esteemed there. In New England the Puri-

---

[1] Franklin, *Writings* (Smyth, *ed.*), vi, 43–44.
[2] Eggleston, *Transit of Civilization*, 186.

tan settlers had been hostile to music, and what they permitted must have "conscience rather than elegance." Lest it should prove an instrument of the devil to charm godly minds from holy thoughts, the Puritan had been wary of music for its own sake. In New York and Charleston the singing of hymns was from the first accepted without controversy, but in New England, church singing gained approval slowly, and the strong prejudice against instrumental music caused the church organ to be barred in some districts until well into the nineteenth century. Nevertheless the real beginning of truly American music was probably in the psalm-singing of the Pilgrims; though Old-World music had been sung earlier by the Virginians. The old "Bay Psalm Book" with not more than eight or ten tunes was not likely to allure with "syrenes sounds," and even Williams's "New Harmony of Zion" (1769), and Flagg's collection of one hundred and sixteen tunes and two anthems might be resisted by the pure in heart. Flagg admitted, "We are obliged to the other side of the Atlantic chiefly for our tunes." Yet America was progressing. As early as 1740, Philadelphia had a "Musical Association." Choir singing began about 1750, and twenty years later, William Billings, the first American composer, and a good type of the provincial crudity, published "The New England Psalm Singer." There were concerts in New England forty years before the Revolution. Later in Charleston, Philadelphia, and New York sporadic musical entertainments were given, but in Charleston, at least, it seems to have been necessary to mingle tight-rope dancing, magic, and other thrills with the more sober musical entertainment.[1] Before the Revolution a few professional musicians eked out an existence, and one in Virginia advertised instruction in the "true method of Singing Psalms." [2] Individuals throughout America indulged a crude taste in an amateur way. John Adams was in his youth tempted by the fiddle, and both Henry and Jefferson yielded to its charms. Every cultivated young lady must play the harpsichord or the spinet, which were to be found in the homes of prosperous merchants and planters. Jefferson ordered a "forte Piano" of solid mahogany, "worthy the acceptance of a lady for whom I intend it." "Councillor" Carter had "an Armonica, one of the new fashioned musical instruments invented by B. Franklin," but his uncle, Langdon Carter, less "moved with a concord of sweet sounds," complains in his diary of a "constant tuting" from one instrument or another in the town of Williamsburg.[3]

"The cultivation of music is rather rare as yet," wrote Mittelberger about 1750. "In Philadelphia, no music is made either in the English or in the German Churches. Some English men give occasional concerts in private homes with a spinet or harpsichord. I came to this country with the first organ, which now stands in a High German Lutheran Church in the city of Philadelphia, and which was built in Heilbronn . . . many people came from a great distance, 10, 20, 30, 40, and even 50 hours'

---

[1] O. G. Sonneck, *Early Concert Life in America, passim.*
[2] M. N. Stanard, *Colonial Virginia*, chap. XII.   [3] *Ibid.*

journey to see and hear this organ. . . . As I became more and more known in Pennsylvania, and the people learned that I had brought fine and good instruments with me, many English and German families came 10, 20, and 30 hours' journey to hear them . . . and they were greatly surprised, because they had never in all their lives seen or heard an organ or any of these instruments." [1] In appreciation of music as in art, the colonies trailed far behind England. America was only at the beginning of the ascent to Parnassus, and the muses hardly knew of her existence.

Intellectual attainment in its higher spheres was in America far below that in contemporary England. A polite literature created by native authors did not even exist in the colonies in a generation for which Sterne was writing his "Sentimental Journey," Sheridan, "The Rivals," and Goldsmith, "She Stoops to Conquer." At a time when Johnson and Burke and Cowper were delighting a cultivated English public, America could boast only a few rushlights of literature which even the inordinate national vanity of historians of American literature has been unable to keep aflame. Ten years before the American Revolution a Boston paper spoke of Michael Wigglesworth's "Day of Doom" as "those divine poems." If not typical of New England taste, it did not shock it to speak thus of a book which describes in doggerel the damnation of non-elect babes for the guilt of Adam's sin, merely granting them "the easiest room in Hell," and which portrays Christ as now a Mo-

[1] Mittelberger, *Journey to Pennsylvania*, 114-15.

loch, now a saintly Dogberry. The Puritan mind,
which took sheer delight in the thought of that
"fiery deluge, fed with ever-burning sulphur uncon-
sumed," preferred Dent's "Plaine Man's Pathway
to Heaven wherein every man may clearly see
whether he shall be saved or damned" to the mere
worldly entertainment of the "Sentimental Journey." On the eve of the Revolution there was much
lyric verse contrasting the charms of Freedom with
the ugliness of Tyranny, but no man of taste would
now give it a place in a collection of the best English
verse of the eighteenth century. In prose most
literary expression was pugnacious. Words were
blows. Mild and pleasing forms of literature were
not in fashion. Even theological literature must not
be mild. The Puritan at least had only censure for
the "smooth divine, unused to wound the sinner's
heart with Hell's alarming sound."

Life in the colonies was too wrapped in the material interests, energy too much spent in the battle
for life. Even a Milton would have been mute and
inglorious where sympathy never turned its genial
face, and where no detached mind gave heed. Not
that the Americans of that day were wholly wanting
in the appreciation of pure literature, but the audience was small, and usually provincial enough not
to recognize talent or genius until it had been ac-
claimed in England. Many who did care for elegant
literature acquired the taste in English schools where
the sons of wealthy planters or prosperous merchants
were apt to be educated, and their minds furnished
in the best English fashion. Lord Adam Gordon,

traveling in Virginia before the war, says in his journal that most of the gentlemen he met there were educated in England.[1] Among such men it was, of course, good form to gain polish and urbanity by a communion with the classics, ancient or modern. Nevertheless, the average Virginia gentleman had not eaten excessively "of the dainties that are bred in a book." It was to some extent in Virginia, as Guevara says of the days of chivalry, "When among knights or gentlemen talk is of arms, a gentleman ought to have great shame to say that he read it, but rather that he saw it." In Boston we are told it was the Loyalists of the North End, whose sectarian bent was shown by the possession of the "English Prayer Book," who read "Tom Jones," "Tristram Shandy," "Sir Charles Grandison," and Addison's "Spectator." With them it was an imported fashion, followed because the path was well worn by those whom they aped in England. Nevertheless, good reading was not a monopoly of the Hutchinsons and the Olivers, the Apthorps and the Amorys, for Abigail Adams knew her Addison and her Pope, her Milton, Dryden, and Shakespeare, and had wit enough to quote them in her devoted letters to her much too absent husband, John Adams. She could not, however, be brought to like Molière, for the good Puritan reason that "he ridicules vice, without engaging us to Virtue."[2] Richard Henry Lee reveals in his letters an acquaintance with

[1] Mereness, *Travels in the American Colonies*, 405. An interesting list of the Virginians so educated, and where, is given in M. N. Stanard, *Colonial Virginia*, 292–94.

[2] *Warren-Adams Letters*, 19.

Shakespeare, Pope, Butler's "Hudibras," and even with the "Junius Letters," which were little liked in America, perhaps because the subtlety of their innuendo and irony made little appeal to the conventional colonial mind. Lee also shows a familiarity, a little pedantic at times, with the Latin language, and with the classic myths.[1] Nathanael Greene, too, read the English poets, and knew well his Plutarch and his Cæsar. Henry Laurens, with no Latin or Greek, and only a smattering of French, had opened his mind to a liberal view of the world by wide reading of the English, or the translated ancient classics. The very names of his slaves, Othello, Tully, Mentor, Valerius, Claudius, Juliet, Lavinia, and many similar would attest that he had at least brought away the scraps from his feast of knowledge.[2]

In spite of the existence in the generation before the Revolution of such institutions of learning as Harvard College, sending forth its average of about forty Bachelors of Arts annually, and of Yale, King's, Princeton, William and Mary, and other yet smaller colleges, the opportunities for acquiring more than superficial learning were few. John Adams, at the age of twenty, wrote sadly in his diary: "I long to be a master of Greek and Latin. I long to prosecute the mathematical and philosophical sciences. I long to know a little ethics and moral philosophy. But I have no books, no time, no friends. I must there-

---

[1] R. H. Lee, *Letters*, i, 5, 129, 161, 167, 175, 187; *The Francis Letters*, i, 112.

[2] Wallace, *Henry Laurens*, 15, 79.

fore be contented to live and die an ignorant, obscure
fellow." Yet he was a Bachelor of Arts from Harvard College.[1] In the yearnings of young Adams
one sees the avidity with which the ambitious youth
of America was reaching for even the scraps of
erudition. Adams improved every opportunity to
seize the crumbs of culture. He tells with pride that
James Otis used to invite him home evenings to
converse "on all subjects of religion, morals, law,
politics, history, philosophy, belles-lettres, theology, mythology, cosmogony, metaphysics,— Locke,
Clark, Leibnitz, Bolingbroke, Berkeley," and other
"subjects as high as Milton's gentry in Pande-
monium." [2]

He, with Otis and Thacher, belonged to the
"Sodalitas," a law club, really a political science
club, which read and discussed Blackstone, Robertson's "History of Scotland," "Lord Coke," and
Rousseau.[3] There was no lack of zest in the intellectual appetite of the most ambitious colonials,
but the pliant hour and the tools of science or
scholarship were wanting. Over a generation later,
Noah Webster sadly admitted, "our learning is
superficial in a shameful degree, . . . our colleges are
disgracefully destitute of books and philosophical
apparatus, . . . and I am ashamed to own that
scarcely a branch of science can be fully investigated
in America for want of books especially original
works. As to libraries, we have no such things.
There are not more than three or four tolerable
libraries in America, and these are extremely im-

[1] John Adams, *Works*, II, 13.   [2] *Ibid.*, x, 285.   [3] *Ibid.*, II, 148.

perfect.[1]   Great numbers of the most valuable
authors have not found their way across the Atlantic." — "As to classical learning," he went on,
"history, (civil and ecclesiastical,) mathematics,
astronomy, chemistry, botany, and natural history,
excepting here and there a rare instance of a man
who is eminent in some one of these branches, we
may be said to have no learning at all, or a mere
smattering." [2] Webster's words were even more true
in Franklin's time, when besides himself and David
Rittenhouse, who said of himself that "he would
probably be slain making a telescope as was Archi-
medes, while tracing figures on the sand," there were
very few who had the least reputation in science.[3]
Franklin himself, in order to satisfy his hunger for
scientific knowledge, was obliged to correspond with
English or French scientists such as William Her-
schel, Nevil Maskelyne, or Antoine Court de Gébelin.

It was not that the common people of America
were more unlettered than the masses in England,
for, at least in New England, the people were probably better cared for in the rudiments of education
than in the mother country; but in the higher
aspects of intellectual life, English attainment
towered far above that of America.   There was, of

---

[1] For libraries in Philadelphia, see Schoepf, i, 86–87; in the treasure
room of the Widener Library on the exhibition board is a list of books
in the Harvard Library in 1764 (in a newspaper account of a fire at
Harvard).   For lists of books in Virginia libraries, see M. H. Stanard.
Colonial Virginia, 295; see also *Libraries and Literature in North Carolina in the Eighteenth Century*, Washington, 1890.   Also American
Antiquarian Society, *Proceedings*, v, 171.

[2] Henry Adams, *History of the United States*, i, 63.

[3] Pennypacker, *Historical Sketches*, 65.

course, nothing uncivilized about the colonists, for, after all, they were only transplanted Europeans, and as far as possible had carried with them the letters and arts and science of the Old World; but in the early days only the ruder forms took root, while the higher drooped and died. The colonists had, in fact, made remarkable progress and already possessed a culture admirably suited to the needs of their simple life, but in the eyes of the English connoisseur, their science and art and letters seemed boorish and rustic in a contemptible degree.

This cultural difference extended even to the very language which was their common heritage. Noah Webster wrote a few years after the Revolution, "a new country, new associations of people, new combinations of ideas in arts and sciences, and some intercourse with tribes wholly unknown in Europe, . . . introduce new words into the American tongue." He even ventured to prophesy that in time American English would differ from that of the British Isles as Dutch or Swedish from German. Many easily traced influences had brought this to pass. In addition to the many new words learned from the Indians for new objects unknown to the European world, there were words and phrases culled from the speech of the Dutch, French Huguenot, or German settlers, and even from the negro slave. Their "succulent and nervous speech" drew some of its aberrations from the climatic conditions, some from the nervous haste of Americans, urging them to short cuts for verbal expressions. If their speech was vehement and brusque, the strain of frontier life

explained it, and if they were unusually contemptuous of the rigors of grammar, that too might be explained by their being cut off from the corrective
influence of books.

Witherspoon, who came from Scotland in 1769 to
be President of Princeton, asserted, "I have heard
in this country, in the senate, at the bar, and from
the pulpit, and see daily in dissertations from the
press, errors in grammar, improprieties and vulgar-
isms which hardly any person of the same rank
would have fallen into in Great Britain." [1] That
commentary was perfectly in keeping with the
opinion of most colonial governors and their coterie
of subordinate colonial officers.

English travelers, like cultivated Easterners wandering in the benighted West to-day, were wont to
regard their own English as the "pure and limpid
stream," and to denounce American divergences as
the turbid waters of a wild and swollen torrent.
They listened with ill-concealed disdain to amateur
botanists who were not only ignorant of Latin
names, but of their English equivalents, and who
had invented *poke-weed*, *eel-grass*, *egg-plant*, *huckle-
berry*, and *Johnny-jump-up*. It was not enlighten-
ing to have the landscape described by their colonial
host with outlandish terms such as *run*, *fork*, *bluff*,
neck, *notch*, and *bottom-lands*. It depended upon the
English visitor's sense of humor whether he was
pleased to find that *mush* had driven out *porridge*,
or that he was expected to eat Indian *succotash*,

[1] The Druid No. 5, in Witherspoon, *Collected Works* (Green, ed.,
1800), IV.

German *noodle* soup, or Dutch *crullers* and *cookies*. It grated even on the royal ear to hear what seemed the careless use of good English words. When the loyal Hutchinson used the word "corn" in conversation with George III, the King stopped him testily with "What corn?" "Indian corn," Hutchinson explained, "or as it is called in authors, maize."

Jonathan Boucher, who came from England to Virginia, and who for years preached to George Washington, wrote spitefully, after he was driven back to England for his loyalism, that the Americans were "making all the haste they can to rid themselves of the |English| language." He had encountered in Virginia the droll Indian words, *opossum*, *chipmunk*, *papoose*, and *pow-wow*, and had heard new and odd combinations of familiar English words like *fire-water* and *war-path*. His Brahmin sensibilities had been offended, no doubt, by the term *hired man*, a term coined in America to avoid the word *servant*, much resented by the frontiersman of the late colonial period. A highly cultivated mind like Boucher's was certain not to approve of the bold, extravagant American humor and grotesque imagination, nor would he like colonial contempt for grammatical authority. And yet he might have found preserved in the colonies choice words that had become archaic in England. "Our ancestors," Lowell laments with his dry humor, "unhappily could bring over no English better than Shakespeare's," and in colonial times, as to-day, in remote places where the stream of change has been little felt, one could hear the " gypsy phrases," the "loose and brilliant syntax" of the Shakespearean vocabulary.[1] And yet Jonathan Boucher was very naturally not pleased. America was the refuge of the uneducated and those not delicate in an æsthetic sense. John Pory, annalist of early Virginia, found the incoming vessels freighted more with ignorance than other merchandise. These uncouth settlers had no respect for the keepers of the sacred vessels of the English language. They were cultural image-breakers, knowing more of the axe and the plough than of spelling books and grammar. To New England, too, there came in time men with only contempt for the high-browed Puritan divines — blackguard sailors, and workmen — ready to coin, with loutish wit, new words from English materials such as *bull-frog, hog-wallow, razor-back, garter-snake,* and *lightning-bug.*[2] When such forces had been at work for one hundred and fifty years, it was not strange that Franklin drew up (1768) a scheme of spelling reform which should conform to the standards of spelling and pronunciation in the New World.[3] Eleven years later, when Ambassador to France, he was instructed to use the "language of the United States in communications to Louis XVI." This order was given in the heat of strife, but betrayed that the members of the foreign committees of Congress were conscious of a difference between American and English speech.

The peculiarities of language and colloquial slang

---

[1] H. L. Mencken, *The American Language,* 58, quotes *Dialect Notes,* iv, iv, 283-97.

[2] *Ibid.,* 44, 45.   [3] Franklin, *Writings* (Smyth, ed.), v, 169.

in New England during the colonial period are nowhere more naïvely reproduced than in the journal
of Madame Knight kept on a journey from Boston
to New York.[1] Travelers usually derided such torture of the King's English in private, but in 1775,
in the midst of debate in the Commons on the state
of American affairs, Colonel Grant, who had served
in America and claimed to know the colonists well,
made merry with them before Parliament; and, Hansard says, "repeated many of their common-place
expressions, ridiculed their enthusiasm in matters
of religion and drew a disagreeable picture of their
manners and ways of living." [2]

In but one direction did American intellectual
attainment gain respect in England. American State
papers such as the resolutions of the Stamp Act
Congress, the Massachusetts Circular Letter, and
the Virginia Resolutions did much to enlighten
Europeans about the state of American civilization.
These "law-defying backwoodsmen" showed no
mean amount of cultivation in political matters and
minds moulded by political literature, law, and
history to a sober political conservatism worthy even
of the Old World. Few of the writers on politics
were unknown to the American leaders before the
War of Independence. Burke declared in 1775, "I
hear as many Blackstones are sold in America as in
England." John Adams read and quoted Harrington, Hooker, Sidney, Selden, Locke, Hobbes, Montesquieu, Rousseau, Grotius, and Pufendorf. In

[1] *The Journals of Madam Knight*, etc. (N.Y. 1825 ed.).
[2] Force, *American Archives* (4th Ser.), I, 1543.

Franklin's library were Locke, Hoadley, Sidney, Milton, and Montesquieu. John Hancock owned Milton, and Beccaria on Crimes. Josiah Quincy bequeathed to his son, Sidney and Locke's Works. Jonathan Mayhew knew well his Locke and Milton's "Defence of the People of England." President Stiles read with approval Harrington's "The Commonwealth of Oceana." Samuel Cooper, writing to Thomas Pownall, bolstered an argument by referring to Jean Jacques Burlamaqui, the Swiss author of "Principes du Droit Naturel" (1747). Selden, and Montesquieu's "Spirit of the Laws" are quoted by Richard Henry Lee. Robert Carter's library of 1066 volumes contained, in 1772, Locke, Sidney, Hume, and Hobbes.[1] Samuel Adams had read Grotius, Hooker, Hume and Locke, Montesquieu, Sidney and Vattel; and Alexander Hamilton, youth that he was, showed that he was grounded in Grotius, Hobbes, Hume, Locke, Montesquieu, and Puffendorf. John Dickinson prepared for his "Farmer's Letters" on a diet of Hooker, Hume, Locke, and Montesquieu. This "catalogue of the ships," though it makes Homer seem to nod, is of great significance, if one would understand the source of American liberal political philosophy. The wide acquaintance with such literature was the one green oasis in the arid desert of American intellectual

---

[1] John Adams, *Works*, ii, *passim;* Sears, *John Hancock*, 109; *American Historical Review*, viii, 328; R. H. Lee, *Letters*, i, 20; ii, 95; Stanard, *Colonial Virginia*, 304. Mr. Goshorn, a graduate student, tabulated the number of times certain famous political writers were quoted before 1776 by the political leaders of America. Locke was quoted 22 times, Hume 20, Selden 11, Montesquieu 10, Grotius 8. Harrington 8, Hooker 4, Vattel 4, Pufendorf 4, Hobbes 2, Sidney 6.

attainment. No sensible English statesmen would speak disdainfully of colonial accomplishment in that branch of learning.

The other ways, however, in which the colonists were inferior to the English in the externals of civilization, or at least different in a marked degree, tended not only to create misunderstandings, but actually a new nation. Not only was there the contrast of country and town life, the differences in wealth and the distribution of it, which brought in their train the glaring moral dissimilarity and the disparity in intellectual attainment, but there was actual difference in the ethnic make-up of colony and mother country. Whatever combination of peoples had in centuries past formed the English race, the inflow of alien blood during the last two centuries had made little change, while into America during the last century had poured hundreds of thousands of Germans and Scotch-Irish, many thousands of French Huguenots and Dutch, until fully two fifths of America's white population was of other than English extraction. This same movement, together with religious unrest in England, had brought a variety of religious sects, and had made America, like the Netherlands, a "great mingle-mangle of religions," very unlike the comparative uniformity in England. This immigration had brought also not only foreign tongues, but some of the changes in the English language itself which have just been noted. It was the great sum of all these differences which created conditions foreshadowing an independent America.

CHAPTER XIII

RELIGIOUS AND SECTARIAN FORCES WHICH THREATENED IMPERIAL UNITY

A SPY traveling in the colonies in 1765 in the employ of the French Government made in English a summary sketch of the various religious sects in America, closing with the observation, "In Boston they are ranck bigoted presbitarians, of these sort of people preserve me O Lord."[1] This fact and the historical tradition, fixed in the Puritan mind, that from their first settlement in New England they had resisted the attempt of the British Government to transplant into their midst the seeds of privilege and the institutions of feudalism, became a secondary cause for desiring to break the bonds uniting them to the homeland. Early in the history of Massachusetts Bay, Archbishop Laud, hoping to supplant the Puritan with the Anglican Church, had aided Gorges, aristocrat and supporter of the Stuarts, in an effort to set up as a feudal proprietor in the Puritan midst.[2] The plan failed, but the fear remained, and after 1700 the suspicions of the colonists were often aroused. Once the Anglican Church supported a plan to subject all corporate and proprietary colonies to the direct control of the Crown, and that was taken as an attempted blow at the Puritan

[1] Paris Archives, *Service Hydrographique de la Marine*, vol. 76, no. 2; *Journal of Travel in American Colonies*, July 9, 1765.

[2] Bradford, *History of Plymouth Plantation* (Original Narratives Series), 315–16.

and Quaker power. Often the dissenting sects noted the zeal of that good shepherd, the Bishop of London, in getting political plums for members of his Anglican flock. The same apostolic figure in lawn sleeves was known to have secured a veto of laws which had seemed good to dissenting colonial legislators. Andros, with that prelate's approval, had tried to place marriages solely in the hands of Anglican clergy. In Virginia, indeed, this was the case, although some who held the holy monopoly were, we are told, such as would "babble in a pulpit and roar in a tavern." [1] Nevertheless, though the Board of Trade was not above aiding the interests of the Established Church, the graven image of commerce was not permitted to be injured by the zeal for the true God. [2] For this reason the Board enforced toleration, but even that was hateful to bigoted dissenting colonists who wished to assail Anglican rivals. To an American public long nagged by fear of intrusion by Episcopalian officialdom there came, nearly at the same time with the Stamp and Townshend Acts, a threat of setting up an American Episcopate. [3]

The Anglican Church, during the colonial period, had legal establishment only in the colonies south of Pennsylvania and in three counties of New York. The Episcopal clergy in these colonies were obliged

---

[1] *Pennsylvania Statutes at Large*, II, 450, 480, 490; *Colonial Records of North Carolina*, VI, 716; Hutchinson, *History of Massachusetts Bay*, I, 318; Johns Hopkins University Studies, XII, no. 4.

[2] Dickerson, *American Colonial Government*, 231–33.

[3] Since the publication of Dr. Cross's exhaustive and scholarly study of the *Anglican Episcopate and the American Colonies*, it remains the last word on the subject.

to secure ordination from the Bishop of London, whose jurisdiction was extended over the colonies. The journey of six thousand miles in a sailing vessel "to interview a cross old gentleman" in London was a serious matter enough to check the rise of a native American clergy.[1] Those sent from England were often the sort that had failed at home, and who only disgraced the cloth in America. In Virginia, they were reputed to be the sort to whom the sheep look up and were not fed.[2] On the spiritual side, there was much to be said for bringing Mahomet to the mountain — for bringing a bishop to America — and thus making ordination easy. Against this excellent spiritual argument fought two very important political objections. In the North, the sending of bishops on the authority of Parliament — and only by its act could the American Episcopate be founded — would seem to the dissenting sects to threaten their overthrow; while in the South, where the Anglican Church was established, the Episcopalians preferred local to imperial control.

Beginning with an unsuccessful plan of Archbishop Laud's in 1638,[3] to send a bishop to New England,

---

[1] Some of those who, "inwardly moved by the Holy Ghost" — to use Mayhew's sneering phrase — "have taken a trip across the Atlantic to obtain Episcopal ordination," were Rev. S. Johnson, President of King's College; Rev. Timothy Cutler, President of Yale; Rev. S. A. Peters, author of the *History of Connecticut;* Rev. E. Apthorp, missionary "in foreign parts, at Cambridge, Mass." Thornton, *The Pulpit in the American Revolution*, 100.

[2] W. S. Perry, *Historical Collections relative to American Colonial Church*, IV, 128; H. A. White, *Southern Presbyterian Leaders*, 106. But see on the other side, *William and Mary College Quarterly*, XIX, 13.

[3] According to the assertion of Heylyn, *Cyprianus Anglicus*, 347, quoted by Cross, *Anglican Episcopate*, 21.

and to back him with some force to compel obedience, there were isolated, still-born plans of this
sort, from time to time, for the next half-century.
In 1701, there was incorporated the "Society for
the Propagation of the Gospel in Foreign Parts,"
and this heavenly-minded society began very soon
to urge, from what were at first, no doubt, spiritual motives, the establishment of an Episcopate
in America. They just missed being successful in
Queen Anne's time, but, thereafter, George I was
found to be cold toward the project, and the shrewd
Sir Robert Walpole was too wise to attempt it. For
a quarter of a century the idea dwindled, but revived
again when the Bishop of Oxford, Thomas Secker,
preached a notable sermon in its favor, which was
vigorously confuted by Rev. Andrew Eliot in America. From 1748 to 1761, Thomas Sherlock, meanwhile Bishop of London, strove without ceasing for
an American Episcopate. In 1763, Jonathan Mayhew, whom John Adams sought to designate as the
spiritual director of the American Revolution, began
his famous attack upon the Society for the Propagation of the Gospel. This Society, he declared, was
trying to "root out Presbyterianism" in America by
getting Parliament to establish a bishop in America.
He was answered by Secker and others; and this
controversy, says John Adams, "spread an universal
alarm against the authority of Parliament." Next
occurred (1767–71) a bitter pamphlet war between
Thomas Bradbury Chandler and Charles Chauncey,
in which the former's appeal for an Episcopacy was
sanctioned by a convention of his Episcopalian

brethren from New York and New Jersey. He was accused of aspiring after a complete Church hierarchy with revenues, and bare toleration for dissenters. A newspaper war characterized this controversy, in which figured William Livingston, John Dickinson, and others who later became prominent in the Revolutionary struggle. So bitter was the attack on the Episcopacy that the dissenting writers themselves seemed barely to refrain from that ceremonial, the laying on of hands, which in their ministration would have had no spiritual significance.

In the course of this paper war many improbable perils were conjured up by the opponents of Episcopacy. Some of the pamphleteers had "lived long on the alms basket of words." Bishops, who in Archbishop Laud's time had been denounced by their Puritan enemies as "knobs and wens and bunchy popish flesh," now became "Apostolical monarchs," "right reverend and holy tyrants"; they would, it was said, introduce "canon law — a poison, a pollution."[1] The Congregationalists of New England were warned that they would "be consumed by the flames or deluged in a flood of Episcopacy." Mercilessly the Puritan Juggernaut was dragged over every scheme for an American Episcopate. Mayhew told his New England readers that the "People have no security against being unmercifully priest-ridden but by keeping all imperious bishops, and other clergymen who love to lord it over God's heritage, from getting their feet into the stirrup at

[1] Samuel Adams, *Writings*, II, 236. One said "the court of probate might get into their hands." John Adams, *Works*, II, 284.

all."[1] These prophecies of evil were the very thing to appeal to the masses of the people who read them in their newspapers. Moreover, after the Stamp and other revenue acts, the economic aspects of the religious question were dwelt upon. Set up a bishop in America, and he must be supported. If the colonial assemblies refused, Parliament would be called upon to tax. In 1768, it was artfully asked, "At this time when we are suffering from the restrictions on our trade are we to be involved in ecclesiastical bondage into the bargain; Is this the time to think of episcopal palaces, of pontifical revenues, of spiritual courts and of all the pomp, grandeur, luxury and regalia of an American Lambeth?"[2] To these hints of tithes and spiritual courts were added prophecies of the assumption of secular functions by the bishops.[3] As to their attitude in politics, it was pointed out that five bishops had joined the Lords in their protest against the repeal of the Stamp Act. All of these terrors were very real to many good people; and it does not matter that the English State authorities did not consider the Episcopate project seriously,[4] for they were suspected of doing so; and it was the American "state of mind" that wrought the mischief. It was, as the Massachusetts House of Representatives put it (1768), "very alarming to a people whose fathers, from the

[1] Cross, *Anglican Episcopate*, 145. [2] *Ibid.* 196, 213.
[3] Thornton, *The Pulpit of the Revolution*, 204; Richard Henry Lee, *Letters*, I, 59; Mass. Hist. Soc., *Collections* (2d Ser.), II, 209, 210; Samuel Adams, *Writings*, II, 272.
[4] Cross, *Anglican Episcopate*, 199, 258; *Literary Diary of Ezra Stiles*, I, 238.

hardships they suffered, under such an establishment, were obliged to fly their native country into a wilderness." [1]

In the North, the opposition to the plan of American bishops was almost universal outside the pale of the Episcopalian Church,[2] and even in the South, the Anglican laity of Virginia were opposed, for they already had State control, and did not want intrusion by the British Government.[3] Even some of the Virginia clergy recognized that that agitation would "infuse jealousies and Fears into the Minds of the Protestant Dissenters," and the House of Burgesses, though almost wholly Anglican, approved of this objection.[4] Arthur Lee, a Virginian, regarded the scheme of an American Episcopate "as threatening the subversion of both our civil and religious liberties." [5] Part of the Virginia clergy, however, and

[1] Samuel Adams, *Writings*, I, 149. Franklin expresses the same idea, *Writings* (Smyth, *ed.*), v, 403. William Pitt had a similar view. But see Franklin's denial, *Writings* (Smyth, *ed.*), v, 207.

[2] The synods of New Jersey and New York Presbyterians joined the Congregational Association of Connecticut in frustrating the efforts of Episcopal organization. Cross, *Anglican Episcopate*, 216; Trent, in Jameson, *Essays*, 234; *Literary Diary of Ezra Stiles*, I, 24 (note). It would not have been more desirable, perhaps, had they known that Dean Swift asked to be sent out as a bishop over the Virginia Lilliputians. Cross, *Anglican Episcopate*, 91–92.

[3] Cross, *Anglican Episcopate*, 200.

[4] *Ibid.*, 233, 235; Franklin, *Writings* (Smyth, *ed.*), v, 404–05; *Literary Diary of Ezra Stiles*, I, 116, 138; Samuel Adams, *Writings*, II, 236.

[5] Thornton, *The Pulpit of the Revolution*, 110. As to forebodings such as this, Dr. Cross says: "The fact that the leaders of the Church of England in America thought and acted in concert, and furthermore, that many of them held well-known loyalist sympathies, makes the supposition possible that they held some ulterior motive in the introduction of bishops, which boded no good to the religious liberties of their fellow-colonists." Cross, *Anglican Episcopate*, 166.

all, apparently, of the Maryland clergy did petition the British Government for an American bishop.[1] Some who favored this were accused of looking up to the British Government "for an American episcopate, and a pair of lawn sleeves." [2] One should note that most of those in Maryland who had a part in this petitioning later went into the Loyalist party.

As to the effect of this controversy in bringing on the Revolution, we have the assertion of Jonathan Boucher, a Loyalist, that it was "clearly one great cause," and of John Adams, a Patriot, that the apprehension contributed "as much as any other cause, to arouse the attention, not only of the inquiring mind, but of the common people, and urge them to close thinking on the constitutional authority of parliament over the colonies." [3] Dr. Cross, the leading authority on the subject, takes a cautious tone, saying: "If the question of the establishment of the Episcopate did not contribute a lion's share in causing that enmity to England . . . it is involved in the struggle and deserves to be regarded as an important part of it," and again, "it was at least one of the causes tending to . . . alienation." [4] Looking at the matter from another angle, he says later: "the strained relations which heralded the approach of the war of independence strengthened

[1] *Literary Diary of Ezra Stiles*, I, 91.

[2] John Adams, *Works*, II, 358.

[3] Jonathan Boucher, *View of the Causes of the American Revolution*, 150; John Adams, *Works*, X, 185, 188, 288.

[4] M. Chamberlain, *John Adams*, 23, 47, 25 (note); Brooks Adams, *Emancipation of Massachusetts*, 314 *et seq.*; Cross, *Anglican Episcopate*, 157, 214; Thornton, *The Pulpit of the Revolution*, 109–10.

the opposition to Episcopacy, rather than that religious differences were a prime moving cause of political alienation." [1] In the light of the date (1750) of the bitter Mayhew controversy — quite as envenomed as any later contest — it is hard to agree with this last opinion unless it is limited solely to the Anglican Episcopate controversy, and does not include other religious differences, cumulative in effect and creating a general spirit of discontent. Different issues were at different periods uppermost in men's minds, and, though they might at times seem most concerned with economic grievances, the religious one was deep and abiding. Moreover, Dr. Cross himself points out another way in which this quarrel surely had great influence, when he says: "It is at least a tenable hypothesis that the bitterness of the controversy brought out so sharply the latent hostility between Episcopalian and Puritan, that many churchmen who might otherwise have taken the side of their country, were, by the force of their injured religious convictions, driven over to the loyalists' ranks." [2]

If one looks only at this opposition to an American Episcopate, one misses the full influence of religious and sectarian forces in causing a desire for independence. One notable fact in addition was the large number of Presbyterian and Congregationalist ministers preaching in various parts of America, during several generations, the doctrines of political liberty which they had learned from their study of seven·

---

[1] Cross, *Anglican Episcopate*, 271.
[2] *Ibid.*, 214.

teenth-century apostles of free institutions.[1] Jonathan Mayhew tells us "that as a youth he was initiated in the doctrines of civil liberty as taught by Sidney, Milton, Locke and Hoadly; and he had learned from the holy scriptures that wise, brave and virtuous men were always friends to liberty"; and that "where the spirit of the Lord is there is liberty."[2] New England preachers regarded themselves and their flocks as lineal descendants of the rebellious Puritans of Cromwell's time, and they felt bound to defend the Puritan Revolution.[3] For such a purpose these bookish men found an arsenal of argumentative weapons in the writings of Locke and Milton. Though their sermons might have no hint of discontent, no incitement to rebellion, yet they would often state Locke's theories more clearly than Locke himself. Their people, living in an open-minded frontier, fed on a political pabulum like this, would be certain never to endure an arbitrary government distant three thousand miles.

The pulpit, in the northern provinces at least, was in colonial times the most direct and effectual way of reaching the masses, far outrivaling the newspaper, then only in its infancy. In New England, moreover, a sermon was always preached as a part of the imposing ceremony of the election. This was not a mere compliment to religion, for after 1750, the sermons were listened to as a source of political instruction. By legislative resolution they were

---

[1] See lists of sermons in my article in *American Historical Review*, **xix**, 48 *et seq.*
[2] Tudor, *James Otis*, 144. [3] John Witherspoon, *Works*, I, 326.

published in pamphlet form, and were scattered through the colony, becoming in some cases a sort of text of civil rights. Preachers like Mayhew and Cooper seem to have known as much of the science of government as Otis and the Adamses. They boldly attacked the question of the nature of compacts and charters as they affected the relations of the colonies to England. They discussed the origin, nature, and end of government, and the rights of man, and asserted that all laws were designed for the good of the governed.

In these sermons, the congregations were told of Locke's doctrine that it was the people's right to choose their own rulers and to fix the bounds of their authority. They were taught that government was accountable to the people, and that the New England charter had been a compact between the sovereign and the first patentees. Samuel Davies, the eloquent Virginia preacher, to whom Patrick Henry listened from his eleventh to his twenty-second year, taught that the British Constitution was "but the voluntary compact of sovereign and subject." [1] Henry gave proof that he had learned his lesson when later he declared, "government is a conditional compact between king and people . . . a violation of the covenant by either party discharges the other from obligation." Nearly one hundred years earlier, a Connecticut preacher taught that "the choice of public magistrates belongs to the people, by God's

---

[1] Samuel Davies, *Sermons*, III, 80. There is little doubt that Davies was Henry's model in public speaking. *Ibid.*, I, 21; H. A. White, *Southern Presbyterian Leaders*, 52–56, 104.

own allowance. They who have the power to appoint officers and magistrates, it is in their power, also, to set the bounds and limitations of the power and place unto which they call them." [1] Among the tracts reprinted just before the Revolution was one first issued by a Massachusetts pastor in 1687, which bore the title, "Democracy is Christ's Government." [2] Two tracts, by the Reverend John Wise, of Ipswich, more than half a century old, one of which was entitled the "Vindication of the Government of New England Churches," so clearly set forth the leading principles of democracy that they were republished by subscription of laymen in 1772,[3] and two editions soon exhausted.

New England ministers, along with their "three mile prayers and half mile graces" at which their critics jeered, were preaching, too, that people were justified in rising even against the sovereign himself in order "to redress their grievances; to vindicate their natural and legal rights; to break the yoke of tyranny." [4] This they reasoned from the natural freedom of man, basing their arguments upon the ideas of Milton, Sidney, and Locke. From the earliest times, in fact, the ministers had taught the duty to God and the fear of offending God, but had not worried their flocks about their duty to kings or with the fear of offending them. "Honor . . . and obedience to good rulers, and a spirited opposition

---

[1] Lord Acton, *Lectures*, 311. Mayhew, more than one hundred years later than the Connecticut preacher, makes the same argument. Thornton, *The Pulpit of the Revolution*, 61.

[2] Dunning, *Congregationalism in America*, 275.   [3] *Ibid.* 270.

[4] Thornton, *The Pulpit of the Revolution*, 62.

to bad ones," was the burden of some New England preaching, wrote John Adams.[1] "If," he said again, "the orators on the 4th of July really wish to investigate the principles and feelings which produced the Revolution, they ought to study . . . Dr. Mayhew's sermon on passive obedience and non-resistence."[2] This famous sermon of Mayhew's attracted Adams' attention because of its boldness, but the thesis was an old one, and much dwelt upon later by the dissenting ministers of England. They were driven to it out of mere oppugnance to Episcopalian teachings. The young candidates for the Anglican clergy were taught at Oxford that submission and obedience, clear, absolute, and without exception, was the badge and character of the Church of England.[3] The Anglican clergy were compelled to read, on the anniversary of the death of Charles I, the Oxford homily "against disobedience and wilful rebellion," or to preach a sermon against that sin. Mayhew indulged in only modest hyperbole when he charged the Anglican clergy with teaching that if kings oppress, and prayers and entreaties fail, we must all "suffer ourselves to be robbed and butchered at the pleasure of 'the Lord's annointed,' lest we should incur the sin of rebellion and the punishment of damnation."[4]

The scorn of the Puritan for such doctrines is also

---

[1] John Adams, *Works*, ii, 167–68.

[2] *Ibid.*, x, 301. See *A discourse concerning unlimited Submission and Non-resistance to the Higher Powers*, etc., by J. Mayhew (Boston, 1750), 55 pp.

[3] Thornton, *The Pulpit of the Revolution*, 41; John Adams, *Works*, x, 187; Evans, *American Bibliography*, 3282.   [4] Thornton, 63.

well shown in John Adams' article in the Boston "Gazette" (1765) wherein he asserts that the New England Puritans " . . . had an utter contempt of all that dark ribaldry of hereditary, indefeasible right, — the Lord's annointed, — and the divine, miraculous, original of government, with which priesthood had enveloped the Feudal monarch in clouds and mysteries, and from whence they had deduced the most mischievous of all doctrines, that of passive obedience, and non-resistance." [1] Adams did not like it when the Reverend Mr. Gay on the day of Thanksgiving said, "the ancient weapons of the church were prayers and tears, not clubs." This, he thought, inculcated submission to authority in pretty strong terms.[2]

In refutation of the submission doctrine, Mayhew preached the right of people to free themselves from inglorious servitude and ruin. "It is upon this principle that many royal oppressors have been driven . . . into banishment, and many slain by the hands of their subjects . . . that Tarquin was expelled from Rome, and Julius Cæsar . . . cut off in the senate-house . . . that King Charles I was beheaded before his own banqueting house . . . that King James II was made to fly the country which he aimed at enslaving." [3] When Patrick Henry, a few years later, expressed such ideas in the Virginia House of Burgesses, the Speaker thought he had spoken treason. Mayhew declared: "The hereditary, indefeasible,

---

[1] John Adams, *Works*, III, 454; see also Samuel Adams on this subject; Wells, *Samuel Adams*, I, 245.

[2] John Adams, *Works*, II, 167-68.

[3] Thornton, *The Pulpit of the Revolution*, 62-63.

divine right of kings, and the doctrine of non-resistance which is built upon the supposition of such
a right, are altogether as fabulous . . . as trans-
substantation." [1] Again he asked who can prove
"that those who resist a lawless, unreasonable
power, which is contrary to the will of God, do
therein resist the will and ordinance of God." [2]
He ridiculed the rôle of Charles I as "blessed saint"
and "royal martyr." Rather was he a "man black
with guilt," and "laden with iniquity," a "bur-
lesque" upon saintship and martyrdom. A tyrant,
such as he, was "a messenger of Satan to buffet
us." [3] It was such fearless attacks that made serious
breaks in the citadel of superstition wherein sat the
"dread and fear of kings."

Some of the political doctrines quoted were inculcated in New England's early days when political
leadership as well as moral guidance was doubtless
with the clergy. Only the commandments of God
took precedence then over their teachings. Even
in the eighteenth century, when the influence of the
elders had declined, their counsel and advice were
eagerly sought.[4] Pownall, who had been governor
of Massachusetts as late as 1760, warned Parliament
nine years later that it was arousing a spirit in New
England that would resist by force all efforts to tax,

---

[1] Thornton, *The Pulpit of the Revolution*, 84; see also 86, note a,
and 70, 73, 75, 78, 82. See Witherspoon on the same subject, *Works*,
I, 326.

[2] Twenty-five years later, John Adams was proclaiming the same
doctrine. Thornton, *The Pulpit of the Revolution*, 75, and note.

[3] Thornton, *The Pulpit of the Revolution*, 73, 74, note 99. Stiles has
a like attitude in his *Literary Diary*, I, 34, 35.

[4] *American Historical Review*, XIX, 54, note 48.

and "if the ministers once fall in with this spirit, if the people once call upon them, they must take the lead, . . . the people will be led by Moses and Aaron, by the civil and religious." Once that is come to pass, Pownall warned, "The spirit of their religion . . . will, like Moses' serpent, devour every other passion and affection." [1] John Adams testifies that the clergy were "jealous friends of liberty"; that when he sought their advice they were "zealous in the cause." In 1770, the "Merchants and other Sons of Liberty" gave a banquet to the ministers in Faneuil Hall. [2] Again Whig gatherings were held in garrets "crowded with patriots, mechanics and lawyers, porters and clergymen, huddled promiscuously into them." [3] Peter Oliver, Loyalist, recorded that Otis early urged the securing of the "Black Regiment," meaning the dissenting clergy. "Where better could he fly for aid," sneered Oliver, "than to the horns of the altar?" As a result, he adds, the clergy "unceasingly sounded the yells of rebellion in the ears of an ignorant and deluded people." "*In nomine Domini incipit omne malum,*" Oliver cynically concludes. [4]

When the Stamp and Townshend Acts and other measures plagued the colonies, John Adams records that the Puritan pulpits "thundered" and dwelt more and more on the right of resistance. Against the Stamp Act preached Charles Chauncey, one of

[1] Hansard, *Parliamentary Debates*, xvi, 498.
[2] John Adams, *Works*, ii, 329, 424; *Literary Diary of Ezra Stiles*, i, 54, 55.
[3] Frothingham, *Life and Times of Joseph Warren*, 50–51.
[4] British Museum, *Egerton MSS.*, 2671 F 18.

the most eminent divines in America. When it was repealed, his memorable sermon on the text, "As cold waters to a thirsty soul, so is good news from a far country," was filled with liberal political doctrines.[1] Samuel Stillman, a Boston Baptist preacher, denounced the same act from his pulpit, and John Zubly, a German Lutheran minister, denied the British right to tax, using as his text the proverb, "A house divided against itself cannot stand."[2]

The "Boston Massacre" was piously magnified by New England divines; the Reverend John Lothrop preached upon the "Innocent Blood Crying to God from the Streets of Boston."[3] The Reverend Samuel Cooke's sermon on this occasion was filled with the doctrines of Locke, and the Massachusetts House of Representatives resolved that it be printed in the public press.[4] On the anniversary of the "Massacre," in 1772, Dr. Chauncey preached a sermon in the Old South Church, and then Joseph Warren stepped into the pulpit, which was hung with black cloth, and delivered an oration on the danger of standing armies. In a sermon preached before the Governor and Council, the Reverend Mr. Tucker

[1] My article in *American Historical Review*, xix, 52-53.   [2] *Ibid.*

[3] Hearing that Governor Hutchinson would pardon the soldiers, Dr. Chauncey in his pulpit cried, "Surely he would not counteract the operation of the law both of God and of man . . . surely he would not make himself a partaker in the guilt of their murder, by putting a stop to the shedding of blood of those who have murderously spilt the blood of others." Hutchinson, *History of Massachusetts Bay*, iii, 329, note.

[4] Thornton, *The Pulpit of the Revolution*, 147, 155. The text was: "He that ruleth over men must be just, ruling in the fear of God." It was listened to by the Lieutenant-Governor, Council, and House of Representatives.

discussed the origin and design of government, and the sacredness of compacts. "The people," he declared, "as well as their rulers are the proper judges of the civil constitution they are under. . . . Unlimited submission is not due to government in a free state." [1] Upon every event in the series that led to a war for independence, the influence of New England's dissenting clergy may clearly be seen.

The Episcopal ministry did not meanwhile sit with bridled tongue, mute and unprotesting. In the North, however, they preached to a small minority of the people, while in the South, especially in Virginia, they were in bad repute, and had, moreover, little influence over their congregations, made up of a planter aristocracy which took its religion not overseriously. Jonathan Boucher, who later became an ardent Loyalist, preached up to the eve of the Revolution to his Episcopalian parishioner, George Washington, who soon became the patriot leader. In the Southern uplands, however, the Scotch-Irish Presbyterian preachers were spreading the same anti-monarchical doctrines as the New England clergy. Nor was this conflict between Anglican and dissenter confined to colonials of English extraction. From those dissenting preachers, Germans or French Huguenots, who had not come from the British Isles, there came not so much a political opposition to the Anglican Church, as one that was spiritual. Burke suggested it when he asserted that "even the stream of foreigners which has been constantly flowing into

[1] *Literary Diary of Ezra Stiles*, I, 218; Headley, *Chaplains and Clergy of the Revolution*, 26.

these colonies, has for the greatest part, been composed of dissenters from the establishments of their
several countries and have brought with them a
temper" like that of the British dissenters with whom
they mingled in America.[1] These non-English dissenters were often little concerned with the political
antagonism between Anglican and dissenter, but
spiritually it was with the latter that they were fairly
sure to sympathize.

North of Virginia, the political hostility between
Church of England men and dissenters grew apace
as the period of open revolt drew near. Alexander
Mackrabie sensed it keenly in 1768 in New York.
He wrote to Sir Philip Francis:[2] "Among the many
disputes in this and the more northern parts of
America, the religious are not the least. The zealous
members of the Church of England are full of Apprehensions at the great and growing power of the Presbyterians. Don't imagine that I mean in any matters that regard Salvation; that Affair might have
been left to shift for itself at Doomsday. The Alarm
was taken at an Election lately; since which the
Parties have raged with tolerable violence. The
Church People, conscious that the Presbyterians,
who have the Appointment of their own Ministers,
must always outnumber them, are desirous of having
some Person here vested with the Power of Ordination — but they don't like a Bishop, nor Ecclesiastical Courts, in short they don't know what they
want. You remember Dean Swift was to have been
made Bishop of Virginia. The Presbyterians should

[1] Burke, *Works*, II, 123.   [2] *The Francis Letters*, I, 98-99.

not be allowed to grow too great. They are all of Republican Principles. The Bostonians are Presbyterians."

To the accuracy of Mackrabie's observation there is a cloud of witnesses. In the following year, in New York, the election conflict was between the Livingston and Delancey factions, the former being supported by the lawyers and dissenters and the latter by the Anglican Church and the mercantile interests.[1] At its close, Peter Van Schaack, predestined by his character, conservatism, and affiliations to become a Loyalist, wrote with joy: "Our election is ended and the Church triumphant . . . in spite of all the efforts of the Presbyterian interests combined with some other dissenting sects." [2] Lieutenant-Governor Colden wrote the Earl of Hillsborough a year later that the opponents of the British Government "consist chiefly of Dissenters, who are very numerous especially in the country and have a great influence over the country members of Assembly. The most active among them are independents from New England or educated there, and of Republican principles. The friends of the Administration are of the Church of England, the Lutherans and the old Dutch congregations. . . . From this the reason will appear of some bills having passed the House of Assembly in favour of the Dissenters, and in prejudice to the few ministers of the Church of England, who have stipends by a law of

---

[1] Becker, *Political Parties in the Province of New York*, 18–19, 60; Sedgwick, *William Livingston*, 107, 115.
[2] Van Schaack, *Life of Peter Van Schaack*, 10.

this Province." Again Colden declared that all the popular leaders of his day were both lawyers and Presbyterians.[1] The struggle, dissenter against Anglican, was much older than the days of colonial resistance to British taxation; as early as 1751 was begun a struggle between these factions as to which should dominate King's College.[2] Ten years later, Peter Van Schaack commented upon the fear of the Presbyterians because of the growing power of the Anglican Church in the legislature; "the other branches of power [Governor and judges] being at the disposal of the Crown and out of reach of those who are disagreeable to mitred heads." [3]

The clash between the sects took place on every occasion. Ezra Stiles noted in his meticulous "Literary Diary" that, at dawn on March 18, 1769, the anniversary of the repeal of the Stamp Act, a large flag was hoisted to the top of the "tree of Liberty" by the "Sons" of that same divinity, and the bell in his church and that of the First Congregational Church began and continued to ring, but the bell of the Episcopalian Church struck a few strokes and then stopped, "the Episcopalians being averse to the celebrations." Next year the Anglican politicians tried "to confuse the Cause of Liberty," by some bell-ringing and color-hoisting on Sunday, the 18th, instead of Monday the 19th, the day agreed

---

[1] *Ecclesiastical Records of New York*, VI, 4181. The offensive laws were vetoed in the Council where the Anglicans were strong. *American Historical Review*, I, 239.

[2] Sedgwick, *William Livingston*, 80, 82, 95. King's College became Columbia University.

[3] Van Schaack, *Life of Peter Van Schaack*, 11.

upon by the Sons of Liberty in Newport, Boston, and New York. A year later the two Presbyterian bells struck, but the Anglican was silent at first.[1] Then, as a Loyalist sadly recorded, the face of public affairs became melancholy, "altar against altar in the Church, and such open bold attacks upon the State, as, I believe the English annals do not furnish us with the like since the reign of King Charles I."[2]

A royal governor's view of this conflict, altar against altar, we have in a letter to the Earl of Dartmouth written by Governor Martin of North Carolina on the very eve of open rebellion.[3] "I cannot therefore, help observing to your Lordship the congeniality of the principles of the Church of England with our form of government. To the reproach of the professors of Christianity on both sides . . . distinctions and animosities have immemorially prevailed in this country between the people of the established Church and the Presbyterians on the score of the difference of their unessential modes of Church Government, and the same spirit of division has entered into or been transferred to most other concernments; at present there is no less apparent schism between their Politics than in matters appertaining to religion, and while Loyalty, Moderation and respect to Government seem to distinguish the generality of the members of the Church of England, I am sincerely sorry to find that they are by no

---

[1] *Literary Diary of Ezra Stiles*, i, 6–7 (note), 16, 42, 96; see also i, 30, 31, 294–95.

[2] Sabine, *Loyalists*, 333.

[3] North Carolina, *Colonial Records*, ix, 1086.

means the characters of the Presbyterians at large, whence ... the people of this denomination in general throughout the continent are not of the principles of the Church of Scotland, but like the people of New England, more of the leaven of the Independents, who according to English story have been ever unfriendly to Monarchical Government." [1]

[1] See also Grigsby, in *Washington and Lee Historical Papers*, no. 2, p. 6.

CHAPTER XIV

THE BOSTON "TEA PARTY"

AFTER the climax of feeling due to the "Boston Massacre" the colonial public grew weary of the "group of gloomy mortals" who still saw visions of tyranny. Then came the cooling of colonial tempers due to the repeal of the Townshend measures, except as to the tax on tea; and finally the break-down of the great mercantile combination against British trade. For three years thereafter the shops were filled with merchandise, business throve, ships plied briskly over the customary trade routes, and farmers were busy cultivating their lands. The alliance between the merchants and the radicals was severed. "All Men of property," wrote Lieutenant-Governor Colden, "are so sensible of their danger, from riots and tumults, that they will not rashly be induced to enter into combinations which may promote disorder for the future, but will endeavor to promote due subordination to legal authority."[1] All friendship between John Hancock, merchant, and Samuel Adams, agitator, was "suddenly at an end," wrote Hutchinson, and it is certain that on several occasions Hancock threw his influence against the efforts of Adams to stir the embers of discontent.[2] "Officious Patriots" prated in vain about slaves groaning from lack of liberty; the merchants were tired of six years of agitation and bad business.

[1] *New York Colonial Documents*, VIII, 217.
[2] Wells, *Samuel Adams*, I, 469, 470.

They fairly basked in the sunshine of better times, and rejoiced in the political calm. They saw gold actually being imported from England.[1] Floods in France and Spain and Italy increased the call for American grain, and with the profits from that trade colonial merchants paid off long-standing debts in England. It was true that as a result of non-importation more products of colonial industry were to be obtained than ever before, but that did not diminish trade with England, and the domestic industry only increased colonial prosperity. Shoes from Lynn, paper from Milton, sails from Boston, watches and bar-steel from Philadelphia were the boast of men who would have America industrially independent.[2] The old trade restrictions and the old revenue laws lost their power to nettle the sensitive nerves of the colonial trader. Even Parliament's legal tender laws were modified in May, 1773, to ease the currency stringency. Finally, tea itself lost its power to stimulate the patriotic soul, and John Adams confessed to dining with Hancock and drinking "green tea from Holland, I hope, but don't know." Only in New York and Philadelphia, the centers of tea smuggling, was any heed given to the boycott of dutied tea.[3] In two years over half a million pounds of the "enervating leaves" passed through the colonial customs houses, and yet it seems to be true that more than nine tenths of the tea consumed in that time was smuggled.[4]

---

[1] Schlesinger, *The Colonial Merchants*, 240–42, 255.
[2] *Ibid.*, 243, 244.   [3] *Ibid.*, 244, 246, 247.
[4] *Ibid.*, 249. See also abstract prepared in the office of Inspector of Imports and Exports. Channing, *Hist. of the U.S.*, III, 128.

The incentive to the tea smuggler grew out of the efforts of the East India Company to recoup their losses by advancing the price of tea at their public auction sales in London. As a result of this the smuggler could afford, Hutchinson declared, "to lose one chest in three"; and even after such a possible loss, he could undersell the honest tea merchant who had bought at the London auctions and paid the tax in America. In order to put a stop to this widespread evasion of the laws of the empire, the activity of ships-of-war off American harbors was redoubled. The zeal of the customs officers stirred the fury of the mob. There were outbreaks at Falmouth and at Philadelphia in 1771, and in June of 1772 the "outrage" of the burning of the *Gaspée*. Lieutenant Dudingston, who patrolled Narragansett Bay with that vessel, had found the harbors of Rhode Island most inhospitable to minions of the law. The numerous coves and inlets made smuggling easy, and among the people nobody loved a customs officer. If the commander went ashore he risked "insult" by seizure to answer the suits of traders whose craft had been accused and held for smuggling. Even Governor Wanton asked him to answer complaints against the presence of his "piratical vessel." [1] To crown his troubles he ran aground on a sand spit near Providence; at midnight boats approached with fifty to one hundred and fifty men who clambered on board, set Dudingston and his sailors ashore, burned the vessel and vanished as they came. The wrathful British authorities ordered

[1] Channing, *Hist. of the U.S.*, III, 125.

an investigation by a commission; but though a cloud of witnesses knew the names of the mob, and the details of the exploit were common gossip, yet only one runaway negro servant could be got to testify, and he disgraced the inquiry. The main effect of the commission and of the intent of the British Government to bring the offenders to England for trial was to fan a flame of colonial wrath which blazed with only brief respite until it destroyed the bonds which knit the empire.[1] During the evolution of the *Gaspée* affair, Samuel Adams, keenly alive to the cool temper of the Boston merchants, realized that the cause of colonial freedom must not be left dependent upon the selfish interests of the merchant class, but that all the people must be roused to sense the danger. When Samuel Adams looked for "mighty grievances and intolerable wrongs" he was famously successful. He knew how to recite old grievances in the newest kind of ways. Seizing upon the report, in September, 1772, that judges' salaries were hereafter to be paid by the British Government out of the revenue collected in colonial customs houses, he urged in the press that every social club, every town assembly, every association consider the topic whether the people were to be "freemen or slaves." Merchants, he warned, were submitting to "the Indignity of a Tribute," the body of the people looked on unconcerned while "*Pensioners*" multiplied "like the Locusts in Egypt." Was everything dear and sacred to be submitted to the decisions of pensioned judges?

[1] *Calendar of Home Office Papers* (1773–75), no. 80.

Were they to become "*Hirelings*" and help the
"iron Hand of Tyranny to ravish our Laws?"
"Merciful God! Inspire Thy People with Wisdom
and Fortitude and direct them to gracious Ends,"
he implored.[1]

But Samuel Adams was one of those prudent
mortals who, while much given to such pious appeals, kept his powder dry. He brought great pressure to bear on the selectmen to call a town meeting,
and overcoming all opposition he gained his end.
In meetings in Faneuil Hall Adams brought about
a colloquy with the Governor on the judges' salary
matter. At its height, designing to spread the results of the debate, Adams introduced his famous
motion for a committee of correspondence of twenty-
one men.[2] Its duties were "to state the Rights of
the Colonists and of this Province in particular, as
Men, as Christians, and as Subjects: to communicate
and publish the same to the several Towns in this
Province and to the World as the sense of this Town,
with the Infringements and Violations thereof that
have been, or from time to time may be made —
Also requesting of each Town a free communication
of their Sentiments on this Subject." It passed
without opposition, and thus was born, in the wrathful words of the Tory pamphleteer, Daniel Leonard,

[1] Samuel Adams, *Writings* (Cushing, *ed.*), II, 334–37.

[2] It is not meant that Samuel Adams invented the idea of Committees of Correspondence, for there had been similar committees at
the time of the Stamp Act in both Massachusetts and New York.
Moreover, Mayhew and others had long before suggested it, but this
time the idea was to grow and bear fruits of great importance. Becker,
Political Parties in the Province of New York, 45–46; Thornton, *The
Pulpit of the Revolution*, 44; R. H. Lee, *Letters*, I, 29, 106, 113.

"the foulest, subtlest, and most venomous serpent ever issued from the egg of sedition."

Governor Hutchinson wrote to Pownall that the committee was composed of "deacons," "atheists," and "black-hearted fellows whom one would not choose to meet in the dark." These dangerous persons were James Otis, Samuel Adams, Joseph Warren, Benjamin Church, Nathaniel Appleton, Oliver Wendell, Josiah Quincy, John Bradford, Nathaniel Barber, William Molineaux, and Robert Pierpont. James Otis was at first the chairman, but when madness again came upon him, he was succeeded by "the Grand Incendiary of the Province." We have no knowledge that Samuel Adams read Bacon's Essay entitled "Of Seditions and Troubles," but he understood as well as the "wisest and brightest of mankind" that "common people are of slow motion, if they be not excited by the greater sort," and "the greater sort are of small strength, except the multitude be apt and ready to move, of themselves." Adams used this new "engine of sedition" most adroitly to awaken the people to the "violations of their rights." A paper written by Adams and endorsed by the town meeting was soon sent to all the towns in the province. It drew from the political Pandora's box every ill real or fancied, which the colonies had suffered, and conjured up perils yet to come. Many of the charges against the British Government, later included in the Declaration of Independence, make their appearance here. The customs officers with writs of assistance, the presence of fleets and armies, the bogy of the American Episcopate, the capricious and dangerous powers of the admiralty courts, the restrictions on manufactures, and the interference with home rule by means of royal instructions to colonial governors, all were exhibited with frightful mien in this circular letter to which every community was invited to reply through a like committee of correspondence to be appointed by town meetings throughout the province. Radicals everywhere in the colony were now given an organization hitherto unknown, and over against the governmental machine, fairly in the control of British officials, stood a revolutionary organization full of sinister potentialities.[1] As time went on, similar committee systems were established in other colonies and everywhere became a powerful force working on popular sentiment within each province. It represented the radical faction and was its agent to resist the will of the British Ministry. Moreover, as Burke declared in 1775, "The new institution is infinitely better obeyed than the ancient government ever was in its most fortunate periods. Obedience is what makes government and not the names by which it is called." [2] General Gage wrote the British Ministry that these committees were "assuming to themselves more power and authority than any body of men ever did, looking upon Government as at an end, and making rules and orders for the regulation of the people of the country. In truth the people here have taken the

---

[1] E. D. Collins, *Committees of Correspondence*, in *Annual Report*, American Historical Association (1901), I, 245-71. See criticism of Collins' view in J. M. Leake, *The Virginia Committee System* 88-92.

[2] Burke, *Works*, II, 128.

government into their own hands and whoever does not comply with everything proposed by them, their persons and properties are not safe." [1] The committees did not exercise such powers at first, but once created, the march of events was sure to bear them onward. For a time after the first organization in Massachusetts their chief activity was to fan the embers of discontent, or, as Samuel Adams expressed it, arouse people from "stupor and inaction to sensibility and activity." The merchants as a class held aloof at first from this popular clamor prescribed and directed by Samuel Adams. After July, 1773, apathy seemed once more to reign. [2]

Lord North now became responsible (April 17, 1773) for a measure which roused the colonial merchant when all of Adams' demagogic devices had failed. Once more he tried to save the fortunes of the East India Company by helping them to sell their ever-growing surplus of tea, which had mounted to seventeen million pounds. His device, passed by Parliament without opposition, amounted to no less than giving the company a monopoly of the business of selling tea in the colonies. It was that fact which made the trouble rather than that the Government, as Chatham said, had dressed "taxation, that father of American sedition, in the robes of an East Indian director." [3]

As far as taxes were concerned there was no new inroad on American rights, but the English tea

---

[1] *Calendar of Home Office Papers* (1773-75), p. vii.

[2] Schlesinger, *The Colonial Merchants*, 260, 262.

[3] Becker, *Political Parties in the Province of New York*, 96-102; Hansard, *Parliamentary History*, xvii, 1355.

merchant and the American tea merchant, who as middlemen used to make profits by buying at the public auctions in London and then selling to the American retailer, were swept aside, leaving the East India Company to be its own exporter to its own branch tea houses in the colonies. The tea, free of duty in England, reached American consumers at half its old price even with the three pence duty added in the American customs houses, and cheaper even than smuggled tea; but the powerful interests of both the honest and the illicit colonial traders were utterly opposed.[1] Once more the colonial merchant, conservative by nature and interest, lashed himself into a fury and recklessly joined with the radicals whose dangerous passions were so hard to control.

Since the public would actually profit as far as the cost of its tea was concerned, the injured merchants were careful not to confine their agitation too closely to the true issue of their own prospective losses. The hygienic arguments were not neglected, and it was astonishing how clearly it could be shown that "spasms, vapors, hypochondrias, apoplexies of the serous kind, palsies, dropsies, rheumatisms, consumptions, low nervous miliary and petechial fevers" were all due to the drinking of tea.[2] The old political arguments against taxation without representation

---

[1] For further details and qualifications see Schlesinger, *The Colonial Merchants*, 262–64; also 133 Geo. III, c. 44. See M. Farrand article in *American Historical Review*, III, 266. It should be noticed that "non-importation" was impossible under such an arrangement, for the East India Company itself would do the importing. Colonial merchants would have no say in the matter.

[2] Schlesinger, *The Colonial Merchants*, 276.

were dressed up and paraded by the merchants themselves, but if the true objection to the plan, the monopoly, was exploited in the press, the articles were signed "Mechanic," "Patriot," "A citizen," or some Roman or English defender of liberty. Lest other than tea merchants lose interest it was hinted that this was only the entering wedge; that if the East India Company was allowed to "pilfer the trade" from the tea merchants, soon its other importations from India, spices, drugs, silks, chinaware, and all other Oriental goods would be taken from the traders in the commodities.[1] The company's bad record in India was recited to show that it would have no conscience as to the rights of its fellow-men. John Dickinson pointed out how little it regarded "the Laws of Nations, the Rights, Liberties, or Lives of Men. They have levied War," he declared, "excited Rebellions, dethroned lawful Princes, and sacrificed Millions for the sake of Gain. The Revenues of Mighty Kingdoms have centered in their Coffers. And these not being sufficient to glut their Avarice, they have, by the most unparalleled Barbarities, Extortions and Monopolies, stripped the miserable Inhabitants of their Property and reduced whole Provinces to Indigence and Ruin." [2] Destroy the merchants, it was argued in order to broaden the basis of the popular appeal, and the shipbuilding would cease and other industries follow in their train. Long before any of the "pernicious leaves" arrived in America, the rhetoric of pam-

---

[1] Schlesinger, *The Colonial Merchant*, 269, 273, 275.
[2] *Life and Writings of John Dickinson* (P. L. Ford, *ed.*), II, 459-60

phleteers had been changed to the action of city mass meetings, one of the first of which, apparently on the initiative of the merchant aristocracy, was held at the State House in Philadelphia, where it was voted that any one who should aid this last ministerial plan against American liberty should be denounced as "an enemy to his country." The merchants selected by the East India Company to receive the expected tea were forced to resign, and at a second meeting the entry of tea ships at the customs house or landing of the tea was unanimously disapproved.[1]

One of the worst mistakes of the East India Company was that it did not choose as its agents the colonial merchants who had been accustomed to handle the tea trade. In Boston, where the danger signals had long been flying; where Samuel Adams was on the alert for some better issue than judges' salaries to stir the public wrath; and where he was preparing to supersede the orderly Boston town meeting with an irresponsible mass meeting of radicals from Boston and the neighboring towns; in this true cave of Adullam, the Company had given their prospective tea business to sons of the unpopular Governor Hutchinson and to his nephew, Richard Clarke, the detested men who had opposed the late non-importation agreement. Hutchinson himself was interested and doubtless influenced by his interest.[2]

---

[1] Schlesinger, *The Colonial Merchants*, 281.
[2] *Ibid.*, 281–83; Channing, *Hist. of the U.S.*, III, 130. There were five consignees.

By this error of judgment the Company made it certain that the body of Boston merchants, though hating and fearing mobs and violence, would nevertheless support, if not actually direct, any measures against the importation of tea in a manner that menaced their business. If they tried to prevent mob violence they were outwitted by Samuel Adams, who seemed bent on committing his colony to revolution if not actual independence.[1]

Boston was one of four cities to which the East India Company sent consignments of tea. Four ships sailed thither, one being "cast away on the Back of Cape Cod," the rest, under Captains Hall, Bruce, and Coffin, dropping anchor in Boston Harbor between November 28th and December 8th. Before the "baleful" tea was halfway across the ocean, placards had appeared on almost every corner calling the freemen of Boston and the near-by towns to meet under the "Liberty Tree" to hear the consignees resign their offices and swear to reship the "fateful" tea to London. When the offending agents of the East India Company failed to appear at the rendezvous, a committee, reënforced by a large concourse of people, waited upon them; but they still refused, and a fortnight later a mob visited the house of Richard Clarke, one of the tea agents, and broke all his windows.[2]

The merchants as a class were alarmed by this mob action: they had tried to use the legal town meeting as their vehicle of protest, and therein had

---

[1] Schlesinger, *The Colonial Merchants*, 283–84.
[2] *Letters and Diary of John Rowe*, 252–57.

adopted the Philadelphia Resolutions and agreed
that dutied tea was not to be imported. Once more
they asked the resignation of the tea agents and
were refused. At this point Samuel Adams took
matters out of the hands of the merchant-led town
meeting, and controlled the march of events through
a joint meeting of the committees of Boston, Brook-
line, Cambridge, Dorchester, and Roxbury, more
radical and less restrained by men of property. To
these committees were added the inhabitants of the
towns represented. The lowest as well as the highest
came, and there were no legal qualifications as at
town meetings. It was an irresponsible mass meeting which became too large for Faneuil Hall, and
some twenty-five hundred people adjourned November 29th to Old South Meeting-House.[1] They
had been summoned by "papers stuck up," ad-
dressed to "Friends! Brethren! Countrymen!" The
"worst of Plagues, The Detestable Tea," had arrived, and tyranny, the people were told, stared them
in the face. When the bells rang, every friend of
his country and posterity was urged to meet at the
hall.

At the meeting, a single person, Hutchinson believed, directed all. "Adams was never in greater
glory," he sneered. The first resolve was that the
tea must not be landed or duty paid. The meeting
only hissed the sheriff who brought Hutchinson's
command that they disperse and "surcease" their
proceedings. The people's blood was up. When
John Rowe was chosen a committee man, he con-

[1] Schlesinger, *The Colonial Merchants*, 284-85.

fessed to his diary that it was "much against my will but I dare not say a word." [1]

"The flame is kindled and like lightning it catches from soul to soul," wrote Abigail Adams.[2] The Governor remained obdurate against the demand of Rotch, the owner of the first tea ship, that he sign a permit for the ship to leave before unloading the tea. In fact he caused the guns at the fort to be loaded and two warships to stand on guard at other channels by which the vessel might escape. On December 17th, under the law the tea on this ship must be seized by the customs officer and sold at auction if at that date the tea had not been landed and the duty paid. The officer would not blink the law; the consignees having taken sanctuary in the Castle held that in honor they could not resign; the Governor bound to his oath of office, as he pleaded, would not yield. The refusal of the consignees was sent from their safe retreat at Castle William, where, surrounded with cannon, they could do things, as Hutchinson confessed, which they "would not have dared to do in any other situation." It was best to keep close, they decided, "until the infernal spirit is layd or at least cool'd." [3] If the tea were offered at auction, it was dubious whether Boston patriotism could stand the strain. A guard of twenty-five men was set day and night to prevent clandestine landing of the tea. On December 16th the largest gathering ever known, five to seven

---

[1] *Letters and Diary of John Rowe*, 256.
[2] *Warren-Adams Letters*, 18.
[3] British Museum, *Egerton MSS.*, 2659 F 56.

thousand people, came in and about Old South
Meeting-House. By fifties and hundreds they
flocked in from outlying towns. A committee made
a last demand at the customs house, and poor dis-
tracted Rotch was sent once more to try his Quaker
eloquence upon the Governor, who was at Milton,
his country seat.[1]

Both missions failed. The news was reported at
dusk to the nerve-strained crowd in the dimly
lighted Old South. During two sessions the people
had been harangued by Samuel Adams, Dr. Young,
and Josiah Quincy, Jr. John Rowe had wondered
"how tea would mingle with salt water." Samuel
Adams arose, and solemnly declared, "This meeting
can do nothing more to save the country."[2] At
once there was a shout outside, and a band of men
disguised as Indians hastened to Griffin's Wharf,
where the tea ships lay. For two hours they hoisted
the chests from the holds of the vessels, broke them
open, and threw them overboard. It was bright
moonlight and crowds of people watched from the
wharves. There was no clamor, no talking, no
injury to any property but tea. Having finished,
the decks were cleaned, order restored, and the
"Indians" vanished "into Egyptian darkness."
Next morning tea lay strewn like seaweed along
Dorchester beach. The Bostonians had "made tea
for all the cod-fish on the banks of Newfoundland,"

---

[1] Mass. Hist. Soc., *Proceedings*, VIII, 325–26.

[2] Drake, *Tea Leaves*, LXIV. This book contains a mass of contemporary materials concerning the "Tea Party." *See* minutes of the
Tea Meetings. Mass. Hist. Soc., *Proceedings* (1st Ser.), XX, 10–17.

wrote a London Whig.[1] Property of the East India Company to the value of fifteen thousand pounds had been destroyed by not only masons, farmers, barbers, and blacksmiths, but by citizens of high position, merchants who may have thought better of it when the excitement was over.

Governor Hutchinson's ill-repute in Boston reached its climax with this incident. But it had been greatly augmented by Samuel Adams' clever use of some letters written by Hutchinson to friends in England and secured by Benjamin Franklin in a manner which left it possible for enemies to question his sense of honor. Franklin sent them to the political leaders in Massachusetts, stipulating that they were not to be copied or printed. After they had been handed about for a few days, Samuel Adams rose in the Massachusetts Assembly and dramatically asked to have the galleries cleared that he might read certain letters inimical to American liberties, tending secretly to alienate the affections of the King. The Assembly having listened, resolved that the letters tended "to undermine the Constitution." Soon the public was mysteriously made aware of the existence of letters damaging to Governor Hutchinson, it being "buzzed about" that they would amaze everybody. When the demand to see them increased, Hutchinson was given the dates of some of the letters, and was asked for copies which might be published without violation of the stipulation made by

---

[1] *Serious considerations on the Political Condition of Lord North*, 54 For a Philadelphia "Tea Party" at a later time see Friends Historical Society, *Bulletin*, vol. III, no. 1, pp. 21-49.

Franklin. This he refused, because, he declared, all the views therein expressed were known through other channels, and the letters were private. Copies were spread about meanwhile, and at last by a process of curious ethical reasoning the House authorized the printing. The publication was preceded, however, by resolutions explaining what was iniquitous in the letters and asking for the removal of the Governor.[1] Moral obliquity having been thus subtly insinuated into letters which in fact contained nothing new, seventeen of them were published. The result gave support to the sophist's assertion that there is nothing either good or bad but thinking makes it so, for the poisoned public mind found them full of "evil and treason." The contents were no longer the essential thing, but what they had been said to be. The Boston Committee of Correspondence sent them out with the pious comment: "The providential care of the gracious Being who conducted the early settlers of this country to establish a safe retreat from tyranny, for themselves or for their posterity, in America, has again wonderfully interposed to bring to light the plot that had been laid for us by our malicious and insidious enemies." In England, meanwhile, as a result of Franklin's confession that he had gotten possession of the letters, he was called before the Privy Council, where, as he says, "all the courtiers were invited, as to an entertainment," and Wedderburn, the Solicitor

---

[1] This was unanimously rejected by the Privy Council and Hutchinson's letters judged meritorious. British Museum. *Egerton MSS.* 2659 F 68.

General, made the aged philosopher the "butt of his invective ribaldry for near an hour."[1] General Gage who was present says: "I suppose no man's conduct and character was before so mangled and torn, as Dr. Franklin's was at this time. People wondered he had confidence to stand it with the contemptuous looks of the audience upon him."[2] Charles Fox remembered long after how the Council came away "throwing up their caps and exulting ... at the speech," in which Franklin had been "most uncommonly badgered." But, Fox declared, we paid very dear for those "Tropes, figures, metaphors and hyperboles ... all our American colonies, a hundred million of money, and a hundred thousand of our brave fellow subjects." Wedderburn was ironically complimented afterwards as "the nobleman whose talents were so eminently useful in procuring the emancipation of our American brethren."[3]

In New York, when Paul Revere arrived with an account of the "Boston Tea-Party," "vast numbers of the people collected, and highly extolled the Bostonians." Ringing bells and "universal huzzas" greeted the news in the Quaker City. The thoughtless masses in general seem to have applauded an act whose very daring commended it to the popular imagination, but individuals differed widely in their reactions. John Adams in his diary recorded: "Last night three cargoes of Bohea tea were emptied

---

[1] Franklin, *Writings* (Smyth, *ed.*), vi, 189.

[2] British Museum, *Egerton MSS.*, 2659 F 69.

[3] Franklin's own story of this episode is most entertaining. See *Writings* (Smyth, *ed.*), vi, 81, 108, 109, 172, 183–92.

into the sea. This morning a man-of-war sails, This
is the most magnificent movement of all. There is a
dignity, a majesty, a sublimity in this last effort
of the patriots, that I greatly admire. The people
should never rise without doing something to be
remembered, something notable and striking. This
destruction of the tea is so bold, so daring, so firm,
intrepid and inflexible, and it must have so important consequences, and so lasting, that I cannot but
consider it as an epocha in history." To have let
it be landed, he argued, was to lose "all our labor for
ten years," and to subject "ourselves and our posterity forever to Egyptian task-masters." [1]

Henry Laurens, with the merchant's feeling for
the sacredness of property, wrote: "I won't say the
people have proceeded too far in drowning and
forcing back the tea; possibly it may prove to have
been the most effectual and therefore wisest method;
but at present I commend the proceeding at Charlestown in preference to all the rest; the consignees
refuse the commissions; the people will not purchase
the commodity; it must remain in store and perish
or be returned at the expense of those who sent it
There is a constitutional stubbornness in such conduct which must be approved of every true Englishman and open the understanding of those whose
stubborn attempts to ensnare America are supported
by no other plea than power." [2]

Benjamin Franklin looked upon the "tea party"
as "an act of violent injustice." An out-and-out
Tory, Harrison Gray, believed God would punish

---

[1] John Adams, *Works*, II, 323–24.   [2] Wallace, *Henry Laurens*, 194.

the unrepentant tea-destroyers in "the lake which burns with fire and brimstone." [1] The sober judg- ment of the merchant class in general was shocked by the anarchy at Boston. Though there was less sympathy for the great East India Company's loss than there would have been for that of an individual, yet there was remorse and fear in the hearts of the conservative merchants. They agreed with an Eng- lish writer who said, "There is a strange Spirit of Licentiousness gone forth in the World, which shel- ters itself under the venerable and endearing Name of LIBERTY, but is as different from it as Folly is from Wisdom." [2]

Boston was not alone in showing its antipathy to East India Company tea. In Philadelphia, when the tidings came that Captain Ayres with a tea ship was on his way up the Delaware, some eight thousand people gathered in the square and resolved that he put about and sail back whence he came. By his obedience Philadelphia was saved the Boston di- lemma. [3] At the port of New York the approaching danger was sensed by the radicals who resorted to an "Association of the Sons of Liberty." This document signed by "lawyers, merchants, land-

[1] Channing, *Hist. of the U.S.*, III, 133.
[2] Schlesinger, *The Colonial Merchants*, 299.
[3] *Ibid.*, 290–91. Perhaps his obedience was quickened by the warn- ing sent him by a committee. "What think you, Captain, of a halter around your neck, ten gallons of liquid tar decanted on your pate with the feathers of a dozen wild geese laid over that to enliven your appearance? Only think seriously of this and fly to the place from whence you came; fly without hesitation; without the formality of a protest; and above all, Captain Ayres, let us advise you to fly without the wild geese feathers." *Calendar of Home Office Papers* (1773–75), p. iv.

holders, masters of ships and mechanics," promised to boycott all who aided the bringing in of dutied teas. The radicals, led by John Lamb, made the most of the news from Boston and assembled two thousand people, who agreed to a committee of correspondence to keep in touch with other colonies. Fear of mob action seized the conservative merchants, Isaac Low and Jacob Walton, who resented the intrusion of unprivileged classes into political affairs. They were circulating a paper pledging the signers to avoid violence when the news of the "Boston Tea Party" stopped them. The consignees meanwhile resigned and warned the incoming tea ship *Nancy* under Captain Lockyear to return to sea. By his great caution he saved the East India Company a second loss; for another tea ship, the *London*, arriving about the same time with a private consignment, was boarded by an impatient mob who stove in the tea chests and mingled more tea with salt water.[1] Next day Captain Lockyear started upon his return voyage, while a band at the wharf played "God Save the King." The mechanics and cobblers and tailors had again driven New York to radical action. Nowhere in the northern ports was the tea landed, though at Portsmouth and Newport action was belated and tame, and the province of Connecticut could not be made to sense the danger.

In Charleston, South Carolina, no great impression was made at first by the new measure of Lord North. There were few smugglers, the local Scotch merchants were not popular, and if they lost their

---

[1] Becker. *Political Parties in the Province of New York*, 104–10.

business to the East India Company consignees, what did consumers care? The merchants were often only factors with a like relation to great London merchants as tea consignees had to the East India Company. When a tea ship actually arrived. however, the people were summoned by hand-bills and in a great assembly framed a pledge by which merchants would agree not to import dutied tea. Christopher Gadsden and a committee of planters had little success with this agreement, and while efforts were being made through meetings of the planters and mechanics to devise a plan agreeable to the merchants, the tea was removed to the Government warehouse, and there it remained for three years until independence of England made it safe and proper to dispose of it at auction.[1]

Except in Massachusetts where, after the "Tea Party," the radical spirit burst all the chains with which conservative merchants sought to have it shackled, there was no universal uprising as at the time of the Stamp Act. Soon after the thoughtless approval of Boston audacity by a few mass meetings there seemed to be a general ebbing of the radical power everywhere. Things were going badly for the "Saviors of the people," when to their delight the British Government changed the whole aspect of the struggle from a dispute over trade regulation and tax methods to a clear-cut issue as to whether the British Parliament had the political right to punish Boston by acts which ruined their commerce and radically altered their government.

[1] Schlesinger, *The Colonial Merchants*, 295–98.

CHAPTER XV

LORD NORTH'S EFFORT TO PRESERVE
IMPERIAL DIGNITY

WHEN Grafton's headship of the Ministry had given way to that of Lord North, there had been a still greater increase of the power of the King already waxing with the growth of his personal faction. Lord Chatham's illness had led during Grafton's régime to the development of government by departments, and during Chatham's absence the King had simply stepped in and maintained a balance between factions entrenched in the several departments. When also, in the effort to *"find a medium between the violence of George Grenville and the madness of Lord Chatham,"* [1] the resignation of Lord Shelburne was brought about and Lord Hillsborough was made Secretary of State for the Colonies, the malign influence of the Bedford faction on American affairs was determined. It grew thenceforth in its effect upon the King until it reached full fruition in the severance of the empire.

In Lord North, the King found a man of Tory principles skilled in giving his royal master petty governmental tasks so pleasing to a meticulous mind like that of George III, and whose boast was that in seven years he had never given a vote for popular measures.[2] Though North was a skillful warrior in

---

[1] *Grenville Papers*, IV, 250.

[2] Alvord, *The Mississippi Valley in British Politics*, II, 38; Winstanley, *Lord Chatham and the Whig Opposition*, 322.

the parliamentary lists, to the King he was all amiability and obedience. For twelve years he bent all of no inconsiderable talents to raising George III to a zenith of royal influence. North was in office, the King ruled. Able and industrious, a remarkable debater and possessed of a wit of no mean order, Lord North might have been a statesman of note but for his subservience to a stubborn, self-willed monarch who used him as a tool. He had good sense, plenty of tact, and a remarkable sweetness of temper which with his other talents marked him for leadership which he preferred to let George III employ to his own ends.

It was this Minister who was in power when the news of Boston's rash conduct reached London. Some very old and tried friends of the colonies were surprised into words of resentment and censure. "Clamour against the proceeding is high and general," wrote Franklin. Colonel Barré admitted that his "sons of liberty" ought to be punished. Chatham wrote that Boston's conduct was "certainly criminal," and admitted in Parliament that the whole affair was "turbulent and unwarrantable." The Bostonians, he said, had violated "the most indispensible ties of civil society." He would not "adopt their passions and wild pretensions." Franklin wrote home his disapproval, and hoped for a speedy and "voluntary reparation." [1] "All our friends here wish this," he asserted. He thought the eyes of all Europe were on Boston, but an examina-

---

[1] Chatham, *Correspondence*, IV, 336; Hansard, *Parliamentary History*, XVII, 1354–55; Franklin, *Writings* (Smyth, *ed.*), VI, 179.

tion of the letters of contemporary leaders on the Continent showed that the European world was much more interested in the papal bull for the suppression of the Jesuit Order than in the Boston "Tea Party."

Lord North lost no time in asking Parliament (March 7, 1774) to vote measures for securing obedience to the laws in America. A week later he moved for leave to bring in what has come to be known as the Boston Port Bill.[1] It aimed to remove the customs houses from Boston and to stop all landing and shipping of goods in that harbor until the town made full reparation to the East India Company for the tea destroyed. Lord North believed "that the people of Boston had begun many years ago to throw off all obedience to this country." Now is the time, he cried, to stand out, to defy them, to proceed with firmness and without fear. Four or five frigates will do the business without any military force, he held. The rest of the colonies would "not take fire at the proper punishment" of disobedient Boston.[2] Boston had been the ringleader thus far, but the rest would be peaceable enough if she were punished. As Franklin commented, "Divine Providence first infatuates the power it designs to ruin."

Parliament then entered upon a series of debates which exceeded by a thousand pages of Hansard's reports any previous debate on colonial matters during all of their existence. Lord North had back-

---

[1] Pickering, *Statutes at Large*, xxx, 336.
[2] Almon, *Debates of the House of Commons*, ix, 92-94.

ing enough from among those whose patrons were the "King's Friends" and from those who sat for royal boroughs. All were obsequious now, for a new election was near. Mr. Herbert said that "the Americans were a strange set of people and that it was in vain to expect any degree of reasoning from them; that instead of making their claim by argument, they always chose to decide the matter by tarring and feathering." Mr. Van was more ferocious and wanted to "destroy that nest of locusts." "Boston ought to be knocked about their ears and destroyed, *delenda est Carthago.*" There must be no more talk of that "attribute to awe and majesty." He would "burn and set fire to all their woods" as in the time of the ancient Britons.[1] The historian Gibbon wrote a little later with the confidence of one who had settled half a millennium of Roman problems, "I am more and more convinced that we have both the right and the power on our side, . . . we are now arrived at the decisive moment of persevering or of losing forever both our Trade and Empire."[2]

It was safer to talk that way than to defend the colonists. Burke declared that those who opposed the bill were menaced. "Look, sir, . . . into the public papers, you will see Cinna, and a thousand other Roman names, throwing out their invectives, and tarring and feathering all those who oppose the bill."[3] He ridiculed the punishment of Boston to

---

[1] Almon, *Debates,* IX, 91–101, 141.
[2] Gibbon, *Correspondence,* I, 248.
[3] Almon, *Debates,* IX, 106.

preserve British dignity. "This dignity of yours is a terrible incumbrance to you. It has of late been ever at war with your interest, your equity, and every idea of your policy." He begged the Government to pause and take a reckoning of the point to which it had drifted. He pleaded with Parliament to note how general was the distemper, not "one port in America where the goods have been landed and vended." Had they the power, he asked, for a universal proscription of the trade of America? Punish individuals, he urged, not all the innocent with the guilty.[1] Barré, too, cautioned them to realize that this was "the first vengeful step," that they were "becoming the aggressors and offering the last of outrages to the people of America." "Let the banners of rebellion be once spread in America, and you," he cried to his British colleagues, "are an undone people." He would vote for the Port Bill, which "was a bad way of doing what was right," because he thought Boston had gone too far, but he would seize this opportunity to point out that if the British Ministers would "keep their hands out of the pockets of the Americans," they would be obedient subjects.

Some members of Parliament, like the Bishop of St. Asaph, neither approved of the Boston riots nor of their punishment. General Burgoyne favored persuasion rather than the sword, and he was roundly abused for his mercy. All warnings were in vain, however, and the bill with "so mild an appearance" in Gibbon's view, passed "with but

[1] Almon, *Debates*, ix, 107.

very few negatives." [1] Parliament saw in Boston's exhibition of temper no reflection upon ministerial follies in government, no hint that there might be actual grievances. As Parliament's power overtook and passed that of the King, that body began to conceive of itself as having acquired the "divine right" with the power.

Lord North was not content with closing the Port of Boston. On March 28th, he informed Parliament that the Massachusetts government was all wrong. For years, as he well knew, Bernard and Hutchinson had pressed for a change in the Massachusetts government which would make it conform to that of New York or that of Virginia. "There appears to be a *total defect* in the constitutional power throughout," he declared. "If the Governor issued a proclamation, there is hardly found a magistrate to obey it, the Governor of his own authority can do nothing." Now, Lord North announced, he proposed "to take the executive power from the hands of the democratic part of the government." "Every gentleman," he said, "will naturally see the impropriety of such irregular assemblies or town-meetings which are now held in Boston." [2] Yes, indeed, chimed in Lord George Germain, who for his insight into their affairs was soon to become Secretary of State for the Colonies. He approved of putting an end to town meetings. "I would not have men of a mercantile cast, every day collecting them-

[1] Force, *American Archives* (4th Ser.), ɪ, 113; Almon, *Debates,* ɪx 102, 116, 133.
[2] Almon, *Debates*, ɪx, 117–18.

selves together and debating about political matters;
I would have them follow their occupation as Merchants, and not consider themselves as ministers of
that country." You have there no government, no
governor, only a "tumultuous and riotous rabble"
which ought to stick to trade and leave "politics
and government which they do not understand." [1]
North expressed his approval of such ideas, and he
would "effectually purge the constitution of all its
crudities." He soon introduced bills which gave to
the King the appointment of Massachusetts councillors. Jurors, who hitherto had been chosen in
town meeting, were thereafter to be summoned by
sheriffs, agents of the Governor. Town meetings
would, thenceforth, only be held by permission of the
Governor. The appointment and removal of judges
and sheriffs were also to be in his hands.[2] No heed
was given to the Bishop of St. Asaph, who declared,
"The Americans have the same veneration for their
Charters that we have for the Magna Charta."
The Duke of Grafton declared long after, "as for
the alterations in the Massachusetts charter which
envenomed the people, perhaps forever by this
violation of the law of nature, I opposed myself to
that with all my power, in public and in secret." [3]
Mr. Dunning in vain taunted the Ministry with
having made alterations in the government of Mas-

[1] Force, *American Archives* (4th Ser.), I, 67–68; Almon, *Debates*, IX,
120, 121.

[2] Pickering, *Statutes at Large*, XXX, 381–90. See Historical MSS.
Commission, *Reports, Various*, VI, 257, for Knox's statement that Sir
Francis Bernard put these ideas about juries and the town meeting
into North's head.

[3] *Archives des Affaires Étrangères; Angleterre*, tome 515, no. 4.

sachusetts without the previous ceremony of knowing the old one. He claimed that the Governor had
power enough, but did not know it. Few listened
to Barré's warning that the Government had been
"goading and teasing America for these ten years
past . . . you are continually harrassing and beating
into their ears the word rebellion, till at last you will
find nothing but real rebellion in it." He asked
ominously, "If we in this country had not resisted
such arbitrary laws in certain ancient times, whether
we should have existed as a House of Commons here
this day." [1] He saw nothing in the measures but
"inhumanity, injustice and wickedness." Pownall
disputed Germain's judgment and gave the Americans the character of a "conscientious, good, religious, peaceable set of people"; doubting whether
there were "in all His Majesty's dominions a more
respectable set of persons existing." [2] All such protests of men who had seen and who knew America
were brushed aside and the bills were passed by a
large majority.

Meanwhile, Lord North had been advancing another bill to its third reading, one for "the impartial
administration of justice." Whenever the Governor
of Massachusetts might think that a fair trial could
not be had there for an officer or soldier questioned
for his conduct while suppressing riots or tumults,
he might with consent of his council send them for
trial to a sister colony or to England.[3] This plan, it
was hoped, would make for a more effective execu-

---

[1] Almon, *Debates*, IX, 134, 249.   [2] *Ibid.*, 123.
[3] Pickering, *Statutes at Large*, XXX, 367.

tion of the customs laws as well as an aid to the keeping of order. A petition from Mr. Bollan, the Massachusetts agent in London, urging that this and the "Government Act" be delayed until he could get his colony's pleas in defense, was refused consideration. In vain was the fair trial recalled which Captain Preston and his soldiers were accorded after the "Boston Massacre." In vain were the protests of Savile, Burke, and Dowdeswell, and the warning of Mr. Sawbridge that a minister who would enslave America might later do the same with England. While the Opposition abused him, Lord North sat there somnolent and unashamed. Under attack he always had an easy insolence which warmed the hearts of his friends, but was gall and wormwood to his enemies. He was unmoved, confident now in public approbation, and probably right as far as the politically active part of the nation was concerned. Mr. Fuller, of the Opposition, said that much against his will he believed that the country approved the bill, that the people of England were misled. "If ever there was a nation running headlong to its ruin, it is this," he cried. There was no staying the eager zest of the majority of the Commons to do Lord North's bidding. On May 20, 1774, "His Majesty being seated on the Throne, and the Commons attended with their Speaker," the royal assent was given.[1]

The Lords had meanwhile advanced another act whose object it was "to facilitate the establishment of a temporary military government in Massa-

[1] Force, *American Archives* (4th Ser.), I, 79-80, 118, 126, 129.

chusetts." This "Quartering Act" aimed to remove
the difficulties which Colonel Dalrymple had met
when he arrived with his troops in Boston in the
days before the "massacre." Then the city fathers
chose to interpret the old Quartering Act to require
that he lodge his troops in the barracks on an island
in Boston Harbor, where they would have been quite
useless to quell riots within the city. Now it was
provided that, when the barracks were not in the
places where the soldiers were needed, the local
authorities must find suitable quarters for them. If
they neglected their duty, it would be lawful for the
Governor to direct the use of inns, alehouses, or
any uninhabited building for that purpose.[1] Except
Chatham's speech against clapping "a naval and
military extinguisher" over Boston Harbor, there
was almost no opposition. Though Chatham condemned "in the severest manner" the riots of Boston, yet he begged his colleagues to recall the follies
of Government which had roused their passions.
The destroying of the tea was the effect of despair,
he urged, "an act which in their cooler hours, they
would have thought on with horror."[2] He begged
for an amnesty on all her youthful errors. As for
himself, his prayers would always be for America's
welfare — "length of days be in her right hand, and
in her left hand, riches and honor; may her ways be
ways of pleasantness, and all her paths be peace."
All such exhortation seemed to the Ministry like
mere sentimentality, safe enough for the Opposition,

---

[1] Pickering, *Statutes at Large*, xxx, 410.
[2] Hansard, *Parliamentary History*, xvii, 1354–55.

but only pointing the road to ruin for a responsible administration. The bill passed, and on June 2d, the King's reason being temporarily under a cloud, the royal assent was given by Commission, which consisted of "three of the Lords Commissioners, being in their robes, and seated on a form placed between the Throne and the Woolsack, the Lord Chancellor in the middle, with the Lord Archbishop of Canterbury on his right hand, and the Earl of Sandwich on his left." [1]

The Quartering Act was the fourth, and really the last, of the measures which the Ministry thought of as undertaken to punish Boston and perhaps to bring the colonies to their senses. The Quebec Act, however, passed nearly at the same time with no thought of giving offense to the English provinces, and not thought of as one of the punitive acts, was soon classed with the other four by the Americans, and all became known as the "Five Intolerable Acts." Yet the provisions of the act which roused almost universal execration in the colonies, and which was supposed to have had vital connection with the punitive measures directed at Boston, had in fact been fully decided upon years before that event, the Boston tea episode, which the colonists suspected was its cause.[2] Indeed, Chatham, the great friend of America, had been during his administration committed to three out of four of its important provisions. Had the measure been passed seven years earlier it would have differed little from

[1] Force, *American Archives* (4th Ser.), I, 170.
[2] V. Coffin, *The Province of Quebec and the American Revolution* 530.

the Act of 1774.[1] The Quebec Act was passed with the desire to put an end to that injustice done by the hasty Proclamation of 1763, which by including the eighty thousand French-Canadians with the people in the area west of the Alleghenies established English courts, procedure, and law in French Canada.

Lord Mansfield had said of that mistake, which was due to the ignorance of Lord Hillsborough when using in haste the plans of Lord Shelburne, "The history of the world don't furnish an instance of so rash and unjust an act." Attorney-General Thurlow called it the "grossest and absurdest and cruellest tyranny that a conquering nation ever practiced over a conquered territory."[2]

The English-speaking subjects in Quebec had used the courts to seize the property of the French, who, being Roman Catholics, and subjected to legal disabilities as if in English courts, were left helpless.[3] All this after more than ten years was swept away by a statesmanlike measure which may well soften the judgment of history on Lord North, Lord Mansfield, Wedderburn, and even on the much-maligned George III. The King as he signed the bill declared it was founded "on the clearest principles of justice and humanity."[4] In granting the French colonists the free exercise of their religion, the British Parliament made a commendable, forward step in the

---

[1] V. Coffin, *The Province of Quebec*, 411–31, 432–36, 450–56, 531.

[2] *Grenville Papers*, II, 467; Cavendish, *Government of Canada;* Almon, *Debates* (1774), 29.

[3] Alvord, *The Mississippi Valley in British Politics*, I, 253–54.

[4] *Ibid.*, II, 247.

progress of religious toleration.[1] The liberality of
Mansfield aided this measure greatly. The reaction
in New England to this phase of the Quebec Act was
not creditable to those men whose ancestors had
fled to the wilderness that they might worship as
they chose. The Whig leaders and the clergy fanned
the flames of rebellion by much talk about holy
water and papal bulls. Thus they aroused the latent
Puritan bigotry until pre-Revolutionary literature
is filled with denunciation of this wise recognition
of the Roman Catholic religion in Quebec.[2] Samuel
Adams sought to stir even the religious passions
of the Indians. "Brothers," he cried, "they have
made a law to establish the religion of the Pope in
Canada, which lies so near you. We much fear some
of your children may be induced, instead of wor-
shipping the only true God, to pay his dues to images
made with their own hands." He always endeavored
to make "Popery and Slavery" seem synonymous.
It was not hard to rouse this traditional fear. No
farther back than 1745 the Puritan expedition
against Louisburg was a crusade. On their flag was
the motto, "Nil desperandum, Christo duce." One
of the chaplains is said to have carried a hatchet
to destroy images in Catholic churches, and one old
deacon wrote: "Oh that I could be with you and dear
Parson Moody in that church, to destroy the images
there set up." It was a regular colonial custom at
the time of the Revolution that the Pope and the

[1] See, however, Coffin's criticism of this act in *The Province of
Quebec*, 532-37.
[2] See my article in *American Historical Review*, XIX, 59.

Devil were religiously burned on Guy Fawkes Day. Calvinists were ready to believe anything concerning Catholic deceit and cunning. William Livingston (1755) stoutly affirmed that the French persuaded the Indians that the Virgin Mary was born in Paris. and that our Saviour was crucified at London by the English.[1] To Jeremy Belknap, the Church of Rome was "the mother of harlots and abominations." Samuel Adams, in 1768, "verily believed" that "much more is to be dreaded from the growth of Popery in America, than from Stamp-Acts or any other Acts destructive of men's civil rights."[2] John Adams, too, was alarmed (1771) that "the barriers against popery, erected by our ancestors are suffered to be destroyed, to the hazard even of the Protestant religion."[3] He was much pleased that "the rascally Roman Catholics" of Braintree did not dare show themselves. Jonathan Mayhew and Ezra Stiles, powerful ecclesiastical figures in New England, were both violently prejudiced against the "Romish Church."

It is not surprising, therefore, that a favorite device on the banners carried by Puritan mobs, after the Quebec Act, was the demand "no popery," and that one of the motives animating the captors of Ticonderoga was to secure the colonies from the incursions of the Roman Catholics, "those children

[1] Sedgwick (*William Livingston*, 97-98) spoke of the "superstitious rites and fantastic trumperies of popery." See also John Adams, *Works*, II, 5.

[2] Samuel Adams, *Writings*, I, 201-03.

[3] John Adams, *Works*, II, 252. His antipathy toward Catholics appears repeatedly. *Ibid.*, II, 5; III, 254, 268; x, 188.

of darkness." Ezra Stiles was astonished that the King and Lords and Commons, a whole Protestant Parliament — even the bishops concurring — should establish the Romish Church and "Idolatry" over three quarters of their Empire. Judge Drayton, in South Carolina, having in mind the Ministry's effort to establish the Roman Catholic religion, pictured "the flames which are lighted, blown up, and fed with blood by the Roman Catholic doctrines; doctrines which tend to establish a most cruel tyranny in Church and State — a tyranny under which all Europe groaned for many ages." [1] Even John Jay looked upon the Quebec Act as a menace to Protestantism. Public assemblies, too, made their solemn protest against this last act of the "lurking spirit of despotism." The New York Assembly expostulated with the British Government, and the famous "Suffolk Resolves" deprecated the act as "dangerous in extreme degree to the Protestant religion." The Continental Congress approved of these resolves and took the same ground as to the Catholic menace in their addresses to the people of Great Britain and to the colonies. It does not matter that Congress, a few months later, when it saw the advantage of allying Canada with the American Union, "perceived the fate of the Catholic and Protestant to be strongly linked together," for the earlier sentiments were the real, and the latter the feigned ones. The immediate reaction of the Puritans to the religious provision of the Quebec Act caused them much embarrassment at a later time.

[1] Force, *American Archives* (4th Ser.), I, 959; (5th Ser.), II, 1048.

Aside from the provision as to religion, the new act ameliorated the political system. The Quebec government, which was placed in the hands of a governor and legislative council, was left to establish English criminal and French civil law. Trial by jury in civil cases was not provided.[1] Even some of these worthy provisions gave offense to the English colonies, as the history of the next year will disclose, but Massachusetts, Virginia, and Connecticut, with their claims to land north of the Ohio, were greatly incensed by another provision extending Quebec southward to the Ohio and westward to the Mississippi, as if, the Patriots complained, to prevent the extension into that region of the free institutions of the Atlantic colonies. The only motive of the British Government was in fact not to "establish idolatry over all that space," but to extend the protection of the imperial power over that part of the Mississippi Valley. For the past ten years the British Government, changing with kaleidoscopic rapidity, had altered and mended and varied its plans for the western lands. The well-matured plans of Lord Shelburne, ascendant in 1767, looking to the gradual settlement of the domain under imperial direction, had been set aside by 1772 for the ill-digested scheme of Lord Barrington wherein the dominant idea was the "inutility of imperial expense in the West."[2] The trans-Allegheny region was to be a great Indian reservation devoted to the fur-trade, but with the duty of controlling it transferred to the colonial

---

[1] The law is given in full in Coffin, *The Province of Quebec*, 544–57.
[2] Alvord, *The Mississippi Valley in British Politics*, II, 50, 51.

government, which was ordered by imperial decree
to keep their citizens in bounds. Pitt's dream of a
teeming West, rich in farms and towns, growing
markets for British goods, was indefinitely put off.
By royal decree, moreover, the hopes of George
Washington, and many other land speculators not
so destined to immortality, were blighted.[1] Now in
1774 the ever-shifting policy of the British Government changed again. Under the local autonomy
of the colonial government lawlessness had been increasing in the West. The North Ministry was
alarmed. In the Quebec Act it made another effort
to give imperial protection, at least in the northern
part of the Mississippi Valley, to this Indian reservation already created. In so doing, they took away
the control lately exercised by Virginia, Massachusetts, and Connecticut in the western regions to
which their charters gave them claim. To these
colonies, and to all colonial land speculators anywhere, the Quebec Act seemed, therefore, only one
more of those punitive measures such as had already
been visited on Boston.[2] In the effort to solve its
western problem, as in its solution of problems in the
eastern colonies, the British Ministry seemed to have
failed. The climax of failure was reached at the same
time in the East and in the West, and the enraged
colonists were ready to take upon themselves the
solution of imperial problems affecting America.[3]

[1] Alvord, *The Mississippi Valley in British Politics*, ii, 112–14.
[2] Another act which aroused feeling in America was one putting a
stop to the exportation of tools for the manufacture of cotton, linen,
woolen, and silk. Force, *American Archives* (4th Ser.), i, 220–22.
[3] Alvord, *The Mississippi Valley in British Politics*, ii, 249–50.

In the midst of the debates on the coercive bills and the Quebec measure, a debate took place on a motion for the repeal of the duty on tea. Burke made a noble and compelling speech on American taxation which might have given pause to a body free to think. He pointed out the "shifts and devices" of the Ministry "full of meanness and full of mischief," by which they had tried to "pilfer piecemeal" the repeal of an act which they had not the generous courage to admit was an error. As a result "so paltry a sum as three-pence in the eyes of a financier, so insignificant an article as tea in the eyes of a philosopher, have shaken the pillars of a commercial empire that circled the whole globe." [1] But it was all in vain that he pleaded. Besides the inability of the official mind, guided by its rigidly legalistic advisers, to turn its gaze from the accepted principles governing trade control, or those touching the exercise of the royal prerogative, there was truth in the assertion of one of the high servants of the Lord North Ministry to Josiah Quincy: "You can have no idea of the taxes of this kingdom and the distress of our poor. I don't mean our *manufacturers*, but our hedgers and ditchers and threshers . . . they are extreme poor and wretched indeed: everything here is taxed to the utmost. The colonies must relieve us, they must ease us of our taxes." [2] Moreover, when their friends of the Ministry told Quincy that the British Government had no desire "to injure much less to oppress the Colonies," and

[1] Burke, *Works*, II, 14–15.
[2] Mass. Hist. Soc., *Proceedings*, L, 446 (Quincy's London Journal).

"no wish but that of seeing the Americans free and happy," and that the Administration was inclined to "lenity and mildness," they meant every word of it, and could not understand the cold cynicism which repelled the idea.

Furthermore, the Ministry could not believe that actual resistance would follow their measures. Lord Chatham was not so complacent. "America sets heavy on my mind," he wrote sadly. "There where I have garnered up my heart, where our strength lay, and our happiest resources presented themselves, it is all changed into danger, weakness, distraction, and vulnerability." Franklin and Quincy and other colonists in London were cautioned against the folly of resistance. The Americans must fail, they were told, in a contest with this "great and powerfull people." They were warned that "no power in Europe ever provoked the resentment or bid defiance to the Powers of this Island but they were made to repent it." [1] Was this not "the sceptered isle, the seat of Mars?"

To this pass the affairs of the British Empire had come. Immediate causes of its approach to the verge of war had been a series of misjudgments. Nor was it strange that a ministry, day after day puzzled by the unexpected, had at last committed an unpardonable error. Well-meant efforts to stop colonial evasion of the tea tax led to the unfortunate *Gaspée* incident. While Samuel Adams was toiling with committees of correspondence to stir the dying

[1] Mass. Hist. Soc., *Proceedings*, L, 442–43 (Quincy's London Journal).

embers of discontent, the North Ministry came to his aid with a badly thought-out effort to save the East India Company by a measure giving them a monopoly of colonial tea trade. The American tea importers resented the loss of their business and ventured again to bring to their support that turbulent monster — the rising democratic forces in the greater towns. In Boston that venture led straight to the Boston "Tea Party." From that violence the conservative property-holders in general revolted, but there was mass approval for the moment at least. Even the friends of the colonists were angered at first and the North Ministry pressed by the Grenville and Bedford factions, which had always stood for stern methods with the colonies, took up and carried through the punitive measures which became known as the "Five Intolerable Acts." All this came to pass because, as far as the Ministry was concerned, it could not rise to Burke's wisdom: "It is not what a lawyer tells me I may do, but what **humanity, reason and justice** tell me I ought to do."

CHAPTER XVI

UNION FOR RESISTANCE

WHEN Henry Laurens presented a petition against the Boston Port Bill, signed by thirty Americans resident in London, the Earl of Dartmouth asked his opinion of the proposed act. He replied: "That if the bills respecting America then pending in Parliament should pass into Acts the people of the several colonies from Georgia to New Hampshire would be animated to form such a Union & Phalanx of resistance as he had theretofore believ'd that nothing less than a divine Miracle could establish." [1] He knew that Americans were as stiff-necked people as ever the followers of Moses. Moreover, even those colonists that disapproved of Boston's riotous conduct resented, as Governor Penn wrote from Philadelphia, the effort to intimidate all America. "Their delinquency," he said, "in destroying the *East India* Company's tea is lost in the attention given to what is here called the too severe punishment of shutting up the port, altering the Constitution, and making an Act, as they term it, screening the officers and soldiers shedding *American* blood." [2] "Parliament by their proceedings," resolved Hanover County in Virginia, "have made us and all North America parties in the present dispute."

On May 10, 1774, news of "the severest Act ever

[1] Wallace, *Henry Laurens*, 197.
[2] Force, *American Archives* (4th Ser.), I, 514.

was penned against the town of Boston" arrived with the *Harmony* just from London, and a week later General Gage, who was acting as commander-in-chief of the British forces in America, landed from the Castle, to which the ship *Lively* had brought him the day before. He was received at the Long Wharf by Colonel Hancock's Company of Cadets, and at "the Town House had his Commission read by the Secretary, and took the Usual Oaths," as the new Governor of Massachusetts.[1] He was "escorted to Faneuill Hall, where a good Dinner by his Majesty's Council" gave no suggestion that Gage had come to execute an act of Parliament of which Samuel Adams with customary moderation said, "for flagrant injustice and barbarity, one might search in vain among the archives of *Constantinople* to find a match for it." [2]

Gage had plenty of proof that thousands welcomed his coming, and as he looked about him and saw the natural resources of Massachusetts enriched by the labor and thrift of a hardy, self-governing people, he must have thought with Dr. Johnson that "if the rascals are so prosperous, oppression has agreed with them, or there has been no oppression." He could honestly think too that it was mere moonshine to assert that if the British Government were allowed to tax without representation slavery would surely result. To him the auguries of tyranny which an Adams arrived at by a logical deduction from principle were absurdly improbable. Such

---

[1] *Letters and Diary of John Rowe,* 269–70.
[2] Force, *American Archives* (4th Ser.), **i**, 332.

thoughts hardened his soldier heart, and made him
feel that he was dealing with an ungrateful people.
Perhaps he came to agree with Earl Percy who at
first was kindly disposed, but within a few months
wrote home: "the people here are a set of sly, artful, hypocritical rascalls, cruel and cowards. I must
own that I cannot but despise them compleatly."

Though the amiable Governor Gage had married
an American wife, a tender tie which it was hoped
would soften the rigors of his administration, he
showed no gentleness in executing the orders of his
royal master. Soon it was reported that the Boston
wharves were desolate, "entirely deserted; not a
topsail vessel to be seen either there or in the harbor
save ships of war and transports." The execution
was beyond the rigor of the act itself, thought
Samuel Cooper. Men believed that the town was
to be made a desolate wilderness and grass to grow
in its streets.[1] Yet Gage was conciliatory, almost
deferential toward the civil authorities, and impatient military men began to say that he was no better than "an old woman." He allowed agitators to
speak their minds, and patriot papers, uncensored,
bitterly assailed him. But when it came to obeying
the letter of the law, he abated not one jot. Though
nine thousand bushels of wheat and corn were sent
from sympathetic Virginia and two shiploads of rice
from South Carolina, all was forced to enter the city
by way of Salem or Marblehead and thence around
through Cambridge by wagons, "Lord North's coast-

[1] Andrews' Letters, in Mass. Hist. Soc., *Proceedings,* VIII, 328-30;
American Historical Review, VIII, 328.

ers," as they were dubbed. The distance, twenty-eight to thirty miles, made the expense eight dollars a load, since the wagoners, "whipping their horses and damning Lord North alternately," were not allowed to carry any merchandise on the return trip. The use of Charlestown ferry was not permitted because the goods would then be water-borne, contrary to law. A thousand bushels of grain from Weathersfield, Connecticut, and a thousand barrels of flour from the Quaker City, came by the same devious route. Even the "donation of the sympathizing brethren of Marblehead," meat, fish, and sweet oil, came in eleven carts instead of the easier way by water. Nevertheless, Massachusetts "did not sit solitary," but with the support and sympathy of sister colonies she was "a princess among the provinces." Boston people endured all with astonishing calmness and resolution, "neither dismayed nor tumultous." [1] Public works were planned, streets paved, docks cleaned, and ships built to employ the laboring men, who only grumbled a little because they were thus compelled by the distributing committee to earn what they held had been sent them as a free gift.[2]

Such currents of sympathy had never swept through the colonies. If a town hesitated to give aid to Massachusetts, it was at once scorned as a Tory town. Yet, beneath the surface harmony of applause for martyred Boston, there was a deep

---

[1] Andrews' Letters, in Mass. Hist. Soc., *Proceedings*, VIII, 329; Mass. Hist. Soc., *Collections* (4th Ser.), IV, 1–278; Thornton, *The Pulpit of the Revolution*, 213.

[2] *Boston Town Records* (1770–77), 174–89.

discord resulting from the change in the nature of the contest with Parliament. Hitherto the colonial merchant class had been calling upon Parliament for reform in its trade laws and had used the mechanic or any radical element in society as a powerful tool, dangerous but necessary, and which it hoped to drop when the ends were attained. Now the dispute with Parliament had become wholly political. Trade reform was no longer the issue. The leaders of riots, the "Jack Cades" who controlled the "lower orders of mankind," were now a menace to men of property. As Gouverneur Morris wrote, "the heads of the mobility grow dangerous to the gentry." The "daring coxcombs," who "roared out liberty . . . and religion" and other cant terms, and were able to rule the simple flock, set out to gain their own aims — an independent America and the "rights of man." [1] At such aims the merchants were alarmed. Protection of their trade by the powerful British Empire was not to be sneered at in a world wherein every great nation had its restrictive trade laws. British laws might be offensive in some aspects, but, when they subsidized colonial industries, fostered colonial shipping, and in the British markets shielded American merchants from competition with French or Dutch or Spanish traders, it was clear that membership in the British Empire was a valuable asset. Any merchant trading across the seas could easily compute the value of Britannia's rule of the watery wastes of the earth, and of new markets won each succeeding year, it seemed, by British

[1] Force, *American Archives* (4th Ser.), i, 342.

arms.[1] Many of the mercantile class began to see through British eyes. Law and order began to look more attractive than "liberty" marred by violence. Now that no commercial principle was in question, and it was only mob rule that was to be put down, a merchant found his heart with the North Government.

But the very measures which gave the merchants pause made other men hasten on to a radical position. William Henry Drayton, who had tried to stem the popular current in 1769, now asserted his freedom, "at the risk of life itself," *against the malignant nature* of the late "five acts of Parliament." [2] Others had a like change of heart, and radicals everywhere, from Samuel Adams at the North to Christopher Gadsden in the South, seized the moment of high feeling to carry America beyond the point where there could be any going back.

In Boston "the merchants who either will not or cannot" pay their debts, "the smugglers, the mechanics, and those who are fascinated with the extravagant notions of independency," opposed compensation to the East India Company and favored coercion of the British by withholding all trade.[3] The conservative merchants and the moderates in general regarded the "Tea Party" as a reprehensible act of mob violence for which Boston was responsible and ought to pay. A town meeting was called on May 13th, and a resolution not too fiery

---

[1] Schlesinger, *The Colonial Merchants*, 308–09.
[2] Gibbes, *Doc. Hist.*, ii, 12–13.
[3] Force, *American Archives* (4th Ser.), i, 506–08.

for the moderates in other colonies was adopted, urging all America to unite in stopping trade to or from Britain and her West Indies until the Port Act was repealed. To fail in this, Boston urged, would leave "odious oppression" to "rise triumphant over right, justice, social happiness and freedom." [1] This resolution, with a circular letter from the Boston Committee of Correspondence, went forth to become famous throughout all America. Many Boston merchants in the first heat of passion had signed agreements to join the merchants of other colonies in severing relations with Great Britain, but in cooler moments they repented, and rejoiced when it later became known that the merchants in other colonies were cool toward trade restrictions. The Boston merchants went two or three hundred strong to a town meeting and endeavored to get the tea paid for. Failing there, they took the occasion of Governor Hutchinson's departure to send him an address, which before long became "infamous" in Massachusetts as a list of "traitors to their country." Sixty-three merchants and shopkeepers, a dozen royal officers and others less exalted, but dependent upon the favor of the men of property, signed this protest against popular tumults, endorsing Hutchinson's "wise, zealous and faithful" régime, and offering to pay their share of the East India Company's indemnity.[2]

A week later the radical Committee of Corre-

---

[1] *Boston Town Records* (1770–77), 172–74.

[2] Mass. Hist. Soc., *Proceedings* (1869–70), xi, 392. The signers are grouped as to occupation and place of business. Thirty-one are starred as not natives of America.

spondence countered with a Cromwellian "solemn League and Covenant," wherein all signers, solemnly, "in the presence of God," agreed to suspend all trade relations with the British at once and not to buy or use their goods after October 1st.[1] By a sly artifice the committee tried to have the covenant appear as a spontaneous outburst of the non-mercantile public. Many merchants signed a protest against it as "a base, wicked and illegal measure," meant for their ruin. The legality of the committee and its action was challenged, but in town meeting was upheld by a large majority.[2] Approval of the covenant swept all the county conventions, and finally a provincial convention, called in October to rule the colony until Parliament should restore "constitutional government," commended the covenant to the whole colony. The rest of New England was not so warm for the plan, but preferred to elect delegates to a Continental Congress which might settle the policy for all America.[3]

Meanwhile Gage was finding Boston a most inhospitable place for his regiments gathered from Canada and the other frontiers. Idle workmen would not build barracks, but, inspired by the Sons of Liberty, preferred to ruin the lumber sent for that purpose. Gage was forced at last to get most of his labor from far Nova Scotia. None would sell wood to the troops nor straw for their bedding.[4] The

[1] Schlesinger, *The Colonial Merchants*, 315–19.
[2] *Letters and Diary of John Rowe*, 277.
[3] Schlesinger, *The Colonial Merchants*, 323–27.
[4] *Boston Gazette*, October 3, 1774. New York radicals prevented carpenters being sent to Boston when that was attempted. Force, *American Archives* (4th Ser.), I, 782, 802–04, 814.

councillors appointed under the "Massachusetts
Government Act" were declared by the Boston
Committee "unconstitutional," and Daniel Leonard,
an appointee, had "six balls and some shot fired into
his house," which hastened his seeking sanctuary in
Boston. Timothy Ruggles, another councillor, fled
to the same asylum after his house was attacked
and cattle maimed. Others resigned in haste their
unpopular offices. To defeat the new method of
choosing jurors, the mob at Great Barrington so
filled the court-house as not to leave room for either
judges or jurors.[1] Before this rising specter of rebellion Gage quailed, and wrote home urging that
the acts be suspended until 20,000 Hessians and
Hanoverians could be hired to make an entire conquest of New England. When told of town meetings
being held in spite of the law, he replied testily,
"Damn 'em! I won't do anything about it unless
his Majesty sends me more troops."[2] To this he
had come from his early assurance that the Bostonians would be very meek if he with four regiments
took a resolute part.

When the proposal in Boston's circular letter was
borne to New York by Paul Revere, who appears
in Revolutionary literature like a centaur ever on
horseback,[3] the final struggle began there between
the radicals and the principal merchants. Neither
John Morin Scott nor John Lamb, the mob leaders,
was the equal of Samuel Adams. They were reckless

[1] Mass. Hist. Soc., *Proceedings*, VIII, 346.   [2] *Ibid.*, 348.
[3] *New England Magazine*, April, 1902; C. F. Gettemy, *Paul Revere;*
E. H. Goss, *Paul Revere.*

enough, but lacked ability. Neither they, nor the committee described by its opponents as "flaming patriots without property or anything else but impudence," could dominate the situation.[1] The "most considerable merchants and men of cool tempers" got a new committee of fifty nominated, with conservatives in a majority,[2] and this committee was later confirmed by a citizens' mass meeting, which conceded one more radical, making a committee of fifty-one. This committee had a running fight with the radicals until five delegates to a provincial congress were finally elected, all moderates, two fated even to become Loyalists.[3] The significance of the struggle was fairly expressed by Gouverneur Morris in a letter to Mr. Penn: "Yesterday I was present at a grand division of the city, and these . . . my fellow citizens . . . fairly contended about the future forms of our government, whether it should be founded upon aristocratic or democratic principles. I stood in the balcony, and on my right hand were ranged all the people of property, with some few dependents, and on the other all the tradesmen."[4] His sympathies were not with the "poor reptiles," the mob which had begun to think and reason; he was ready to say, "Farewell aristocracy," as he saw them basking in the sunshine of their vernal morning, and with the other "gentry" he began to fear that "ere noon

---

[1] Force, *American Archives* (4th Ser.), I, 300.

[2] Becker, *Political Parties in the Province of New York*, 112–15 Nineteen members later became open Loyalists.

[3] *Ibid.*, 115–35.   [4] *Ibid.*, 115.

they will bite."[1] Beyond some half-promises, however, the radicals gained little in this contest except organization. The rural counties responded coldly to the request of the "Committee of Fifty-One," to send delegates; not twenty men were present in Orange County, and in King's two men met and one was u..nimously elected by the other to the provincial congress. In general a small faction took any active part in the election, and six counties kept out of the election altogether.[2]

In Pennsylvania was found a situation not unlike that in New York, the masses pitted against the great merchants, with whom stood the majority of the peace-loving Quakers. The latter preferred memorials and remonstrances to trade restrictions and gestures of defiance; or, as their enemies said, "one cargo of British goods to the salvation of America." Charles Thomson, who was courting a lady related to John Dickinson, and who was "the Sam Adams of Philadelphia," led the radicals.[3] Joseph Reed and Thomas Mifflin shared this leadership and they sought to enlist Dickinson, who had looked askance at Boston's "Tea Party." In a town meeting, called after Paul Revere rode into Philadelphia with Boston's plea for succor, Dickinson, gently restraining Thomson, gave his voice for moderation, a petition for redress rather than full acclaim of the Massachusetts plan. Under his in-

[1] Sparks, *Gouverneur Morris*, I, 23–26.
[2] Becker, *Political Parties in the Province of New York*, 139–40.
[3] John Adams, *Works*, II, 358. The lady had £5000 sterling, John Adams says.

fluence a committee of nineteen, weighted on the moderate side, was chosen, which with a Quaker primness chid Boston by implication, and declared in favor of a general congress with "non-intercourse" as a last resort. The Pennsylvania Assembly also was to be called that it might petition the King, but the Governor frustrated that plan, and a new public meeting forced the hand of the committee of nineteen and brought about an enlargement of the committee to forty-four members, reduced to forty-three by the resignation of Joseph Pemberton, "a pillar of the Society of Friends." [1] Of this Dickinson was chairman, and he prevented conflict between its radical and moderate members.

Both factions faced a hostile, conservative body in the lower house of the legislature, led by its speaker, Joseph Galloway.[2] That "loyalist politician," aristocratic by inheritance, was fearful of the noisy elements among the people, and the recent growth of "republican ideas." He believed in the "American rights" up to a certain point, but stopped short of the "anarchy" of popular movements. He had money and property enough to dread excessive taxation, but he did not court the aid of democracy, "enemy of true liberty," in bringing the British Government to terms.[3] Knowing his power the "Forty-Three" tried to conciliate, but moved also to thwart him. They asked him to summon the House, but at the same time called a convention of

[1] Schlesinger, *The Colonial Merchants*, 341–50.
[2] Baldwin, "Joseph Galloway," in *Pennsylvania Magazine of History*, xxvi, 161–91.
[3] *Ibid.*, 440.

county committees, sure to be radical because the
western counties would there have far greater representation than in the regular legislature where an
unproportional system cheated them of a proper
influence.[1] Moreover, the Scotch-Irish Presbyterians and German Lutherans disliked the dominatior
of the Quaker more than they feared "British
tyranny." If the convention could dictate the terms
to which delegates would be committed, the choice
of them might be left to the Galloway-ridden House.
That was what the convention undertook when it
met in Carpenter's Hall and chose Thomson as its
clerk, Thomas Willing as chairman, and agreed to a
petition to the King as a first act of the general Congress soon to convene. It was declared to be the
purpose of Pennsylvania to join the other colonies in
wholly sealing up the trade with Great Britain if the
Congress so decreed and to support even more dras-
tic steps. The Congress was to demand at least the
repeal of the "Intolerable Acts" and all pretense to
a right to tax or to regulate America's internal
affairs. Finally, to appease the radicals, it was
agreed that Pennsylvania did not mean to restrain
its deputies from joining any measures the Congress
might approve.[2] In a body the convention presented these instructions to the House of Representatives, which thereupon, ignoring the suggestion that Willing and James Wilson and Dickinson

---

[1] Lincoln, *Revolutionary Movement in Pennsylvania*, 40–52. Three
Quaker counties, Philadelphia, Chester, and Bucks, with one half the
population of Pennsylvania, elected twenty-four of the thirty-six
deputies in the assembly.

[2] Schlesinger, *The Colonial Merchants*, 351–53.

be chosen, selected seven of its own members, including Galloway, as delegates to a Continental Congress. Nothing was said of the convention's instructions, but the delegates were told to seek redress and also harmony with Great Britain, avoiding anything indecent or disrespectful to her.

The Galloway faction had expressed in a broadside its doubt of the convention's authority. It was simply "setting up anarchy above order — it is the beginning of republicanism." All of their devices failed to stem its rising tide. They resisted every advance, for they believed with Hume that the only way to make the people wise was "to keep them from uniting into large assemblies," mere mobs, as a loyal writer declared them, all swayed by the absurd ideas of any member who might try to heat his audience with that blaze of patriotism with which he conceived himself inspired.[1] But it was these leaders of the masses who were gaining control, and under their direction a new class, formed within a decade, growing rapidly in numbers, was rising to power. In Pennsylvania, as in a number of other colonies, it consisted of small farmers in the back country, Scotch-Irish and German immigrants, reënforced by the voteless laborers and artisans of Philadelphia or other seaboard cities. Clever young lawyers with a gift for mob oratory led some, and Presbyterian preachers whose very dissent made them enemies of England with its Established Church, led others. For over a decade this rising democracy had struggled for power against the little seaboard aristocracy

[1] Force, *American Archives* (4th Ser.), I, 607–08.

of wealth and accepted social leadership; which hob-
nobbed with the Governor, aped the English gentry,
and patronized jewelers, lapidaries, chaise-makers,
and portrait-painters, whose interests thus became
linked with this privileged group since they knew
well "where thrift would follow fawning." It was
from this class that royal governors chose their councils, and even the assembly was often controlled by
its "interests." These men, who were not too modest
to speak of themselves as the "better sort," looked
with alarm at this pushing, aggressive class which
did not have "that repose which marks the caste of
Vere de Vere," but pressed without dignity into high
places. The colonial masses could no longer be controlled by reverence for the high-born. The Quaker
merchants of Philadelphia, the holders of manors on
the Hudson, the tobacco and rice planters of Virginia
and South Carolina, and even the great merchants,
clergy, and professional men of New England, could
no longer rule without question their social inferiors.
The velvet coat, neckerchiefs, and wrist falls of
Irish lace, satin trousers and silver embroidered
cocked hat, no longer enabled Daniel Leonard to
awe the Massachusetts mob who questioned his
loyalty to the colony. Thus, in 1774, came the
climax in the struggle between rich and poor, East
and West, those with a vote and those who were
voteless, between privilege and the welfare of the
common man. The two classes might work in harmony or might clash on the question of resistance
to Great Britain, but they were pretty sure to be in
opposition on the issue of individual rights. A mer-

chant clad in London clothes, and whose mansion walls were decorated with the oil portraits of his ancestors whose Christian names he could recall at will, might welcome the support of the mechanics and small shopkeepers against a grievous tax by the British Government, but the price, a right to vote and to hold office, he was sure to resent, and he grew more and more alarmed as the pressure became more insistent. Some yielded in time, even if ungraciously, but the more conservative, like Galloway, were forced eventually to abandon the colonial cause rather than try to win it at the cost of the loss of privilege.

This class conflict existed in the South, as well as in the North, but in the plantation section the merchants had been consistently on the conservative side during all the decade of controversy. The planters, however, were more aroused in 1774 than ever before, for while they might be Laodicean as to trade reform issues, they were easily heated in a tilt over constitutional rights and personal liberty. Moreover, the planter's business was so conducted that he was always deeply indebted to British merchants, and his crops pledged long ahead for goods he was already enjoying. The most honest tobacco and rice planter could not be unaffected by a proposal to suspend the collection of debts at a time when he was very hard-pressed.[1] Virginia and North

---

[1] The British Government (1791) asked the English merchants for the total debt owed them by various colonies in 1776, with interest. The totals reported for Virginia and North Carolina were £2,305,408 for the former and £379,344 for the latter. South Carolina's debt was £687,953. Public Record Office, *Chatham MSS.*, 343.

Carolina, therefore, resorted at once to the most radical measures yet ventured upon and Maryland followed closely.[1] The Virginia House of Burgesses was in session when the Boston Port Act news came. June 1st, when the act would go into effect, was fixed upon as a day of fasting, humiliation, and prayer, showing that Puritan piety existed in the South as well as in New England, and was a sentiment to be reckoned with. Governor Dunmore, who had constantly irritated the burgesses from the first days of his administration, dissolved the House because of this effort "to inflame the country," but the members, undismayed, met in the Apollo Room of the "Raleigh" Tavern, made Peyton Randolph chairman, and resolved on a boycott of all East India commodities; it then instructed its Committee of Correspondence to invite all the other colonies to a general Congress.[2]

For this step the committee had prepared the way over a year before, when, under instructions from the House, it had at the time of the *Gaspée* affair urged upon the other colonial legislatures the formation of inter-provincial committees of correspondence. Nine colonies had responded to that suggestion, and there existed the parts of a great machine which only needed to be assembled at Philadelphia or some other convenient point to form a union of all the forces of discontent in America.[3] When the Continental Congress met, there is

[1] Schlesinger, *The Colonial Merchants*, 359–61.

[2] Lingley, *The Transition in Virginia*, 81–82.

[3] Leake, *The Virginia Committee System*, 134–38.

good reason to believe that it was looked upon as a meeting of the committees of correspondence of the several colonies; indeed, its members were in most cases the members of the committees of correspondence in the respective provinces.[1] In later generations, when States and sections quarreled as to whom the honor belonged of having been the first to rebel, Virginia or Massachusetts, North or South, there was much ado over the origin of the committees of correspondence.[2] The truth seems to be that Samuel Adams, inspired perhaps by Otis or Mayhew, established the first system of local committees. That of Boston corresponded with those in other towns of that province, and soon other provinces imitated that radical machine. It was Virginia, however, imitating at first standing legislative committees already existing in England, which set up various like committees in the House of Burgesses, and at last (1759) a "committee of correspondence" to keep in touch with Virginia's agent in London.[3]

Out of this experience Virginia was inspired on the eve of the Revolution (1773) to establish and to urge other colonies to set up legislative committees of correspondence which would keep each other informed as to the state of the public mind and strive to preserve unity. From this committee now came the first invitation of one colony to others to meet

---

[1] Leake, *The Virginia Committee System*, 73–75, 147–48.

[2] *Ibid.*, 65–66; E. D. Collins, "Committees of Correspondence," in American Historical Association, *Report* (1901), I, 247.

[3] Leake, *op. cit.*, 11–15, 89–90; J. F. Jameson, "The Origin of the Standing Committee System," in *Political Science Quarterly*, IX, 262–63.

in an all-American Congress, though many town gatherings here and there in America had already proposed that plan.[1] Indeed, the time was ripe and the logic of events put the idea in every fertile mind.

The Virginia Burgesses, who ventured the call to all the colonies, sent a circular letter to the rest of their fellow-members to sound their constituents and then, on August 1st, to come to a meeting at Williamsburg. This appeal to the county meetings revealed a spirit in those fountains of power more radical than that of their representatives in the assembly. Only the Scotch merchants opposed, giving as a reason "the injustice and perfidy of refusing to pay our debts" to British creditors.[2] Many of the merchants, whom a British visitor found "very genteel people," planned "quitting the country as fast as their affairs would permit." In spite of them, the provincial convention met, chose delegates to Congress and declared for an association to enforce a boycott of British goods. This was going no farther than the county meetings had zealously urged them to go.

In North Carolina, in defiance of Governor Martin's proclamation against "illegal meetings," there were like county gatherings followed by a convention at New Berne in which one of the fiery spirits was William Hooper, a law pupil of James Otis, who, with James Hawes and Richard Caswell, carried through a series of measures not much different

---

[1] Schlesinger, *The Colonial Merchants*, 363–93. Many men in private letters and in newspaper articles had suggested the plan even earlier.

[2] Hunt, *Writings of James Madison*, I, 26.

from those of Virginia.[1] An English "Lady of Quality" visiting in Wilmington at the time thought that "noble country" . . . which "owed more favors to its God and King . . . than any other in the known world," was "equally ungrateful to both," and hoped that Governor Martin, whose "gentle methods" with "these infatuated people" she marveled at, would leave the colony as he found it, "a habitation to wolves and bears." [2]

South Carolina took fire less easily owing to the resistance of the merchants and factors and of the rice planters, who were afraid of having their rice crop left on their hands as a result of non-exportation. The resourceful Christopher Gadsden, one of the several "Sam Adamses" of the time, who seems to have been quite regardless of his large business interests, directed the radical plans. In a large meeting of irregular origin and composition, which gathered at Charleston on summons from the General Committee of the city, a "non-intercourse" resolution failed, but the radicals secured a compensating victory by carrying a resolve that delegates to a "Continental Congress" were to have "full power" to agree to "legal measures" for redress of grievances. Thereupon the struggle centered on the election of conservative or radical delegates. Both sides resorted to dubious methods, but the radicals carried the day and elected Gadsden, Thomas Lynch, and Edward Rutledge, in addition to Henry Middleton and John Rutledge, approved

---

[1] Ashe, *History of North Carolina*, I, 420–22.
[2] British Museum, *Egerton MSS.*, 2423 F 102.

by both factions. Edward Rutledge had been a moderate, but he was the son-in-law of Gadsden and the radicals were content. Later the Commons House of Assembly in an early morning session, before Governor Bull was awake, gave the election the stamp of legality and voted money for expenses.[1]

The frontier and infant colony, Georgia, with its annual subsidy from Parliament and its many royal officers under British pay, with the "Haughty Creeks" at their backs and with the consequent need of Government protection, was not easily stirred to rebellion. There was a mere handful of radicals in the province, largely centered in St. John's Parish; while St. Paul, the most popular parish of the colony, was almost wholly loyal. It proved impossible to get delegates sent to represent Georgia in the Continental Congress.

[1] Schlesinger, *The Colonial Merchants*, 373–78.

CHAPTER XVII

THE CONTINENTAL CONGRESS AND THE FIRST BLOODSHED

EXCEPT that the Continental Congress was not authorized by the Crown, the "Friends of Government" were not necessarily opposed to such a general council. It might be the best way for securing a conciliation, and would at least prevent lawless action. Samuel Adams feared it, and tried his best to get the colonies committed in advance to a rebellious plan. Dickinson wished it, that war might be avoided; while Josiah Quincy was afraid it might be the source of timid or lukewarm counsels. New York and Philadelphia merchants thought it might at least postpone or soften non-intercourse, and might even prevent such a blow to mercantile interests.[1] General Gage contented himself with the thought that Boston might "get little more than fair words" from such a congress. Its apparent limitation to trade restrictions, John Adams, a delegate, regretted. "But what avails," he asked, "Prudence, Wisdom, Policy, Fortitude, Integrity, without Power, without Legions? When Demosthenes (God forgive the Vanity of recollecting his Example) went Ambassador from Athens to the other states of Greece, to excite a Confederacy against Phillip, he did not go to propose a Non-Importation or Non-

[1] Schlesinger, *The Colonial Merchants*, 393-95.

consumption Agreement ! ! !" Adams hoped for
"Something a little more sublime and mettlesome." [1]

While the Massachusetts House locked the door
on the Governor's message of dissolution, delegates
were chosen, September 1st determined as the date,
and Philadelphia the place, for a Continental Congress. James Bowdoin, Thomas Cushing, Samuel
and John Adams, and Robert Treat Paine were
chosen as delegates.[2] John Adams for the moment
lost confidence. "We have not men fit for the
times," he wrote in his diary. "We are deficient in
genius, in education, in travel, in fortune, in everything. I feel unutterable anxiety. God grant us
wisdom and fortitude!" Still he was not without
devices. "I could," he wrote his wife, Abigail,
"turn the course of my reading and studies to subjects of Law, and Politics, and Commerce as may
come in play in Congress. I might be furbishing up
my old reading in Law and History, that I might
appear with less indecency before a variety of gentlemen, whose educations, travels, experience, family,
fortune and everything will give them a vast superiority to me, and I fear even to some of my
companions." He might well be concerned about
Samuel Adams, who had never left the bounds of
Massachusetts until he went as a delegate to the
first Continental Congress.[3] The journey to Philadelphia was full of edification; nothing was lost, not

[1] *Warren-Adams Letters*, 29.
[2] Force, *American Archives* (4th Ser.), I, 421-23. On June 15th,
Rhode Island, first of all the colonies, had chosen delegates; Massachusetts was two days later.
[3] Wells, *Samuel Adams*, I, 5.

even the view from the church steeple at Wethers-
field. At New Haven all the bells in town were set
to ringing, and the people, men, women, and children, crowded at doors and windows as if to see a
coronation. Roger Sherman, "a solid, sensible man,"
one of Connecticut's delegates, waited on them at
Isaac Bear's tavern, and pleased Adams, because he
would not concede that Parliament had a right to
make any laws whatever for America. The delegates
visited Yale College, but doubtless took especial
delight in seeing the gravestone of Dixwell, the
regicide.[1] On they went to New York, stopping at
the tavern, "the sign of the Bunch of Grapes," but
soon they were invited to private lodgings, where
they were made familiar with all the ins and outs
of New York politics, chiefly from the radical point
of view, though they met, on good terms seemingly,
a number, like Peter Van Schaack, who later became
Loyalists. They met the New York delegates, "all
Episcopalian" except Philip Livingston, "a great
rough, rapid mortal," who "blustered away so that
one could not converse with him." He had no more
delicacy than to remind John Adams that Massachusetts hanged the Quakers and that New Yorkers
feared the leveling spirit in New England. Two
New York delegates, Duane, "with a sly, surveying
eye," and Alsop, "a soft sweet man," gave Adams
recent news about the bad state of mind in England.
A week of entertainment greatly impressed Adams
with the grand houses, the rich and splendid furniture, the quantities of silver plate, but the breeding

[1] John Adams, *Works*, II, 340–45.

he thought inferior to his beloved New England;
and he had not seen "one real gentleman, one well-
bred man." They talked "loud, very fast and altogether" paying no attention to one another — and
perhaps not to John Adams. He would rather, in
his Puritanical zeal for improving his mind, have
seen the college, the churches, and the booksellers'
shops,[1] and at the last moment part of his desire was
granted.

At length the party crossed Paulus Hook Ferry
into New Jersey and pressed on to Princeton, where
they saw the college and Rittenhouse's planetarium,
showing most of the motions of the astronomical
world. The president and the students were all
"Sons of Liberty." Passing on through Trenton and
over the Delaware, the delegates arrived at last near
"the happy, the peaceful, the elegant city" of
Philadelphia, where they were met by carriages
filled with other delegates and gentlemen from the
city. Tired, dusty, and fatigued they rode into
town. It had been a long journey for many of the
delegates, but all agreed with Bland that they would
have gone "if it had been to Jericho."

Life for the next few weeks was a round of that
lavish hospitality for which the city has been famed
from that day to this. There was no rest. "A most
sinful feast again," John Adams wrote after ten days
of such a life, "everything which could delight the
eye or allure the taste; curds and creams, jellies,
sweetmeats of various sorts, twenty sorts of tarts,
fools, trifles, floating islands, and whipped sillabubs."

[1] John Adams, *Works*, II, 353.

"Parmesan Cheese, punch, wine and porter, beer, etc." Again, when he dined with Chief Justice Chew, there was "turtle and every other thing, flummery . . . sweetmeats of 20 sorts . . . and then a dessert of fruits, raisins, almonds, pears and peaches. Wines most excellent and admirable. I drank Madeira at a great rate, and found no inconvenience in it." [1] Either the Madeira or the social intercourse broadened the views of all the delegates, and to some extent dispelled the mists of religious or sectional prejudice. John Adams, the stern Puritan, attended the Baptist and Methodist, the Moravian and the Episcopalian Churches and even the "Romish Chapel," where he conceded "the scenery and the music are so calculated to take in mankind, the paintings, the bells, the candles, the gold and silver; our Saviour on the cross, all his wounds bleeding," that he wondered the Reformation had ever succeeded. He even summoned up diplomacy enough to move, on the second day of the Congress' meeting in Carpenter's Hall, that the session open with prayers by Mr. Duché, the Anglican clergyman; though he could not resist flattering himself that he was no bigot. [2] It was a good stroke, and disarmed much prejudice against Puritan New England.

John Adams' comments upon the delegates from other colonies betrayed the New England bias. He was meeting most of the delegates for the first time,

---

[1] John Adams, *Works*, ii, 370–81.
[2] *Ibid.*, 364, 368, 369, 378, 395. Duché later disappointed Adams and became a "Tory."

as was true, perhaps, of most other members, for only six had served in the Stamp Act Congress. Dickinson, Adams wrote, "is a shadow, tall, but slender as a reed; pale as ashes"; he was "agreeable and modest." The elder Rutledge "had no keenness in his eye, no depth in his countenance, nothing of the profound, sagacious, brilliant or sparkling" and "maintains the air of reserve, design, and cunning." Lee was "a tall, spare man; Bland a learned, bookish man." Edward Rutledge, "good natured but conceited," was "young, sprightly, but not deep; he has the most indistinct, inarticulate way of speaking, speaks through his nose." "A perfect Bob-O-Lincoln, — a swallow, a sparrow, a peacock; . . . excessively weak and excessively variable and unsteady." Cæsar Rodney "is the oddest looking man in the world; he is tall, thin and slender . . . pale; his face not bigger than a large apple, yet there is sense and fire, spirit, wit and humor in his countenance."[1] Joseph Galloway, a "sensible and learned but cold speaker," the greatest enemy of the Adamses' cause, remembered Samuel Adams as "equal to most men in popular intrigue and the management of a faction. He eats little, sleeps little, drinks little, thinks much and is most decisive and indefatigable in the pursuit of his objects." All these were surface, first impressions, but were what any casual observer who was somewhat critical and censorious might have gained had he enjoyed Adams' or Galloway's opportunities.

Of the delegations to the Congress, four were in-

[1] John Adams, *Works*, II, 360–61, 362–64, 401.

structed to procure the harmony and union of the
empire, to restore mutual confidence or to establish
the union with Great Britain. Three were instructed
to report the breach made in American rights, and
to preserve American liberty. Two were to seek a
repeal of the obnoxious acts or to determine on
prudent and lawful measures of redress. Three were
simply to attend the Congress, or "to consult to
advance the good of the colonies." North Carolina
alone bound her inhabitants in honor to obey the
acts of the Congress, to which she was sending
delegates. New Jersey and Delaware, with chiefly
farming interests, were the only colonies to recommend a plan of complete restriction of incoming
and outgoing trade, but the southern plantation
provinces stood plainly for a two-edged plan of commercial war on England to which the northern
commercial interests were cold. As there were only
eleven merchant members, and the lawyers, together
with the representatives of agricultural interests,
predominated, some plan of trade restriction was
assured. Finally, the Congress was not thought of
as a lawmaking body, but was regarded as a convention of emissaries from distinct communities
who wished to take counsel among themselves concerning their common relations to England. It was
decided that each colony should have one vote.
Fifty-five members from twelve colonies attended,
and Arthur Lee, with a flourish of his pen, calculated that the Congress represented two million
people. Peyton Randolph was chosen president, and
Charles Thomson, secretary.

At first the Congress, under a rule of secrecy, proceeded with "flattering tranquillity." Finding that the New England members had "numberless prejudices" to remove, the Adamses kept out of sight, felt pulses, sounded depths, and insinuated their sentiments through other persons.[1] The great obstacle to realizing the radical wishes was Joseph Galloway and his strong group of moderates, "possessed of the greatest fortunes in America," seeking a clear definition of imperial relations and peaceful petitions rather than some irritating trade coercion. These men were startled when, on September 17th, the radicals suddenly carried over their protest an endorsement of the bold resolves of Suffolk County, Massachusetts, nullifying Parliament's "Intolerable Acts," calling for a "people's government" and a defensive militia, and advocating a complete severing of all trade bonds with Great Britain, Ireland, and the West Indies.[2] Then Congress continued "nibbling and quibbling," as Adams impatiently wrote. Debates were "spun out to an immeasurable length." "There is no greater mortification," he declared, "than to sit with half a dozen wits, deliberating upon a petition, address or memorial . . . these subtle critics, these refined geniuses, these learned lawyers, these wise statesmen are so fond of showing their parts and powers." "The art and address . . . of a conclave of cardinals at the election of a Pope, or of the princes in Germany at the choice of an Emperor would not exceed the specimens we

[1] John Adams, *Works*, ii, 382, 391.
[2] Schlesinger, *The Colonial Merchants*, 411–13.

have seen." [1] His "patience and long-suffering" were particularly tried when Joseph Galloway countered the stroke of the radicals with a plan of union, a wise and worthy effort to save the empire, endorsed by Duane and Jay and Edward Rutledge, with other men of fortune and property, and only defeated by a majority of one in a vote of eleven colonies. Then and there, Galloway asserted long after, "the measures of independence and sedition were ... preferred to those of harmony and liberty." [2]

Day after day the conservative forces weakened and radicals had their way. October 14th, Congress approved a "Declaration of Rights," calm, moderate, and filled with the political theory and ideals of the colonists. [3] Colonial rights to life, liberty, and property were secured, they declared, by the principles of the British Constitution, the unchanging laws of nature, and their colonial charters. They were not and could not be properly represented in Parliament, but only in their local assemblies where must reside, therefore, the exclusive power of legislation. Nevertheless, for the good of the empire as a whole, they would accede to acts of Parliament regulating their external commerce if there was no "idea of taxation, external or internal," but would no longer submit to such oppressive acts as had

[1] John Adams, *Works*, II, 391–401.

[2] *Ibid.*, 387–90; Galloway, *Candid Examinations of the Mutual Claims of Great Britain and the Colonies*, 53. The plan is in *American Archives* (4th Ser.), I, 905–06.

[3] *Journal of Congress* (Ford, *ed.*), I, 63. No documents of the time better reveal the colonial ideas of government.

vexed them since 1764.[1] They asked, in a word, to be restored to what had come to look like the golden age before the Seven Years' War. Five colonies denied all right of Parliament to regulate trade, five admitted the right, and delegates from Massachusetts and Rhode Island were not agreed. Into the Declaration of Rights was written their compromise. A like political philosophy, and no little argument and declamation as to America's wrongs, were embodied in addresses to the British people, to the King, to the Province of Quebec, and to the inhabitants of the several colonies. When Chatham saw them, he could think of no political expression of any body of men which could rival these papers in solidity of reason, force of sagacity, and wisdom of conclusion under a complication of difficult circumstances.[2]

The real accomplishment of the Congress, however, was the Continental Association, making national and uniform the devices for commercial coercion which hitherto had been local and spasmodic. It bore marks of strong southern influence in its name, its basic likeness to Virginia's Association adopted two months earlier, and in its expedients for forcing the merchants to obey its provisions.[3] When this Association was signed by all members of the Congress, as it was on October 20, 1774, it bound

---

[1] *Journal of Congress* (Ford, *ed.*), I, 71–73.

[2] Force, *American Archives* (4th Ser.), I, 917–38; Hansard, *Parliamentary History*, XVIII, 155.

[3] Schlesinger, *The Colonial Merchants*, 423–24. In the North in general the merchants had previously enforced their own agreements.

them and their constituents at home to an industrial attack upon England to be carried on until redress should be granted by the British Government. A stringent non-importation would begin December 1, 1774, and non-exportation September 10, 1775. There was to be no profiteering, and local arts and manufactures were to be encouraged. There was, finally, a ban upon extravagance and dissipation, gaming, cock-fighting, horse-races, and all expensive diversions. Even the luxuries of mourning were to be reduced.

Since the Congress could give no legal sanction to its acts, it invented penalties and created administrative and judicial organs to enforce the proposed boycott. There were to be chosen, in every city, town, and county, committees whose duty was to secure signatures to the Association and to declare "enemies to American liberty" all who refused to sign or who violated its regulations. Its penalties were not "the gallows, the rack and the stake . . . but infamy" which is even "more dreadful to a freeman." The Association was not a mere compact applying only to the parties to the covenant, but applied to all persons and even to whole provinces. Moderates could no longer go their own way, but had been driven into the position of being traitors to the general cause if they were guilty of the least deviation from the resolves of the Congress.[1] Yet they need not have felt, as many like Galloway did, that they had made a mistake in lending countenance to the Congress, which, dominated by radi-

---

[1] Schlesinger, *The Colonial Merchants*, 428, 432, 433.

cals, had pushed the colonies farther on the road to rebellion; for they should have remembered that the radical measures taken by the Congress had all been warmly endorsed before by provincial conventions and assemblies, and before that by county and town meetings. Moreover, the measures of the Congress were quickly endorsed, with the exception of a few towns and small sections, by the same political bodies which had created the continental gathering.[1] The spirit of the Congress, indeed, was mild compared with that of the people behind them, who filled the papers with stories of rioting and burning and of tarring and feathering those who opposed their will. An almost universal protest found voice in the letters of individuals and the resolutions of towns and of county and provincial conventions. All America was in a rebellious mood. Lord North was "cursed from morn to noon, and from noon to morn by every denomination of people." As Chatham expressed it, "Mal-administration . . . has not a move left — it is check-mate."[2] George III and his Minister could no longer be excused for thinking of Boston or even of New England as the only contumacious region in America.

The "salvation" of the colonies through the effects of the Continental Association soon seemed assured. There had been a rush to buy British goods before the boycott should begin and English importations into New York increased from £289,214

[1] Schlesinger, *The Colonial Merchants*, 435–72.
[2] Hansard, *Parliamentary History*, xviii, 160; Mass. Hist. Soc. *Proceedings*, viii, 341.

in 1773 to £437,937 in 1774, but in the next year, during the operation of the Association, trade fell off to only £1228.[1] Reductions in trade totals were not so great in all other ports, but were sufficient to alarm the British merchants and manufacturers by the prospect of depression and dull days ahead. The buying in advance had merely tied up their capital in America. Only a turn in European affairs which drew British goods into new channels, into Germany and Spain and the Baltic lands, robbed the Continental Association of its logical effect.[2] Nevertheless, before their deliverance through the new twist in Europe's affairs, the merchants of England had been quickened to action by the startling vision of closing American markets. Petitions rained upon Parliament from Belfast, Leeds, Manchester, Glasgow, Birmingham, and many other factory towns and shipping centers, foretelling bankruptcy and ruin unless the Americans were conciliated by a repeal of the obnoxious acts. The Ministry only hardened its heart, and refused to let the Americans rebel and then slip behind their creditors for security. Lord North's only reply was that " as the Americans had refused to trade with this kingdom, it was but just that we should not suffer them to trade with any other nation." [3] Bills to that end were passed first against New England and then extended to five other colonies.[4]

The enforcement of the Association in America

---

[1] Macpherson, *Annals of Commerce*, III, 549, 564, 585.
[2] Schlesinger, *The Colonial Merchants*, 474, 475, 539–40.
[3] *Ibid.*, 537, 538.
[4] 15 Geo. III, cc. 10 and 18.

had not been difficult. Its administrative machinery had been quickly set up in every colony but Georgia, and men obeyed the decrees of the Congress more faithfully than the laws of the provincial legislatures. The almost doubling of importation, just previous to the boycott going into action, softened the early effect on living conditions; and open war came so soon as to make any guess as to its ultimate probable effect mere speculation. In Massachusetts the Provincial Congress made rules for all emergencies under the Association and urged the ministers of the gospel to instruct their people to cleave to the Association. Under these rules, if cargoes arrived after December 1st the local committees reshipped the goods or sold them at auction, reimbursing the owner for his actual investment. Non-consumption was harder to enforce, but there were numerous cases where the committee forced buyers of tea to burn it in the presence of a crowd, and then to ask the pardon of the offended citizens. The greatest trouble was with wandering peddlers and petty chapmen who sold tea, and who tempted " women, girls and boys with their unnecessary fineries." Home manufactures were encouraged and all forms of extravagance and needless games like cards and billiards were shunned. In Connecticut the tendency of prices to rise gave the most trouble and the profiteering was hard to prove, since many goods came from neighboring colonies. Offenders seemed to have a fair trial before local committees and convincing proof was required. In New York the enforcement was almost wholly in the hands of the city Committee of Sixty which was very active, and used the devices noted in New England, but, as was also true of the Philadelphia Committee, it seemed less concerned about the raising of prices. They were more rigid in the matter of insistence upon simple funerals and the curtailing of dissipations like puppet shows. Lieutenant-Governor Colden grudgingly admitted that the Association was rigidly maintained in New York. The aristocratic Quaker merchants of Philadelphia were hostile to the Association and the Society of Friends was made use of for opposing propaganda. Friends' meetings resolved that Quakers would act contrary to their religious principles and to the rules of Christian discipline if they opposed government by the devices of the Association. Other meetings testified against "every usurpation of power and authority in opposition to the Laws and Government." Many members from varied motives disagreed with this stand, and it is safe to say that the Quakers were divided. In spite of their opposition, the Committee of Sixty-Six which enforced the Association could truthfully say that they had "not met with the least impediment or obstruction" in carrying it into execution.[1] Local manufacturing, moreover, made a great advance at this time.

South of Pennsylvania the old antithesis between the interests of planter and merchant created the only obstacle to enforcement of the Association. Merchants and factors, chiefly Scotch in Virginia and North Carolina, sought to coerce the over-

---

[1] This paragraph is based entirely upon Schlesinger, *The Colonial Merchants*, chap. XII.

zealous planters by pressing the collections of debts in the provincial courts. Thereupon the provincial conventions in the Carolinas and Virginia, dominated by the planters, closed the courts and forbade lawyers, witnesses, and suitors to take part in civil cases.[1] This put a stop to the harassing of debtors. Governor Dunmore declared that in this high-handed measure "the men of fortune and preëminence joined equally with the lowest and meanest." [2] The next device of the Scotch factors in Virginia and North Carolina was to discredit the Association by a rapid elevation of prices. They supported one another, and "even at the expense of their souls" clannishly swore to each other's lies, as the radicals declared. The committees met this problem by fixing maximum prices. As a result of this opposition there was a widespread antipathy to the Scotch merchants, whose good faith was suspected even when they signed the Association which in Virginia was required of all inhabitants, thus forcing every individual into a position of active friendship or of open hostility. So high was the spirit of the community that "The Laws of Congress," as Dunmore glumly admitted, got "marks of reverence which they never bestowed on their legal Government." In South Carolina not so much attention was paid to the sumptuary rules of Congress as in Maryland, Virginia, and North Carolina where there was a cessation of balls, and the races of the Jockey Club

[1] In certain cases the local committee might give permission for civil actions.

[2] Force, *American Archives* (4th Ser.), I, 1062. This letter of Dunmore's is most important as revealing the Loyalist point of view.

were called off. A traveler saw the ladies of Wilmington burn their tea in solemn procession, but commented dryly that they had delayed "until the sacrifice was not very considerable, as I do not think anyone offered above a quarter of a pound." In Virginia gambling was deep-rooted. "Colonel Burd," as a French spy relates, was "never happy but when he has the box and Dices in hand, . . . from a man of the greatest property of any in America [he] has reduced himself to that degree by gameing that few or nobody will Credit him for Ever so small a sum of money." [1] Yet, in such a community where men of this character were not rare, committees made every effort to stop gaming. Outside of these special problems, committees in the South displayed about the same kind of activities as those in the North, and all both North and South soon discovered that they must coöperate with each other to prevent evasions of the Association under the guise of coastwise trade.[2] In both North and South the few weak attempts of the conservatives or Loyalists to organized opposition to the will of the Congress failed because of the much better organization of the radicals.

It was this period of great activity of radical committees which witnessed the most rapid formation of the Loyalist Party. Many individuals had been hanging back, and a few had openly opposed the forward push toward rebellion, but beginning with 1774 these men had been drawing together, looking

---

[1] French Archives, *Service hydrographique de la Marine*, v, 76, no. 2.

[2] This paragraph is chiefly based upon Schlesinger, *The Colonial Merchants*, chap. XIII.

anxiously into each other's faces, and in confidential tones asking each other where it would all end. Few realized up to 1774 that the quarrel between America and England would end in violence. Men could argue before on one side or the other without calling for pistols and coffee for two. Many of the ablest conservative writers and speakers had had little to say in public until 1774.[1] Then opinion suddenly crystallized and Daniel Leonard, Joseph Galloway, Samuel Seabury, and Jonathan Odell began to write their powerful arguments to show that America's best interests lay in a union with Great Britain. The period of two years, 1774 and 1775, was the time of the bloom of their polemical literature. In general, they argued as Mansfield or Lord North or old Dr. Johnson argued on constitutional questions, but the main revelation of their argumentation was that they believed in a strong central government, and delighted in the glories of a great empire. To them was given a vision of a vast, powerful British Empire dominating the world, and in which they as citizens might thrill with a sense of superiority. Others, not so ambitious, but having a pacific temperament, dreaded controversy. Still others did not doubt the validity of the American constitutional argument put up to deny Parliament's right to tax America, but they at least disapproved of violent measures to resist Parliament.[2] There were motives as diverse as the variety of human emotions and interests which made men Loyalists when the hour for decision arrived, but

[1] *American Historical Review.* I. 25.　　　　[2] *Ibid.*, I, 24.

there were certain classes foreordained by the logic of their place in society and in the political structure to be the leaders of that faction. During the latter part of the colonial period all of the colonies outside of New England were royal or proprietary colonies in which most of the officials were appointees of the King or proprietor. This created a social caste which imitated England in its social aims. Governors, lieutenant-governors, secretaries, councillors, attorneys-general, and chief-justices looked to England for authority and support, and formed an exalted party looking down on the people of the colony. Their habits were English rather than colonial, and life at the Governor's court was extravagant, graft almost as common as in England. As a result the great officers of government in America were the backbone of the Tory Party. Next in influence was the clergy of the Established Church. These groups received the support of many of the landowners and substantial business men — prosperous men who were satisfied with the existing order of things. The aristocracy of culture, of dignified professions and callings, of official rank and hereditary wealth were therefore in a large measure ultimately found in the Tory Party. Descriptions of them are rich with gold lace, purple and gold, chariots and four horses, wigs after the pattern of that of the Speaker of the House of Commons. One of the motives which determined some of the colonial aristocrats to turn to the Loyalist side was the manifest tendency of the masses to demand, not only the colonial rights from the British administration, but to assert their equal right in the Provincial Government with those to whom they had long submissively yielded obedience. This demand made most true aristocrats recoil with horror.

During the months in which the Congress was elected and convened, and while it devised its coercive Association and left to a thousand willing spirits the execution of it, General Gage with ships of war and five thousand troops was doing his best to carry out the rather rash orders of his King. He may have recalled Tigranes' comment upon the Roman army, which was too many for an embassy and too few for a fight, since he made no effort to disarm the inhabitants or to send Samuel Adams and John Hancock to London for trial. He brought some comfort, however, to Peggy Hutchinson who wrote pathetically that she had "been running from a mob ever since the year sixty-five." [1] Gage was not the "great person of military valor" whom Bacon advised princes to have "near unto them, for the suppressing of seditions in their beginnings," but he did have enough good sense to appreciate the danger of his situation. When he sent out soldiers, September 1, 1774, to seize three hundred barrels of gunpowder which a Massachusetts Committee had laid up against a time of need, messengers went flying far and wide, there was wild excitement, swearing men left their farms, and some three thousand militia who had been drilling for just such an occasion gathered at Cambridge before it could be explained that six Americans had not been killed as

[1] British Museum, *Egerton MSS.*, 2659 F 64.

rumored. It was said that forty thousand started for Boston on that occasion. Little wonder that Gage was glad to let sleeping dogs lie and to seek even Hancock's influence to get barracks built before winter came upon them. A Patriot dubbed him the "Duke of Alva . . . shut up with his troops, and his forlorn mandamus Councillors in Boston." [1]

In the spring Gage grew bolder and sent out disguised officers "in brown cloaths and reddish handkerchiefs" around their necks to locate roads, rivers, defensible places, encampments, and sources of forage. The narrative left by one of them of this reconnaissance gives a graphic picture of the high nervous tension, the bitter hostility throughout the countryside. Suspicion dogged them. When they remarked civilly to a "black woman," who waited on them, that it was "a fine country," she retorted, "so it is, and we have got brave fellows to defend it." So sinister grew the warnings that they all but turned back. "Friends to government" were very rare, but gave the spies brief respites from the long hours of apprehension. An offer of tea was the best proof that the host was Tory. On Sunday, at Worcester, they did not dare stir until evening because nobody was allowed to walk the streets during divine service. At Buckminster a company of militia exercised under the very windows of their tavern, and a commander harangued them, quoting Cæsar and Pompey, urging the men to wait for the British fire. That over, they all entered the tavern and

[1] *The Remembrancer*, i, 60. The "Mandamus Councillors" were those appointed under the Massachusetts Government Act.

heated their valor with pots of ale. As the spies pushed on, they were harassed by horsemen scouring the country and asking very unpleasant questions. The party barely escaped the Committee of Correspondence at Marlborough, who searched their host's house from top to bottom, and warned him that had the spies been found the house would have been pulled down about their ears.[1] As a result of this or a similar expedition, it was learned that at Concord was one of the many stores of arms and provisions gathered by the Committee of Safety, appointed by the Provincial Congress and led by Samuel Adams and Joseph Warren. In spite of the failure, late in February, of an effort to seize brass cannon at Salem, Gage resolved to destroy the stores at Concord, and on the evening of April 18th, troops for that mission gathered at the waterside.

The Committee of Safety was alert, and Joseph Warren dispatched Joseph Dawes, and later Paul Revere, to warn the town people and farmers on the route. Prearranged signals in the tower of the Old North Church gave the alarm to many, and the riders reached the rest. As the British force marched up into the country, the ringing of bells and firing of signal guns and the boom of cannon made it clear that the expedition was no secret. As they neared the green at Lexington in the early dawn, they saw "a body of country people drawn up in military order, with arms and accoutrements." A shot was fired, but by which side or by whose order is one of

---

[1] Mass. Hist. Soc., *Collections*, IV, 204–14.

the unsolved questions of history.[1] It was probably
not heard around the world as some authorities
state. General firing then began, and when the
British soldiery passed on to Concord, they left
eight dead militiamen and ten wounded in Lexington. The village of Concord was occupied, a few
stores not yet removed were destroyed, and there
were a few casualties in a brief fight between the
minutemen and the British picket at the bridge over
the river. But meanwhile the embattled farmers
were rising. Fighting, as some had fought the Indians, from behind trees and rocks and stone walls
they poured a deadly fire into the red-coated British
regulars, so that with all their bravery they were
nearly ready to surrender when they entered the
welcome hollow square formed by the soldiers under
Lord Percy who had been sent with fifteen hundred
men to give them succor. After a rest the whole
force set out again for Boston, galled by a furious
fire from behind houses and stone walls. The maddened "red-coats" stopped at times, broke into
houses, killed all who were therein, and burned the
dwellings when they could. This only enraged the
"rebels" whose number and fire increased as Cambridge was neared.[2] The official report says that
"notwithstanding a continued skirmish for the
space of 15 miles receiving fire from every hill, fence,

[1] An excellent collection of the best evidence with the many conflicting stories is in *Source Problems in United States History*, by A. C.
McLaughlin *et al.*, 13–54. The essential source bibliography is there,
and in Winsor's *Memorial History of Boston*, III, 101. See also F. W.
Coburn, *The Battle of April 19, 1775.*

[2] Mass. Hist. Soc., *Proceedings* (2d Ser.), v, 393.

house, barn, etc., his Lordship kept the enemy off and brought the troops to Charleston" and from there they were ferried over to Boston.[1] There was a crimson trail from Concord to Boston. Some seventy-three of the British soldiers had been killed and one hundred and seventy-four wounded, while the Americans had lost forty-nine killed and thirty-nine wounded. Gage wrote to the War Department three days later that he had nothing to trouble them with, "but of an affair that happened here on the 19th. Inst." He reluctantly admitted that "they were at length a good deal pressed."[2] He forgot to mention that the next day Boston was a besieged town, that from all New England men were hurrying to the camp-fires of the besiegers.

To this point at last had come the relations of the British Government and the American colonies, all because the matter of right had been "kept perpetually on the anvill."[3] It was contrary to nature that conciliation would be possible now. It needed no gift of prophecy to see that war had begun between Britain and her colonies. That it would last seven years and involve the greatest nations of the world was a cosmic catastrophe which even the most dismal prophets did not foresee.

[1] Public Records Office, *War Office* (*In-letters*), **II**, F 179.   [2] *Ibid.*
[3] *American Historical Review*, **VIII**, 327.

CHAPTER XVIII

THE FREEST OF PEOPLES WERE THE FIRST TO REBEL

To understand why England of all countries in Europe should have been plagued with a rebellion of her colonies, one must compare in some detail the political and social conditions in the several States of that continent. It will then appear that the American Revolution was one of the glories of British history, rather than a blot upon her fair political record. The colonies of no other nation in that age had progressed so far in the attainment and enjoyment of political liberty as to have "snuffed" the taint of tyranny in those acts of the British Government which precipitated the struggle. What political liberty American colonies enjoyed, they had, in a large degree, inherited from the mother country. "The flood of British freedom, which . . . from dark antiquity hath flowed 'with pomp of waters unwithstood,'" found even more generous channels in the American colonies. All the conditions of colonial life in the forest border of the settled Atlantic coast, on the frontier of the British Empire, tended to encourage radical views, and to resist any backward political step of the more conservative homeland. They were the heirs of all the political accomplishment of England, and they had increased their heritage. As British political progress had outstripped the other lagging nations of Europe, so had that of the American colonies run on ahead of English political advance. A brief survey of European political conditions, besides furnishing a background to the Revolutionary history, will give body and definiteness to these general assertions.

When the Revolutionary War began, Englishmen had behind them over five hundred years of struggle for political liberty. From Simon de Montfort and Edward I, the creators of the House of Commons, striving to secure the rights of the knights and burghers, to the days of Burke, Pitt, and Fox, the great liberal leaders of the eighteenth century, England had made an almost ceaseless advance toward control of Government by the people or their representatives. Sometimes the progress was made under the leadership of a great, wise, and liberal king like Edward I, sometimes under the direction of the titled aristocracy, but more and more, in the later periods, through the impulse of wider and wider circles of common men who were constantly increasing their political experience. To tell every step in the slow growth of English freedom would be to tell again England's political history. It is not the purpose here to recount the facts which establish beyond cavil the assertion of the British historian, that Englishmen were the inventors of political liberty on the scale of the great nation-state, as Greece was the inventor of political liberty on the scale of the little city-state. It suffices to recall that when in the seventeenth century the Bourbons, Hohenzollerns, and Hapsburgs were eliminating all popular influence in European Governments,

the English were decapitating Charles I, enticing
James II into exile, and putting on firm foundation
the principle that the people's representatives were
sovereign. In the eighteenth century, when benevolent despotism triumphed on Europe's mainland,
England perfected a Parliamentary system which
took away all the King's legislative power and most
of his executive power. This gain for liberal government was made by the leaders of the English people,
and not for them by a benevolent despot.

The century preceding the American Revolution
had seen the English Whigs annihilate the ancient
legal powers of the Crown by forcing it to act
through ministers responsible to Parliament.[1] The
transfer of this power had been obscured under conventions which continued the appearance of power
where, in truth, there was obedience. The evolution
of these conventions — party government, the cabinet and a responsible ministry — solved the problem
of attaining Parliamentary Government while re-
taining the King. As early as the time of Queen
Anne, the mystic halo of the divine-right sovereign
had vanished, though interested men did not cease
to deceive the masses with that royal aureole. Not,
perhaps, before 1760 had this revolutionary state,
legitimate in law before, become truly so by usage
and sentiment.[2] It was the Whig Party, aristocratic
and even oligarchic as it was, that had wrought this
change, the harmonizing of monarchical principles
with Parliamentary supremacy. No King Edward,

---

[1] C. G. Robertson, *England under the Hanoverians*, 162.
[2] *Ibid.*, 163.

no benevolent despot of the type so common in continental Europe of that age, had decreed these reforms, but rather the leaders of a freedom-loving people, becoming ever more conscious of their power.

Nevertheless, it was certain that great families, a socially privileged class, a commercial hierarchy (such was the make-up of the Whig Party) could not and did not give England the real essentials of a liberal government — religious toleration, a humane criminal code, a truly representative legislature, a free press and the right of the common man to vote.[1] In a society struggling up toward political freedom, such limitation on personal liberty could not long survive. A new England politically was emerging by 1760. The grave defects still existing in England's Parliamentary system were openly attacked. Reformers ere long were pointing out that the House of Commons, because of a moth-eaten suffrage law, did not properly represent its constituencies. Sarum was a sheep-walk, Droitwich, a by-gone salt pit, Dunwich was half under the sea; yet these wild places helped to outvote the nation's centers of trade and industry.[2] Moreover, low ethical standards, the barter and sale of Parliamentary seats, representatives under "wages" from the King, made corruption easy and lent power to an unscrupulous monarch. Stars and ribands, pensions, offices in the royal household, and sinecures in the Government services, were all resources of an inexhaustible treasury of corruption. All put power in the King's

[1] C. G. Robertson, *England under the Hanoverians*, 163.
[2] *Ibid.*, 172–73.

hands. Indeed, such resources helped George III to hold the Parliamentary Opposition at bay for twenty years. In a word, as things were in 1760, the Ministry was responsible to the Commons, but the Commons was not effectually responsible to the majority of the people. The executive part of the governmental machine had been reconstructed, but it was a re-modeling of the social and economic organization that was needed. Even this requisite reform, England was, by 1792, to be on the verge of making when the excesses of the French Revolution arrested the reformers. Their work, however, was merely delayed and was to reach its fruition in 1832, when the Revolutionary storm was spent.[1]

This "realm of England," advanced to the very bounds of an era of liberal government, was still too handicapped by tradition to advance the little remaining way that would have preserved her union with her American colonies. Yet, compared with the political régime in the countries of continental Europe, the liberalism of England seemed radiant perfection. England had already passed along the highway to political liberty along which less favored nations were not to pass for half a century. In France and Spain the Bourbon kings were bent on preserving the personal authority of the monarch in absolute despotism, and in the latter, at least, the King's views were generally supported by all classes of society. In France Louis XVI expressed the faith that was in him when he said, "It is God's will that whoever is born a subject should

[1] C. G. Robertson, *England under the Hanoverians*, 174.

not reason but obey." [1] With all their absolutism, however, the Bourbons were less autocratic than the Hapsburgs. In Spain, Philip V started the custom of allowing Government officers of the higher class to sit when discussing affairs of state with their august master.[2] The Hapsburgs required them to remain on their knees as if in the presence of the Deity. Though merely a form, it was indicative of the real absolutism in government. In the Hungarian portion of the Hapsburg dominions, there was a chancellery, responsible to none but the King, and reflecting merely the light of the royal sun.[3] In Prussia, though Frederick, called "the Great," talked sententiously about the King being the "first servant of the state," and the people "not being there for the sake of the rulers," but "the rulers for the sake of the people," yet he was utterly skeptical of the intelligence and reliability of the common man. He deliberately trained his subjects to expect everything governmental to be done for them, nothing by them. He rejected their political cooperation and "postponed indefinitely their training and education in state affairs." The depth of their abject submission we may see in the expression of thanks by the citizens of Grieffenberg for relief funds sent them when their city was burned:[4]

"The gratitude of such dust as we, is, as we are aware, of no moment or value to you. We shall,

---

[1] Parkman, *The Old Régime in Canada*, 232.

[2] Chapman, *A History of Spain*, 426.

[3] Marczali, *Hungary in the Eighteenth Century*, 332.

[4] Preuss, *Friedrich der Grosse*, IV, 484.

however, implore God to grant your Majesty his divine favors in return for your royal bounty."

Frederick nursed his divine right and his absolute rule with all the solicitude of less benevolent despots. He bestrode his narrow political world "like a Colossus," and even chief ministers were hardly more than secretaries to him. Frederick was Prussia. Nor were the citizens of other German States admitted to greater political freedom or experience. Incompetent and wicked Governments still lingered in Bavaria and Württemberg. Ignorant, impoverished people in serfdom bore not only the weary loads imposed by luxurious and tyrannical rulers, but by an equally selfish priesthood.[1] In these, as well as smaller States of Germany, men might be imprisoned at the mere whim of the ruler or hired out to fight for any cause which would pay their masters best.[2] Most of the large number of petty princes possessed and exercised the power of life or death over their subjects. Certainly in Spain, Austria, or Germany, there was nothing comparable to the political progress made in England.

Politically, it is hard to take seriously Italy of the eighteenth century. There, that age was a "happy, lotus-eating time," when Goldoni could happen upon his colony of the "Arcadia of Rome" and solemnly accept from his new friends the gift of the Fegean fields in Greece, becoming thus a shepherd

---

[1] Priest, *Germany in 1740*, 28.

[2] Six States of Germany let out their soldiers to Great Britain in the American Revolution. Lowell, *Hessians in the American Revolution*, 2.

of the "Colony of Alpheus." [1] It was of Italy's careless, amiable, and entertaining society that Goethe wrote to a friend, "Would that I could pass on to you but one breath of this delightful existence!" [2] As Sedgwick says, "Italy was still like a comedy of Goldoni, dukes enjoying taxes and mistresses, priests accepting oblations and snuff, nobles sipping chocolate and pocketing rent, while the poor peasants kept behind the scenes, sweated and toiled for a bare subsistence." [3] Italy alone, perhaps, in that age, could have offered the myriad romantic situations suited to evolve such geniuses as Casanova and Goldoni. One must read Monnier's pages in order to realize how much of life, and even happiness, there might be in a country wholly without political liberty. [4]

Italy was "a name and not a nation." She was broken into numerous small states, of which Milan, Sardinia, Sicily, Naples, Tuscany, and Parma were used as so much small change to adjust the bargains among the Great Powers — especially the Bourbons and Hapsburgs. With Italy's heritage, they "haggled and bargained, offered and counter-offered when they did not battle and lay siege and pillage and devastate." Small despots did their own will when they were not doing that of greater despots. [5] Perhaps the worst condition was in the Papal States where there was a debased people, no order, and a

---

[1] H. D. Sedgwick, *A Short History of Italy*, 354.
[2] Monnier, *Venice in the Eighteenth Century*, 32.
[3] H. D. Sedgwick, *A Short History of Italy*, 36.
[4] Monnier, *Venice in the Eighteenth Century*.
[5] Vernon, *Italy*, chap. III

government scandalously bad. Dumas, in "Monte Cristo," hardly exaggerates the power of the brigand chiefs. That vocation alone promised fortune if a man were not an officer of the Church. In Rome, itself, life on the economic side was easy, but, in the country, famine, war, official oppression, and a low state of agriculture made life wretched.[1] With each brief Papal reign there was a change of officers eager to enrich themselves by monopoly, and in a hurry to get in the harvest. Italy surely was no rival of England in the race for human liberty.

Eastern Europe, especially Russia during the eighteenth century, was but just emerged from a kind of magnificent Oriental barbarism. It lagged two centuries behind England in all those characteristics by which we measure degree of civilization or advance in political liberty. Except among a few nobles there was in Russia hardly even a struggle for political liberty. It was said that Peter the Great by blows with his cane taught his nobility to feel themselves free men and Europeans.[2] In the reign of Empress Anne, while yet the century was young, the leaders of the Russian nobility, as if emulating the English nobles in the days of King John, had forced the Czarina's assent to certain reforms that would secure their liberties. There was to be a High Council which would bridle her power, and which would have made of Russia a sort of oligarchic republic. With the backing of a group of the lesser nobles, who offered to lay at her feet the

[1] Vernon, *Italy*, 389.
[2] Rambaud, *History of Russia*, chaps. v–ix.

heads of the ambitious reformers, Anne tore into bits that "scrap of paper," the already signed "conditions," and with executions and exile disposed of the would-be makers of Russia's Magna Charta.[1] During ten years of her reign, thirty thousand people were exiled to Siberia and five to seven thousand were condemned to death.[2] In a single year, four hundred and twenty-three men were put to torture. The people of Russia paid little attention to their rulers except to obey their laws. While rightful Czars and proper heirs to the throne were murdered or imprisoned during forty years of shameful intrigue among rulers or pretenders to supreme power, all Russian people of every class except a few courtiers and guard officers remained perfectly indifferent. The Russian subject remained, even in Catherine II's time, not so much a citizen as a taxpayer.[3]

That immortal feminine despot, Catherine II, who reigned in Russia at the time of the American Revolution, possessed absolute power such as no other sovereign of her time pretended to exercise. Yet Catherine was enlightened and tolerant, even while she was welding the chains of her absolute power. She succeeded in making the Russian nobility the pillar of her autocracy. Her despotism became firmly established because that class were self-interested allies. She took very seriously Montesquieu's dictum, "Nobility is the natural support of monarchy."[4] To her nobility she granted the ex-

[1] Kovalevsky, *Russian Political Institutions*, 119.
[2] *Ibid.*, 122.   [3] *Ibid.*, 127.   [4] *Ibid.*, 128, 135.

tension of serfdom and she gave them the monopoly of the right to acquire inhabited estates.[1] The Russian nobility, by this securing of its economic wealth to the detriment of the people, lost its chance of being supported by them in its demands for personal liberty and control of public affairs. They could not, as King John's nobility, become leaders of a move ment for political emancipation.[2] Not in Russia, surely, was there any such advance toward political liberty as in England.

Poland, in a very different sense, fell far in arrears in humanity's forward movement toward freedom. It was during Catherine's reign that Poland, with no cohesion in the State, with its anarchic constitution, the most vicious ever devised by man, and with its paralyzed Diet and helpless executive, went headlong to political ruin. As King Casimir had long before warned the Diet, no human society can stick together on these terms. "This glorious republic," he cried, "will get torn into shreds, . . . [and] be stuffed into the pockets of covetous neighbours." In two partitions, one on the eve of the American Revolution and one just after its close, Casimir's prophecy was fulfilled. Poland disappeared as an independent kingdom.[3]

The very success of the three robber monarchs, Frederick, Catherine, and Maria Theresa, measured the impotence of democracy in continental Europe. All the world saw that strong and greedy despots

---

[1] Large areas of Russia in that day were uninhabited.
[2] *Ibid.*, 130, 131.
[3] Eversley, *Partitions of Poland*, 25.

had conspired to plunder a feeble State, with little more regard for common honesty or mere decency in method than might be shown by an Assyrian or a Redskin. To Frederick II, Poland was Naboth's vineyard, and both Catherine II and Maria Theresa saw it in the same light. When the Prussian King blasphemously invited the two empresses to partake with him of his Holy Eucharist, Maria Theresa shed some tears over the iniquity of the robbery, but she adapted her morality to the "Reason of State" and "sought compensation for the violence done to her feelings by insisting on a larger share of the spoils." [1] Though democratic Europe was against the partition, it was powerless before this caprice of absolutism. The political system of Europe was shaken, public morals were lowered, and public law was weakened by the act, but the forces of democracy were helpless. [2]

This slight sketch of continental European conditions would leave a false impression if we failed to include with it a brief survey of the tremendous forces making for political betterment. France, enjoying in that day as to-day a spiritual leadership like that of Greece in the ancient world, gave the intellectual impetus. [3] It is an open question whether the revolutionary spirit originated in, or was merely taken up by the French intellectuals. Certain it is

---

[1] W. A. Phillips, *Poland*, 69.

[2] Lecky, *England in the Eighteenth Century*, v, 217. The truckling Voltaire approved it; Rousseau denounced it. Years later Carlyle could see in it only "the operation of Almighty Providence and of the eternal laws of nature."

[3] Rocquain's *The Revolutionary Spirit Preceding the French Revolution* is a treasure house of contemporary evidence.

that by the middle of the eighteenth century the people were in a dangerous mood. They talked of burning Versailles, erected at their expense. Two thousand women surrounded the Dauphin and Dauphiness at Notre Dame crying, "Give us bread, we are dying of hunger"; and, "Dismiss the harlot who governs the nation." Men were heard to express pleasure that the Government used violent measures, for that would "hasten the revolution." In 1753, when the Parliament was disgraced, Paris was in an uproar. There was a cry, "Long live the Parliament! Down with the King and Bishops!" A chief magistrate thought the Parisians were in a highly inflammable state, and prophesied the shutting of shops, and barricades. There were patrols of French and Swiss guards in the streets. A sudden tack in the course of the Government — a tack said to have been suggested by Madame de Pompadour — averted revolution. Still, it was force alone that sustained the Government, and within ten years the Paris Parliament was warning the King that "to sustain a Government by force, was to teach the people that force could overturn it." In France, at least, the initiative of her people and not of her sovereigns promised political advance.

But it was not the revolutionary temper of the French people which was to exercise the greatest influence on the outside world. By the middle of the eighteenth century, the forward-looking, vision-seeing spirits in France were shaking every foundation on which complacent conservatism sat enthroned. Nothing seemed firm. The Advocate-

General of France expressed his opinion (1747) of a book entitled "Morals." "Reason is exalted," he solemnly warned,[1] "as the sovereign judge of Religion." "Humility, mortification, penance, celibacy, the indissolubility of marriage, and all Christian virtues, are decried by the author. . . . He even censures the penalty which human justice attaches to the crimes of theft and homicide." In this case the author was obscure, but soon Voltaire and Diderot with more power and less crudity were attacking the props of established society. Formal religion and morality were first assailed, but the old political faith and governmental forms soon felt the shock of battle. As early as 1747, D'Argenson was asking, "In view of the slight esteem in which Royalty is held, will anyone dare to take any steps toward the introduction of a Republican Government? . . . These *ideas are coming*, and new customs make their way rapidly with the French."[2]

By 1762, a period of French history when the significant events were books not acts, appeared Rousseau's "Social Contract." It advanced the startling theory of the sovereignty of the nation, of appeal to the people as the court of last resort. Even radicals thought it important that a book of this kind should not be allowed to ferment in minds easily excited. An earlier work on human "Inequality" Voltaire declared was a new book against the human race. "When we read your book," wrote the philosopher, "we feel like going on all fours." Two years later, Voltaire raised a prophetic voice,

[1] Rocquain, *The Revolutionary Spirit*, etc., 49.   [2] *Ibid.*, 48.

"All I now see sows the seeds of a Revolution which will infallibly spring up, but I shall not be a witness of it." Another year passed and the General Assembly of the French clergy declared publicly: "A multitude of fearless writers have trodden under foot all laws, both human and divine. . . . Nothing has been respected, either in civil or spiritual order. The majesty of the Supreme Being and that of the King is outraged. . . . In the realm of faith, in that of morals, and even in the State itself, *the spirit of the century seems to threaten a Revolution that presages on all sides total ruin and destruction.*"[1] Voltaire, Helvetius, Diderot, Rousseau, and Montesquieu were the leaders of these fearless writers.

Horace Walpole, in the year 1765, found philosophy and free-thinking all the rage in Paris. Even the women discussed "public rights," and their salons became "miniature States-General." At private gatherings and supper-parties, the chief topic was the "violation of the constitution,"[2] The Encyclopædists furnished the talkers with their themes. Members of the Parliament wished to arrest Voltaire as a warning to authors against too great license, but he, more cunning than Socrates, and having no desire to emulate him in the drinking of hemlock, publicly took communion in church, an act received as a recantation. A *lettre de cachet*, ordering Diderot to give up all his manuscripts, warned him to flee Paris in haste. Marmontel's "Belisarius," a plea for tolerance, was condemned by the

[1] Rocquain, *The Revolutionary Spirit*, etc., 94.
[2] Walpole, *Letters*, vi, 301, 309.

Faculty of Theology. Yielding to their complaints, the Government ordered the new edition of the Encyclopædia to be taken to the Bastille. The crime of the writers of the incarcerated volumes was described by the Advocate-General of France: "The Philosophers have constituted themselves the preceptors of the human race. 'Liberty of thought' is their cry, and this cry has made itself heard from one extremity of the earth to the other.... *Revolution, so to speak, has been accomplished.* Kingdoms have felt their ancient foundations totter, and nations, astonished to find their principles annihilated, have asked themselves by what fatality they have become so different from their former selves. [Religion is attacked by the Philosophers.] In writings without number, they have poured forth the poison of unbelief. Eloquence, poetry, histories, romances, and even dictionaries have been infected [from Paris they have spread like a torrent to the country]. The contagion has penetrated even to the workshops and cottages" [1]

During the four years in which Madame du Barry reigned by the side of Louis XV, the prestige of royalty faded away. While the monarch, "shut up in his seraglio and plunged in debauchery," insisted that he owed an account of his conduct to God alone, monarchy by divine right became almost universally condemned. Much read authors were declaring that "the King and the Law received their authority from the same source ... the unanimity of the wishes of the 'Nation.'" In a pamphlet, "The

[1] Rocquain, *The Revolutionary Spirit*, etc., 103–04.

Maxims of Public Right," it was asserted that "kings were made for people and not people for kings." The Government dared go no further than the mere suppression of the "Philosophical Reflections upon the System of Nature," which held that it was not the people's right alone, but their duty to rise up against despotism. Abbé Raynal's "Philosophical and Political History of the Establishment and Commerce of the Europeans in the Two Indies," wherein he attacked ministers, priests, and kings with equal violence, was merely suppressed by a Decree of Council. In France at least the Revolution in political ideas had already taken place — that in governmental forms and institutions was not far off.

But the influence of the French intellectuals did not stop at the frontiers of France. In Spanish libraries were found the works of Voltaire, Diderot, Mirabeau, Montesquieu, and Rousseau, as well as those of the English thinkers, Locke and Hobbes, whose influence most of the French writers had felt.[1] Even the heretical Encyclopædia was there and some of these works were in translation. The Spanish Minister, Aranda, corresponded with French reformers. The Duke of Alba wrote letters to Rousseau, the Marquis of Miranda to Voltaire. The Inquisition failed to bar this flood of democratic ideas. The Bourbons, like other "benevolent despots" of that age, gave much attention to intellec-

---

[1] Voltaire said of Locke, "Never was there perhaps a wiser or more methodical spirit, a more exact logician than Locke." Lowell, *The Eve of the French Revolution*, 56–61. The French censor objected especially to this admiration.

tual, social, and economic reforms, though meanwhile holding fast to their royal prerogatives. "Enlightened despotism" was a fad of the age. All reform must come from above. The Cortes in Spain was kept unimportant, and all governmental machinery of a democratic character was viewed with suspicion.[1] "Everything for the people, but nothing by them," was the slogan of the Bourbons. All ameliorations came in the form of royal orders. "For such is my will" ran the royal decrees. It was the monarch and not the people that progressed politically. Spanish kings could not realize that "man is not changed by whitewashing or gilding his habitation."

Italy also felt the French influence. The jurist Beccaria, its most distinguished liberal writer, declared, "I owe all to French books." D'Alembert, Diderot and Condillac, Montesquieu and Helvetius were, he wrote, "the object of my preoccupation during the day and of my meditation during the night."[2] Italian rulers, too, felt the spell of these reformers either directly or through Beccaria. Leopold of Tuscany abolished the death penalty, burned the gallows and instruments of torture, carried through economic reforms which restored prosperity, and removed tiresome taxes. He even talked of granting a constitution and becoming a constitutional monarch.[3] Yet his government was frankly absolute, and he believed that only an autocratic

[1] Chapman, *History of Spain*, 426–27, 436–37, 441.
[2] *Great Jurists of the World*, 505
[3] Vernon, *Italy*, 428–29, 430.

government could effect reform.[1] "Liberty" did
not mean to benevolent despots that their subjects
were to have a share in government, but merely
safety of their persons and equality before the law.

In Lombardy, then under Austrian rule, Joseph II
put an end to farming out taxes, which had been
collected with much tyranny. "In the time of the
Gospels as well as today," he said sententiously,
"the farmers of taxes have always been odious to the
people."[2] In Austria, Joseph abolished serfdom,
secured civil rights and freedom of worship to all
Protestants.[3] Toiling "with uncontented care" he
tried to rule better than he knew. Traveling, reading, picking up ideas from the Encyclopædists, im-
bibing liberal opinions from every source, he "did
good with a cudjel" until his reformed subjects,
like those of Leopold, looked upon him as a senseless
ruler with a mania for innovation. Verri, the reformer, said of him, "He disregarded public opinion,
and exhibited to men the despot who knows no other
rule than his own will." Had Mazzini lived a hundred years earlier, he might have taught Joseph that
"the Utopist may see afar from a hill the distant land
which will give to society a virgin soul, a purer air,
his duty is to point it out with a gesture and a word
to his brothers; but he cannot take humanity in his
arms and carry it there in a single bound; even if
this were in his power, humanity would not therefore
have progressed." Few of the reforms of the benevolent despots made the people happier. The ignorant

---

[1] *Cambridge Modern History*, vi, 602.   [2] Vernon, *Italy*, 415.
[3] Priest, *Germany since 1740*, 27

Ferdinando of Naples who undertook no reforms
could say truthfully to Joseph II, "When I go trav-
elling I can hardly tear myself from my people, your
subjects are pleased when you are far off. . . . Do
take a little rest and let others do the same." To
the other Italian reformer, Leopold of Tuscany, he
pointed out the people's dullness. "Florence was
gay in the time of the Medici," he jeered. "Believe
me, and govern them a little less; all your learning
makes them dull." [1]

Of all the benevolent despots of the eighteenth
century, perhaps Frederick "the Great" was the
most intelligent. This "Spartan in the morning,
Athenian in the afternoon," pensioned Voltaire,
offered a stipend to Rousseau. He read and applauded their liberal books and corresponded with
both. The works of most of the French liberal
writers were known to him, but his own liberalism
was that of a despot. His reforms in Prussia were
numerous. He ordered the courts to render decisions to noble and peasant alike, and he proclaimed
religious tolerance — that "every man was to go to
Heaven in his own way"; but it was his despotic
will and not the free will of the people that determined these reforms. The nature of Frederick's
religious tolerance was not badly described by Less-
ing when he wrote that "Berlin liberty...merely
consists in the liberty of circulating as many witti-
cisms as you like against religion." [2] Some small
States of Germany imitated the reforms in Prussia.
The administration of justice was improved, class

[1] Vernon, *Italy*, 410.   [2] *Cambridge Modern History*, VI, 713.

distinctions were softened, and the burdens of the peasantry lightened, but in all cases a command by a despot to a submissive people secured the reforms.[1] Maria Theresa granted political and social reforms — in education, trade, religious toleration, and laws affecting the condition of the peasants — but only so far as it might not weaken the authority of her absolute government. In the Hungarian portion of her empire, at least, there was the form of a parliament, but the prerogatives of the Crown practically annulled its power.[2]

In Russia, Catherine II played with liberal ideas, and took pride in her familiarity with the works of the French philosophers. She had a romantic admiration for Charles James Fox, and she knew Blackstone so well that Sir James Harris, himself a lawyer, admitted that she soon had him beyond his depth in the discussion of the laws and constitution of his own country. In her instructions to her commission (1766-68) to make a "new code of laws for Russia," she confessed to have "pillaged" the philosophers of the West, Montesquieu and Beccaria.[3] Indeed, her Minister, the cautious Count Panin, declared that these instructions contained "axioms enough to knock a wall down." They were so liberal that Catherine boasted to Voltaire that the "Instruction" came under the interdict in Paris. Yet she found an excuse for breaking up the "Commission" saying that she had gotten hints and knew

[1] Priest, *Germany Since 1740*, 28, 29.
[2] Marczali, *Hungary in the Eighteenth Century*, chap. **v.**
[3] Rambaud, *History of Russia*, 101.

now what to do herself. She was the State. In
Russia as elsewhere in continental Europe, the State
was developed by rulers like a private property, for
its own good and that of its masters. All seemed
imbued with the idea that the more they governed
the better off the people would be. Nothing should
be done by the people, but everything for them.
As a result the people everywhere seemed to prefer
the ills of an old régime than to be driven to set up
a new and better one.

Viewing these political conditions in continental
Europe and comparing them with the political attainments of contemporary England, one may see
that Burke was uttering the truth, and not a foolish
boast, when he told the British House of Commons
that freedom was a "commodity of price" of which
Englishmen "had the monopoly." Slavery, Burke
told them, "the sons of England may have anywhere.
It is a weed that grows in every soil. They may have
it from Spain, they may have it from Prussia." In
England alone had the power of the King been so
curbed that he could not, by his despotic will, oppress the people, but that he could act only through
ministers responsible to the legislature. Burke
begged Parliament to keep its sovereign authority as
the sanctuary of liberty, the sacred temple conse-
crated to the common faith in freedom. "Do but
that," he cried, "and English colonists wherever
they may live will turn their faces toward Westminster. The more they multiply, the more friends
you will have." He was merely urging what was
fated to become a splendid realization, that the more

the British Empire should grow, the more freedom would be established on the face of the earth. It was the failure of a Parliament, corrupted by George III, to heed the warning of England's greatest living statesmen, Burke and Pitt and Fox and Camden and Barré, that brought about the rending of the empire. No doubt, a majority of the politically active people of England for a time were opposed to these great statesmen. The nation was, therefore, on the eve of disaster, as any nation is like to be when its greatest minds and characters are forced to defy and to try to defeat the convictions of a majority of their countrymen. The British Empire was doomed to be broken asunder, but it was brought to that disaster by the insistent demand of Englishmen in America for the full enjoyment of those liberties which England had fostered beyond any other country of the world.

THE END

INDEX

INDEX

Absolutism, Spanish, 93 *n.*; in continental Europe, 460–67; reforms imposed by despots, 473–77. *See also* Divine right; Monarchy.

Acts of Navigation and Trade, restriction on tobacco, 63; beginning, 64; classes of restriction, results, 64–68; and colonial shipbuilding, 65; and royal navy, 67; and natural trend of trade, 130; payment of duty at English port, 195; Townshend's administrative measure, 247; customs efficiency under it, 256, 267, 282; *Liberty* riot in Boston, 283; other violence, 283; conditions after cessation of non-importation, 369, 370; controversy absorbed in larger issue, 390; Continental Congress on, 440, 441; closing of colonial ports, 444. *See also* Board of Trade; Commerce; Mercantile system; Molasses (Sugar) Acts; Smuggling.

Adams, Abigail, culture, 335.

Adams, John, on beginning of Revolution, 1; heroics, 43; prophecy of American greatness, 110; on Sugar Act, 128; and Stamp Act, 159–62; and Stamp Act riots, 167; on Sons of Liberty, 170, 194, 293; on Otis, 173, 174, 181; in Sodalitas, 174, 337; on Writs of Assistance case, 177–79; and Pitt's attitude, 200; on virtual representation, 211, 212; on natural rights, 225 *n.*; on British Constitution and liberty, 231; on *Liberty* riot, 283; on troops in Boston, 286, 288; counsel for "massacre" soldiers, 288; on Samuel Adams, 291; on subsidence of agitation, 311; American brag, 317; New England conscience, 325, 326; and culture, 336, 433; and political study, 343; on clergy and liberty, 358, 360, 361; drinks tea, 370; on Tea Party, 386; on Quebec Act, 404; attitude toward Continental Congress, 432, 433; delegate, 433; journey to Philadelphia, 433–35; on Philadelphia hospitality, 435; disarms prejudice, 436, 439; comments on other delegates, 436, 437.

Adams, Samuel, Sr., and Land Bank, 292.

Adams, Samuel, on governor and civil list, 41, 42; provincialism, 72, 433; and imperial representation, 215; on natural rights and power of Parliament, 225–27; on fixity of Constitution, 230, 235; on British Constitution and liberty, 232; on non-importation, 262; Hutchinson pension incident, 274; on control over salaries, 275, 372; on riot compensation, 280; on troops in Boston, 286; and Boston Massacre, 289, 290; character, 291–96; Circular Letter, 296; attitude toward Hutchinson, 311; keeps agitation alive, 311, 312, 372, 376, 409; political study, 344; Hancock abandons, 369; committees of correspondence, 373–76, 428; and Tea Party, 379–83; and Hutchinson Letters, 384; on Quebec Act, 403, 404; on Port Bill, 412; fears Continental Congress, 432; delegate, 433; journey to Philadelphia, 433–35; Galloway on, 437; conduct at Congress, 439; Committee of Safety, 453.

Addison Joseph, on British merchant, 66.

Administration of colonies, parliamentary control, 24, 137, 179–81, 188; inefficiency, 68–70; efforts to strengthen, 70, 71; and union, 71–74; policy of compulsive centralization, 84–86, 105; British, not anachronous, 87, 88, 100, 104, 105; but colonies in advance of times, 88–90, 456, 477, 478; Spanish, 91–93, 98; French, 94–99; Dutch, 99; Portuguese, 100; Greek, 100, 101; Roman, 102; candor of new British policy, reason for failure, 107, 144, 145; as separate cabinet department, 116; character of Shelburne, 116–18; attitude of Bedford Ministry, 125; Grenville as minister, 127; acquiescence in parliamentary control, 137. *See also* Coercive Acts; Colonial government; Commerce; Imperialism; Standing army; Taxation; Union; West.

Admiralty trials under Sugar Act, 127.

Agitation, character of Samuel Adams, 291–96; subsidence (1770), 310, 311, 369, 370, 390; Samuel Adams keeps it alive, 311, 312, 372, 376; revival by *Gaspée* affair, 372; committees of correspondence as instrument, 374–76; importance of Coercive Acts, 390; promotion by English ministry, 409, 410; results of wholly political, 414–16; New York radicals.

INDEX

in cabinet, 116; and royal veto, 151; and religious matters, 347. *See also* Acts of Navigation.

Bollan, William, and Regulating Act, 399.

Boroughs, Sir John, on sea power, 56.

Boston, non-importation (1765), 164; Stamp Act riots, compensation for, 166–68, 280; portraits of Conway and Barré, 195; non-importation (1768–70), Mein incident, 256, 258, 260–62, 269–71; antagonism to customs officials, 282; *Liberty* riot, 283; troops sent to, 283–85; lodging and subsistence for troops, 285, 418, 452; attitude towards troops, 286–88, 299; literary conditions, 335; Sodalitas law club, 337; committee of correspondence, 373, 374; Quartering Act (1774), 399–401; siege begins, 455. *See also* following titles, and Massachusetts.

Boston Massacre, troops sent to Boston, 283–85; conduct toward them, 285–88; "massacre," 288; trial of soldiers, 288; forced withdrawal of troops, 289, 290.

Boston Port Bill, debate and enactment, 393–96; petition against, 411; and union, 411; enforcement, conditions under, 412–14; colonial sympathy and relief, 414; and political agitation, 414–16; Boston's attitude and circular letter, 416–18. *See also* Coercive Acts.

Boston Tea Party, consignees of tea, 379; arrival of tea, 380; agitation and meetings, 380–83; destruction, 383; colonial reception of news, 386; colonial opinion, 386–88; effect in England, 392. *See also* Boston Port Bill; Tea.

Botetourt, Lord, as governor, 303, 304.

Boucher, Jonathan, on colonial music, 330; on colonial speech, 341; on episcopal controversy and Revolution, 353; and Washington, 363.

Bouquet, Henry, forbids settlements, 114.

Bowdoin, James, delegate to Continental Congress, 433; journey to Philadelphia, 433–35.

Boycott of British goods, non-importation as protest on Stamp Act, 163–65; effect in England, 186; abandoned (1766), 194; New England non consumption measures against Townshend Acts, 254, 255; attitude and purpose of merchants (1768), 255, 268; failure of attempted non-importation league, 255–58; non-importation by large northern cities, 258, 259; carrying out, opposition, 259–63; effect, 262, 263, 266; by other northern cities, 263 n.; in South, 264–68, 305; breakdown, 268–71, 369, 370; effect in England, 271; Boston non-consumption agreement (1774), 418; attitude of Pennsylvania (1774), 423; Virginia nonintercourse resolves and association, 427, 429; in North Carolina, 429; question in South Carolina, 430; instructions to delegates in Congress, 438. *See also* Commerce; Continental Association.

Braddock's Defeat, causes, 79.

Bradford, John, committee of correspondence, 374.

British Constitution, colonial conception, 224–28; English conception, 226, 229; source of colonial view, 228, 229; colonial deduction of fixity, 230, 231; colonial appreciation, 231; English attitude toward parliamentary absolutism, 232–34; constitutional results of divergent theories, 234–36; divergent ideals and independence, 236–38; development to 1775, 457–60, 477, 478.

British debts of colonials (1776), 426 n.

Bruce, James, tea ship, 380.

Buckingham, Duchess of, on Methodism, 240.

Buethner, J. C., on sea passage, 13.

Bull, William, outwitted by assembly, 431.

Burgoyne, John, and Boston Port Bill, 395.

Burke, Edmund, on effect of distance, 10, 13; on colonial inheritance, 22; on control of colonies, 71; and Shelburne's plan, 119; on whale fisheries, 129; on Acts of Trade, 135; on timely warning of Stamp Act, 140; on colonial lawyers, 159; on Rockingham and repeal of Stamp Act, 190; as representative, 203; and imperial representation, 214; on colonial legislative rights, 218; on dangers in centralization, 222; on American spirit of liberty, 237; mistaken idea of colonists on, 239; on aristocratic leadership, 240; on Chatham-Grafton Ministry, 243; on Chatham, 243; on partial repeal of Townshend duties, 308; on non-English colonists, 363; on committees of correspondence, 375; on Boston Port Bill, 394; on bill on soldiers' trials, 399; on American taxation (1774), 408; on legality versus humanity, 410; on British freedom and colonies, 477.

Burlamaqui, J. J., colonists read, 344.

Burnaby, Andrew, on colonial provincialism, 82; on Virginians, 146.

Burnet, William, as governor, 44.